THE LIBRARY
ST. MARY'S COLLEGE

W9-ADE-576

ST. MARY'S CITY. MARYLAND   20686

# China:
# Liberation and
# Transformation
# 1942-1962

# China:
# Liberation and
# Transformation
# 1942-1962

## Bill Brugger

CROOM HELM LONDON

BARNES & NOBLE BOOKS
TOTOWA, NEW JERSEY

© 1981 Bill Brugger
Croom Helm Ltd, 2 – 10 St John's Road, London SW11

British Library Cataloguing in Publication Data

Brugger, William
   China.
   1. China — Politics and government — 1937 – 1949
   2. China — Politics and government — 1949 – 1976
   I. Title
   951.05    DS777.53

   ISBN 0 – 7099 – 0605 – 6
   ISBN 0 – 7099 – 0606 – 4 Pbk


First published in the USA 1981 by
Barnes & Noble Books,
81 Adams Drive,
Totowa, New Jersey, 07512


ISBN: 0 – 389 – 20086 – 7
Printed and bound in Great Britain

# CONTENTS

# ACKNOWLEDGEMENTS

To the many students who commented on the first edition of this book. To colleagues at Flinders University and elsewhere who pointed out the shortcomings and errors in that text, and especially to Graham Young, Dennis Woodward, Steve Reglar and Michael Sullivan. To the many reviewers who persuaded me to change the book's organisation and approach. To Michelle Grieve for her help on the first edition and to Ron Slee for carrying on her good work into the second. To Andrew Little for map work. To Catherine Cameron for logistic support, through both editions, and to Marie Baker, Heather Bushell, Anne Gabb, Linda Kelly, Elizabeth Neil and Mary Saunders for typing the latest manuscript. Finally, to Suzanne Brugger for the many hours I spent closeted with the text and for her refreshing criticism.

Once again, I can only reiterate that it would be presumptuous for me to claim responsibility for a work which contains so much plagiarism. I must, however, carry the burden for the many errors which remain. Once again, I can only express adherence to the Chinese slogan 'collective initiative and individual responsibility'.

Bill Brugger

*The Flinders University of South Australia*
December 1979

# ABBREVIATIONS

| | |
|---|---|
| ACFL | All China Federation of Labour (later translated as ACFTU) |
| ACFTU | All China Federation of Trade Unions |
| *BR* | *Beijing Review* (formerly *Peking Review*) |
| *CB* | *Current Background* |
| CC | Central Committee |
| CCP | Chinese Communist Party |
| CIA | Central Intelligence Agency |
| CPSU | Communist Party of the Soviet Union |
| *CQ* | *The China Quarterly* |
| *ECMM* | *Extracts from China Mainland Magazines* |
| *FBIS* | *Foreign Broadcast Information Service* |
| *FEER* | *Far Eastern Economic Review* |
| FLN | Front de la Libération Nationale |
| GAC | Government Administration Council |
| *GMRB* | *Guangming Ribao* |
| GNP | Gross National Product |
| *JPRS* | *Joint Publications Research Service* |
| NATO | North Atlantic Treaty Organisation |
| NCNA | New China (Xinhua) News Agency |
| NEP | New Economic Policy |
| NPAD | National Programme for Agricultural Development |
| NPC | National People's Congress |
| PFLP | Peking Foreign Languages Press |
| PLA | People's Liberation Army |
| *PR* | *Peking Review* |
| *RMRB* | *Renmin Ribao* |
| SC | State Council |
| *SCMM* | *Selections from China Mainland Magazines* |
| *SCMP* | *Survey of China Mainland Press* |
| SEATO | South East Asia Treaty Organisation |
| *SW* | *Selected Works* |
| *SWB* | *Summary of World Broadcasts* (British Broadcasting Corporation) Pt 3 *The Far East* |
| UN | United Nations |
| URI | Union Research Institute |
| US | United States |
| USSR | Union of Soviet Socialist Republics |

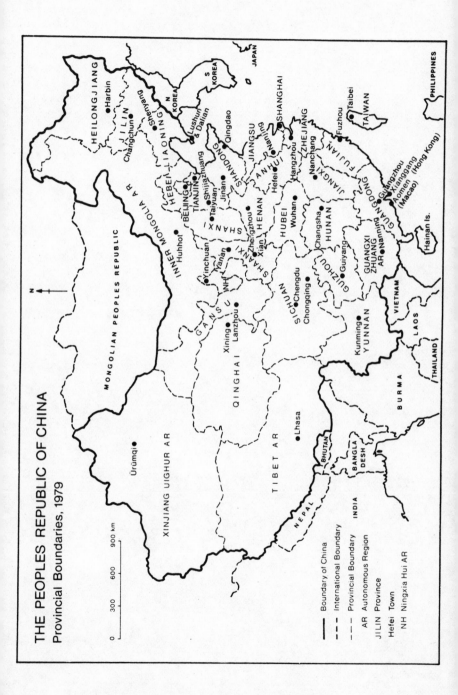

# THE PEOPLES REPUBLIC OF CHINA
Provincial Boundaries, 1979

| | |
|---|---|
| —— | Boundary of China |
| —·— | International Boundary |
| — — | Provincial Boundary |
| AR | Autonomous Region |
| JILIN | Province |
| Hefei | Town |
| NH | Ningxia Hui AR |

N

0   300   600   900 km

# PREFACE

The first edition of *Contemporary China* was written in 1974 and revised for publication in 1975. I concluded the book by noting that it would soon be out of date. Sure enough, it was—several months before it was published. By the time the book appeared, Mao Zedong was dead, the 'Gang of Four' had been arrested and China's leaders were engaged in a total reassessment of developmental strategy. That reassessment was to lead to a rewriting of much of Chinese history since 1949. By 1979, new evidence had been produced to support the reversal of the official verdicts on a whole series of historical incidents. Statistics had been released, moreover, to show that many of the achievements of the past had not been so great as many people had supposed. Revising one's conclusions is always painful. In this case, it was extremely difficult, since some of the new official documents omitted key passages in the original versions which had become available through Red Guard sources in the Cultural Revolution. In deciding which version to choose, one could not fail to develop a heightened scepticism concerning both the old and the new evidence. Surely no one, familiar with the criticism of von Ranke, would be contented by Chinese assurances that, this time, they were writing correct factual history. Scepticism towards one's evidence, of course, is a quality which should always characterise the scholar, but, to be honest, if one carried the rules of evidence to the optimum, scarcely anything about China would have been written in the West.

The major characteristic of the new official writing on contemporary Chinese history is a complete reversal in the assessment of the roles of the major protagonists in past debates. Mao Zedong has, to some extent, been spared this treatment, though the late chairman's reputation has not remained untarnished. Many of the other 'heroes' of pre-1976 China are, however, now portrayed as villains. Such an inversion of roles has, it seems, delighted many Western commentators who have been willing to accept the current version of the 'two-line struggle'. But I, who was somewhat too willing to accept the old version of the 'two-line struggle', have now developed a more cautious approach. I have, therefore, revised many of the views about 'two-line struggle' which appeared in the first edition of this book. No longer will the reader find consistent radicals pitted against diehard conservatives and pure 'ultra-leftists'. Such, indeed, was not my original intention in the first edition but, quite clearly, the book was sometimes read in that spirit. This is not to say, however, that I will eschew the terms 'conservative' and 'radical'. The category 'radical' will be used to signify a person who wishes to accelerate the process of social change, whilst a conservative is one who places much greater importance on maintaining the economy in a state of balance. But when I use these terms, I shall attempt to indicate on which issue a particular leader might have been radical, and on which conservative. It will be noted, therefore, that sometimes Mao and other leaders adopted a conservative position and at other times they adopted a radical position.

Though I have modified considerably the 'two-line struggle' conception of Chinese politics in my treatment of the period up to 1962, the approach is still based on a depiction of conflict. The model of administration, worked out by the Communist Party in the revolutionary base areas, centred on Yan'an, was profoundly different from that copied from the Soviet Union in the 1950s and, at times, there was conflict between adherents to these two approaches. Once the Soviet model was abandoned, in the mid-1950s, there was conflict also between an approach which developed into the Great Leap Forward and one which resembled more the economic reforms practised in the Soviet Union and Eastern Europe. But with one or two notable exceptions, this conflict did not result in an irreconcilable split within the senior leadership of the Party.

But this book is not only about the leadership of the Chinese Communist Party. At lower levels, throughout the period covered, there was much conflict and much antagonism, not all of which might be seen according to the view of class struggle put forward by the Communist Party. Indeed, by 1958, just to criticise the Great Leap Forward was enough for one to be branded a 'rightist'. To be sure, the Party considered such behaviour to be a manifestation of class position, but classes themselves were often seen purely in behavioural terms. Such, I will suggest, was to lead to dissatisfaction, and one major theme of this volume will be Mao Zedong's attempt to reconceptualise the nature of class formation and class struggle in socialist society. By 1962, Mao had reached a new position. Thus, that date is a convenient cut off point for the first volume. I will, therefore, take quite seriously the way the Chinese Communist Party, as a Marxist organisation, saw the nature of socialist transition—how it moved from what I shall call the Stalinist positive model of socialism, through what was known as 'uninterrupted revolution' (*buduan geming*) to what was eventually described as Mao's theory of 'continuous revolution' (*jixu geming*). Such a transition was, however, not to be made without much theoretical confusion.

Nevertheless, this book is not a work of political theory. It is an introductory textbook with quite modest aims. If offers no fundamentally new insight into the dynamics of Chinese politics, nor any new information based on a study of primary sources. Primary sources have, of course, been used but the bulk of the material is drawn from secondary sources. But that is what a textbook should do. Because it is a textbook, I do not anticipate that it will make good bedside reading. Its primary purpose is to provide a source of reference for an introductory course in politics or history. It is, thus, not meant to be a gripping story to be devoured at one sitting. But the material it uses is profoundly exciting and the book's aim will be achieved if it persuades students to turn to some of the secondary sources on which it is based. Since the appearance of the first edition, a huge amount of secondary literature on China has been produced. This, as much as the release of primary material, has caused me to modify my position.

In the new edition I have not only revised my views on 'two-line struggle' but have also chosen to play down the cycles of radicalisation and consolidation which loomed large in the original text. In the first edition, each chapter constituted a discrete cycle. This made for very large and indigestible chapters and experience of using the book for teaching purposes over three years has led me to the view that smaller chapters are preferable. What appeared as the first five cycles in that edition, now appears as the ten chapters of this volume. When I say I have played down the notion of cycles, however, it does not mean that I have abandoned them and I have attempted a defence of this categorisation in the conclusion. The point is, however, that the depiction of cycles raised more theoretical questions than it was proper for an introductory textbook to explore. Secondly, as one of my perceptive reviewers pointed out, the notion of cycles made a lot of sense in the period up to 1962 but not much sense thereafter.[1] Once I accepted that criticism, it seemed pointless to organise the first volume in cycles and not the second.

The utility of this textbook to the undergraduate student will depend upon the academic tradition and intellectual milieu in which he finds himself. I anticipate that those who will be most at home with my approach will be political scientists or sociologists. A student brought up in the world of classical sinology will probably find it alien, for the stress is on change rather than continuity. Those who seek modern *gurus* will perhaps be affronted by my suggestion that Mao did not foresee the whole course of Chinese history. Those whose *guru* is Leon Trotsky will be annoyed that, in my view, Mao was not in the least like Stalin. Those who adhere consistently to the current Chinese line will be annoyed that I have one or two good things to say about the Great Leap Forward and one or two bad things to say about 'market socialism'.

No doubt this book will also soon be out of date. But what will continue to be relevant are the lessons learned in China about issues at the core of the Marxist project—about 'base' and 'superstructure', 'relations of production' and 'forces of production'; or, if one doesn't like Marxist terminology, about that Marxian contradiction which is understandable from any perspective—the contradiction between freedom and necessity.

## NOTES

1. Addis, *Times Literary Supplement*, 1 April 1977, p. 407.

# INTRODUCTION

There was a time when most writing on contemporary China began with the statement that China had enjoyed a degree of social and political continuity for two millennia and that such continuity was unparalleled. We now know enough about the process of development to beware of using the residual category of 'traditional society' and indulging in the ahistorical assumption that basic features of a society had not been subject to radical change. In the two millennia that precede our century, China had experienced many changes in the system of land tenure, had at times been politically unified and at others fragmented, had for periods experienced a level of scientific and technological sophistication far in advance of the West and had been the object of both the praise and vilification of foreign observers.

## Feudal Society

Change within China during the last three decades has been away from a society which the Chinese Communist Party describes as 'feudal' (*fengjian de*). Those Western historians who see feudalism essentially as a phenomenon that either precedes or follows a bureaucratic empire and in which land ownership is based upon a tradition of military service would disagree with the use of this term. They would assert that the real 'feudal' period in Chinese history occurred before the second century BC when a number of military states vied with each other for power, in much the same way as in medieval Europe. These states were to be replaced by the empire of Qin, from which the English name 'China' is derived. Nowadays, however, when Chinese historians used the word 'feudal', all they mean is a social system based upon the primacy of landownership, which applies to the warring states, the Qin empire and, for that matter, the following two millennia.

Whether properly classified as 'feudal' or not, early-twentieth-century China was governed by a disintegrating traditional bureaucracy. In its heyday, the Chinese bureaucracy had constituted an élite of educated amateurs dedicated not to expertise but to virtuous models of the past. They had been recruited by an elaborate examination system[1] consisting of four degrees, for which some candidates might study for the greater

17

part of their lives. The system had been abolished at the beginning of the twentieth century but the values which it enshrined were remarkably persistent and, in many places, local Confucian 'mandarins' remained in power until the 1940s.

Confucian philosophy meant different things to different social groups and had been subject to repeated change since the time of the Sage (sixth century BC). In its ideological form, however (that is in the form which legitimised the rule of a landed élite), Confucianism was a highly static value system. It reduced human behaviour to moral determinants. Social turmoil or prosperity was seen as due to the moral qualities of individuals and groups rather than material conditions. Indeed, in its extreme form, natural calamities such as flood or drought were seen as due to human wickedness. The *moral* was considered more important not only than the material but also than the *intellectual*. In short, it was better to be 'good' than 'knowledgeable'. Wisdom was not the knowledge of necessity nor the overcoming of necessity but the knowledge of what was prescribed by the Confucian classics which harked back to a 'golden age'.

The normative model was one of 'Great Harmony' (*Datong*) rather than struggle. In contemporary social science jargon, what was aimed at was not a mode of conflict resolution nor conflict stimulation but of *conflict avoidance*. Since the laws which governed Nature were essentially the same as the laws which governed men, men should be in harmony not only with themselves but with Nature.

Within the Confucian scheme, great stress was placed on education and the creation of 'superior men' (*junzi*) who labour with their minds rather than their hands. This did not mean that the system was geared to the creation of individualistic supermen, for the 'superior man' was one who realised the continuity of the Confucian tradition and subordinated himself to his peers. Freedom consisted in the subordination of the self to the community of good men and to Nature. Indeed, when the word 'liberty' was translated into Chinese, it was associated with licence, for the Western negative concept of liberty was freedom *from* rather than freedom *to*. In theory, the Chinese positive conception of freedom applied to all men, though in practice it applied to those 'superior men' who, through education, had reached élite status.

One's adherence to the moral precepts of Confucianism was evaluated according to outward behaviour. In terms made popular by Riesman,[2] one measured an individual's moral commitment and moral rectitude not in terms of his *inner direction* (to what extent he had internalised the prescriptions of the classics) nor in terms of *other direction* (to what extent his public image corresponded to current values) but in terms of *tradition direction* (to what extent his conduct measured up to his worthy ancestors). In this kind of situation, we can talk of society being essentially a *shame* culture (where people did what they ought out of fear of being shamed) rather than a *guilt* culture (where people did what they ought because they would feel guilty for not doing so). One result of this tradition direction was a considerable respect for age (made practicable by the scarcity of old men) and a gerontocratic organisation of society. Another result was an essentially patriarchal form of organisation which gave women inferior status.

The establishment of an educational hierarchy based on Confucian ideology led to a view of this world and the next (when Confucians bothered to think about such problems) as essentially organised according to the same kind of traditional bureaucracy which characterised Imperial China. As far as most peasants were concerned, however, the ideology of Confucianism took on more overtly religious forms such as ancestor worship mixed with animism (the vesting of spiritual qualities in inanimate objects). At different levels of society, Confucianism mixed also with Buddhism and Daoism (the fusion of the self with the indefinable 'way' and the total integration of the self with Nature). At times, these religions served to legitimise revolt, as did Islam amongst national minorities. On occasions, heterodox Christianity even took on a Confucian hue. It would be inappropriate to go into all these transmutations here. Suffice it to say that a society based on land developed a static ideology that stressed not challenging the status quo but was sufficiently elastic to accommodate a right of rebellion justified only by success.

Just as the values of the traditional bureaucracy changed little during the early twentieth century, rural social and political structure was also relatively static. The formal apparatus of Imperial government did not extend much below the level of the two thousand odd *xian* (or counties) into which China was divided. There existed, however, in places, the remains of a system of mutual responsibility known as *baojia*, in which each group of families was organised into a unit collectively responsible for the conduct of its members. There was also a level of local government lower than the *xian*, known as the *xiang*, at which most local dignitaries or 'gentry' (*shenshi* or *shidafu jieji*) operated. Here the 'gentry', who consisted of official aspirants or their landowning relatives, undertook the task of local administration and the settlement of disputes according to customary law.

It is probable that most *xiang* were coterminous with what anthropologist G.W. Skinner has referred to as 'standard marketing areas'.[3] Applying a version of the central place theory of Cristaller and Lösch to the Chinese situation, Skinner divided the whole country into a number of these standard marketing areas, each of which consisted of a group of villages (divisible usually by six) arranged around a market. By 1949, he calculated that there were some 58,000 standard marketing areas which themselves were grouped into intermediate marketing areas and which, in turn, were grouped into central marketing areas at *xian* level. There has been much discussion as to the applicability of Skinner's theory and whether or not the marketing areas correspond to administrative divisions. It does seem reasonable to me, however, that the horizon of a peasant's existence would be bounded by the area in which he could sell his produce rather than simply by the natural village in which he lived.

Within the villages, grouped together as *xiang* or standard marketing areas, there existed a number of organisations which cut across class lines. An example of such an organisation would be the lineage (or clan—*zu*) based on real or imagined family ties and usually dominated by those of its members who had larger holdings of land. One should note here that the popular myth of a traditional Chinese society characterised by huge extended families living under one roof is largely untrue. Such families did, of course, exist, particularly among the wealthy, but in general the most common form of family organisation was the *famille souche* (or stem family) which consisted of husband and wife, their children and one or two grandparents,[4] forming a unit that would fit very neatly into clan or lineage.

Though the family was quite small (consisting on average of between four and six persons),[5] the clan or lineage was a significant organisation (particularly in South China), occasionally providing a primitive system of social security and a forum for the settlement of disputes.

Another organisation which cut across class lines, though this time characterised by *simulated* rather than real kinship, was the secret society which fed upon a long tradition of anti-bureaucratic dissent. During the seventeenth and eighteenth centuries, many secret societies were organised around resistance to the alien Qing (Manchu) dynasty and had as their professed aim the restoration of the last great Han dynasty—the Ming (overthrown in 1644). Whatever the original political aim, however, many of these societies became religious organisations in their own right, probably because a religious organisation is better able to survive periods of repression than a clearly political organisation. Like their Western counterparts, these quasi-religious bodies, based upon patterns of simulated kinship, easily turned to crime.

Though the bulk of the Chinese population still lived in the countryside in the early twentieth century, some 10 per cent did, in fact, live in towns. The development of the urban population in China had been markedly different from that in the West. There has been much discussion as to why China, which in the seventeenth century was technologically more advanced than the West, did not produce an indigenous urban bourgeoisie. One reason is quite clearly that Confucian ideology accorded the merchant a low status though this, I believe, is only a partial explanation. A more fruitful line of enquiry is to be found in the pattern of social mobility.

It has been suggested that the development of a bourgeoisie in the West and a quasi-bourgeoisie in Japan depended upon the fact that class structure was relatively closed. There were few mechanisms in England, for example, whereby merchant classes might be absorbed into the land-owning aristocracy and this led to the development of a bourgeoisie in independent towns with a consciousness of itself as a class for itself. Similarly in Japan, the Meiji Restoration of the 1870s depended upon the association of merchants and *samurai* which constituted two unassimilated middle-class groupings in a closed-class situation and which could do nothing but assert their independence. In both Britain and Japan, the absence of a violent revolution might be explained by the subsequent blending of aristocratic elements into the new bourgeoisie whereas, in France, non-assimilation resulted in violent upheaval.[6] In China, on the other hand, the class structure was more 'open'. By 'open', I do not mean that there was much upward peasant mobility, merely that the land-owning class could co-opt merchants. It was not until the impact of Western imperialism that anything like a bourgeoisie developed and such a bourgeoisie as existed in the twentieth century was shaped by that imperialism.

## The Impact of Imperialism

In the 80 or so years after the First Opium War in the 1840s, China was repeatedly humiliated by the Western powers. Over 90 'treaty ports' were established in which foreigners were immune from Chinese law. Spheres of influence were created which at one time looked like being turned into actual colonies, and Japan manifested direct colonial ambitions. A Maritime Customs Service under foreign control ensured the payment of foreign debts and the infamous indemnities wrung out of China at bayonet point. The Chinese tariff was fixed by treaty at a low 5 per cent, favourable to foreign business. Missionaries reached over half of the two thousand-odd *xian* and, regardless of individual goodwill and intentions, were often the instruments of foreign powers. Overall, a plethora of limitations on Chinese sovereignty caused resentment which was frequently explosive.

Though food production may have kept pace with population increase during the nineteenth century,[7] the various risings that took place at that time, which cannot be dissociated from foreign impact, produced areas of intense privation exacerbated by monetary inflation. By the early twentieth century, there had been a sharp increase in the numbers of poor peasants forced to mortgage their land to pay, to warlord régimes, taxes demanded often a decade in advance. The exactions of these warlords drove many peasants into the arms of bandits who found it fairly easy to operate in the fragmented political structure. Though one cannot directly assign the phenomenon of warlordism to the foreigner, some warlord régimes were backed by foreign powers who were not sympathetic to the forces that sought national reunification.

As far as traditional handicraft industries were concerned, it is probably true that foreign-manufactured equivalents of Chinese handicraft goods did not seriously dent the domestic market overall but the effect of foreign competition on certain industries was dramatic. Between 1870 and 1910, for example, the handicraft spinning of cotton yarn declined by over 50 per cent and, although weaving held its own, it could only absorb one-tenth of the labour released from spinning. Though, by the early 1920s, some 78 per cent of factory output in China south of the Great Wall came from Chinese-owned factories, the bulk of the extractive and transport industries was under foreign control—a characteristic of early imperialist penetration. Foreign mines produced 99 per cent of the pig iron and 76 per cent of the coal mined by modern methods. In 1920, 83 per cent of the steamer tonnage cleared through Maritime Customs and 78 per cent of that on China's main waterway—the Changjiang (Yangtze)—was in foreign ships. Railway control was brought about through foreign loans and, according to one estimate, foreign capital controlled 93 per cent of China's railways in 1911.[8]

Such a situation, so different from Japan, is all the more remarkable in that China had embarked upon its own version of the Meiji Restoration at the same time as its eastern neighbour.[9] The modern industries of the 1860s were set up with little capital. Most of them were initiated by governors-general (in charge of one or several provinces) with funds milked from any available source (such as the local defence budget). Government officials placed in charge of them were expected to be major shareholders in their own right and to sell shares in the treaty ports to raise more capital.[10] It was thus impossible to separate the state from the private sector of the economy, especially when those industrial concerns established tenuous links with individual manufacturers organised along traditional lines. There was pressure throughout the latter part of the nineteenth century (especially from Beijing) to increase the size of private investment in state-run factories and this frequently led to a situation where foreigners became majority shareholders. Perhaps the paradigm case here was the Hanyeping Coal and Iron Company which commenced operation before the first Japanese iron and steel works (Yawata) and which, within half a century, had become completely a Japanese subsidiary.[11]

The government officials who were also major capitalists became known in the twentieth century as 'bureaucratic capitalists' (*guanliao zibenjia*) and depended for funds on a new class grouping which began to develop in the treaty ports—the comprador capitalists (*maiban zibenjia*), oriented towards the economy of the overseas imperial countries. By the early twentieth century, however, there also began to develop a third group of domestic or 'national capitalists' (*minzu zibenjia*) whose links with foreign countries were much weaker.

The expansion of foreign-controlled industry contributed much to the growth of an industrial working class. Half a century after the establishment of state-run factories, there existed a small number of workers who had few ties with the countryside. But since the bulk of industrial expansion took place during the First World War boom, the majority of workers had arrived recently from the rural areas. They had been recruited by the notorious 'gang-boss system' (*batouzhi*).[12] Gang-bosses were not merely labour contractors but also remained as supervisors of their contractees after they had been signed on. They took a sizeable cut from workers' wages[13] and developed personal relationships with members of their gangs, expressed in terms of 'family' with all the obligations which that word implied in contemporary Chinese society. As one might expect, the labour gangs established links with the larger and more powerful organisations characterised by the same patterns of simulated kinship—the secret societies. In fact, some secret societies such as the 'Green Gang' (*Qingbang*) specialised in the field of labour control and provided major obstacles to the development of labour unions.

### The Early Years of the Chinese Communist Party[14]

The China in which the Communist Party was founded in 1921 was politically, economically, socially and ideologically fragmented. Warlord régimes vied for power. Modern capitalism coexisted with a 'feudal' agrarian economy. The wealth and social position of rural classes was subject to sudden and extreme variations as intermittent civil war took its toll. The working class was divided by complex patterns of simulated kinship and different types of capitalist continually swallowed each other up. Traditional Confucians mixed with Western and Japanese trained intellectuals. Buddhists and Daoists rubbed shoulders with Marxists and anarchists.

In such a confusing situation, there is little wonder that the ideological coherence of the young Party depended on the Comintern (Communist International) in Moscow whose advisers had helped set it up. By the early 1920s, the Comintern was convinced that the struggle in colonial and semi-colonial countries should be directed against imperialism and that Communist parties should unite with the 'national bourgeoisie'. It had some difficulty, however, in deciding who exactly in China represented the 'national bourgeoisie'. By 1923, the Guomindang (Nationalist

Party) of Sun Zhongshan (San Yat-sen) seemed to fill the bill but the Soviet-Guomindang alliance and the United Front between Communist Party and Nationalists was to be short-lived.

Following the death of Sun Zhongshan in 1925, the Nationalists embarked upon a series of military campaigns against the warlords. These were to give China some kind of unity. During the course of the campaigns, the Communist Party switched from its earlier concentration on mobilising the industrial workers to developing a peasant movement and a radical programme of land reform. This, amongst other things, alienated the right wing of the Guomindang and resulted in the massacre of Communist Party members, first by the Nationalist commander, Jiang Jieshi (Chiang K'ai-shek) in Shanghai and then by the official Guomindang government in the central Chinese city of Wuhan.

During the resulting Civil War (1927–37), the Communist Party went from crisis to crisis. In 1971, Mao Zedong referred to ten major crises in the fifty-year history of the Party.[15] Six of them occurred in this first Civil War. The first crisis (1927) was the direct outcome of Comintern advice to the Chinese Party to maintain an alliance with the Guomindang at all costs.[16] It resulted in the inauguration of a series of military engagements in the countryside in anticipation of decisive risings of the urban proletariat.[17] When the risings failed to develop, a second crisis occurred (1927) which produced a new leadership but continued much the same strategy.

By 1930, a guerrilla base area had been built up by Mao Zedong in Jiangxi province, defended by a Workers and Peasants Red Army. An attempt, however, to use this army to capture major cities resulted in military defeat, another change in leadership (the third crisis),[18] a breakaway movement of what was left of the urban Party (the fourth crisis) and eventually the consolidation of a Chinese Soviet Republic in Jiangxi. In the early years of the Jiangxi Soviet, Mao Zedong evolved a distinctive approach to fighting the Civil War. Three Guomindang campaigns of 'encirclement and suppression' were beaten off by a strategy expressed as 'the enemy advances, we retreat; the enemy camps, we harass; the enemy tires, we attack; the enemy retreats, we pursue'. Large bodies of Red Army troops were concentrated to attack enemy units one by one and war along fixed fronts was avoided. By the fourth encirclement campaign in 1933, however, the Party switched to a 'forward and offensive line' on the grounds that Mao's strategy invited enemy reprisals. The result was disastrous.

The 'forward and offensive line' together with a new Guomindang strategy, led to the defeat of the Red Army in the fifth encirclement campaign of 1934. During the course of the ensuing Long March[19] the fifth and sixth of the major crises occurred. The fifth crisis centred on the unsuccessful policies of the Wang Ming leadership whose influence was drastically reduced at a Politburo meeting in Zunyi in January 1935. The Zunyi meeting elected Mao as Politburo chairman, though arguments over strategy still continued and the sixth crisis occurred soon after the meeting when Zhang Guotao, the former vice-chairman of the Jiangxi Soviet, broke with Mao over the destination of the march. It was, therefore, only part of the Red Army which reached an isolated soviet in north Shaanxi in the autumn of 1935 though, before long, Mao's main force was joined by troops who had made a detour through Sichuan.

Most of the crises outlined above concerned military strategy and several crucial lessons had been learned. Mao's principles of people's war had been vindicated and any future strategy would rely on flexible guerrilla tactics to build up a network of rural bases with which to surround the cities. There were to be no premature assaults on the cities and what was left of the urban movement would subordinate its activities to those of the rural base areas. Secondly, several of the crises had been, in no small measure, the result of faulty advice from the Comintern in Moscow. Though the Comintern could not have prevented the massacres of 1927, its advice to maintain the United Front at all costs had made the debacle much worse than it need have been. At least one of the abortive risings of 1927 had been the direct inspiration of Stalin[20] who seemed to have little appreciation of the actual Chinese situation. The attempt to capture major cities in 1930 and an extravagant faith in the Chinese proletariat's willingness to rise in revolt was due in some measure to the Comintern's mystical faith that a global 'high tide' was in the offing. Finally, the inexperienced Wang Ming leadership which dominated the Party in the early 1930s had actually been sent to China from Moscow together with its Soviet mentor, Pavel Mif. By 1935, Mao had developed a contempt for Soviet-trained intellectuals who attempted to import into China prepacked models of revolution.

### The Second United Front

Although, by 1935, Mao was wary of Comintern advice, there was one policy which the Comintern adopted in that year which was very welcome—the call for a broadly-based United Front against imperialism. In 1931, the Japanese had turned north-east China into the puppet state of Manchukuo and, since that time, Jiang Jieshi had been under pressure to make peace with the Communist Party in order to resist Japan. As early as 1933, the Communist Party had called for a United Front though it had been wary of uniting with Jiang Jieshi. In December 1935, a series of demonstrations in Beijing[21] protested against Japanese attempts to establish a puppet régime in north China and, in 1936, Nationalist forces in north-west China refused to fight the Red Army. When Jiang Jieshi flew to Xi'an to investigate the situation, he was captured by Nationalist generals and forced to enter into negotiations with the Communist Party.[22] An agreement was finally concluded in September 1937 after the inauguration of total war with Japan. The Soviet régime in north Shaanxi was reorganised as a 'special region' of the Republic of China. The Red Army was incorporated into the national forces (at least in theory) under the new name 'Eighth Route Army' and land reform ceased.

Immediately after the reorganisation, the Eighth Route Army crossed the Huanghe (Yellow River) and joined battle with the Japanese. Limited in strength to 45,000, it fought in small units of one thousand behind the Japanese lines and helped create guerrilla units. In the south, a New Fourth Army was also formed in September 1937 out of people left behind in the old Jiangxi Soviet. As anti-Japanese sentiment swelled, a solid base of recruitment was established amongst intellectuals in the towns as well as among peasants in the countryside and an Anti-Japanese University (*Kangda*) was set up to train them. Meanwhile the Guomindang resistance crumbled and, after a holding operation at Taierzhuang, the Nationalist government pulled back to remote Chongqing.

By 1940, the United Front had begun to fall to pieces. The Communist Party suspected that Jiang Jieshi was about to do a deal with the puppet government which the Japanese had set up in Nanjing[23] and the Guomindang government looked with alarm upon the rapid growth of the Eighth Route and New Fourth Armies, well beyond the limit imposed by the 1937 agreement. In early 1941, tension gave way to open hostilities as Guomindang troops attacked the headquarters of the New Fourth Army after it had proved slow in obeying an order from Chongqing to withdraw north of the Changjiang.

The United Front was effectively at an end and an already existing embargo on goods transported to the Communist border regions from areas under Guomindang control was strengthened. At the same time, a fierce campaign of suppression know as the 'three all' (*san guang*—burn all, kill all, loot all) was launched by the Japanese. The result was dramatic. The population of Communist-controlled areas in north China fell from 44 million to 25 million and, in the country as a whole, from 100 million to 50 million.[24]

The situation in the border regions was critical. The tightening of the Guomindang blockade, together with the Japanese policy of ringing individual areas with blockhouses, resulted in a shortage of goods. Now that the Communist government in Yan'an (the capital of the major border region of Shaan Gan Ning) received no subsidies from Chongqing, a crushing burden of taxation was imposed upon the residents. In 1941 alone, taxes were doubled and such a situation could surely not be tolerated if the government were to retain the support of the peasants and continue to call itself revolutionary. Secondly, the political situation deteriorated considerably. The rapid expansion of the border regions during the early part of the war had led to large numbers of people moving to places such as Yan'an out of purely patriotic motives. They consequently did not have much understanding of Marxism-Leninism or Communist Party policy. A top-heavy bureaucratic structure had been created which was staffed by unreliable personnel without much contact with ordinary people. The bureaucrats had imposed a formal education system based on current practice in the coastal cities without much regard for the special needs of the border regions and a peasantry which had to be convinced that education was not a waste of time. Thirdly, with the abandonment of land reform in 1937, the former rural élite strove to regain not only its political influence but also its property and vied with the cadres from the cities in a struggle which left the peasants untouched.[25] New policies were called for and, in 1942, a process was instituted which resulted in a new and very different model of political administration and economic management—a model which went a long way towards guaranteeing success in the war and which has been the starting point for the policies of the radical leadership of the Communist Party ever since. The adoption of the Yan'an model, which marked the maturity of the Communist Party, is the starting point of this book.

## NOTES

1. See Ho, 1962.
2. Riesman, 1953.
3. Skinner, 1964.
4. See Levy, 1949.
5. Buck, 1964, p. 368.
6. Moore, 1967.
7. This is the view of Myers, 1970, p. 124, who held that such was the case until 1937.
8. Based on Esherick, 1972.
9. For a discussion of the Chinese Tongzhi Restoration, see Wright, 1957.
10. See Feuerwerker, 1958.
11. See Feuerwerker, 1964.
12. Discussed in Brugger, 1976, pp. 42–5.
13. Fong, 1937, pp. 40–1.
14. A number of standard introductory histories exist for the period 1921–42. On the career of Mao Zedong, see Schram, 1966, Ch'en, 1965, Schwartz, 1966, Snow, 1961. On the career of Zhu De, see Smedley, 1972. On the early years of the Party, see Meisner, 1967, Schwartz, 1966. On the early labour movement, see Chesneaux, 1968. On the student movement, see Israel, 1966. On the events of 1927, see Isaacs, 1961. On the Jiangxi Soviet, see Rue, 1966, Swarup, 1966, Waller, 1973. For an interesting collection of excerpts from various writings, see Schurmann and Schell, Vol. II, 1968.
15. Mao Zedong, August–September 1971, Schram, 1974, p. 290.

16. See Isaacs, 1961.
17. See Guillermaz, 1962; Wilbur, 1964; Hofheinz, 1967.
18. See Harrison, 1963.
19. For a graphic account, see Wilson, 1971.
20. See Hsiao Tso-liang, 1967.
21. See Israel, 1966, Chapter V.
22. See Snow, 1961, Part XII.
23. Schram, 1966, p. 217.
24. Selden, 1971, p. 179.
25. For a description of the crisis, see ibid., Chapter V.

# I
# FROM YAN'AN TO VICTORY
## (1942 – 1949)

Doubtless the brutality of the Japanese invasion after 1937 contributed to the success of the Communist Party.[1] The focus here, however, will be on internal developments in the border regions and the positive appeal of the Party's policies. These policies took the form of what later became known as the Yan'an model.

### The Yan'an Model of Administration and Participation[2]

The crisis in the border regions in 1942 revealed a defective local leadership. With the expansion of the Party from some 40,000 members to some 800,000 in 1940, the competence of leaders had declined markedly. The first aim of the Yan'an model, therefore, was to improve their quality in a process known as 'rectification' (*zhengfeng*). In the rectification movement of 1942, leaders learned how to apply Marxist-Leninist theory to their work situation and were made to answer for their daily conduct. Launching the movement in February 1942, Mao directed his attention not only to intellectuals from the coastal cities who had a poor knowledge of Marxism but also to 'dogmatists', such as Wang Ming:

We do not study Marxism-Leninism because it is pleasing to the eye or because it has some mystical value, like the doctrine of the Daoist priests who ascend Mao Shan to learn how to subdue devils and evil spirits. Marxism-Leninism has no beauty, nor has it any mystical value. It is only extremely useful. It seems that, right up to the present, quite a few have regarded Marxism-Leninism as a ready-made panacea; once you have it you can cure all your ills with little effort. This is a type of childish blindness and we must start a movement to enlighten these people. Those who regard Marxism-Leninism as

29

religious dogma show this type of blind ignorance. We must tell them openly, 'your dogma is of no use' or, to use an impolite phrase, 'your dogma is less useful than excrement'. We see that dog excrement can fertilise the fields and Man's can feed the dog. And dogmas? They can't fertilise the fields nor can they feed the dog. Of what use are they?[3]

Clearly, one of the major targets was blind worship of the Soviet Union. During the course of the movement, all cadres were submitted to 'struggle' within small groups under psychological stress; the object of struggle was then reincorporated into the group. The metaphor, which was drawn, was 'curing the sickness to save the patient' which was vastly different from the metaphor, often drawn by Stalin, of the surgeon amputating the diseased limb. The movement, therefore, was not a 'purge' but a method of internalising prescribed group norms. The mode of conflict management here was not the traditional conflict *avoidance* but conflict *stimulation* within the individual. Conflict within the individual was prescribed, as was competition and conflict between groups and classes, but not between individuals (the dominant Western pattern).[4]

One of the primary aims of the rectification movement, which was centred around 27 documents[5] (of which only four derived from the Soviet Union), was to create a new leadership type—the 'cadre'. The nature of this second feature of the Yan'an model may best be understood in terms of the characterisation made by Franz Schurmann. Whereas the traditional bureaucrat operated in a network of human solidarity (between human beings and groups of human beings), he was committed to preserving the status quo. The ideal cadre also operated within a network of human solidarity but was committed to *change*. Both these types of leadership differ considerably from those types with which we are more familiar in our own society characterised by technological solidarity (between roles and structures)—the manager (committed to change) and the modern bureaucrat (committed to the status quo). In simple form, Schurmann's matrix is as follows.[6]

| Type of social solidarity | Commitment to change | Commitment to status quo |
|---|---|---|
| HUMAN | CADRE | TRADITIONAL BUREAUCRAT |
| TECHNO-LOGICAL | MANAGER | MODERN BUREAUCRAT |

The ideal cadre was preferably to be young. He was to be a leader rather than a conciliator, but was required to persuade rather than command. He had to participate in 'criticism and self-criticism' both as part of the rectification process and in the course of his normal work. He was enjoined to be responsive to those amongst whom he operated and their reactions to him were to be recorded in a dossier which might be scrutinised by the Party leadership during a rectification session.

The commitment of the cadre was to the Party as the symbol of socialist transition rather than to the Party as an *organisation*. Perhaps a religious analogy might clarify this notion. The cadre was like the Protestant whose commitment was directly to God rather than the Church and who sought inspiration in the *Word* which was not interpreted for him but which only had meaning in practical life. He was not like the Catholic, whose commitment to God was through the Church and who dealt with a number of agents who interpreted the Word for him and mediated between him and God. The cadre's guilt orientation was not absolved in the private confessional but in his work within a group.

Precisely because the cadre operated in a network of human solidarity, as opposed to technological solidarity, his commitment was first to 'virtue' (*de*—self-awareness of action and motive) rather than 'ability' (*cai*—knowing how to do things and having the talent to do them).[7] Though he might serve very different classes and groups in society, this pattern of commitment was precisely the same as the traditional bureaucrat and there was always a possibility that the cadre might slip back into this traditional leadership type. Hence the need for rectification.

This sociological characterisation of cadre leadership has been made only recently because of the dominant and erroneous assumption of the 1950s that institutional leadership and personal leadership were mutually exclusive. It leads us to the third feature of the Yan'an model—the relationship between leaders and led known as the 'Mass Line'. In its 1943 form, the Mass Line was spelt out as follows:

In all the practical work of our Party, all correct leadership is necessarily from the masses, to the masses. This means: take the ideas of the masses (scattered and unsystematic ideas) and concentrate them (through study, turn them into concentrated and systematic ideas), then go to the masses and propagate and explain these ideas until the masses embrace them as their own, hold fast to them and translate them into action, and test the correctness of these ideas in such action. Then once again concentrate ideas from the masses and once again go to the masses so that the ideas are persevered in and carried through. And so on over and over again in an endless spiral with the ideas becoming more correct, more vital and richer every time. Such is the Marxist theory of knowledge.[8]

What this meant in practice was that each leader at each level of organisation was required, as part of his job, to explain policy to those he operated amongst and to collect their opinions for processing into future policy. The cadre was required to tread the narrow path between 'commandism' (relying too much on central policy directives) and 'tailism' (just doing what the masses wanted without regard to central policy). Although (like all leadership strategies) this process was open to manipulation, it was intended to prevent cadres behaving in a routine manner. It provided material for the criticism and self-criticism to keep the cadre on his toes. It also dealt squarely with what Mao felt was a *contradictory* relationship between leaders and led and avoided the convenient assumption of Stalinists that, given the right class composition and the right political line, one could assume identity between all members of an organisation who were not actively counter-revolutionary. Indeed, it was this assumption which led Stalin to brand even minor deviations as counter-revolutionary acts maliciously contrived.

To facilitate the operation of the Mass Line, there was the assumption of a dichotomy between broadly determined *policy* and routine or specific *operations*. For this reason, policy tended to be kept general and unspecific to allow for optimum flexibility and leeway. There was also the assumption that cadres would not remain in their offices but would go out and solicit mass opinions. This leads us to a fourth feature of the Yan'an model—the *xiaxiang* ('to the countryside') movement. During the course of this movement, large numbers of office workers and intellectuals were required to spend a period of time in the countryside to integrate with ordinary people. As well as educating the cadres, this movement fulfilled a number of other functions. It helped get the harvest in when there was a labour shortage. It provided personnel to counter the influence of those landlords and members of the old rural élite whose power had increased following the cessation of land reform. It brought senior leadership into contact with local poorly educated cadres deprived of their leading position once the great influx of new people began with the arrival of the Long March. It helped form peasant organisations to complement the centrally controlled work-teams, which hitherto had constituted the major instrument for dealing with rural problems, and also provided a supplement to the inadequate supply of teachers in the border region.

As one might have expected, the process of *xiaxiang* generated some hostility amongst members of the former rural élite and among local cadres who felt that the movement was aimed at usurping their position. Some of the rusticated personnel did not regard their new position with equanimity but most accounts of the time speak of the exhilaration of participating in a historic mission.

In addition to the above, one of the more important functions of the *xiaxiang* movement was connected with a fifth feature of the Yan'an model—the movement to streamline administration (or as it was known the 'movement for crack troops and simple administration'), since the *xiaxiang* process could absorb many retrenched cadres. During the streamlining movement, the number of full-time cadres in mass organisations (labour unions, Women's Federation etc.) was halved. The number of cadres located at sub-region, *xian* and *qu* (the next level down) was reduced by 15 per cent and militia cadres were deprived of their separate salary. For example, of 55 cadres in Yanchuan *xian*, 17 were retrenched of whom 11 resumed full-time work in production, four became heads of *xiang* and two were sent to Yan'an to study.[9] As a consequence of this reduction of personnel, there was a partial move to what some sociologists refer to as *functional* as opposed to *staff-line* leadership. That is to say, there was a greater tendency for a person who had a particular skill to be deployed when and where he was needed rather than to locate him at a particular point in an administrative hierarchy where he could only advise a leader at one position in the direct line of command. One of the drawbacks of functional leadership, in such a situation, was that a person fulfilling a particular role might increasingly see his own position defined only according to that role and this would militate against social solidarity defined in *human* terms. Here again was need for constant rectification and constant retrenchment and at least temporary exchange of roles. Such was Mao's practical application of a commitment to socialism which attempted to reduce the alienation[10] caused by the division of labour; a problem which the Soviet Union never really solved.

The retrenchment of cadres made available people to penetrate the natural village.[11] Such a policy, which no government administration had succeeded in carrying out for many hundreds of years, was one of the major achievements of the Communist Party. To prevent, however, the development of a system of attenuated lines of command, which would have made the Mass Line unworkable, a sixth feature of the Yan'an model was introduced—the principle of *dual rule*.[12] This system may best be understood by examining first what it replaced—the system of *vertical rule*. Prior to 1942, specialised chains of command, staffed almost exclusively by 'outside' intellectuals, reached right down from top to bottom according to what was known as a branch (*bumen*) principle. In practice, this meant that the local education office or the local finance department was a subdivision of a higher-level education or finance department and responsible only to that level. Thus, if two offices at a local level wished to co-ordinate their activities, they could only do so through higher-level organs at that point where the matter in hand was authorised to be settled (which might be at the very apex of the hierarchy). As a result of such a system, lateral co-ordination was difficult, resources tended to be concentrated at higher levels of administration and there was considerable delay in the transfer of materials across branch lines. Anyone who has studied Soviet administration will be familiar with such a system which, in that country, led to severe bottlenecks in production and delays in decision-making. In the wartime situation in China, such inefficiency and delay could not be tolerated, and the new principle of dual rule specified that each office at each level of administration should be responsible not only to higher levels in the same system but also to local government via a co-ordinating committee. These co-ordinating committees were, in practice, the local Party branches. Such a system would make local administration dynamic so long as the Party remained a directing organ with as little formal structure as possible. If the Party itself were to become bureaucratised or fuse with the state bureaucracy and management, then co-ordination would suffer. Similarly, the considerable powers now given to local Party branches might produce a situation where *co-ordination* became *direction* and specialised vertical chains of command atrophied. A careful balance had to be maintained therefore between, on the one hand, the fusion of Party with bureaucracy and, on the other, the Party organisation taking everything on to its own shoulders. Here was another important need for on-going rectification.

The decentralisation of decision-making power to local areas and the strengthening of the power of co-ordinating committees leads us to a seventh feature of the Yan'an model—user control of an increasingly informal education system.[13] The pressing educational need in the border region was seen to be not skilled labour but rather a literate workforce. In the late 1920s, the literacy rate in the Shaan Gan Ning area was between one and three per cent and superstition was widespread with over 2,000 spirit mediums in operation.[14] Peasants in these rural areas were always suspicious of those who advocated extending education—particularly when it came to women who, by infanticide, were made relatively scarce and to whom peasants were unwilling to grant the means for independence. With the onset of fighting and the economic blockade, the exigencies of the war made the establishment of a formal education system very difficult, especially when imports of paper were cut off. Despite these difficulties, however, some progress was made, in the early years, in establishing a formal school system based on structures and methods currently employed in the eastern coastal ports and run by intellectuals from those areas. The stress was on formal lectures, strict entrance examinations and the standardisation of curricula. Despite the phenomenal rise in the numbers of students engaged in formal education (the number in primary schools in the region leapt from 5,600 in 1937 to some 22,000 in 1939),[15] the impact was inadequate and the peasant hostility towards book learning had not been overcome. In 1943, therefore, following administrative decentralisation, the bureaucratic educational hierarchy was broken down and a large portion of the educational effort handed over to *xiang* and village cadres. The number of courses was reduced and courses were made more relevant to the needs of agriculture and the war effort.

The stress now was on mutual learning among the peasants who were invited not only to give talks based on their experiences but to take part in school administration and help establish schools attached to units of production. Such was the origin of the *minban gongzhu* ('people run, public help') schools. The idea was that everyone could in some way participate in the educational process as student or teacher. The peasant associations could assist with housing; the spinning and weaving co-ops could provide for the clothing of students and teachers; the schools could run their own agricultural enterprises and could thus attune themselves to the harmony of rural life. In short, the approach was to produce an education system which sought to *create* the environment for mass education rather than to *select* an educated élite. If formal standards suffered in the process, then surely these would be offset by the long-term gains in mass literacy, without which many other features of the Yan'an model such as the Mass Line and the training of cadres would suffer. There was, however, to be a serious problem. Although *minban* education was considerably expanded, the formal school system coexisted beside it. Thus there was always the danger that this 'two-track' system might make the *minban* idea merely subsidiary to the effort of selecting trained personnel.

The breakdown of the division of labour within the border region leads us to an eighth feature of the Yan'an model. The severe economic privation in 1943 was countered by the insistence that, wherever possible, military and civilian organisations should merge and that each unit of administration, whether civilian or military, should engage in production and aim at self-sufficiency. Back in 1936, some moves had been made in this direction but it was not until 1943 that the Party insisted that *all* cadres should take part both in productive labour and management and that military units should seek self-sufficiency when not in combat. The model here was the 359th Brigade under Wang Zhen (subsequently Minister of Land Reclamation) which opened up new land around Nanniwan and managed to recover 82 per cent of the cost of its upkeep. Enthusiastically, Mao called upon all units to strive for 80 per cent self-sufficiency and most managed to achieve one-third or one-half. Some indication of the achievement is provided in the 1944 budget which was worked out as the equivalent of 260,000 *dan* (piculs) of millet (this being the currency standard) of which 100,000 was to be produced by units and agencies of government themselves.[16] Though the stress on self-sufficiency and ingenuity was, in many ways, dictated by a particular objective situation, Nanniwan was to serve as a model for the next three decades.

But, in the main agricultural field, any attempts at radical reform were hampered by the provisions of the United Front whereby outright confiscation of landlords' property had been replaced by periodic campaigns aimed at rent reduction. With the breakdown of the United Front, these campaigns became tougher and the strengthening of Party branches at village level made the campaign style of politics much easier. Nevertheless, the rent ceiling was still set at the remarkably high figure of 37.5 per cent of crop (deliberately chosen, for this had been the stipulation of an old Guomindang law which that party had been unable or unwilling to put into effect). If landlords resisted, occasional coercion was employed but such coercion often had merely a temporary effect. A campaign would establish a rent ceiling but rents might be raised again once the campaign was over. In such a situation, despite the view commonly held in the West at the time that the Communists were no more than 'agrarian reformers',[17] the original aim of the Party to break the power of the landlords was never far from people's minds and, as an initial step towards its realisation, a programme of co-operativisation was launched.

In the early years of the border regions, attempts to effect a rudimentary form of co-operativisation had been undertaken by *work-teams* sent down from above which were regarded correctly by peasants as agencies of central government. With the reforms of 1942–3, newly formed peasant associations (*nonghui*) were given the task of forming co-operatives and the role of the work-team sent down from above was merely that of initiator. A policy of Mao, attempted in the Jiangxi Soviet, to transform existing patterns of organisation from within now came to the fore once again and traditional forms of labour organisation were incorporated into the peasant association structure with a minimum of interference from the outside. By the beginning of 1943, only some 15 per cent of the full-time labour power of the Shaan Gan Ning border region had been organised into various forms of mutual aid team. By the summer of 1943, 25–40 per cent had participated in the co-operativisation movement and, in 1944, 50–75 per cent.[18] This figure declined in 1945 to 28–45 per cent with the rapid expansion of the region and the consolidation of previous gains. By that time, however, the institution of peasant associations had been firmly established and, once radical land reform was resumed again during the Civil War, these associations were to play an important part in restructuring the countryside. Co-operativisation, therefore, was the ninth feature of the Yan'an model and indeed one of its most significant.

The final feature of the Yan'an model we shall consider here concerns industry which was comparatively underdeveloped in the border regions during the war. I mentioned earlier that the operation of the Mass Line involved a separation between broadly defined *policy* and specific *operations* and the tendency in organisation towards functional patterns of leadership as opposed to the Soviet-style staff-line systems. In industry, this took the form of a policy known as 'concentrated leadership and divided operations' (*jizhong lingdao fensan jingying*), whereby general targets were set centrally but where scattered units of production were allowed operational independence. In such a system, expertise might be deployed over a wide area rather than concentrated in a particular location. The dispersal of industry was useful in time of war when transport costs were high and there was a danger of enemy air attack. More importantly, the dispersal of industry led to the spreading of technical skills and the development of a rudimentary intermediate technology which married in with the traditional handicrafts and what little modern industry there was. Such a policy probably owed much to experiments in industrial co-operation carried out independently of the Communist Party.[19] It was to develop, however, into a cardinal element of Mao's economic strategy. Bringing industry to the peasants and decentralising operational decision-making was a significant break from the Soviet tradition.

Some features of the Soviet experience were, however, employed in the Yan'an area such as the fostering of labour models based on the Stakhanovite system.[20] Though this policy was often individualistic, the stress was usually on the *collective* dimensions of incentive rather than the *individual* dimensions and the wartime situation generated a significant degree of *moral* incentive to counter *material* incentive. Subsequent chapters will explore the extent to which the above pattern was seen to be a temporary expedient and the extent to which it offered a blueprint for the whole of a modernising society.

Disagreements on the peculiar nature of the Yan'an experiences were later to loom large in the polemics within the Chinese Communist Party. In assessing those experiences, one must beware of the revisions of Party history which occurred in the subsequent Cultural Revolution of 1966–9 which was the example *par excellence* of 'open Party rectification'. At that time, it was said that conflict existed within the Party not only concerning the 'dogmatism' of Wang Ming and on the nature of the United Front but also concerning the relationship between Party and masses. Mao was portrayed as a leader who invariably appealed to mass initiative whereas Liu Shaoqi was an organisation man who strove to create a Party élite. Though Liu's view of the Party was more 'organismic' than that of Mao,[21] the difference between the two leaders was only one of degree. For both leaders, rectification was essentially an inner-Party affair[22] and the implementation of the Mass Line, whilst providing material to be used in the rectification campaign, was not essentially part of the rectification process. The Yan'an movement was not an example of 'open rectification'.

Similarly, one should beware of the view that Liu was, at that time, the advocate of control by work-teams sent down from above whilst Mao had a greater faith in the efficacy of the peasant associations. Such a claim, which was made in the first edition of this book, projects the experiences of the early 1960s back to the 1940s. On reflection, it seems that there is no evidence that major differences of opinion existed in Yan'an on the role of work-teams as initiators of social change. It is true that Mao wished to effect social transformation from within, but there was a danger inherent in such an approach. Although such a policy might prevent peasant *anomie*, there was always the possibility that the Party might fail to take over existing leadership and existing organisations, and those leaders and those organisations might, in some cases, take over the Party. Most leaders, therefore, saw a continued need for work-teams.

A third problem in the subsequent reinterpretation of the Yan'an experiences concerns Mao's policy of 'curing the sickness to save the patient'. Though it is true that there were no major witch-hunts and mass expulsions from the Party in Yan'an, policy towards writers and artists was often quite harsh. In his 'Talks at the Yan'an Forum on Literature and Art' (1942), Mao demanded that, in assessing a work of literature or a work of art, both political and artistic criteria should be applied.[23] In fact, all too often, only political criteria were applied and writers and artists suffered some degree of repression.

### The Japanese Surrender

The Yan'an model constituted a rejection of alien models of development and prepacked strategies from which China had suffered all too much in the past. In that sense, the model was implicitly critical of the Soviet Union. The role of the Soviet Union as the first socialist state, however, was consistently upheld and the writings of Lenin and Stalin figured in the rectification campaign.[24] By the 1940s, Mao had also written a number of introductory philosophical works,[25] which meant that the newly literate peasant's introduction to Marxism-Leninism would henceforth be via the writings of Mao which were firmly rooted in the Chinese situation. It was, appropriately, at this point that the Comintern was dissolved (1943) and Stalin's major preoccupation became, quite naturally, the war in his own country.

In 1943, the war in China was not a major concern of the Soviet Union, which had yet to declare war on Japan. It was, however, of crucial importance to the United States. In that year, the Americans beheld an enigmatic Jiang Jieshi going through a Confucian metamorphosis[26] though in practice his military inactivity, in the mountain fastness of

Sichuan, was more akin to the Daoist doctrine of *wuwei* (doing nothing). As the Guomindang contribution to the Allied war effort sank to almost zero, Jiang was challenged by an exasperated American General Stilwell[27] and was prodded firmly, but more diplomatically, by the American government. The Americans began to realise that the brunt of the war with Japan in China was being borne not by Jiang but by the forces led by the Communist Party in the north.

Not long after the Yan'an *Jiefang Ribao* (*Liberation Daily*) published its 4 July 1944 editorial on the parallel between the Communist Party's struggle and that of George Washington,[28] an American mission was sent to Yan'an.[29] When President Roosevelt sought to achieve the appointment of General Stilwell as supreme Allied commander, he was supported by, of all people, Mao Zedong against the opposition of Jiang Jieshi. In the end, however, Jiang was to be victorious. Wedemeyer replaced Stilwell and a new American ambassador to China, Patrick Hurley, proved singularly inept at negotiating between the Guomindang and the Communist Party. An agreement, concluded between Hurley and Mao to support a coalition government, was vetoed by Jiang to whose camp Hurley eventually gravitated. A chain of events was then set in motion which culminated in increasing enmity between the United States and the Chinese Communist Party and the eventual purge of those American officials who had gone to Yan'an in 1944.

By the Seventh Congress of the Chinese Communist Party in April 1945, it was clear that the Party depended on the support of no outside body. The mood was confidently defiant. The Thought of Mao Zedong as the practical application of Marxism-Leninism to the Chinese situation was given particular prominence in the new Party constitution[30] and it was claimed that the oppressed peoples in all countries could profit from a study of the experiences of the Chinese revolution. Now that the forces led by the Communist Party were approaching one million and areas under the various Communist Party-led governments contained a population of some 100 million, Stalin feared that, once the war with Japan was over, the Chinese Civil War would erupt once again and go on for a very long time. In such a war, he felt, the Chinese Communist Party had a very slim chance of success.[31] In the meantime, a weakened China would leave the long Sino-Soviet frontier exposed to any future enemy. The best policy of the Soviet Union, therefore, was to conclude an alliance with Jiang Jieshi and attempt to prevent the Chinese Civil War.

With the dropping of atomic bombs on Japan and the Soviet declaration of war, the Russian Red Army poured into the former state of Manchukuo in an attempt to secure an area that had been strategically important since the Russo-Japanese War of 1904–5. On the very day of Japan's surrender (14 August), an alliance was concluded between Moscow and the régime of Jiang Jieshi which stipulated that, once Soviet troops were withdrawn from north-east China, the area would be handed over to the Guomindang government.[32] To cap it all, the Soviet government had stressed the urgency of an alliance on the grounds that any delay would allow the forces led by the Chinese Communist Party to get there first.[33] Although this was clearly a diplomatic ploy, it did not attest to the reliability of the socialist ally of the Chinese Communist Party.

With the surrender of Japan, the Guomindang and Japanese armies co-operated in preventing Japanese troops from surrendering to those led by the Communist Party. In some cases, the Japanese continued to fight Communist Party-led troops with the tacit support of the Guomindang. As civil war seemed imminent, Mao and Jiang met in Chongqing to negotiate a *modus vivendi*.[34] An agreement was concluded on 10 October 1946 but, almost immediately, Jiang's forces intensified their attack on the base areas and hurriedly availed themselves of American transport to ferry troops to the Soviet-occupied north-east. The Soviet response was inexplicable. Despite certain sympathy expressed to Jiang in August, the Red Army proceeded to give aid to the Communist forces until November and then changed to a policy of actively aiding Jiang Jieshi. By spring 1946, the Soviet position had changed yet again.[35] Meanwhile, vast amounts of industrial equipment in north-east China were dismantled and shipped off to the Soviet Union.[36] The American position was equally confusing. Considerable aid was given to Jiang Jieshi, yet, at the same time, an American mission under General Marshall proceeded to negotiate between the two sides.[37] By mid-1946, however, the Civil War was on in earnest, and the initial struggle centred on control over the north-east in the wake of the withdrawing Soviet troops.

It is not my intention here to go into the many campaigns of the Civil War.[38] I shall, however, devote some attention to the various and different policies put forward by the Communist Party during the war which provide a background for the establishment of the People's Republic. In the very early period, these policies were to be far more radical than any of those implemented in Yan'an.

### Rural Policy (1946–9)

With the onset of the Civil War, Mao's policies on 'people's war' emerged in their fullest form. In the early period, attention was devoted to building up strength in the countryside and the fighting consisted largely of guerrilla engagements. To facilitate this, a huge militia was created[39] which fed recruits into the guerrilla forces and these, in turn, provided recruits for the regular forces which, in 1947, were to be renamed the Chinese People's Liberation Army (PLA). The notion of unity of work and arms, which had been developed in Yan'an days, received a new emphasis but the situation was somewhat different from the early 1940s. The co-operatives which had been formed at that time were frequently identical with units of the people's militia and such a situation facilitated the initial penetration of the natural village and the financing of the war effort. Soldiers on the march had been given work tickets which expressed a certain period of active service as the equivalent of so many days' farm work and which were repayable according to a millet standard of currency.[40] When no fighting was necessary, soldiers might return to farm work or at least help train the local militia units which were also engaged in political work. Such a system worked best when the regular army was relatively small, when its area of operations was concentrated and where armies remained near their place of original recruitment. But, after 1946, it became increasingly difficult for troops to return to farm work. On the one hand, there were fewer breaks in the fighting and, on the other, troops were moved over great distances with the result that their knowledge of the area in which they operated was not as great as their old Eighth Route Army predecessors. Consequently, the Party had to rely more and more on the rapid development of village activists (*jijifenzi*) to instigate rural reforms.[41] This was particularly important for three reasons. First, the enemy was no longer a foreign aggressor but Guomindang troops which often had close relations with landowners in their areas of operation. Secondly, at the beginning of the war, these Guomindang troops far outnumbered those of the Communist Party. In the old Japanese occupation days, the enemy was greatly overextended and resorted merely to periodic (though savage) 'mopping-up' (*saodang*) operations. Now, the resources at the disposal of the Guomindang allowed for permanent instruments of repression to be continually buttressed by Guomindang military force. Thirdly, as the Civil War erupted, a new land reform policy was instituted which no longer favoured the rich peasants. As the focus of attention switched to 'poor and lower-middle peasants', intensive mass mobilisation was seen as imperative.

The new period of land reform commenced with a Party directive of May 1946. Though more radical than anything which had existed in Yan'an, this document did not call for the confiscation of landlords' land. It sought merely to purchase land for redistribution.[42] But the radicalism of local cadres, in areas where it was felt necessary to break the power of pro-Guomindang élites, was such that some land was, in fact, confiscated. Such actions were to win peasant support and the Land Reform Law, passed at an agricultural conference in September 1947, reflected the new climate. This law stipulated that all property of landlords and land owned by the (Guomindang) state was subject to confiscation; additionally all property above the general average (which included that of rich peasants) was redistributed but peasants still retained the right to buy and sell land.[43]

To implement the new policy, it was necessary to mobilise the peasants. In some areas, where actions had already anticipated the change in Party policy, this was a relatively easy task. In other areas, however, there were immense problems. Traditional social structure frequently cut across class lines. Institutions such as the lineage (clan—*zu*) or the secret society would contain both landlords and poor peasants and the network of loyalties within them frustrated any attempt by an outside organisation to penetrate the villages. The Yan'an method had been to utilise existing members of these organisations to weaken the structure of loyalties and, over a period of time, heighten consciousness of the class divisions within them. This task had been facilitated by the relatively mild land reform policy. Now with the occupation of vast expanses of new territory and with a new land reform policy, cadres frequently encountered a situation where peasants were unwilling to be mobilised, either because they did not perceive their class interests or because, in a wartime situation of rapidly shifting fronts, they feared Guomindang reprisals once the PLA withdrew. Participation in land reform was a commitment to the whole process of revolution and was not made lightly.

Considerable skill, therefore, was needed in the process of mobilising the peasants and, to ensure that local cadres had such a skill, the land reform programme was accompanied by a new rectification movement. The main target in that movement was, at first, slothful and bureaucratic cadres. It was considered that such cadres came from 'impure backgrounds' and many cadres, who were not poor peasants, were denounced and removed from office. Yet it was often the case that the slothful cadres were, in fact, poor peasants and the rectification movement frequently resulted in a 'commandist' persecution of the most active. During land reform, work-teams were enjoined to form peasant associations and poor peasant bands (*pinnongtuan*) to carry out the struggle. In practice, they all too often descended upon the village and imposed policies from above.[44] This violation of the Mass Line was to generate some hostility.

Where commandist deviations were avoided, problems could still occur because of the way commitment was fostered. Because of the risks involved in participating in the revolution, peasants could not drift into the process of rural reform as had been possible in Yan'an days. A conscious act of repudiation of traditional loyalties was required. Such an act tended to be made suddenly and in a highly charged emotional atmosphere which the Communist Party cadres sought to create. 'Struggle sessions' were held at which landlords stood with heads bowed and were humiliated. As more and more peasants joined in the process of denunciation, they symbolised their irrevocable commitment by burning land titles and mortgage agreements. The result was a snowball effect; or,

Killing landowners

as one writer put it, the process was a veritable 'hurricane'.[45] Peasants, who for a long period had resisted mobilisation, now took the law into their own hands and were often as unresponsive to Party cadres as they had been in the early days of mobilisation. The Land Reform Law had stipulated that only landlords guilty of certain crimes should be punished and that others should be given a share of land after redistribution. But what was the Party to do in a situation where decades of bottled-up hatred and resentment finally exploded and resulted in the victimisation or summary execution of landlords? A 'tailist' solution, whereby inexperienced rural cadres just went along with spontaneous peasant action and random seizure of land, was clearly not what was required. Yet if controls were applied harshly by work-teams sent down from above, peasants might be alienated and further administrative reform made difficult.

The problem was compounded by the fact that, due to the exigencies of war and the concentration on areas of actual conflict, the Party network in rural areas was weak. Moreover, a situation might occur where cadres adopted a radical approach to land reform and a highly conservative attitude towards other issues such as the rights of women.[46] Pending adoption of a Marriage Law, cadres had to deal with knotty problems such as what to do with a woman who was formerly half-owned by her husband and half-owned by a landlord. With the demise of the landlord, was she wholly owned by her husband or owned by neither? The answer was obvious, one might assume, but not to the cadre who had thought about nothing but the problem of land.

As one might expect, there was consensus in the Party that something had to be done about what the Party historian He Ganzhi called 'erroneous dispersionism, lack of discipline and anarchy at work' and situations where inexperienced cadres were guilty of 'free actions in political affairs, a dislike of Party leadership and supervision and a disrespect for the decisions made by the Central Committee and higher echelons'.[47] It was generally felt, in early 1948, that the rectification movement should be intensified but the attitude towards that movement varied amongst different cadres. The crucial question centred on exactly what kind of behaviour was to be rectified. Some people continued to see the movement as directed against those cadres who took a cautious approach or simply those who came from 'impure' backgrounds, whilst others saw its major target as 'ultra-leftist' indiscipline. In the mid-1960s, the view of official Party historians was that the Party leadership deliberately confused the main target of the movement. Mao had apparently warned against 'ultra-leftism' in December 1947,[48] but Liu Shaoqi, no longer the organisation man who remained aloof from the masses, persisted with 'ultra-left' policies. In his study of the process of rectification, however, Frederick Teiwes has challenged this view, suggesting that there was no discernible difference between Liu and Mao on rural policy. In fact, neither leader really perceived how bad the situation had become until April 1948 when both of them came down on the side of caution. Liu Shaoqi, therefore, was responsible for 'ultra-leftism' only in the sense that he was head of the land reform department and directed rural policies in areas where there had been considerable resentment against those who had collaborated with the Japanese and where peasants feared the return of Guomindang-backed élites. Contrary to my previous writing on the subject, I find Teiwes's argument quite convincing and tend to support his hypothesis that when a revolutionary party, during the struggle for power, suffers from a divided leadership or when the environment it operates in is hostile, it tends to adopt coercive techniques of internal control; when the organisation is unified and when its environment is secure, it tends to adopt methods of persuasion. Thus, it is argued, the Yan'an rectification movement adopted techniques of persuasion because, despite the Japanese threat, the enemy could not disrupt the rectification process and the régime was relatively secure. In 1947–8, however, during a period of much sharper class struggle, coercion became the rule.[49] Yet this resulted in a loss of Party control and China's first attempt at 'open Party rectification' was not particularly successful. The result was eventually a change in policy. With the Second Plenum of the Seventh Central Committee in March 1949, the Party announced that the main focus of its work was to shift from the rural areas to the cities[50] and, by late 1949, a new land reform law had been formulated which was much less radical than that of 1947.[51] Stability was, for the moment, considered more important than radical reform. Such was the genesis of what was later referred to as 'the rich peasant line'.

## Urban Policy (1946 – 9)

In the urban and industrial sectors, a similar pattern of radicalisation followed by deradicalisation occurred, with rank-and-file cadres tending to be somewhat more radical than the centre. In the early part of the Civil War, a considerable amount of industrial equipment had been removed either by the Soviet armies occupying north-east China or by the retreating Guomindang. Machinery too had been destroyed by Communist Party-led troops guilty of 'left deviation' or to prevent it falling into enemy hands once a particular town was abandoned. By December 1947, however, it had become clear that, from then on, cities would be occupied permanently and a clear policy was enunciated by Mao Zedong that the takeover (*jieguan*) of industry was to cause as little disruption as possible.[52] Nevertheless, the same lack of discipline which had manifested itself in the rural areas, together with the confused military situation, led to considerable damage. The mammoth Anshan Iron and Steel Works, for example, which was later to be the keystone of China's First Five Year Plan (1953–7), did not resume production after the war with Japan until 1947, after which it changed hands no less than seven times between February and November 1948.[53] As it had already been ransacked by occupying Soviet troops, this further damage was disastrous.

The increasingly mild policy towards industrial takeover was reflected in the resolutions of the Sixth Labour Conference which met in Harbin in August 1948[54] and which attempted to establish a transitional structure for industrial enterprises; but, even at that late date, the north-east bureau of the Party was reluctant to employ Guomindang members in senior management positions.[55] The Party was particularly suspicious of those Guomindang government appointees who had been sent to take over industrial concerns from former Japanese management in 1945.[56]

The great problem which faced the new administration in China's heavy industrial heartland, north-east China, was not only that much of industry was not operational but that many senior management personnel had been transferred to the south by the retreating Guomindang forces. Regional government, therefore, was required to appoint new and inexperienced people to senior management positions, often from outside the industrial sector. These people were occasionally attacked for maintaining 'the line of the poor peasant and hired hand' (they paid no attention to orderly planning).[57] But, as more senior management and administrators were found still at their posts as the PLA moved south, the policy of industrial and urban takeover became more and more restrained. An urban equivalent of the 'rich peasant line' was apparent.

### The Collapse of the Guomindang

By the end of 1947, the numerical superiority of the Guomindang over the People's Liberation Army had been reduced from four to one (in 1945) to two to one and, from then on, smaller towns tended to be occupied permanently.[58] In late 1948, parity in forces had been reached, in part due to large-scale defection of Guomindang troops to the side of the PLA. Up to that year, two-thirds of recruits were from the peasants and only one-third from Guomindang defectors but the situation was to change so drastically that, by the end of the war, it was reckoned that two-fifths of the PLA strength of five million were from the Guomindang.[59] There was no course but to retain such troops since there was often nowhere to demobilise them, and one of the plagues of China's history had been demobilised soldiers who had turned to banditry.

To counter the influence of Guomindang defectors and also as a consequence of the Yan'an tradition, a system of 'military democracy' prevailed in the PLA ranks. When not in combat, the most important figure in a military unit would be the political instructor or commissar who was frequently also the secretary of a military Party branch. At such times, soldiers were encouraged to criticise their officers and might nominate non-commissioned officers (if that term has any meaning in an army which had appointments but no ranks), though such nominations were subject to ratification by higher levels. The old Eighth Route Army tradition of not appropriating the property of civilians was maintained, though it was often difficult to enforce at a time of rapid expansion and increasing defection from the enemy. Relations with the mass of the people were, on the whole, very good and in the major campaigns, especially as the focus switched to east China, peasants provided large numbers of auxiliaries.[60] Yet gradually the expanded army took on a new character: a large conglomerate army was not the small, well-disciplined force which had fought the Japanese.

The turning point of the Civil War came in the autumn of 1948. By that time, not only had the PLA achieved parity in numbers with the Guomindang forces but the international environment had begun to change. In the early stages of the Civil War, the United States had given considerable aid to Jiang Jieshi and the degree to which that country should prop up the Guomindang became an important issue in the United States presidential election. With the unexpected defeat of the pro-Jiang candidate Thomas Dewey, Mao Zedong could see that large-scale aid was a thing of the past. In the United States, the talk was of negotiations and peace and influential journals such as the *New York Times* and *Business Week* urged that their government should stop supporting Jiang for fear of driving the Communist Party further into the arms of the Soviet Union.

The Chinese Communist Party's perception of the change in United States policy was not that imperialism was any less of an ultimate threat, merely that, in the immediate future, the United States was unlikely to intervene in China, in its offshore islands such as Taiwan or for that matter in Korea. Indeed, by mid-1949, United States forces had been removed from Korea and even such a 'hawk' as General MacArthur, who had fostered policies such as the rearmament of Japan, declared that it was not America's intention to fight a war on the Asian mainland.[61]

In the autumn of 1948, the PLA swung into a massive offensive in north-east China. Following the capture of the north-eastern capital of Shenyang, the policy was to seize the major cities. As the Communist Party leaders constantly updated their estimate of the end of the war, the Guomindang régime crumbled. Beiping (soon to be renamed Beijing) negotiated a surrender and, in a last bid to reach a settlement, Jiang resigned in favour of his vice-president, Li Congren. In April 1949, the terms proposed by the Communist Party were rejected and the PLA crossed the Changjiang (Yangtze). A demoralised south China, ruined by catastrophic inflation and having lost its confidence in the Guomindang's military ability, fell rapidly to pieces. By the time of the inauguration of the Chinese People's Republic on 1 October 1949, Jiang Jieshi had retreated to Taiwan.

## Conclusion

The Guomindang régime had shown little inclination to fight the Japanese or to ally itself effectively with forces which were pursuing the war. By the late 1940s, it was riddled with corruption and had allowed a catastrophic inflation to develop. It had been co-opted by old rural élites and even the United States government was convinced that continued aid would be money cast down a bottomless well. Opposition to the Guomindang came from many different groups of people—workers, peasants, frustrated businessmen, dispirited generals and even those Nationalists who still maintained the ideals of the 'revolutionary Guomindang'. The Communist Party did more than offer an alternative régime tried and tested in the wartime border regions; it offered also the vision of an alternative society which promised to redress the humiliations of a century.

The alternative régime built up around Yan'an, however, was the product of peculiar historical conditions. As the Civil War expanded after 1946 many of these conditions changed and the close link between leaders and led, so carefully fostered in Yan'an, became weaker. At the same time, the switch from national to civil war changed the composition of the Party's United Front and resulted in some extreme leftist activities. As the Civil War drew to a close, therefore, priority was accorded to maintaining control rather than mass mobilisation and a period of rather moderate policies was ushered in.

## NOTES

1. See Johnson, 1962.
2. This section is based on Selden, 1971, with some ideas from Schurmann, 1966.
3. Mao Zedong, 1 February 1942, Compton, 1966, pp. 21–2.
4. This idea courtesy of Bill Jenner.
5. Compton, 1966.
6. Schurmann, 1966, p. 236.
7. This was later redefined as 'red' (*hong*) and 'expert' (*zhuan*).
8. Mao Zedong, 1 June 1943, *SW* III, p. 119.

9. Selden, 1971, p. 215.

10. Note, Mao did not speak specifically of alienation.

11. Schurmann, 1966, pp. 415–16, 422–7.

12. Ibid., pp. 188–94.

13. See Seybolt, 1971.

14. Ibid., p. 644.

15. Selden, 1971, p. 269.

16. Ibid., pp. 253–4.

17. See Shewmaker, 1968.

18. Selden, 1971, p. 246.

19. These were the Chinese Industrial Co-operatives. At one time, these co-operatives received some support from the Guomindang government but, with the collapse of the United Front, were frequently considered to be too radical. With the expansion of the Communist Party base areas during the war, many of these co-operatives were swept into the orbit of the Communist Party and given a new lease of life. See Alley, 1952.

20. The Stakhanovite movement in the Soviet Union was named after A.G. Stakhanov whose team of three workers attained, in the mid-1930s, the remarkable output of 102 tons of coal in a shift of 5¾ hours at the Irmino Mine in the Ukraine. The team went on to break new records and a nationwide movement was launched to emulate it. The term 'Stakhanovite worker' was applied thereafter to those who broke output records.

21. Young, 1979, pp. 7–93.

22. Teiwes, 1979, pp. 73, 78 and 99.

23. Mao Zedong, 23 May 1942, *SW* III, p. 88.

24. Compton, 1952, pp. x–xi.

25. E.g. 'On Practice', July 1937 (*SW* I, pp. 295–309), 'On Contradiction', August 1937 (*SW* I, pp. 311–47).

26. See Jiang, 1947.

27. Tuchman, 1970.

28. Schram, 1966, pp. 225–6.

29. Barrett, 1970.

30. Text in Liu, 1950, pp. 155–204.

31. Mao Zedong, 24 September 1962, Schram, 1974, p. 191; Djilas, 1969, p. 141.

32. Tsou, 1967, pp. 284–5.

33. Ibid., p. 283.

34. See Mao Zedong, 17 October 1945, *SW* IV, pp. 53–63.

35. Tsou, 1967, pp. 327–40, for one explanation.

36. During the 268-day Soviet occupation, the value of installations damaged or shipped away from north-east China to the Soviet Union has been estimated at $US 635,649,000 (Pauley's statistics cited in Cheng, 1956, p. 266) and $US 845,238,000 (statistics compiled by Japanese technicians, cited in ibid., p. 266).

37. See Beal, 1970.

38. See Chassin, 1966.

39. *PR* 34, 21 August 1964, p. 22.

40. Lindsay, 1970, p. 3.

41. W. Hinton, 1966, p. 115.

42. CCPCC, 14 May 1946, Selden, 1979, pp. 208–14.

43. Text with supplements in W. Hinton, 1966, pp. 615–26; Selden, 1979, pp. 214–18.

44. Discussed in W. Hinton, especially Chapters XLI–III.

45. The title of a novel by Zhou Libo (Chou Li-po).

46. W. Hinton, 1966, p. 398.

47. He Ganzhi, cited in Schurmann, 1966, p. 433.

48. Mao Zedong, 25 March 1947, Mao, 1949, pp. 20–41.

49. Teiwes, 1979, pp. 100–1.

50. *Beiping Jiefangbao*, 25 March 1949, p. 1.
51. Text in *CB* 42, 22 December 1950, Selden, 1979, pp. 240–3.
52. Mao Zedong, 25 December 1947, Mao, 1949, pp. 20–41, Selden, 1979, pp. 169–75.
53. Cheng, 1955, p. 22.
54. *RMRB*, 10 November 1948, p. 3.
55. Ibid., 7 August 1948, p. 2.
56. Ibid.
57. Ibid., 12 September 1948, p. 1.
58. CCPCC, N.E. Bureau, 10 June 1948, Liu *et al.*, 1949.
59. On Guomindang absorption, see Gittings, 1967, pp. 68–73.
60. Ibid., pp. 65–8.
61. Friedman, 1971, p. 214.

# II
# THE ESTABLISHMENT OF GOVERNMENT
## (1949 – 1950)

The speed with which the Guomindang régime collapsed in 1949 took everyone by surprise. Huge areas of south China were rapidly occupied by the PLA and large numbers of economic enterprises were taken over intact. It seemed, therefore, that economic reforms in the south might proceed without too much disruption. Such a possibility reinforced the moderate tone of Party policy in evidence since 1948. As the war drew to a close, the new régime anticipated that it would enjoy a certain degree of security from external threat. The United States appeared to have cut its losses in Asia and, as the fighting in Indo-China and Korea intensified, it was likely that an American *cordon sanitaire* would be drawn far from China's borders.

## 'Leaning to One Side'

The possibility of relatively peaceful reform in China and the lack of any short-term threat, in 1949, allowed the Chinese Communist Party to think of long-term foreign policy. The United States posed no immediate danger but the activities of General MacArthur in Japan could cause major problems in the future.[1] It is not difficult for us to imagine China's fears about a rearmed Japan which, if anything, were greater than Soviet fears about a rearmed Germany. Thus, mindful of a future Japanese-United States threat, Mao Zedong declared unequivocally that China would 'lean to the side of the Soviet Union',[2] despite the treatment China had received at Soviet hands. In the meantime, however, it was quite possible that diplomatic relations with the United States might have been established, at least on the same partial basis as they were with Britain, not long after the creation of the People's Republic. China showed no intention of intervening in Indo-China or Korea and it seemed that the

50

progress of people's war in those areas would, before long, lead to a result similar to that which had occurred in China without much danger of American intervention.

This view was, of course, quite wrong but, as Edward Friedman has argued, it was not an irrational one.[3] One cannot blame the Chinese, not skilled at that time in 'Washingtonology', for not understanding the erroneous view gaining currency in the United States that north-east China was in the grip of the Soviet Union and what was happening in Asia was part of some international Communist conspiracy hatched by the Cominform[4] after its establishment in 1947.[5] To the Chinese, such a view was manifestly ludicrous, especially since relations with the Soviet Union were not particularly good.

We have noted the ambivalent attitude of the Soviet Union during the occupation of the north-east at the start of the Civil War when a treaty was concluded with the Guomindang government. In 1949, relations were still not good despite the fact that an agreement had been signed between Moscow and the Communist Party administration in north-east China.[6] When Mao himself went to Moscow, late in that year, to conclude a new treaty, he noted that the atmosphere remained quite cool and it was not until the Korean War that Stalin was to have any confidence in the new Chinese leadership.[7]

A thirty-year Sino-Soviet treaty was, however, concluded in February 1950[8] and reflected very clearly the fear of a rearmed Japan. The two sides agreed that, if either were attacked by Japan or any state allied with it (a reference to the United States), the other would immediately render military and other assistance by all means at its disposal. In a separate agreement, the Soviet Union granted trade concessions and a $300 million loan. In return, China agreed to preserve the special rights of the Soviet Union granted by the former Guomindang government. Joint Sino-Soviet administration was established over railways in the north-east and over the port of Lushun and Dalian pending the conclusion of a peace treaty with Japan, or, failing that, until 1952. A number of joint-stock companies were established in petroleum, non-ferrous metals, shipbuilding and civil aviation and the *de facto* independence of the Mongolian People's Republic (Outer Mongolia—formerly claimed by China) was guaranteed.

## The 'New Democratic' Government

The independence of China from the Soviet Union may be clearly seen in the theoretical discussions concerning the new form of government. Back in 1940, Mao Zedong had articulated the principles of a 'new democratic' stage of development which was much wider in scope than Lenin's 'democratic dictatorship of workers and peasants'. These principles were reiterated in 1949 in Mao's 'On People's Democratic Dictatorship'.[9] They held that the revolution which the Communist Party led should not be seen as a socialist revolution, in the Marxian sense,[10] but as a new democratic revolution (*xin minzhuzhuyi geming*). Under this formulation, the workers were defined as 'masters' (*zhurenweng*) but were joined in their 'dictatorship' over the landlords and bureaucratic capitalists by three other class groupings—peasants, petty bourgeoisie and national capitalists. This four-class bloc was defined as the 'people' and was represented as the four smaller stars on the new Chinese flag.

The new democratic revolution was seen as a process rather than an act. The act by which the régime changed was referred to as 'liberation' (*jiefang*) and, in its individual dimension, was known as 'turning over' (*fanshen*). Likewise, the construction of socialism (*shehuizhuyi jianshe*) was also seen as a process, during which the concept 'people' (95 per cent of the population at that stage) would change according to the pace of transformation (*gaizao*). The key questions then were: how quickly should this process develop, what was the structure of the United Front during each of its stages and what were the policy implications of that structure?

The principles of new democracy were enshrined in official state documents in September 1949 by a body known as the Chinese People's Political Consultative Conference. The members of this body were chosen to represent the current United Front and the formal delegates represented a number of political parties and groups sympathetic to the Communist Party, geographical areas, religious bodies, national minorities, overseas Chinese and mass organisations (such as the All China Federation of Democratic Women).

The three major documents passed by the conference, which were to serve as an interim constitution, were the Common Programme, the Organic Law of the Chinese People's Political Consultative Conference and the Organic Law of the Central People's Government.[11] The first of these outlined the formal content of new democracy, stating that citizen rights would be given only to those who formally qualified as the 'people' and prescribing 'dictatorship' over the former exploiting classes and groups which constituted the remainder. The document stipulated the abolition of imperialist privileges, the pressing need for industralisation and the importance of friendship with the Soviet Union. It stated that the Political Consultative Conference was only to serve as a temporary body until a National People's Congress might be elected by all citizens (such a body was to meet in 1954). Until such time, a Central People's Government Council would be elected by the conference and a National Committee (with a smaller Standing Committee) would be set up to conduct conference affairs when the large body (with over 500 delegates) was not in session. The second document outlined the functions of the conference in the rehabilitation of the country and procedures for the selection of delegates and the third prescribed the initial organs of state.

The supreme government organ of the new régime was to be the Central People's Government Council, which was simultaneously a legislative, executive and judicial organ. It supervised a number of committees, the most important being the Government Administration Council headed by the premier, Zhou Enlai. This latter body, which consisted of five deputy premiers, a secretary-general and 16 members, controlled all government ministries under three very powerful committees—Political and Legal Affairs, Finance and Economics and Culture and Education. In addition, there ranked equal to these committees a People's Control Committee charged with checking up on the operation of all ministries. Alongside the Government Administration Council, the Central People's Government Council established a Revolutionary Military Council, a Supreme People's Court and a Supreme People's Procuratorate. These institutions were based on Soviet models—especially the Procuratorate which was required to ensure the observance of the law by all government officials.

Until 1954, the powers of the central government were considerably limited by those of the six large administrative regions which were set up during and after the Civil War. Of these, the first to be established, and probably the most powerful, was that of north-east China under Gao Gang, a former leader of the North Shaanxi Soviet area before the arrival in that area of the Long March. Devastated by war, the north-east was still the centre of China's heavy industry and the area with the closest links with the Soviet Union. In 1949, part of the region (Lushun and Dalian) was still occupied by Soviet troops and the administration in that area was to serve as a model of industrial rehabilitation for those who inclined toward the Soviet Union.[12] In this region, and later elsewhere, the initiative in creating a state structure was taken by the army. The Fourth Field Army under Lin Biao, having successfully completed its campaign in the north-east, proceeded to the Guangdong area in south China where a Central South Administrative Region was carved out with its capital in the central China city of Wuhan. Throughout the next 20 years, key government and Party personnel in these two regions remained Fourth Field Army men with, it is alleged, some kind of attachment to their former military commander, Lin Biao. A similar pattern has been posited for north-west China (the First Field Army under He Long and Peng Dehuai), north China (the Fifth Field Army under Nie Rongzhen), east China (the Third Field Army under Chen Yi and Su Yu) and south-west China (the Second Field Army under Liu Bocheng).[13] The six large administrative regions, therefore, corresponded to the zones of operations of these armies. Below them came the traditional administrative divisions—province, special district, *xian* (or urban *shi*), *xiang* (or market town *zhen*) and village. At most of the higher levels, there was initially a military control commission which operated through a number of committees (Party, economic, educational, cultural etc.) set up on an *ad hoc* basis. The control commissions at various levels sent out special task forces to take over various institutions and these task forces, before very long, became absorbed into the institutions themselves.

The life of the military control commissions was very limited. Their function, as described by A. Doak Barnett, was similar to receivers in bankruptcy. In Beijing, where takeover proceeded very smoothly, the control commission was assisted by a joint administrative office consisting of Guomindang officials and Communist Party cadres. Once the Guomindang members of this office had made an inventory of the assets of former government organisations and those of organisations designated as 'bureaucratic capitalist', they handed over power to a newly formed People's Government. This consisted of personnel retained from the old régime, representatives of mass organisations ('red' labour unions etc.) and Party-military personnel.[14]

This triple alliance formula was repeated at lower levels of administration, though the components of the alliance varied from area to area. In north-east China, since many Guomindang government officials had been removed before the cessation of hostilities, the component of retained personnel was comparatively small. The south, where they had concentrated before the advance of the PLA, however, provided greater numbers of experienced personnel who might be retained. Here, many senior government officials and management personnel remained at their posts upon liberation[15] and consequently the triple alliance was more evenly balanced.

Within factories, the military representatives, who had been sent down by military control commissions (or their sub-committees when they were in existence), frequently remained behind and linked the retained personnel with the mass organisations.[16] These latter were frequently the worker pickets (*gongren jiuchadui*), the function of which had been to maintain factory discipline while the fighting had been going on and to undertake policing and patrolling duties pending the arrival of the PLA.[17] Sometimes these pickets maintained a city-wide organisation such as the Shanghai People's Peace Preservation Corps (*Renmin Baoandui*) which was formed by the Communist Party and which consisted of some 60,000 people, of whom 60 per cent were workers. Its members were responsible for some remarkable feats of courage in keeping production going during the battle of Shanghai.[18]

In Shanghai, the resumption of production and the restoration of order was relatively smooth. In some areas, however, disruptions occurred due to what many people felt to be excessive radicalism on the part of the worker picket organisations. In Tianjin, for example, which had been liberated during the last phase of the north-east campaign prior to the siege of Beijing and where there were relatively few retained personnel, worker organisations often disregarded Party policy, took over factory management themselves and created a considerable amount of confusion.[19] In such a situation, the vice-chairman of the Party, Liu Shaoqi, delivered his famous 'Tianjin Talks' designed to restore discipline.[20]

The situation in Tianjin was perhaps an exception but it does reveal that, in an increasingly conservative mood, the Party leadership was prepared to curb radicalism and make concessions to the employees of the former government. Whilst they were in existence, considerable autonomy seems to have been given to military control commissions or takeover groups in deciding who was suitable for re-employment, and the urgent need to establish the organs of state resulted in very elastic standards. In public security work in particular, the disappearance of former policemen was initially made up for by the employment of PLA troops, though a number of former Guomindang government policemen were reinstated.[21] The credentials of these policemen were not always impeccable from a Communist Party point of view. Nor were the former civil servants, who were now employed in civil affairs bureaux, comparable to the former cadres of Yan'an days and it was felt necessary to balance their influence by the recruitment of a large number of activists, often drawn from the ranks of students.[22]

The new conservatism was also evident in the rural sector and took the form of the 'rich peasant line'. During the Cultural Revolution, some 17 years later, the inauguration of the 'rich peasant line' was directly attributed to Liu Shaoqi.[23] It was certainly Liu who made one of the key speeches elucidating the line on 14 June 1950, though perhaps here he was only reflecting a committee decision. In the speech, Liu called for a halt to land reform in all areas where it had not yet started and imposed restraints upon peasants who had already initiated the process.[24] Liu stressed that land reform should in no way harm production and that, where it had been decided on for the winter of 1950–1, every effort should be made to get in the harvest and collect the public (tax) grain before launching the reform. Under no circumstances should land reform be allowed to lead to 'confusion' and on no account should the land of rich peasants be confiscated, for they had moved to a 'neutralist' position. The main theme, therefore, was that production should come before social change, nothing was to be done without authorisation from above and the work-team method of social control should replace the former peasant association approach. Now, 'enlightened gentry' were to be invited to participate in a United Front and all land reform trials were to be handled by the formal court structures.[25]

A new and complex class analysis was employed. The category of 'small landlords' was introduced, being defined as landlords who had supported the revolution, and, to avoid the opprobrium associated with the name 'rich peasants', the term 'prosperous middle peasant' became current. It was frequently the case that several of these different categories might be found in the same family and the problem of implementing the new scheme of categorisation led to a veritable bureaucrat's paradise.[26] We shall return to the problem of bureaucratisation later; in the meantime it should be noted that, by 1949, village administration tended to conform to the triple alliance model—'enlightened gentry' or rich peasants were the equivalent of the retained personnel; what was left of the radical peasant associations were classed as mass organisations and personnel remaining from the work-teams sent down from above, around which Party nuclei were to grow, provided the link.

### The Democratisation of Enterprise Management

One of the most interesting manifestations of the triple alliance formula was in factory management.[27] Military representatives, or Party secretaries who replaced them, were required to establish factory management committees upon which worker delegates and senior management (often retained) also sat. These bodies were to formulate factory policy according to regional plans, as they were drawn up, and were to provide an institutional form for worker participation in management.

The management committees, however, were not very successful for a number of reasons. First, industrial management (and especially in the north-east where much industry was located) was the one area in Chinese society where a Soviet model of organisation was introduced very early on. Although the management committees were similar to the Soviet workers' councils set up after the Bolshevik Revolution, the model of organisation emulated in Chinese industry after 1948 was a current Stalinist one which was extremely suspicious of 'parliamentary' (*yihui*) forms of management. The considerable powers given to line management meant that the effectiveness of other elements in the triple alliance formula was not great. Secondly, the Party representatives and worker delegates were often too inexperienced to curb management. Thirdly, many worker delegates were creamed off into management if they showed any particular skill. Fourthly, the worker component on the management committees often became the nuclei of labour union branches from which the more politically active were transferred to higher union posts. In such a situation, many management committees became little more than audiences for management (*tingting hui*) and lacked any democratic spirit.

Other bodies which were set up in factories to curb the power of management and to foster worker participation were the worker and staff congresses at which factory general managers were required to defend policies, seek suggestions and if necessary undergo 'self-examination'. As time passed, however, these bodies met less and less frequently and caused the Party some concern.

Although leading bodies in factories occasionally manifested some radicalism in early 1949, it was quite clear by 1950 that a more usual development was bureaucratism. At first sight, a manifestation of bureaucratism would seem strange in the atmosphere of euphoria which accompanied liberation, but the transformation of an 'ultra-left' deviation into its opposite was probably quite familiar to cadres schooled in the dialectic. Undoubtedly, the major cause of this change was that cadres were swamped by the complexity and size of the myriad tasks which had to be undertaken.

## The Establishment of Control

The most immediate task which had to be undertaken following liberation was a general stocktaking of all resources both human and economic. Rudimentary census returns had to be made, births reported and residence units demarcated. Particularly active here were citizen groups such as the worker picket organisations who, through controlling grain supplies,[28] not only registered the population and established an elementary system of public security but also took measures to facilitate the regulation of labour and the relief of unemployment.[29]

As the registration of the population proceeded, local authorities were instructed to provide work for the unemployed and relieve the needy. China's cities had for long been afflicted by periodic influxes of rural vagrants (*youmin*) who were now organised to undertake huge labour-intensive construction tasks at low wages. At the same time, measures were taken to ensure that the swollen urban population was fed. Pending the establishment of an effective rural taxation policy, however, the government could do little but despatch work-teams to the countryside to requisition grain and this policy occasioned sporadic peasant opposition.[30]

Along with the registration of the population, the new government made an inventory of all industrial and commercial institutions with a view to controlling resource allocation (in favour of the former). In the early post-liberation period, such control was best effected by the supervision of contracts between economic organisations both in the state and private sectors. The institution of controlled contracts, it was said, was to provide the rudiments of a planning system and local budgeting.

Perhaps the greatest headache was the catastrophic inflationary situation which the new government inherited. As far as wages were concerned, the first step was to extend the wage policy of the old liberated areas to the whole country. According to this policy, a system of wage-points (known either as *xi* or *fen* in various parts of the country) was in operation, whereby a day's labour was calculated in wage-points assessed in terms of bundles of commodities (rice, wheat, edible oil, coal etc.).[31] In effect, this meant greatly extending the millet standard (north China) or rice standard (south China).

A second anti-inflationary policy was to impose strict control over the banking system and to subordinate all financial institutions to the People's Bank. Regulations were issued imposing limits upon private banks and increasing their indebtedness to the People's Bank. Similarly, insurance companies were required to deposit sums of money with the People's Bank and were forbidden to invest in industry.[32] Strict limits were imposed upon all state organs concerning the amount of ready cash they were to retain[33] and the inherited Guomindang taxation system was used to soak up private funds, to channel resources into the public sector and to drive smaller, inefficient private concerns out of business. At the same time, the circulation of foreign currency was forbidden and propaganda teams were organised to persuade holders of foreign currency to pay it into branches of the People's Bank.

Another task of the propaganda teams was to promote the sale of government bonds. When first introduced, these bonds had been specifically designed to support the war effort but continued to be promoted as hostilities lessened. They were issued for five years with (by traditional Chinese standards) a low rate of return of 5 per cent per annum which was probably not very attractive to businessmen. None the less, many were sold though we cannot be sure of the extent to which this was due to patriotic fervour or to pressure.[34]

On the whole, the new government's response to inflation was bold and imaginative and the above were merely the first of a series of measures which eventually stabilised the currency. Before long, new measures were adopted such as the provision of consumer co-operatives in which ordinary people invested at a low rate of interest but which provided daily necessities at low prices. At the same time, a whole stream of regulations was published to achieve economic ends not explicit in their provisions. Sanitation regulations, for example, were used to restrict the number of barbers' shops and other service establishments, though care was taken to see that such restrictions did not lead to unemployment.

Policy was aimed at restricting the operations of the small shopkeeper and businessman and establishing clear lines of ownership and control.

Similarly, in private educational institutions, initial attention was focused not on the content of courses but the degree to which these institutions had any advantage over the government school system.[35] Many teachers did, however, institute new curricula in the new political climate and the degree to which they did so must surely have had some effect on the provision of government subsidies.

All of the above measures, of course, needed people to administer them and the retained personnel were inadequate both in numbers and in political consciousness. To provide such personnel, a massive educational campaign was launched in which the New Democratic Youth League (the youth wing of the Party) played an active part, especially since large numbers of these activists were students. To achieve a greater degree of national integration, the activists undertook a campaign for the teaching of the national language and attempted to become more influential amongst groups other than the intellectuals. More and more housewives, for example, were encouraged to form residents' groups and street committees.

Perhaps the most important sphere to involve housewives concerned the new Marriage Law of 13 April 1950[36] which abolished child marriage, polygamy and concubinage and provided the legal basis for what was to be a fundamental change in the status of women. The earlier Guomindang Marriage Law, while quite progressive, had been a dead letter as far as most of China was concerned because legal reforms had not been matched by economic, social and ideological reforms. As a first step in the implementation of the new law, a propaganda campaign was launched, though traditional ideology and traditional forms of social organisation proved to be major obstacles in the very early period.

The Chinese Communist Party had had a long history of successful propaganda. Now all the stops were pulled out. Millions of pamphlets were issued on every conceivable subject from choosing a marriage partner to the layout of a meeting hall. Mobile theatrical groups toured the country and local units of production organised plays and propaganda meetings to familiarise people with Party policy. It was an exhilarating experience but one which required a considerable amount of work, particularly by those organisations whose job it was to co-ordinate the whole process—the Party and the labour unions.

## Party and Union Bureaucratism

We have noted that the structure of state administration was determined at the highest level by the principle of the United Front and at lower levels, to an increasing degree, by its specific variant—the triple alliance. What is important to look at here is not so much the components of the

United Front but the linkages between them. The main body responsible for maintaining these linkages was the Party although, in the very early period of military government, army personnel performed the linkage function between retained personnel and mass organisations until a regular Party network could be established.

In linking up diverse elements, the Party was to impel policy in a particular direction without exactly giving administrative orders. It was the function of state bodies to formulate *operational* instructions; it was the job of the Party to establish broad *policy*, ideally according to the Mass Line formula. It was vital, therefore, that the Party, defined as embodying the long-term interests of a class, should be kept separate from the state defined merely as its instrument of repression. The state structure was characterised by a hierarchical bureaucratic organisation, the parts of which were linked by a network of technological solidarity. The Party, on the other hand, should ideally be characterised not by structure and organisation (though indeed it must possess these) but by its *direction*. Its internal linkages should be 'human' rather than technological, ideological rather than routinised. Rooted in society rather than in the state, the Party was the instrument that forged the resolution of the contradiction between state and society.[37]

Following liberation, the activities of Party branches had to adhere to the narrow path between the same opposing errors which figured in the rectification movement of 1942. The first of these errors was to usurp the power of the state structure and take everything on to their own shoulders.[38] This 'ultra-leftist' error stemmed often from extreme enthusiasm or from distrust of retained personnel. The second error was for Party branches or committees to subordinate themselves completely to the state structure and to do little more than invest the directives of bureaucrats or managers with moral force. In a situation where personnel were inexperienced, this latter error was probably more frequent than the former. Many Party branches had only come into existence following the end of military rule and the initiative in their formation had been taken by military representatives formerly attached to control commissions. These representatives had, at the same time, to supervise the establishment of regular administrative machinery and it is little wonder that they confused their functions. Such bureaucratism as developed was probably strengthened by the increasingly conservative atmosphere which prevailed after 1949, and was particularly marked in that most important of the 'transmission belts' which were ideally to link the Party with the masses—the labour unions.

Although syndicalism (where unions actually took over the running of factories) occasionally occurred,[39] the newly formed labour unions[40] revealed themselves as extremely pallid bodies. Upon their formation, some union branches simply sided with management both in the state and private sectors.[41] This was due to the fact that many union cadres had concurrent management posts, were subject to repeated transfer (leaving their branches in the hands of inexperienced cadres), were too busy with the sheer paperwork involved in union registration and too busy studying technology to develop any independent position. Many of those who proved themselves to be competent technically were creamed off into management; similarly those who proved themselves to have a high level of political consciousness became specifically Party cadres. Unions were defined as 'schools for management' but, quite clearly, the educational principle which was applied was that described earlier as selective rather than creative. It is not surprising therefore that some union cadres bemoaned the fact that they were considered to be 'fourth class'[42] (the top three classes being 1. Party cadres, 2. government cadres and 3. engineers).

Just as the rapid expansion of union organisations in the period following liberation weakened union branches and the paperwork involved contributed to bureaucratism, so the Party itself was impaired by a similar process. The overall rise in Party membership between October 1949 and mid-1950 was only from 4.5 to 5 million[43] but these figures concealed the fact that, following the Party decision in March 1949 to switch the focus of its work from countryside to cities, there had been a decline in rural Party membership and a staggering increase in the urban areas. Many factories reported increases in Party membership from some three per cent to between 10 and 30 per cent, of whom large numbers were skilled workers and technicians retained from pre-liberation days.[44] In fact, policy was not just to increase the working-class component of the Party but in particular its skilled and managerial component. This process of recruitment, similar to Stalin's 'Leninist Levy', may perhaps have diluted the overall political consciousness of the Party. One must note also that, all too frequently, enthusiasm for production was taken as a sufficient indicator of political consciousness, particularly during China's first major production movement known as the 'movement to create new records',[45] launched in north-east China in 1949 and designed to determine production norms.

By mid-1950, therefore, the composition of the Party, though more orthodox (in a Soviet sense), was very different from two years previously. In the following year when 11.4 per cent of the total industrial workforce in north-east China was enrolled, it was announced that within five years the Party planned to recruit one-third of all the industrial workers.[46] Meanwhile, leaders began to worry about the political health of the Party which, according to Gao Gang, had been affected by 'the depraved ideology of remnant feudal elements and capitalists, petty bourgeois individualism and defects in ideological and educational work'. Gao noted that industrial idlers tended to rationalise their indolent attitude in political terms and, when admonished for relaxing, accused their critics of 'taking a rural viewpoint' and of not realising the importance of the United Front between workers, peasants, petty bourgeoisie and national capitalists.[47]

Clearly the low level of political consciousness was not just confined to new Party members. Many veteran cadres had neglected their political duties while studying new and unfamiliar technical and administrative problems. Others, after entering the cities, were said to be infected with the 'ideology of power and prestige'.[48] The major factor, however, which contributed to the new bureaucratism resulted from the rapid verti-calisation of administrative control according to a scheme very different from the Yan'an pattern of *dual rule*. As the power of central economic ministries grew, local Party and state organs began to abdicate all respon-sibility for economic enterprises and were reduced to merely functional agents in an increasingly staff-line pattern of organisation.

## The Persistence of Simulated Kinship Structures

The simulated kinship structures, such as secret societies and the gang-boss network, proved to be difficult to eradicate for the simple reason that they had considerable success in permeating any government that impinged upon them. Indeed, one of the principal reasons why Party and unions came under criticism in the period following liberation was because they had, in fact, been infiltrated.

Again, the situation varied from area to area. In north-east China, where there were fewer retained personnel, reconstruction could proceed almost from scratch in a somewhat more radical atmosphere than that which prevailed in areas further south, which were not liberated until 1949. In the north-east, a democratic reform movement (*minzhu gaige yundong*) was launched immediately after liberation with, it would appear, much success.[49] South of the Great Wall, however, a policy of maintaining the status quo remained in force until mid-1950. In many mining enterprises, former gang-bosses were still practising extortion at that time and had merely changed the name of their gangs to shifts and teams. In the construction industry, which was still largely dependent upon contract labour, the gang-boss system was rife with as many as seven levels of contractor each taking its cut. Cases are on record of gang-bosses completely dominating mine Party committees and their position was justified on the ground that Party policy demanded the retention of skilled workers.[50] Many union branches were similarly dominated and some gang-bosses had even managed to get themselves chosen as model workers. Various secret societies such as the notorious Green Gang and the *Yi Guan Dao* were still in existence and *banghui* (mutual aid groups), which had degenerated into protection rackets, still operated.[51]

Was the Yan'an pattern of transformation from within adequate to deal with the situation? Athough it had proved remarkably successful in generating commitment to the Communist Party during the war with Japan, the events of 1947–8 seemed to show that it was inadequate to cope with the process of transformation with a diluted Party spread thinly on the ground over the whole country.

It was quite apparent that, in local situations where its organisation had been created from scratch out of very dubious personnel, the Party was far from taking over the existing structures from within. It was rather the simulated kinship structures which were taking over the Party. In such a situation, calls for a more radical approach to social transformation became louder.

## Problems of Defence and the Outbreak of the Korean War

Anyone familiar with the history of the Soviet Union will observe that the moderate policies pursued during the first few months after the establishment of the People's Republic were similar to those of the Bolshevik government after October 1917 and before the commencement of the Russian Civil War. There was, however, one crucial difference: the moderate policies pursued by the Chinese government *followed* a protracted civil war which did not come to an abrupt end. Throughout 1949 and into early 1950, Guomindang air raids continued. In Guangzhou alone, from 3 November 1949 to 24 February 1950, there were 76 'plane incidents' at a time when a PLA air force hardly existed and when air defences were very poor. Indeed, in Guangzhou, it was not until March 1950 that the first enemy aircraft was shot down.[52] At the same time, China was particularly vulnerable to attacks by sea and the Guomindang navy maintained control over the Chinese coast well into 1950. Coastal defence was complicated by the fact that, in south China, communities of boat people had been infiltrated by Guomindang agents. Inland, the Guomindang still maintained a Military Secret Service (*Jun Tong*) which remained active in the anticipation of a Guomindang counter-attack on the mainland from Taiwan.[53]

In early 1950, such a counter-attack was by no means a remote possibility. In contrast to 1949, there was some apprehension that General MacArthur's plans for Taiwan went far beyond defence,[54] despite the proclaimed American intention not to intervene further in the Chinese Civil War and American Secretary of State Acheson's assertion to that effect on 12 January.[55] Despite the massive literature on the origins of the Korean War, it is still not clear to what extent, in early 1950, MacArthur was wagging the American Presidential dog. It is I.F. Stone's contention that the first shots in that war were fired by South Korea as part of an international conspiracy involving MacArthur, President Rhee of South Korea, John Foster Dulles and Jiang Jieshi to provoke a North Korean reaction, enlarge the war and so commit United States forces to a restoration of the Guomindang within China.[56] Others would support a claim that South Korea opened hostilities and that the United States found it extremely difficult to restrain Rhee in early 1950 but the evidence for a conspiracy is rather weak. The conventional Western view, however, is that hostilities were opened by the North. Whatever the situation, it is my view that China was unaware of any intention of either side to cross the 38th Parallel and initiate full-scale war.

China's main military concern in early 1950 was the liberation of Taiwan. The Third Field Army had been mobilised under Su Yu and an intensive programme of training in amphibious operations carried out. Five thousand junks had been assembled, 30 airfields constructed, radar installations set up with Soviet help and 15,000 troops mobilised for the invasion.[57] Surely the last thing the Chinese would have wanted was a war on two fronts.

Despite the intended Taiwan operation, plans were under way in China for large-scale demobilisation. Two-fifths of the five-million-strong PLA still consisted of Guomindang defectors and the sheer size of the army placed considerable burdens on the Chinese exchequer. Military expenditure in 1950 was estimated at 38.8 per cent of the draft budget for that year which was probably a gross underestimate since many military items were not included under the military heading. Gittings estimates that the figure was probably more like 60 per cent.[58] Though a large number of troops had been assigned to production work in their original place of recruitment[59] to ease the burden (units of the Fourth Field Army, for example, were transferred back to the north-east from Guangdong), mass demobilisation was considered to be imperative. By a curious quirk of fate, the decision was taken for large-scale demobilisation on 24 June 1950,[60] the day before hostilities broke out on the 38th Parallel and the Korean War began. The surprised Chinese government could only cancel the demobilisation order and await events. It did not have to wait long, for one of the first acts of the United States was to order the Seventh Fleet into the Taiwan Straits, allegedly to hold back Jiang Jieshi. The previous policy enunciated by Acheson was at an end; the United States was now a direct threat.

### Conclusion

In 1949–50, the first steps were taken to establish a regular form of government over most of mainland China. The central government was based on United Front principles according to the notion of new democracy. It contained, however, a number of institutions copied from the Soviet Union where a very different theory of class representation applied. Regional government was initially in the hands of the military and varied from place to place. Significantly, north-east China under Gao Gang, which was the country's centre of heavy industry, took the lead in implementing Soviet forms of organisation. In other parts of the country, Soviet influence was not so marked. There, cadres busied themselves with the immense task of reforming local government in a situation where often the institutions of the former régime were still intact and land reform had not yet been carried out. Initially, local government took the form of a 'triple alliance' of army, retained personnel and local activists and tensions occasionally developed between each of these components. The overall tendency, however, was towards bureaucratism and inertia and this was facilitated by the moderate and cautious policies emanating from the centre.

The general programme of reconstruction was constrained by the continuance of hostilities with the Guomindang throughout the first few months of 1950. In mid-year, attempts to demobilise the huge army were frustrated by developments in Korea and the forced postponement of the impending Taiwan campaign. In retrospect, the United States action in sealing the Taiwan Straits was the most significant event in the whole of post-war Asian politics. It inaugurated an Asian Cold War which was to last for many years and pushed China much closer to the Soviet Union. With the exception of Tibet, where a Chinese military presence was established following negotiations later in 1950, the Civil War went into cold storage. For two decades, the unfinished business was to exercise a major influence over both China's foreign and domestic policies.

## NOTES

1. Friedman, 1971, p. 210.
2. Mao Zedong, 30 June 1949, *SW* IV, p. 415.
3. Friedman, 1971.
4. The Cominform was a much looser organisation than the old Comintern and was concerned largely with the dissemination of information throughout the International Communist Movement.
5. Gittings, 1971.
6. Schurmann, 1966, pp. 239–40.
7. Mao Zedong, 24 September 1962, Schram, 1974, p. 191.
8. Text of treaty and associated documents in *CB* 62, 5 March 1951.
9. Texts in *SW* II, pp. 339–84, and *SW* IV, pp. 411–24.
10. The word 'Marxian' is used here to signify the writings of Marx rather than the much broader term 'Marxist'.

11. These documents are discussed in Waller, 1970, pp. 81–4. The Common Programme is in *CB* 9, 21 September 1950, Selden, 1979, pp. 186–93.

12. Discussed in Brugger, 1976.

13. Whitson, 1969.

14. Barnett, 1963, p. 340.

15. It was said that as many as 90 per cent of old administrative personnel were retained in Shanghai.

16. Brugger, 1976, pp. 74–5.

17. Shanghai, n.p. n.d., pp. 1–4. The institution of worker pickets had a very long history in China. They fulfilled an important role in the takeover of factories during the abortive revolution of 1926–7. They were again active following the Japanese surrender in 1945 and their very existence in 1948–9 attests to a very significant urban Communist Party underground which had been in existence during the Civil War.

18. Shanghai, n.p. n.d., pp. 1–4.

19. Lieberthal, 1971, pp. 509–12.

20. The situation in Tianjin, in April–May 1949, occasioned a considerable polemic during the subsequent Cultural Revolution. As Party troubleshooter, Liu Shaoqi was sent to Tianjin to rectify the situation. It was claimed that Liu's 'Tianjin Talks' ended the previously moderate radical policy in favour of a 'revisionist' policy which favoured the national capitalists in the private sector and precluded fundamental rearrangement of factory management in the public sector. As such, it was said to be a violation of the programme announced by Mao in his report to the Second Plenum of the Seventh Central Committee of the Party (5 March 1949). The implementation of reform in the spring and summer of 1949 was much less radical than in the earlier period and the 'Tianjin Talks' occupied an important place in the development of policy, but I am not convinced that these 'Talks' constituted a total break from previous policy. The 'Talks' seem only to be the culmination of the previous moderate approach dating from December 1947. What the 'Tianjin Talks' seem to reveal, however, is that Liu's view of the United Front was a much longer-term one than that of Mao (at least on the basis of speeches published in Zhonggong Yanjiu Zazhi she, 1970, pp. 200–20).

21. Vogel, 1971, p. 48; Schurmann, 1966, pp. 371–2.

22. Vogel, 1971, pp. 49 and 53–4.

23. E.g. *SCMM* 652, 28 April 1969, p. 3.

24. Liu Shaoqi, 14 June 1950, Liu, Vol. II, 1969, pp. 215–33.

25. Ibid., pp. 230–3.

26. One might note here that it was extremely difficult to determine ownership in a situation where land had been informally divided amongst members of the same family. In such a situation, the terms 'poor' and 'lower-middle' peasant may not have had much operational significance. For the guidelines for categorisation, see Selden, 1979, pp. 218–25.

27. Discussed in Brugger, 1976, Chapter VII.

28. Vogel, 1971, pp. 72–3.

29. On early labour regulation, see Howe, 1971, pp. 88–94.

30. Vogel, 1971, pp. 78–9.

31. See the examples in Brugger, 1976, Appendix I.

32. Vogel, 1971, p. 75.

33. *Xinhua Yuebao* 7, May 1950, p. 128.

34. Vogel, 1971, pp. 79–80.

35. Ibid., p. 75.

36. PFLP, 1950; Selden, 1979, pp. 193–200.

37. Schurmann, 1966, p. 112.

38. Ling Huachun, *Dongbei Gongye* 56, 21 April 1951, pp. 19–21.

39. Gao Gang, 13 March 1950, *Dongbei Ribao*, 6 June 1950, p. 1.

40. These unions were formed out of the underground unions of pre-liberation days, out of the worker pickets or sometimes *ex nihilo*.

41. *Zhongguo Gongren* 15, April 1951, p. 36.

42. *Gongren Ribao*, 11 January 1952.

43. Schurmann, 1966, p. 129.

44. E.g. *Zhongguo Gongren* 3, 15 April 1950, pp. 32–3. Xiao Feng, *Laodong Chubanshe Bianshenbu*, 1951, pp. 55–67.

45. Brugger, 1976, Chapter IV.

46. An Ziwen, *Gongren Ribao*, 31 August 1951, pp. 1 and 4.

47. Gao Gang, 31 August 1951, Zhongguo Minzhu Tongmeng Zongbu Xuanchuan Weiyuanhui, 1951, pp. 14–25.

48. Li Long, *Xuexi* 7, 1 January 1951, p. 8.

49. E.g. *Gongren Chubanshe*, 1953, p. 36.

50. Lin Li, *Zhongguo Gongren* 3, 15 April 1950, pp. 12–14.

51. Brugger, 1976, p. 105.

52. Vogel, 1971, pp. 61–2.

53. *Huadong Renmin Chubanshe*, May 1951 (for a catalogue of subversive activities).

54. Friedman, 1971, p. 222.

55. Gittings, 1967, p. 41.

56. Stone, 1970.

57. Gittings, 1967, p. 42.

58. Ibid., pp. 26–7.

59. Ibid., pp. 26 and 29–32. For Mao's directive on this task (5 December 1949), see *JPRS*, 1974, pp. 2–5.

60. Gittings, 1967, p. 27.

# III
# MASS MOBILISATION
## (1950–1952)

From mid-1950 to early 1952, a series of mass campaigns took place in China. They were primarily a response to the problems outlined in the previous chapter—Party and union bureaucratism, the persistence of simulated kinship structures and a moderate policy towards education and the private sector of the economy. The inauguration of the first of these campaigns antedates the outbreak of hostilities in Korea but there can be no doubt that the new concern for security, caused by the war, made an active campaign against counter-revolutionaries more urgent and perhaps silenced some people whose attitude toward mass mobilisation was somewhat cautious.

### Party and Union Rectification (mid-1950)

The new radicalism of mid-1950 was ushered in by Mao Zedong at the Third Plenum of the Seventh Central Committee on 6 June,[1] 19 days before the commencement of hostilities in Korea. Directed against bureaucratism and commandism in economic and financial administration, the rectification movement assumed only modest proportions. Perhaps those most severely treated were many former guerrilla cadres who, unable to adapt to routine administration, were sent back to the countryside.[2] In general, however, cadres alienated from the masses, who had succumbed to the 'ideology of the meritorious' or the fleshpots of the cities, were merely required to undergo self-criticism.

Within industry in north China, the process of democratic reform was stepped up. Administrative orders were issued formally abolishing the gang-boss system in various sectors of industry[3] and reports began to appear in the press describing how stubborn and persistent gang-bosses were dealt with.[4] It was soon apparent, however, that Party and union branches within economic enterprises were responding to the movement rather sluggishly. Cadres were unsure how to eradicate the gang-boss system without harming production, how to distinguish gang-bosses among skilled workers[5] or how to deal with the informal structure within factories. I have argued elsewhere that, just as rich peasants in the countryside came to exercise some of the power which formerly belonged to landlords,[6] so a stratum of 'industrial kulaks' appeared in industry following the demise of the more obvious gang-bosses.[7] Such was the consequence of a closed rectification movement which involved inadequate mass mobilisation. Memories of the 'open Party rectification' of 1947−8 had probably made the central leadership somewhat cautious.

Among labour union cadres, the rectification movement of 1950 had results often contrary to what had been intended. In July 1950, Deng Zihui, vice-chairman of the Central South Finance and Economics Committee, criticised the excessive subordination of unions to management in both the public and private sectors of industry and demanded that both sides examine in what way their concrete 'standpoint' (*lichang*) might differ.[8] Deng's cautious speech sought to ensure that the interests of workers were not sacrificed to the goal of merely increasing production, but was not 'economist' in the Leninist sense. The debate which followed, however, was not so cautious[9] and could indeed be described as 'economist'.[10] Some unions began to interpret the demand that they show greater independence as an injunction to devote greater attention to the immediate gratification of material desires. Unions' concentration on benefits for the working class as opposed to those of workers *and* peasants was to precipitate a major union crisis in the following year.

In view of China's increasing concern about developments in Korea, it was particularly serious that the beginnings of radicalisation, in the summer of 1950, lacked vigour and had led labour unions into a reactionary position.

### China's Participation in the Korean War (June–November 1950)

Even after the outbreak of fighting between North and South Korea, the possibility of an active Chinese involvement seemed remote. Opinion in Washington held that South Korea could at least hold its own and, with the sealing of the Taiwan Straits, President Truman had silenced the pro-Jiang Republican 'China lobby' which had complained that he was 'soft on Communism'. At one fell swoop, Truman seemed not only to have rescued his image but looked like securing a $50 billion military budget which had previously been resisted by conservative Republicans.[11]

But with the rapid collapse of the South Korean forces, Truman was forced to reassess the situation and could only explain his miscalculation in terms of 'external aggression'. Two grossly dangerous misconceptions vied for supremacy. In Truman's view, the source of 'aggression' lay in Moscow; this required a strengthening of the United States' position in Europe. In the view of General MacArthur, however, the source of 'aggression' lay in Beijing whither the war should be carried.[12] When American bombers failed to halt the advance of the North Korean forces, the general secured the deployment of American ground troops and initiated a process of escalation which was increasingly rationalised according to his view of 'Chinese aggression'. The return of Korean forces which had fought with the PLA in China was interpreted in terms of such 'aggression', and China's warnings that it would contemplate the despatch of troops if UN forces crossed the 38th Parallel were disregarded, presumably on the grounds that China was thought to be behind the whole operation anyway.

In October 1950, PLA forces moved silently into North Korea[13] accompanied by Zhou Enlai's signal to the United States, via the Indian ambassador, that China would commit troops only if American forces invaded North Korea; in the event of South Korean forces crossing the parallel, China would not react. Though seemingly accepted by Truman, the Chinese position was ignored by MacArthur who continued to push towards the Sino-Korean border—the Yalu River. On 1 November, Chinese and UN forces were to clash.

Even at that point, however, full-scale war could have been averted. With the UN advance on the Yalu River checked, the Chinese forces 'faded away' to allow Truman, it has been argued, to resurrect an earlier idea for the establishment of a buffer zone along the Yalu. MacArthur's response was to escalate the war even further. In receipt of Truman's order not to bomb bridges across the Yalu, MacArthur lodged the 'gravest protest' and Washington gave way. All, however, was still not lost. On 13 November, MacArthur proposed hot pursuit into north-east China but his suggestion was apparently vetoed by six of the powers which made up the UN forces and which appeared to show more resolve than President Truman.[14] It was too late, however, to establish a buffer zone and, with MacArthur's offensive towards the Yalu River in November, China became effectively at war with the United States. In securing Taiwan and occupying Korea, it could only seem to the Chinese that the United States had replaced Japan, which had embarked upon exactly the same strategy half a century previously, as the expansionist enemy.

## Consolidation of Tibet (1950 – 1)[15]

Following its involvement in the Korean War, China became particularly concerned with the security of the frontiers. The pacification of south-west China had been proceeding steadily throughout 1950 but, with the possibility of invasion, all efforts had to be directed towards carrying pacification to a rapid conclusion.

Although the idea of Tibetan independence had been canvassed by some Americans during the Civil War, the position of President Truman (at least prior to his actions in June 1950) had been that the United States would make no commitment on the Tibetan question. As far as the British and Indian governments were concerned, the Simla agreement of 1913 was adhered to whereby Chinese 'suzerainty' over the region was recognised.

In early 1950, there appears to have been some disagreement within the traditional aristocratic governing body in Tibet—the *Kashag*—as to the nature of Tibetan sovereignty and Chinese 'suzerainty', and two courses of action were pursued. In February, Tibet's ruler, the Dalai Lama, despatched a mission to Beijing, via New Delhi, to see what terms would be offered by the Chinese government and, at the same time, a Tibetan army under Ngapoi Ngawang Jigmi set out for the Qabdo (Chamdo) region on the border with Xikang province. The first course of action came to nothing since the Tibetan delegation never left India and the second resulted in a Tibetan defeat at the battle of Qabdo in October 1950. At that time, many Tibetans went over to the side of the People's Liberation Army and later the Tibetan commander was to achieve high rank in the Chinese government.

The victory of Qabdo was not, however, followed by a PLA advance into Tibet proper. On instructions from the Dalai Lama, Ngapoi Ngawang Jigmi proceeded to Beijing to negotiate a settlement and this was concluded in May 1951,[16] after which PLA troops entered Tibet. For its part, the Tibetan government recognised the region's inclusion in the People's Republic and accepted 'regional national autonomy . . . under the leadership of the national government and in accordance with the policy laid down in the Common Programme'. The *Kashag* remained in existence and agreed to institute a reform of the existing system of monastic serfdom. For its part, the Beijing government agreed not to abolish the powers of the Dalai Lama or the other main religious and temporal ruler, the Banqen Erdini Quoiqyi Gyancan (the Panchen Lama). It also agreed not to carry out reform through compulsion and allowed for Tibetan forces to be reincorporated into the PLA (though this, in fact, never happened). In other words, the frontier region of Tibet was now secured, although the domestic social structure remained unchanged with only a vague commitment to self-generated reform.

## The Intensification of Land Reform (late 1950)

Active Chinese participation in the Korean War gave the rather pallid radicalism inaugurated in June 1950 a little more colour. This was nowhere more evident than in the rural sector. The new Land Reform Law which went into effect on 30 June was an extremely moderate one. Rich peasants were allowed to retain their property and landlords were given a share of land in a slow and orderly process of redistribution. Justifying the new situation, Liu Shaoqi argued that radical land reform policies had been necessary during the Civil War when landlords were siding with the enemy, but now landlords were to be encouraged to live by the fruits of their labours.[17] It was not, however, until the autumn of 1950 that the new land policy began to be implemented in the 'later liberated areas' of south China,[18] by which time the situation in Korea looked ominous. With the full-scale Chinese commitment of November 1950, agrarian policy became much tougher.

By that time, the main area embarking upon a programme of land reform was the Central South Administrative Region, based on Wuhan. There, leaders felt that landlord resistance might stiffen now that there was a possibility (however remote) of a renewal of the Civil War on the mainland. At the same time, the rectification movement in the urban sector might have made them aware of the extent to which local cadres had been taken over by traditional organisations. Indeed, it was discovered that landlords in the south had tried to preserve their position by bribing or making concessions to peasants in return for lenient treatment once land reform was undertaken.[19]

The situation in south China was particularly complex. Here land holdings were smaller than in the north. Some land was owned by overseas Chinese who, in the early years, were an important source of foreign currency. Many landlords were involved in commerce and had gone to the cities to sit out agrarian reform. Lineage organisations within the villages were much stronger than in north China which made identification on the basis of class extraordinarily difficult and, most important, there was a much larger number of local cadres within the Party who were related to landowners.

In such circumstances, the authorities in Wuhan were not completely in touch with the situation in rural areas and the further down the chain of command one went, the greater was the resistance to any new hard line.[20] The situation was further complicated by the fact that, at the basic level, many activists were former guerrilla cadres. Their experiences had been very different from the PLA cadres who were sent down in the work-teams from the north and who often did not speak the same language.[21] It was not, however, just a matter of cleavage between higher and lower levels since leaders at most levels divided on the degree of sympathy they showed for either the work-teams or the local cadres. The dimensions of administrative disputes were extremely complex, especially since constant pressure was placed on local cadres to speed up the whole process.[22]

By the end of 1950, this pressure was seen to have been only moderately effective. Just as in the urban sector, the initial moderate radicalism foundered on the rocks of traditional connections, so in the countryside, a somewhat more vigorous movement was similarly obstructed. China's leaders could only pause to consider what to do next.

## *The Beginnings of Mobilisation (late 1950 – 1)*

Although more mass mobilisation was involved in the land reform campaign of late 1950 than in the urban sector, the movements at that time were largely from the top down. The last of these early movements was the campaign for the suppression of counter-revolutionaries, the urgency of which was dictated by security concerns in the new wartime situation. The targets were secret agents (*tewufenzi*) who worked for such organisations as the Guomindang Military Secret Service or the Nationalist Youth Corps (*San Min Tuan*).[23] Numerous accounts of the sabotage of industrial plant had appeared in the press since liberation[24] and now a massive campaign was launched to flush actual or potential saboteurs out. The registration of all spies and Guomindang party members was ordered. If they surrendered within a given period they would be accorded lenient treatment, especially if they gave lists of their associates, but if they did not surrender no mercy would be shown.[25] In fact many people did register under these regulations in late 1950 and early 1951, and a rapid exercise in data collection was undertaken to provide the basis for mass arrests in mid-year. True to its promise, the Communist Party was quite ruthless in the trials and executions which followed. It is said that 28,332 people were executed in Guangdong province alone (one in every thousand of the population);[26] 239 people not classified as counter-revolutionaries also lost their lives and 5,467 were poisoned or injured during the campaign.[27]

One will never be able to ascertain to what extent local cadres broke faith and executed some of those who had registered and who had been promised leniency. It is my own feeling, however, that this latter category was small, since the whole campaign was loudly publicised and much propaganda capital was made even to the point of broadcasting public accusation meetings over the radio. We cannot ascertain, either, the extent to which the campaign might have been used to settle old scores.

In March 1951, Mao demanded that the movement 'be carried out precisely, cautiously and in a planned and methodical way . . . controlled from above'.[28] During the course of the movement, therefore, ordinary workers were not mobilised to denounce gang-bosses and secret society elements which remained in the factories. A concurrent movement which was specifically directed to mass mobilisation, however, was a donation drive to raise funds for the Korean War effort.[29] The drive, which was launched in the autumn of 1950 and intensified in mid-1951, called upon individuals, families and units of production, residence and administration to donate specific sums of money to purchase armaments for Korea.

Contracting individuals or groups might make a donation plan which was expressed in terms of the armaments the contracted sum might buy.[30] The movement was as much political as economic, for it aimed to integrate macro-politics with the day-to-day concerns of ordinary individuals and stress was laid on its educative effect. As the movement unfolded, greater identification was made between donating units and units of work, and units of production competed with each other in concluding 'patriotic compacts' to support the war effort.[31] These compacts were at first somewhat vague but, as time went by, they began more and more to express production targets which were later included in 'increase production and practise economy plans'.[32] In this way, the formation of production plans, mass mobilisation and mass education became fused into a single process.

The slow progress of the Party and union rectification movement and the limited success of the land reform campaign in south China, in the winter of 1950 – 1, were in part compensated for by increasingly successful mobilisation behind the slogan 'resist American aggression and aid Korea.' Towards the end of 1950, following the freezing of foreign (including White Russian) assets, the attitude towards foreign residents hardened.[33] Prior to the Korean War, a few newspapermen and missionaries had been expelled but the majority of foreigners, who had left China at that time, went of their own accord. But with Chinese involvement in the Korean War, greater pressure was placed on foreign firms and businessmen as back debts were assessed and greater numbers of foreigners were persuaded to leave. Cultural, religious, welfare and educational institutions with foreign affiliations were investigated, and people were mobilised to criticise foreigners, a particular target being Roman Catholic convents.[34]

With increasing criticism of foreign religious bodies, the new government began to formulate a policy towards Christian churches.[35] All foreign ties were to be broken and allegiance to foreign organisations was proscribed. The Catholic Church, with an estimated 3.3 million believers, was placed in a very difficult position once it was reorganised as a national body and forbidden to proselytise. It is likely, however, that a good number of the 3.3 million were in fact 'rice Christians' attracted to the Church because of its welfare services and with no lasting commitment. Nevertheless, following the expulsion of some senior prelates accused of espionage, the new national church remained in existence in an uneasy atmosphere of official tolerance and semi-official discouragement.

Accompanying the mass mobilisation against foreign influence was a mammoth drive to create a nationwide propaganda network.[36] In the very early period, activists were divided into 'propagandists' (*xuanchuanyuan*) and routine 'agitators' (*gudongyuan*) along Soviet lines,[37] though soon a new level of propagandist was instituted—the 'reporter' (*baogaoyuan*). He was usually a high-ranking cadre whose job was to invest with authority the activities of lower-level propagandists. Propaganda posts were set up throughout all the mass organisations as well as centres for disseminating a growing volume of literature.

Propagandists were to busy themselves in the escalating campaigns against opium-smoking, prostitution, gambling and alcoholism. They faced particularly arduous tasks in the campaign against 'cultural imperialism' in the field of education. Jazz and romantic ('yellow') music came under attack. Guomindang textbooks were removed and replaced by material which had been prepared in the liberated areas and in Hong Kong. Film circulation began to be controlled, though Western movies were shown throughout most of 1950. Mass criticism was instituted against the notion of 'art for art's sake' and Mao Zedong's 'Talks at the Yan'an Forum on Literature and Art'[38] were widely disseminated. Attempts were made to introduce and standardise political training in institutions of tertiary education, though a more thorough campaign of thought reform (*sixiang gaizao*) did not really get under way until mid-1951, and then only in the older liberated areas. On all these measures, the Party pinned high hopes though, as we shall have cause to remark time and again, the influences it sought to eradicate were remarkably persistent.

In the new atmosphere of mass mobilisation, attempts were made to recapture the spirit of Yan'an with its close bond between soldiers and civilians. An earlier system, whereby the dependents of servicemen were compensated by their neighbours for loss of labour power, was reintroduced and more and more cadres were transferred from the army to help with mass movements such as land reform. Notable successes were achieved in building up a people's militia which was expanded from five million in 1950 to 12.8 million by the autumn of 1951,[39] and this militia provided recruits for the PLA of which initially 700,000 were in active service with the Chinese People's Volunteers in Korea.[40]

The stress now was on the quality of China's armed forces and China's leaders felt sufficiently confident to resume the process of demobilisation, though at first this was probably confined to ex-Goumindang

garrison troops which did not form part of the field armies.[41] Success at
the front had given the PLA a new *élan*, though this *élan* could not
conceal the fact that the war constituted a tremendous drain on the
Chinese economy which had hardly begun to recover from the ravages
of the Civil War. The Soviet Union, convinced now that Mao was not
another Tito,[42] provided more military aid particularly after the autumn
of 1951. Furthermore, China was not short of unskilled labour. The
country lacked, however, skilled workers, technicians and doctors. (The
doctor: population ratio at that time was probably only some 1:10,000 of
whom seven to eight per cent were enrolled for service in Korea[43]). New
military academies were set up, enrolling students with technical and
engineering qualifications who might have been employed elsewhere in
the economy. The cost of the Korean War was quite considerable but
perhaps what is more important, in the light of the subsequent history of
the People's Republic, was that the army was becoming more and more a
professional body, unlike the old army of Yan'an and Civil War days.

## The Further Intensification of Reform (1951)

Following the spring sowing of 1951, attempts were made to bring urban
and rural reform in line with the mass enthusiasm engendered by the war.
Large numbers of ex-Fourth Field Army cadres were moved south from
Wuhan in work-teams to speed up the process of land reform and, in
May, criticism of the 'five kinds of personal relationships' (*wutong guanxi*
—loyalty to those of the same surname, same lineage, same village, same
school and same working place) was intensified.[44] Local cadres who
tended towards conservatism were subjected to criticism and attitudes
towards landlords (including those who had taken up business in the
cities) hardened. As mass mobilisation in the rural areas got under way,
schedules for the completion of land reform were brought forward.

In the urban areas, a major attempt was made in May 1951 to carry the
democratic reform movement to a successful conclusion,[45] this time by
mass mobilisation. Fearing disruption, some people argued that such
mobilisation should not exceed that of the campaign for the suppression
of counter-revolutionaries, of which the current movement was but the
sequel.[46] They felt that it might be sufficient to flush out feudal elements
during production competitions[47] or that registration of workers for
labour insurance might reveal the parasitic.[48] The Party leadership, however, adhered to its new commitment to mass mobilisation and set up
democratic reform committees to lead the movement. Three stages were
designated—'democratic struggle', 'democratic unity' and 'democratic
construction'.[49] The first of these, launched by outside cadres' 'initiation
reports' (*qifa baogao*), concentrated on general issues such as imperialism

and the Jiang Jieshi régime. Before long, attacks became more specific as more and more workers found, through participation in the earlier meetings, sufficient confidence to accuse people with whom they were in daily contact. Once sufficient numbers of workers were involved, groups of activists were formed to conduct discussions and formulate specific accusations against selected targets. As the movement widened in its appeal and narrowed in its criticism, 'speak-bitterness' meetings were held which drew directly on the experiences of land reform. Nevertheless, though gang-bosses were occasionally dragged through the streets,[50] the urban movement was much milder than its rural counterpart.

In both the democratic reform movement and land reform, mass reaction tended to be similar. The fear of retaliation and a long tradition of deference resulted in an initial reluctance to denounce the accused, though, once the accusations got under way, a climate was created where the accused rapidly put an end to their anguish by repenting.[51] Despite the new stress on mass mobilisation, however, both movements proceeded more slowly than anticipated, not only because of the strength of traditional ties but also because of the weakness of lower-level Party branches. In the towns, this situation led to even greater political movements and, in the countryside, to an intensification of land reform in the autumn of 1951.

In most cases the 'struggle' stage of the democratic reform movement went on until the autumn of 1951, though some units did commence the second stage, that of 'democratic unity'. Workers who had previously been forced to join 'reactionary' organisations such as the Guomindang militia or police force, were required to confess their past misdeeds and submit themselves for criticism.[52] Struggle was now to be avoided and errant workers were reincorporated into the community. In such a situation, a new enthusiasm developed for labour union activities[53] though, as had been suggested, the labour unions were, from the Party's point of view, not particularly healthy. As for the final stage of the movement—'democratic construction'—not much could be done until a whole series of mass movements had come to an end. The really radical ones were yet to come.

### The Labour Union Crisis (1951)

With the radicalisation of May 1951, more attention was devoted to the 'economist' trend in the unions. After engaging in intensive debate on the different standpoints of unions, Party and management,[54] the All China Federation of Labour (ACFL) journal, *Chinese Workers* (*Zhongguo Gongren*) was suspended and it became increasingly apparent that peaceful means of dealing with 'economism' (such as linking welfare demands with collective contracts between unions and management) were ineffective. In July 1951, it was estimated that, although over half of all union branches in north-east China were considered to be relatively successful in mobilising workers to fulfil plans and engage in production competitions, they were unable to co-ordinate welfare demands with productivity.[55] The great problem was that cadres, once censured for echoing the 'commandist' demands of management, had now drifted to a 'tailist' position whereby they merely put forward welfare demands without explaining the difficulties in their realisation.

Though 'economism' permeated all levels of the ACFL network, the problem was less serious at lower levels than it might have been.[56] First, vertical links within the ACFL hierarchy were relatively weak and this prevented the effective transmission of an 'economist' line to all union branches. Secondly, labour union cadres were still subject to rapid transfer and were thus prevented from maintaining effective contact with lower levels.

By the second half of 1951, a full-scale reform of labour unions was under way. Now the theme of 'bureaucratism', which had dominated the earlier rectification movement, was joined by that of 'anti-feudalism' (which derived from the democratic reform movement) and 'anti-economism'. A major programme of re-electing union branches was undertaken, though we are not clear with what success, since the key documents relating to the reform, such as Li Fuchun's report to the Party fraction (*Dangzu*) of the ACFL in December, were never published. All we may observe is the official (1953) comment on the proceedings of the second half of 1951 that most cadres had not followed the 'economist line' in the labour unions.[57]

In many ways, the labour crisis of 1951 resembled the Soviet labour union crisis of 1920–1[58] and there were similarities in the approaches of Tomsky and the effective head of the ACFL, Li Lisan who had returned from the Soviet Union in 1948 after a long exile following the debacles of 1930. There were, however, a number of differences, the most crucial of which was that, in China, the crisis took place in an atmosphere of growing centralisation of economic administration, whereas, in the Soviet Union, it originated in an opposition to economic centralisation and took place before the widespread decentralisation of the New Economic Policy.

### The Centralisation of Economic Administration (1949 – 51)

Having outlined the major political movements from mid-1950 to the autumn of 1951, it is possible to draw a few conclusions about them. First each movement was more radical than the one which preceded it and involved a greater degree of mass mobilisation. As far as the rectification of the Party was concerned, there was a move from a relatively closed process of rectification to a more open one. Throughout the movements, however, the stress on vertical control remained dominant and quotas began to be set administratively, specifying how many cadres should be criticised. How far this tendency might be replaced by a vigorous mass movement depended on the extent to which horizontal links were stronger than vertical ones in the 'dual rule' scheme of organisation. Yet to strengthen horizontal links might be to weaken the vertical ministerial chains of command which were seen as necessary for the rehabilitation of the economy. We are confronted here by a classic contradictory situation —between administrative leadership directed towards managerial and bureaucratic goals and Party leadership directed towards political goals. Before considering the greatest of these horizontally mobilised movements, therefore, it would be useful to consider the degree of administrative centralisation by the autumn of 1951.

At the time of liberation, the Party inherited a fragmented adminis- trative system and a mixed economy. As regional administrations were set up on an *ad hoc* basis, the model in the minds of cadres was that of the Soviet Union at the time of the New Economic Policy.[59] Indeed, south of the Great Wall this model was taken sufficiently seriously for people to advocate the establishment of semi-autonomous economic organisations similar to the Soviet NEP trusts. In Tianjin in 1949, for example, Liu Shaoqi had advocated the establishment of ten horizontally integrated corporations and the incorporation of sundry factories, which did not fall into clearly defined production criteria, into 'joint enterprises' (*lianhe qiye*).[60] Liu stated that private firms could enter these organisations, though it is difficult to imagine how this would have worked out in practice.

In the north-east, on the other hand, the model of economic organi- sation which was followed was that of the contemporary Soviet Union, actualised in the occupied areas of Lushun and Dalian. A north-east Industrial Department (*Gongyebu*) was set up which controlled nine administrative bureaux and two corporations—the Anshan and Benxi Iron and Steel Works.[61] The administrative bureaux were the counter- part of Soviet organisational forms known as *glavki* and the corporations were the equivalent of Soviet combines. With the exception of the corpo- rations, the basic economic accounting unit was the economic 'enter- prise' (*qiye*), again similar to its Soviet counterpart. In the economy as a whole, the commercially defined companies and territorially defined factories were redefined administratively according to a process known as 'enterprisation' (*qiyehua*), whereby an internal 'economic accounting system' (*jingji hesuanzhi*) (*khozraschët*) meshed in with the rudiments of a wider planning system.[62]

The aim was to create an integrated Soviet-style planning system, first in the north-east and then throughout the country, though at first this was extremely difficult. Vague annual plans had been in existence in the north-east since 1948[63] but it is doubtful whether these general plans were articulated to operational planning within factories until much later. In the early days of its existence (after 1949), the north-east Industrial Department operated according to ten-day operational plans with controls far tighter than could ever be carried out in the chaotic situation that prevailed.[64] Allocation problems restricted the proportion of the market supply of products controlled by the state. Planning was frustrated by wide cost disparities, even between sectors of the same industry,[65] and supply problems remained serious. Nevertheless, by 1951, there had been established in the north-east a blueprint for national planning which was intended to be implemented over the whole country by 1953.

Reliance on Soviet models of planning was matched by reliance on Soviet methods of industrial organisation. The prescribed model was very clearly one of vertical rule with restricted scope for the operation of the Party branches. Quite unashamedly, former advocates of the Yan'an-style 'dual rule' pattern of control and of 'concentrated leadership and divided operations' now looked sympathetically on Soviet-style 'one-person management' (*danyi lingdaozhi* or *yizhangzhi*).[66] According to this system, each manager at each level of organisation enjoyed exclusive authority and exclusive responsibility for everything that happened in his area of jurisdiction. Cadres in other leading roles, be they technical, financial or even political, were gradually reduced to merely 'staff' status. Advocates of planning concentrated on balancing the books and tended to look askance at political movements which destabilised their operations. Some people began to see production as more important than political awareness and this view militated against movements such as democratic reform which sought to flush out gang-bosses who might also be highly skilled. The contradiction was becoming acute, but the sheer momentum of the movements, set in motion in the second half of 1950 and the first half of 1951, was such that each failure and each short-coming only spurred the drive for more thorough mass mobilisation. The trend towards verticalisation and the reduction in the role of horizontal (Party) linkages was, for the time being, halted.

### The Three Anti Movement (August 1951 to June 1952)

The movement to create new records had been launched in north-east

China in 1949 to formulate production norms. This grew into a movement to increase production and practise economy which was formally begun in August 1951. Like its predecessor, the movement originated in the north-east.[67] It absorbed the drive for donations to help the Korean War effort, merged with the three main political movements in the urban sphere—democratic reform, party rectification and union rectification—and linked up with a parallel campaign in progress in the academic world dealing with ideological reform. This latter movement, under way since the spring of 1951, took on a new intensity following Zhou Enlai's report to a mass meeting of academics on 29 September, after which intensive discussion and criticism took place concerning the 'standpoint' of administrative and teaching staff. In October, the movement was formalised by the Government Administration Council's 'Decision on the Reform of the Education System'[68] whereby the former *laissez-faire* policy towards educational institutions was officially replaced by a greater emphasis on political and ideological training.

By that time, it was impossible to separate all the various movements and parts of movements which were going on. Everything had merged into a nationwide upheaval known as the three anti movement which took as its main targets graft, waste and bureaucratism.[69] At first, an attempt was made to examine the political factors which had led to waste—bureaucratism, the rural viewpoint, and a cavalier attitude towards planning. Then, the scope of the movement was widened to take in all the post-liberation targets for reform—the tendency to relax after victory, to feather one's own nest, tardiness in implementing democratic reform etc. During the early stages one could often find the principal suspect targets of the movement actually leading it, but as the campaign moved closer to the daily concerns of workers, large numbers of activists outside the Party became involved in criticising urban and industrial leadership.

Formal leadership in the movement was usually vested in increase production and practise economy committees (*zengchan jieyue weiyuanhui*) at municipal level, organised according to the United Front principle.[70] In practice, however, leadership rested with the Party which acted through these bodies. Within factories, local Party committees took the initiative, though, at higher levels, retrenchment and economy committees (*jingjian jieyueh weiyuanhui*) were set up to flush out people guilty of bureaucratism[71] and, within the educational sphere, austerity inspection committees began to organise students.[72]

The initial stage consisted of mobilising industrial workers to detect serious crimes and these were dealt with by the courts. In the east China region during this stage, which lasted until mid-December 1951, higher-level courts and organs of the Procuratorate dealt with 179 cases of graft involving some ¥29 million and, according to the East China People's

Control Commission, the amount of money involved in cases of graft and loss of state property in that region, from September 1950 to November 1951, was some ¥124 million. Convictions by the courts in the region numbered 650, of whom 470 were people employed in government departments or financial and economic enterprises. Of the 650, 356 were retained personnel and 133 new cadres.[73] These figures were small, however, for by the end of the movement in mid-1952 it was estimated that 4.5 per cent of all state officials in China had received some form of punishment.[74]

Within the field of education in late 1951, the austerity inspection committees initiated the criticism of professors and other academics. Their efforts culminated in mass criticism meetings, resulting in one or more confessions from each of the accused. The objects of criticism included worshipping the United States, placing research above teaching, individualism, indifference to politics, neglecting political study and clinging to old habits.[75] The results, in retrospect, were not remarkable but it should be remembered that, at that time, the most urgent field for reform was considered to be industry and civil administration and here the movement was to reach new heights in the following year.

In January 1952, the movement was widened to include a larger range of targets. It was discovered that former capitalists, now employed in the state sector, were using economic information to help their relatives and colleagues in the private sector[76] and government officials were said to be taking bribes to treat former capitalists leniently. In the view of Gao Gang, the Party had been relying too much on the bourgeoisie and, unless this reliance was severed, the end of the Party was in sight.[77] By that time, the policy of placing targets of the movement in leading positions was beginning to reveal a situation in which a movement designed to combat bureaucratism was being run itself with undue bureaucratism and Gao Gang was in a position to expose the guilty. At the same time, Li Lisan, under a cloud for advocating too 'economist' a line in the ACFL, castigated the unions for bourgeois thought, bad leadership and an undue concern for status[78] (which, as we have seen, led to union cadres complaining that they were 'fourth class').

By early 1952, all leading personnel in economic administration were involved in the movement in some way, often neglecting their production duties. Particular problems were created when those guilty of graft were flushed out of supply departments with no one to replace them.[79] As a consequence, planned targets for many commodities were not reached in the month of January 1952 and there was occasionally a decline in the quality of products.[80] In the following month, the movement entered a stage of consolidation. A concern for production led to the provision of detailed limitations on the amount of time management might devote to the movement.[81] 'Tiger-hunting' (*dahu*—the flushing out of principal targets) was now combined with production competitions and efforts were directed to making up for the decline in production. By March 1952, steady production in the state sector seems to have been resumed.

### The Five Anti Movement (January – June 1952)

The extension of the three anti movement, in January 1952, into the private sector gave birth to a parallel movement specifically aimed at that sector known as the five anti movement.[82] Here, the five targets were bribery, tax evasion, theft of state property, cheating on government contracts, and stealing state economic information. Responsibility for running this movement again lay with the increase production and practise economy committees, which included industrialists from the private sector, aided by similar committees set up in organisations of private capitalists such as the federations of industry and commerce. In the early stages of the movement, attempts were made to persuade selected businessmen to confess their misdemeanours and engage in 'self-examination', though predictably most of them did not participate willingly in this process and 'defensive alliances' began to form. In February 1952, businessmen in the private sector were subjected to a number of regulations, such as being confined to their place of work and being forbidden to go out of business, to dismiss employees, withhold or lower wages or conclude alliances with dubious elements in the public sector. At the same time, labour unions were instructed to mobilise industrial and shop workers to investigate their employers and write letters of denunciation. Teams were organised to go into key areas where private management was suspect and to propagandise their findings. 'Five anti battle headquarters' were set up, newspaper reading groups were organised and 'five anti broadcasting stations' proliferated, in an all-out attempt to involve the whole working class in the private sector— literate and illiterate alike.

The response of workers and industrialists was similar to the response of peasants and landlords in the agrarian struggle or workers and gang-bosses in the democratic reform movement. After some initial reserve and fear of reprisals, the movement acquired a considerable momentum, often to the point of getting out of hand. Officially, specialist teams were to investigate suspected capitalists, though, by February 1952, workers occasionally took the law into their own hands and initiated inspection themselves.

Paralleling the stress on orderly production in the public sector in March, the five anti movement entered a planned stage. Direct action without the authorisation of the increase production and practise economy committees was now forbidden and new inspection brigades set out on a process of 'key-point testing'. At the same time, 'five anti work-teams', organised on a three-tier basis (urban ward, sub-urban ward, and individual firm), mobilised the workers according to techniques with which we are already familiar—'speak-bitterness' meetings, confrontation meetings etc. As workers gradually developed a sense of confidence, many employers began to change sides and form what was known as a 'five anti United Front'. Such actions split the ranks of the businessmen and gave a tremendous propaganda fillip to the campaign. Capitalists who had 'achieved merit' in this way were treated leniently and sent around the cities advertising the benefits of such action. By early May, the Party could claim 'basic victory' in the movement and, in June, a formal end was called to both the three and five anti movements.[83]

The description above has drawn much on the parallel with land reform, but this is useful only in comparing patterns of mobilisation and response. The treatment meted out to capitalists and landlords was quite dissimilar, even if one considers the earlier, milder period of land reform. All landlords at least lost their land whereas, according to Peng Zhen, only one per cent of the business community was designated as 'big robbing elements' and subject to imprisonment and labour reform. Even then, some of these elements could 'achieve merit' by confession. By May, people's tribunals had been set up to deal with these elements and the most frequent forms of punishment were fines or confiscation rather than more serious penalties.[84]

This is not to say, however, that the effects of the campaign were not profound. The movement increased the dependence of capitalists upon the Communist Party and the People's Government in three important respects. First, capitalists were now fearful of leaving the United Front; they realised the immense power both of organised labour and the state. Financial losses incurred in the movement were frequently made up by loans from the People's Bank which produced indebtedness and facilitated state financial control.[85] There could be no doubt that, although 31 per cent of total production still came from the private sector of the economy,[86] the state sector was supreme. Secondly, the five anti movement strengthened organisations designed to maintain control over private businessmen and industrialists. Among these were the labour-capital consultative conferences which, although set up before the movements, acquired a new importance. These bodies brought unions and management together in the private sector and facilitated the control of the former over the latter.[87] At a national level one of the 'democratic parties', the China National Democratic Construction Association, promoted the extension of ideological reform from the sphere of intellectuals, where it had begun in 1951, to the world of private industry and commerce. The All China Federation of Industry and Commerce, likewise, began to act as a 'transmission belt' between Party and national bourgeoisie and to organise education in new democracy.[88] A third consequence of the five anti movement was the generation of a whole new corps of activists which began to replace the many defective cadres who had hitherto exercised leading roles in the labour unions and who had been responsible for the slow pace of union reform in 1950–1. Utilising the extensive propaganda network established during the movement, these activists advanced the penetration of most aspects of urban life to a new level.

## Consolidation (1952)

The actions taken to stabilise the urban sector in mid-1952 were accompanied by similar moves in the rural sector. With the 'high tide' of the land reform movement in south China in the autumn of 1951, a call had been issued for the completion of land reform in that region by the spring of 1952. After the arrival of the former Fourth Field Army cadre, Tao Zhu, in Guangdong in early 1952, the official policy changed to rectifying conservative and localist (*benweizhuyi de*) cadres in the countryside. As land reform drew to a close, more and more Fourth Field Army cadres, based on Wuhan, were moved south, displacing local cadres and aiding an inexorable drive towards centralisation.[89]

In many other areas, policies which were initially quite radical took on a more cautious note by mid-1952. In December 1951, for example, the Central Committee of the Party had attempted to accelerate the pace of rural co-operativisation[90] but, by mid-1952, not much had been achieved and policy became more gradualist. The implementation of the new Marriage Law underwent a similar change. The new law, which was to free people from the bondage of the traditional family system, had occasionally been promoted far too zealously, with cadres actively engaged in propagandising divorce. One of the results of this was an increase in the suicide rate, while the murder rate also rose as a result of discarded spouses seeking revenge on those who had humiliated them by ending their marriage. It was reported in 1953, by the National Committee for the Thorough Implementation of the Marriage Law, that over 75,000 deaths or suicides in one year could be attributed to marriage differences,[91] though we are not sure of the extent to which these were due to the implementation or non-implementation of the law. As the new period of consolidation began, the keynote was caution. The Yan'an style had been to bring about change from within existing institutions, not to smash them. The family revolution was to take some time.

## Conclusion

The mass movements of 1950 – 2 started as a closed process of rectification and developed, as time went on, into open mass movements where outsiders were able to criticise Party cadres. None the less, throughout the whole period, the central leadership was always concerned to maintain control over what went on and insisted on bureaucratic methods such as the application of quotas. In terms of Teiwes's hypothesis, discussed in Chapter 1, the degree of coercion which occurred might be explained by the extent to which the régime felt itself under threat from Korea. From an economic point of view, there is no doubt that the movements helped to recover a huge amount of embezzled funds and to discourage graft. At the same time, however, their adverse economic effects were considerable and an unemployment problem might have influenced the date of their termination.[92] In terms of the future development of the economy, the subordination of the private sector to that of the state facilitated the move towards more centralised planning, already under way before the movements began. This, in the longer run, was probably much more significant. From an administrative point of view, the plethora of movements strengthened the horizontal component in the 'dual role' pattern of administration and gave local Party organisations a much more effective role. In the years which followed, there was to be rapid decline in that effectiveness due in part, perhaps, to the sheer exhaustion engendered by two years of repeated mass movements.

## NOTES

1. Mao Zedong, 6 June 1950, *RMRB*, 13 June 1950, *SW* V, pp. 26 – 32. For a comprehensive survey of all the movements covered in this chapter, see Teiwes, 1979, pp. 105 – 65.
2. Vogel, 1971, pp. 59 – 60.
3. E.g. *Zhongguo Gongren* 3, 15 April 1950, p. 15.
4. E.g. Lin Li, ibid., pp. 12 – 14.
5. Ibid.
6. Schurmann, 1966, p. 445.
7. See Brugger, 1976, pp. 97 – 9.
8. Deng Zihui, 30 July 1950, *Zhongguo Gongren* 8, September 1950, pp. 1 – 5.
9. Li Nanxing, ibid. 15, April 1951, p. 36.
10. See Harper, 1969, pp. 89 – 99.
11. Friedman, 1971, p. 224.
12. Ibid.
13. Whiting, 1968, Chapter VII.
14. Friedman, 1971, p. 235.
15. Strong, 1965, pp. 43 – 8.
16. Text in ibid., pp. 310 – 15.

17. Liu Shaoqi, 14 June 1950, Liu, Vol. II, 1969, pp. 215–33.
18. Vogel, 1971, pp. 95–6.
19. Ibid., p. 99.
20. Ibid., pp. 101–10.
21. Ibid., p. 53.
22. Ibid., pp. 107–8.
23. *Ganbu Xuexi Ziliao* 37, pp. 28–31.
24. E.g. Huadong Renmin Chubanshe, 1951.
25. Vogel, 1969, p. 63.
26. *CB* 124, 5 October 1951, p. 4.
27. Ibid.
28. Mao Zedong, 30 March 1951, *JPRS*, 1974, p. 8.
29. *RMRB*, 2 June 1951.
30. *SCMP* 112, 8–9 June 1951, p. 2.
31. Brugger, 1976, pp. 175–80.
32. Zhongguo Minzhu Tongmeng Zongbu Xuanchuan Weiyuanhui, 1951, pp. 126–7.
33. Vogel, 1971, pp. 69–71.
34. Ibid., p. 70.
35. See Wilson, 1968, pp. 76–7.
36. CCPCC, 1 January 1951, *RMRB*, 3 January 1951, p. 1.
37. Shanghai Zonggonghui Wenjiaobu, October 1950, Preface, pp. 1–3.
38. 2 May 1942. Text in *SW* III, pp. 69–98.
39. Zhou Enlai, 23 October 1951, *CB* 134, 5 November 1951, p. 8.
40. Gittings, 1967, p. 75.
41. Ibid., p. 77.
42. Mao Zedong, 24 September 1962, Schram, 1974, p. 191.
43. Gittings, 1967, p. 83.
44. Vogel, 1971, p. 113; Selden, 1979, pp. 274–7.
45. See the collection of articles in *Ganbu Xuexi Ziliao* 37, September 1951.
46. Brugger, 1976, p. 106.
47. *Ganbu Xuexi Ziliao* 37, September 1951, pp. 28–31.
48. Ibid.
49. CCPCC, *Zhongnan ju*, 1 August 1951, ibid., pp. 1–16. Expanded at greater length in *Gongren Ribao*, 12 September 1951.
50. *Gongren Ribao*, 30 August 1951, p. 1.
51. Ibid., 12 September, 1951; Selden, 1979, pp. 274–7.
52. Ibid.
53. Ibid.
54. See Li Nanxing, *Zhongguo Gongren* 15, April 1951, p. 35. In ibid. 16 (24 May 1951) the correspondence column on the labour movement was closed. This was the last number of the journal to appear in 1951.
55. *RMRB*, 9 July 1951, p. 2.
56. Harper, 1969 p. 96.
57. *Gongren Ribao*, 11 February 1953, p. 1.
58. See Carr, 1966, Vol. 1, pp. 202–19.
59. ACFL, August 1950, *Zhongguo Gongren* 8, September 1950, p. 6.
60. Liu Shaoqi, May 1949, Zhonggong Yanjiu Zazhi she, 1970, pp. 200–7.
61. Guan Shuixin, *Zhongguo Gongye* 11, 17 March 1950, pp. 18–22.
62. Brugger, 1976, Chapter IV.
63. *RMRB*, 20 November 1947, p. 1, 16 December 1947, p. 1.
64. Dongbei Renmin Zhengfu Gongyebu, 28 February 1950, Zhongguo Quanguo Zonggonghui Shengchanbu, May 1950, pp. 207–17.
65. Perkins, 1968, p. 605.

66. See Brugger, 1976, pp. 188–90.

67. Gao Gang, 31 August 1951, Zhongguo Minzhu Tongmeng Zongbu Xuanchuan Weiyuanhui, 1951, pp. 14–25.

68. GAC, 1 October 1951, *SCMP* 192, 11 October 1951, pp. 13–16.

69. See Zhongguo Minzhu Tongmeng Zongbu Xuanchuan Weiyuanhui, 1951.

70. Rao Shushi, 17 December 1951, *Xinhua Yuebao* 1, 1952, pp. 19–20. The composition of the Shanghai municipal committee is discussed in Gardner, 1969.

71. Rao Shushi, 17 December 1951, loc.cit.

72. Vogel, 1971, p. 85.

73. Rao Shushi, 17 December 1951, loc.cit.

74. He Ganzhi, *Zhongguo Xiandai Geming shi* (*The Contemporary Revolutionary History of China*), Hong Kong, 1958, pp. 366–7, cited in Schurmann, 1966, p. 318.

75. Vogel, 1971, p. 84.

76. Gao Gang, 10 January 1952, *Ganbu Xuexi Ziliao* 44, February 1952.

77. Ibid.

78. *Gongren Ribao*, 9 January 1952.

79. CCPCC, *Dongbei ju*, 20 February 1952, *Xinhua Yuebao* 3, 1952, pp. 7–8.

80. Ibid.

81. Ibid.

82. The following is based on Gardner, 1969.

83. *CB* 201, 12 August 1952.

84. Gardner, 1969, p. 523.

85. Ibid., pp. 524–5.

86. Li Weihan, 27 October 1953, *CB* 267, 15 November 1953, p. 3.

87. Gardner, 1969, p. 526.

88. *SCMP* 405, 29–30 August 1952, pp. 18–20.

89. Vogel, 1971, pp. 116–24.

90. Gray, 1970, pp. 87–8; Selden, 1979, pp. 331–8.

91. Wilson, 1968, p. 81.

92. Howe, 1971, pp. 116–24.

# IV
# THE SOVIET MODEL
## (1952–1955)

Ever since the establishment of government in north-east China in 1948, attempts had been made to emulate some of the experiences of the Soviet Union. It was not, however, until the new period of consolidation, in mid-1952, that any large-scale attempt was made to implement the Soviet model of organisation south of the Great Wall. Undoubtedly, the major factors which led to this move were considerations of defence and the blockade imposed by the United States during the Korean War. That war had brought China and the Soviet Union closer together but it was not until the second half of 1952 that relations between the two countries might be described as cordial.

### The Lean to One Side Becomes More Pronounced (1952–4)

During the first phase of China's involvement in the Korean War (November 1950 to June 1951), the Chinese People's Volunteers were reported to have been poorly equipped[1] and there was a certain resentment, on China's part, concerning the paucity of Soviet aid. None the less, demonstrating Mao's dictum that 'men are superior to weapons', considerable military successes were achieved. The first rapid Sino-North Korean offensive captured Seoul on 4 January 1951. By mid-June, however, vastly superior UN munitions and air power drove the Chinese and North Korean forces back to the 38th Parallel. Truce talks began in July 1951 and, from the end of that year to the armistice on 27 July 1953, both sides remained bogged down around the Parallel. The Chinese forces found themselves fighting a positional war with which they were unfamiliar.

Although some resentment might have been caused by the refusal of the Soviet Union to involve itself in the fighting,[2] the cautious policy of the Soviet Union prevented further escalation and, at least, China was now protected by the Soviet nuclear shield. Following the military stalemate in the second half of 1951, supplies of Soviet military aid to China increased and an effective Chinese air force was created to fight a war which was increasingly being carried on in the air.[3]

With the stepping up of aid, coolness between the two countries dissipated somewhat but a number of bones of contention still remained concerning the degree to which Chinese sovereignty was limited by areas of joint Sino-Soviet control. In the autumn of 1952, serious and hard bargaining began. During the visit of Zhou Enlai to Moscow in September 1952, the two governments announced that control over the north-eastern railways would be returned to China by the end of 1952 but the Russians would remain in Lushun and Dalian, allegedly at Beijing's request[4] (which is not unlikely since the Korean War was still in progress). Upon Zhou's departure from Moscow, a large number of representatives remained behind to continue negotiations and, in October, Liu Shaoqi arrived for the Nineteenth Congress of the Communist Party of the Soviet Union (though we are unsure as to whether he took part in the negotiations). Since China's First Five Year Plan was to begin in 1953, there was a certain urgency about determining the degree of Soviet assistance. Negotiations, however, were to drag on well into 1953 and were complicated by discussions concerning the termination of the Korean War and by the death of Stalin.

There has been much speculation on exactly how the Korean War was brought to an end and the extent to which nuclear blackmail might have been used. Suffice it to note here that the main opponent of armistice was South Korea's Syngman Rhee who still believed, in mid-1953, that he could win.[5] With the Chinese attack on the élite Korean White Tiger Regiment (subsequently the subject of a famous revolutionary Beijing opera), Rhee's hopes were dashed and an armistice was signed.

Meanwhile, after the death of Stalin in March 1953, the Sino-Soviet climate for negotiations improved. There is insufficient evidence to test the claim subsequently made by Nikita Khrushchev that Stalin had actually impeded Sino-Soviet relations.[6] None the less, it is true that, before long, the new Soviet leadership committed itself to providing far greater aid and assistance to China. The Soviet Union promised to supply China with a number of key industrial projects to facilitate the development of the Five Year Plan. Upon the visit of Bulganin and Khrushchev to Beijing in the autumn of 1954, it was finally agreed that Lushun and Dalian should be handed back to China; the number of Soviet aid projects was increased; a new loan was negotiated and agreements on railway construction signed. In the words of Khrushchev, China was now a 'great power' and 'after the Great October Socialist Revolution, the victory of the Chinese people's revolution is the most outstanding event in world history', one which has 'immense significance for the peoples of Asia'.[7] As a Soviet model of development began to be applied in China, Sino-Soviet relations acquired a new warmth, to the point that, at the European Security Conference held in Moscow in December 1954, the Chinese observer Zhang Wentian declared that China would be bound by the terms of the Sino-Soviet alliance to join in the defence of Europe if peace were threatened.[8]

With the Korean War over, improved Sino-Soviet relations and the change of Soviet foreign policy to one of accommodation with newly emerging nations, the government of the Chinese People's Republic, which now enjoyed unparalleled prestige in the socialist camp, began to formulate an independent foreign policy (though not too dissimilar to that of the Soviet Union). As attempts were made to drive United States influence out of Asia by winning over neutrals or quasi-neutrals, an era of peaceful coexistence was to begin.

## The Establishment of a Nationwide Planning Network (1951 – 3)

Although the mass movements of 1951–3 involved a considerable degree of horizontal mobilisation, attempts had been made to see that they proceeded according to plan. By 1953, although bureaucratism still remained a major target for criticism, the other two 'antis' in cadres' minds were 'commandism' and the 'violation of law and discipline'. This shift in targets suggested an even greater concern with orderly planning.

With regard to economic planning, a regional planning commission had been set up in north-east China as early as 1951[9] but it was not until the second half of 1952 that attempts were made to implement the north-east model in the country as a whole. In August 1952, a State Statistical Bureau (*Guojia Tongji ju*) was set up, followed by a State Planning Commission (*Guojia Jihua Weiyuanhui*), in preparation for the First Five Year Plan. The priority given to the establishment of a planning network was reflected in the fact that, on its establishment in November 1952, the State Planning Commission was given status equal to the Government Administration Council, which meant that its head, Gao Gang, who had been transferred from the north-east, was rated, in the formal government apparatus, equal to the premier, Zhou Enlai (though his status in the Party remained lower).[10]

Together with the renewed stress on 'rational' planning went a stress on 'rational' organisation. By late 1952, 'rational' very clearly meant 'Soviet' and large numbers of Soviet advisers were on hand to help China implement the form of 'rational' organisation which had already been introduced into north-east China. It is tempting, therefore, to see the transfer of Gao Gang to Beijing as part of the general strategy of emulating the Soviet Union. After all, Gao had been most successful in emulating the Stalinist model in the north-east. Such a view has, however, been challenged on the grounds that, even in 1952, a close adherence to the Soviet way of doing things was not the best qualification for someone who wished eventually to inherit Mao's mantle.[11] Though the Soviet model was being implemented, it was not done with universal acclaim.

An alternative explanation for Gao's transfer is that the central leadership was worried about Gao's attempt to set up an 'independent kingdom' in north-east China and wanted to keep an eye on him in Beijing. The existence of 'independent kingdoms' was the very antithesis of centralised planning. What better way to solve the problem than to promote the foremost symbol of regional power to the one post which demanded that regionalism be brought to an end. Again, this view has been challenged on the grounds that the evidence that the north-east was an 'independent kingdom', impervious to central direction, is rather slim. We shall perhaps never know the real motives of the central leadership in transferring Gao, but one cannot fail to note that Gao was to be extremely influential in forging the new 'rationality' and articles in the press were not stinting in his praise.

The Soviet procedure for drawing up a plan, which was emulated in China in 1952, was according to the formula 'two up and two down'. The relevant ministry or industrial department would send control figures down through a long chain of command to the enterprise. The enterprise would then work out a draft plan for the approval of the higher level. After undergoing amendments, the plan would descend once again to provide the basis of concrete work plans. Finally, the resulting documents would be sent back to the higher level for approval.[12] Such a procedure involved much discussion which, in the immediate post-liberation period, might have been initiated by factory management committees. By late 1952, however, these bodies were defunct and discussion either concerned mere matters of operational detail or involved an inordinately long period of haggling. In an atmosphere in which efficient and speedy operation was the watchword, the former was more likely and, where discussions were thorough, they resulted in the late appearance of the final document.[13] The role of the Party organisation here was crucial. It could either promote the participation of workers in planning or act as the moral agent of management in securing compliance with predetermined targets. Increasingly, the Party took this latter attitude, despite the injunctions to avoid 'commandism'. This was particularly the case since the lesson of the five anti movement seemed to be that too wide a dissemination of 'economic secrets' might encourage corruption.[14] Such rigidity in the process of planning was exacerbated further in 1953 when the Party advanced the principle that 'the state plan was law'. Acute contradictions occurred, therefore, in the current campaign to combat, on the one hand, 'bureaucratism' and 'commandism' and, on the other, the 'violation of law and discipline'. These contradictions were usually settled in favour of the latter.

## The Soviet Model of Organisation and Administration[15]

To discuss adequately the various features of the Soviet model, which were emulated in China in 1953, an attempt will be made to contrast them with those of the Yan'an model described in Chapter 1. The first feature of the 1942 model was the programme of 'rectification'. The Yan'an rectification movement, it will be remembered, was a closed process of rectification, in contrast to the movement of 1947–8. It was, however, linked with a series of programmes designed to stimulate popular participation in administration. The rectification movement of 1953, which took place in a relatively secure environment, was also a closed movement but it was not linked to measures designed to stimulate mass initiative. What were punished were individual manifestations of 'incorrect behaviour', such as the tendency to create 'independent kingdoms' or rest on one's laurels. Little attempt was made to involve people in experimentation with structural change to prevent the behaviour which was criticised. Nor could there be, so long as prescribed structural forms had already been laid down in the Soviet Union.

Though the rectification movement of 1953–4 was a relatively mild process, the treatment of errant cadres was often quite different from that which pertained in Yan'an. Since the Soviet view of the relationship between leaders and led did not involve any necessary contradictions, there was a tendency to see all opposition as counter-revolutionary. The stress was less on 'curing the disease and saving the patient' than on 'amputating the diseased limb'. Such a state of affairs one might expect in an open movement, carried on at a time of acute class struggle. What was new in the 1950s was that purge tactics took place within the context of a *closed* movement. There was, of course, nothing like the activities of Yezhov, Yagoda and Beria, who, in the Soviet Union, had also operated within closed movements. Nevertheless, labour reform became less a process of remoulding than a form of punishment. Purge quotas, moreover, remained in force, after the turbulent movements of 1951–2.

The rectification movement of 1942–3 had been directed against foreign dogma and ready-made theories not adapted to the Chinese environment. Now, in the early 1950s, despite considerable reservations on the part of many cadres, Soviet forms of organisation and motivation were prescribed without too much thought being given to the problem of adaptation. After 1952, conflict was avoided where possible but competition between individuals was actively encouraged. Production competitions rewarded the advanced producer with both prestige and money. Incentive policy was both material and individual, with huge bonuses accruing to worker and manager alike if they fulfilled production goals. Conversely, a system of individual responsibility assigned all work tasks to specific individuals who were penalised if they failed to achieve them. One does not have to be much of a dialectician to see that such an individual incentive and responsibility system might grow over into what had long been denounced as 'bourgeois individualism' and militate against collective consciousness.

In such an organised individualised system, the concept of 'cadre' leadership gradually changed. 'Rational' organisation, according to the Soviet model, was characterised by technological solidarity with inter-role relationships becoming more important than inter-personal relationships. The leadership type now was at best managerial, when committed to fast technological change, and at worst that of the modern bureaucrat who just went along with the system. The manager and the modern bureaucrat were less responsive to the opinions of those they worked amongst and tended to confine criticism and self-criticism to meetings of those they considered their peers. The commitment of leadership, in this new situation, was still to the Party but increasingly to the Party as *organisation* or to the Party mediated by other organisations. Operating within a network of technological solidarity, the commitment of the new leadership was more to ability (*cai*) than 'virtue' (*de*) or, in those cases where the leader might explain that it was the contrary, the concept 'virtue' was interpreted increasingly in terms of expertise. Within a network of human solidarity, the lax cadre could slip back into the role of traditional bureaucrat—inert but occasionally accessible. In the new network of technological solidarity, the lax 'manager' could slip into the role of modern bureaucrat—inert perhaps, but quite inaccessible.

Now that the operative slogans were 'regularise, systematise, rationalise, and centralise', the Mass Line, though still proclaimed, changed in content. The original idea of 1942 signified a process whereby general policy was integrated with mass demands. By the early 1950s, this formulation increasingly became the integration of general policy with mass support for that policy. Workers participated less in planning; they were more educated as to how to fulfil plans made elsewhere.

Under Soviet-style centralised leadership, the idea of the existence of a dichotomy between policy and operations became weaker. Leaders infrequently went down to the basic level or to the countryside to renew their links with the masses and to discover to what extent policy and operations might be at variance. The working-class identification of leadership was assumed but rarely tested. As a result of this, the gap between urban and rural areas grew not only in a political and ideological sense but also in an economic sense. An urban-oriented leadership now adopted the kind of economic strategy that is the bane of most Third World countries. Though the First Five Year Plan gave considerable attention to industrialising medium-sized cities in the interior, much emphasis was still laid on building up existing industrial areas, such as the north-east and the old treaty ports, and on an élite sector of industry consisting of whole plants imported from the Soviet Union.

The Yan'an model of 1942 – 3 had made much of the principle 'crack troops and simple administration' and, at first sight, it seemed as though a similar principle was to be implemented in 1953. At that time, a movement was launched to criticise what were referred to as 'five too many'. Cadres had too many tasks to perform. They had to attend too many meetings and training classes. They were required to read and write too many documents, reports and forms. There were too many organisations, and activists held too many concurrent posts. In practice, however, the criticism of the 'five too many' resulted not so much in simplified administration but in the replacement of 'multi-headed leadership' (*duotou lingdao*) by a cumbersome staff-line pattern of administration, organised according to the principle of vertical rule. Each leader at each level of administration tended to become exclusively responsible for activities within his sphere of jurisdiction. Within the factories, as has been noted, this pattern took the form of 'one-person management' which replaced the earlier collegial system of decision-making now denounced as 'parliamentary'. Attached to each manager or bureaucrat on the line were a number of technical staff who now could not easily be deployed functionally where needed. It is axiomatic that when staff-line principles of organisation prevail, chains of command tend to elongate and the number of people attached to the line, at middle levels of organisation, tends to increase, effectively insulating the top of an organisation from its base. Even if the will to implement the Mass Line existed under such circumstances, organisational structures were not conducive to such implementation.

In 1953, industry, in the nation as a whole, was reorganised according to the structure of the north-east Industrial Department with ministries taking the place of the former administrative bureaus. Each ministry maintained its own hierarchy extending through the large administrative regions, provinces and cities down to individual productive units or offices. A network of parallel hierarchies was spawned, all subject less to lateral Party committee co-ordination than to further hierarchies of control. As the formal state control system (which culminated in a Ministry of State Control) extended down to the basic level, the nature of control changed from *internal* political control (as practised by the Party during the movements of 1951 – 2) to *external* economic control which consisted largely of checking up on economic performance after the event. In such a structure, the Party, as the supreme co-ordinating body, found it increasingly difficult to operate. At a macro-political level, the Party was becoming fused with a state which it was designed to assist in withering away. As such it was guilty of bureaucratism.

A technological conception of solidarity, a stress on expertise with the engineer as the new culture hero, and a centralised administrative system, resulted in an overwhelming stress on a technocratic and formal education system. The old liberal universities modelled on a Euro-American pattern were not abolished but had the Soviet system of technical academies grafted upon them. In the new idiom of production, education was seen as a resource, just like coal or iron ore, which served as an input into a system which produced goods.[16] It was not seen in the wider sense, which I believe held in Yan'an, as a qualitatively different type of resource which was itself resource-creating. The emphasis was on quality above quantity and the *selection* of an educated élite to serve the new needs of production. Mass fulfilment and other human concerns were considered irrelevant. The school system was indeed greatly expanded but it was the *school* system. Education was equated with *schooling* and *urban schooling* at that. The children of the bourgeoisie were not to be given preference *qua* children of the bourgeoisie, but it so happened that those children more easily fulfilled the entry standards of an examination-based technocratic system.

### The Soviet Model in the Army

In the prevailing climate, the PLA was seen increasingly from a techno-logical point of view. In the early days after liberation, the army was once again involved in agricultural production and, in some cases, the old policy of achieving partial self-sufficiency in food was revived. As the Korean War shifted from mobile to positional warfare, the idea of people's war atrophied. In his army day order on 1 August 1951,[17] Zhu De had called for modernisation but within the tradition of people's war. In his national day (1 October) order of that year, Zhu made no mention of political tasks. One year later, the order called on the PLA to master its profession and, on 1 October 1953, the order had become 'learn from the advanced military science and techniques of the Soviet Union'. The idea of a *professional* army was a disturbing one. I define a professional as one who is committed not just to the values of his calling but one who increasingly uses them to interpret those of other callings. In such a situation, the notion of *esprit de corps*, which is defined in relation to other corps, was profoundly élitist and contradicted the whole Yan'an tradition of people's war.

The former political control system, with dual command exercised by commander and political commissar, began to decline and as more Soviet weapons became available towards the end of the Korean War and thereafter, Mao's fundamental notion that the attitude of the men was more important than the weapons they held was severely weakened. An élitist air force was built up with Soviet help and military academies began to train an officer corps with recruits no longer drawn from the ranks.[18] In 1955, a whole panoply of ranks was borrowed from the Soviet Union together with a system of orders and decorations.[19] By early 1953, plans were well under way for introducing conscription to replace the older militia system which had earned the scorn of professionals. The new conscription system was in force by 1954 with three years for the army, four years for the air force and five years for the navy.[20] The reason for its introduction was not that insufficient recruits were forthcoming, but to make educated youth available for an increasingly technocratic army, to keep costs down and to create a trained reserve which was felt to be more 'modern' than the older militia system.

The last word on this fundamental change in the whole tradition of the People's Liberation Army was said by Minister of Defence Peng Dehuai when he noted that men 'fail to realise that past revolutionary experience, even experience in the Korean War, has a definitely limited value'.[21]

### The Bureaucratisation of the Countryside

While one cannot speak of a Soviet model in agriculture, one can speak of the effect on agriculture of a stress on stability and orderly government. With the winding up of land reform in 1952 – 3, the structure of power in the Chinese countryside had undergone profound changes. In effect, a whole class had been neutralised, though the bodies through which that neutralisation had been effected were but a shadow of their former selves. The poor peasant bands of Civil War days were now defunct and the peasant associations, which had once taken a radical lead in mass mobilisation, were formed into *xiang* people's congresses and *xiang* people's governments.[22] These organs operated largely through proliferating permanent and *ad hoc* committees. Schurmann has noted the case of one *xiang* in Shandong province which had as many as eight permanent committees and 14 *ad hoc* committees, as well as Sino-Soviet friendship clubs, credit communes, statistical teams, tax teams, publishing stations and a few other *ad hoc* bodies designed to check up on the implementation of various policies.[23] By 1953, the press contained many accounts of rural overbureaucratisation with widespread publication of questionnaires. One memorable case, mentioned by Schurmann, was a questionnaire prepared by the Shanxi Provincial Government with 74 pages and 6,307 items.[24] To be sure, 1953 was perhaps an atypical year since it was the year of China's first modern national census; none the less, the sheer amount of paper being generated gives us some indication of the degree of rural bureaucratisation at a time when China's rural literacy rate cannot have been much over 10 per cent.

It would seem, therefore, that the countryside was an important area for implementing the criticism of the 'five too many'. Indeed, the moderate rectification movement of 1953–4, unlike the mass movements of 1951–2, was to have some impact on the rural areas. The new stress on rationalisation resulted in redrawing the boundaries of local government in the countryside in accordance with 'ecological criteria'. This presumably meant that the *xiang*, which at that time contained some two to three thousand people on average, was to approximate even more closely the traditional standard marketing area or intermediate marketing area. Leadership at the next higher level of rural administration (the *qu* or district) was strengthened and provided a home for more cadres, though the lowest level of all (the village), which had been so successfully penetrated since Yan'an days, declined in importance as an administrative unit.[25] A number of reasons have been suggested for this. First, the location of authority at levels higher than the village might have reduced the influence of traditional leadership and, secondly, there were probably not enough cadres to make village administration a workable reality. What the retreat from the village did mean, however, was that the old Yan'an pattern of transformation from within existing structures was very difficult to implement especially as the militia organisation began to deteriorate after the Korean War.

A problem more serious than rural bureaucratisation was a direct legacy of land reform. Land reform had divided the country into small plots of land individually owned and individually farmed. The Party left no doubt that its ultimate policy was to promote co-operativisation, though in the early years following land reform peasant atomisation was quite prevalent. With the removal of landlords and the inauguration of the 'rich peasant line', real political, social and economic power often resided with a stratum of rich peasants whose land holdings were larger and better than those of the poorer peasants. They not only monopolised village leadership in some areas but infiltrated a rather lax Party organisation and sought to consolidate their economic position.[26] Being able to manipulate loans and to buy out poorer peasants who hit upon hard times (the right to alienate land had not been abrogated by the Land Reform Law), these rich peasants took the lead in a process of land concentration.

The initial response of the Party to these developments was actively to promote mutual aid teams and elementary co-operatives but, with superior economic resources in the hands of rich peasants who were reluctant to join, the private sector looked much healthier than the co-operative sector. Though mutual aid teams continued to be formed, many of the earlier co-operatives were dissolved,[27] especially when richer peasants pulled out of them or conducted propaganda against them. In Mao Zedong's view, the situation was extremely serious[28] and, in the new 'regularised' atmosphere, there was a danger that many of the gains of land reform would be lost.

In the field of rural economic policy, the effect of a national plan to emulate the Soviet Union was more direct. It was the peasants who had to bear much of the burden of industrialisation and feed the rapidly growing urban population. By 1953, pressure had been placed upon the peasants to cultivate economic crops to support light industry, thus reducing the amount of land given over to producing grain. At the same time, in addition to the grain tax, the peasants had to bear the cost of compulsory grain purchases made by the state at fairly low prices. As the urban grain supply barely kept up with the growth of urban population, not only was rationing introduced in the cities but further pressure was placed upon the countryside.[29] The price of a lopsided development strategy was beginning to show.

## The Bureaucratisation of Urban Administration[30]

By the time of the three and five anti movements, parts of China's urban population had been organised in street committees which, in turn, were divided into residents' groups. These organisations undertook such tasks as settling disputes, sanitation, literacy work and, of course, mobilisation in connection with the mass movements of 1951–2. The committees tended to be dominated by housewives whose menfolk had been organised elsewhere by labour unions and other bodies and this resulted in some tension. Though never formally part of government, the street committees' functions were very wide, especially in the period of consolidation after 1952 and, in effect, they constituted the lowest level of government administration. Formally, however, the lowest level of government administration in the cities, introduced after the five anti movement, was the street office (*jie gongsuo*) which was articulated to ward (*qu*) and municipal (*shi*) government and which maintained links with the urban police force.

It was these parallel bodies which were responsible for urban registration, made extremely difficult by the massive increase in urban population (40 per cent between 1950 and 1953). They replaced the multiplicity of *ad hoc* committees which had resulted in a confusion of 'multi-headed leadership' and, by 1954, the situation had stabilised to the point that formal regulations could be issued governing street committees and street offices. The provision of appointed street offices now became mandatory in cities of more than 100,000 people and optional in cities of between 50,000 and 100,000. Their area of jurisdiction was exactly coterminous with local police stations (*paichusuo*) which maintained a system of permanent 'household register policemen' (*hujijing*) within each residential area. Each street office supervised a street committee which consisted of the representatives of some 100-600 households and was subdivided into a number of residents' groups of 15-40 households.

The above system was highly formal. However confusing the former system of 'adhocracy' which had been established by radical worker pickets in the days after liberation might have been, it had a certain spontaneity and drive which had now been dissipated. Though the new system was more effective in spreading participation in government to a lower level, its main *raison d'être* seemed to be one of control. As such, Schurmann has noted, it was probably not welcomed by many local Party branches committed to lateral communication and mass mobilisation, and this might explain why the system was introduced slowly.

## The Bureaucratisation of the Legal System

One of the great debates in the Soviet Union after the Bolshevik Revolution had been the extent to which a revolutionary society should possess law or be ruled by *policy*. Some people argued that law was inherently conservative, since it is governed by precedent, and that the revolution should not be unnecessarily fettered, whereas their opponents argued that a body of transitional socialist law might be drawn up. In the old days of Yan'an, the Chinese Communist Party attempted to create a body of law but tried, at the same time, to make it flexible and amenable to mass interpretation. Mass mediation committees of 'fair-minded people' had been set up by village governments.[31] In the confused situation of the Civil War, however, even such a semi-formal system broke down under the strain. Civil disputes were handled more and more on an *ad hoc* basis and criminal cases settled by hastily improvised courts.

Following liberation, the Party attempted to create a formal court system which required low litigation fees to make it accessible to the masses.[32] It was to become *too* accessible especially since a huge backlog of unsettled cases had piled up during the Civil War. When the formal courts almost broke down under the huge burden of work, the Party turned once again to *ad hoc* bodies, new people's mediation committees or to the street committees which sometimes employed mediators; within government organs 'comrades' courts' were established. A plethora of legal bodies began to develop at different levels and predictably, in the new atmosphere of 1952 – 3, calls went out for 'rationalisation'.

In the judicial reform movement of 1952–3, legal cadres were instructed to lead the masses in creating a single system of mediation to relieve the formal court system but, before 1953 was out, the new mediation bodies were functioning in much the same way as the increasingly bureaucratised formal court system. The extension into this field of the movement to criticise the 'five too many' was seen as imperative.[33]

It seems that battle had been joined between advocates of *Gesellschaft* (bargaining) law and formal bureaucratic regulation on the one hand and Yan'an-type *Gemeinschaft* (community) law on the other.[34] The former was to triumph, and by 1954 a system of provisional rules for mediation was promulgated, whereby committees were set up consisting of 'representatives of the residents under the direction of the basic-level people's court'. Apparently of a mass character, these regulations have been described as having more in common with Guomindang legislation than that of Yan'an.[35] The vagueness of the regulations, one commentator remarks, was probably not to allow greater flexibility but reflected the fact that they were seen as a stopgap measure pending their replacement by a formal court system based on legal expertise and without much mass participation.

## The Case of Gao Gang (1953 – 4)[36]

With the new mood of rationalisation after 1952, attempts were made to centralise power at a national level by reducing the powers of the large administrative regions which had, for a time, functioned almost like separate governments. In the Electoral Law of February 1953, which was to prepare the way for the convening of a National People's Congress to replace the consultative bodies set up in 1949, no mention was made of these large administrative regions.[37] This change was intimately connected with the fate of Gao Gang, the most prestigious leader from the most important of these regions, and Rao Shushi, the head of the only other industrially developed region (east China). The crisis concerning these two people was to constitute the seventh of the major crises in the history of the Communist Party, outlined by Mao Zedong in 1971.

The dimensions of the crisis are still very unclear and even their most shadowy outlines were not revealed until long after the event. What we do know is that confrontations, within the top leadership, occurred at a National Conference on Financial and Economic Work in the summer of 1953, at a National Conference on Organisational Work in September and October, at a meeting of the Politburo in December and came to a head at the Fourth Plenum of the Party Central Committee in February 1954. Soon after that, Gao committed suicide. Eventually, in March

1955, the removal of Gao and Rao was finally made public. They were charged with conspiracy to usurp supreme power and with attempting to create 'independent kingdoms',[38] but it was not until the Cultural Revolution of 1966–9 that sufficient evidence was produced to give us any idea of what went on in the years 1953–4. By that time the evidence had certainly been distorted, but various scholars have attempted to piece together an assessment of the main issues in the struggle.

As has been noted, the earliest accusation made against Gao and Rao was that they attempted to create 'independent kingdoms' in north-east and east China. Since developments in north-east China had been somewhat different from those in the rest of the country, there might be some basis for this charge. Nevertheless, north-east China was only implementing policies which were later to be copied by the rest of the country. If there had been a conspiracy to establish regional bases of power, one scholar has concluded, the subsequent removal of officials in north-east and east China would have been much greater than actually occurred.[39] It was true that the commissions for inspecting discipline, set up by the Party to check adherence to the Party line, had been made subordinate to local Party committees and were formally not as responsive to Beijing as they might have been, but there is little evidence that the relatively decentralised pattern of Party authority was used effectively by Gao and Rao to enhance their own power.

A second charge, made against Gao Gang, was that he saw the Party as divided into two parts—a 'Party of the white (Guomindang) areas' and a 'Party of the base areas and the army'. Gao, it is said, saw himself as a representative of the latter whereas his principal opponent, Liu Shaoqi, represented the former less important section of the Party. But what was implied by this division? Was Gao suggesting that all cadres who had worked in the wartime underground should be accorded inferior status in a reconstructed Party? One doubts it very much.

A third charge directed against Gao was that he maintained a special relationship with Stalin and fell from power once the Party endorsed the new Soviet principle of 'collective leadership' after the Soviet leader's death. Gao had built up something of a 'personality cult' around himself in the early 1950s, and saw himself as Mao's successor. He thus rejected the principle of collective leadership and wished to become general secretary of the Party (the position held by Stalin), outranking both Liu Shaoqi and Zhou Enlai. As I have noted, Teiwes, in his recapitulation of the case, discounts the importance of the Soviet connection, despite Mao's comments about the relationship between Gao and Stalin. He does, however, provide evidence for the view that Gao wished to displace Liu and Zhou and notes that this was particularly important in late 1953 because Mao may have been seriously ill. Mao's illness would also help to explain the possible adherence to Gao of other leaders, such as Peng

Dehuai, and their subsequent abandonment of the association. For Teiwes, then, the Gao Gang case was a 'premature succession crisis'.[40]

What is more important, however, is the extent to which policy issues might have been involved. These Teiwes discounts though others have given them more weight. One issue concerns agricultural co-operativisation. Mao, it is alleged, wished to speed up the process whilst Gao favoured gradualism. If this were an issue, one would have expected Gao's demise to have been followed by an acceleration of agricultural co-operativisation. Not only did this not occur but Gao's replacement as head of the State Planning Commission, Li Fuchun, endorsed the gradualist policies after Gao's demise. A second issue concerns the vertical control of the economy. Various leaders, it is alleged, disliked the Soviet model and were very wary of Soviet forms such as 'one-person management'. They wished, therefore, to remove Gao, who was felt to be one of the major exponents of the Soviet model. This view, however, has been rejected on the grounds that 'one-person management' continued to be endorsed after the fall of Gao and his fall actually accelerated the process of economic centralisation.[41]

But before one accepts the rejection of the above views, one might note that there was no point promoting the acceleration of agricultural co-operativisation or ending 'one-person management', unless the Party were strengthened. This could only be done by replacing the commissions for inspecting discipline by a regular Party control network and this initially implied greater centralisation. Secondly, it may be argued, it would only be possible to decentralise economic decision-making power to the provinces once the large administrative regions were disposed of. Thus, greater centralisation had to precede future decentralisation. There is, however, no way of knowing whether Mao or any other leaders had any intention of decentralising the economy as early as 1954, but one should think carefully before endorsing the view that policy issues were not a major feature of the Gao Gang case. One thing is certain, however, Teiwes is correct in noting that the aftermath of the Gao-Rao case saw much greater centralisation.

## *The Establishment of a Permanent Central Government Structure (1954)*

In June 1954, the large administrative regions were abolished, in preparation for the restructuring of central government. The body which was to ratify this process was a newly elected National People's Congress. This was to take over most (though not all) functions of the Chinese People's Political Consultative Conference. As has been noted, the first step in the formation of this body had been the Electoral Law of 1953 which established a 'soviet' principle of election stretching right down to the *xiang* and with each level electing the next highest.[42] The electorate was the section of the 'people' over the age of 18 years and candidature for election was scrutinised by appropriate-level Party branches. The operative principle of democracy was, therefore, one of controlled representation. Such a principle had existed in Yan'an days but, at that time, had perhaps been complemented by a participatory principle of democracy. We are nowadays very familiar with the participatory criticism of representation; it surely applied to China also in 1954.

After some delay in electing lower-level committees, the First National People's Congress finally met in Beijing in September 1954.[43] Its first task was to approve a draft constitution which had been prepared by a committee, set up in January 1953, under the chairmanship of Mao Zedong.[44] By the time the draft reached the congress, it had allegedly been discussed by some 150 million people who suggested amendments. The constitution was an imposing document, similar in many ways to the Soviet constitution of 1936. It discussed types of ownership, policy towards social classes, rights and duties of citizens etc., but only mentioned the Chinese Communist Party in its preamble and then only with reference to its leadership before 1949. Such was the mood of 1954 which was very soon to change.

China was now (unlike the Soviet Union), established as a unitary multinational state with a single legislature, the National People's Congress. The congress was elected for four years and was scheduled to meet once a year. It elected a chairman (Mao Zedong) who was constitutionally commander of the armed forces and chairman of a Council of National Defence. He could, whenever necessary, convene a Supreme State Conference consisting of the vice-chairman (Zhu De), the chairman of the Standing Committee of the National People's Congress (Liu Shaoqi) and the premier of the State Council (Zhou Enlai). The Standing Committee of the National People's Congress was set up to conduct the routine business of the Congress when it was not in session and the State Council was the main executive arm of the government, consisting initially of the premier, a secretary general and the heads of 30 ministries and five commissions. Significantly, one of these commissions was the State Planning Commission which, in the days of Gao Gang, had been ranked equal to the predecessor of the State Council and had now been demoted. The only bodies ranking equal to the State Council in 1954 were the Supreme People's Court (under Dong Biwu) and the Supreme People's Procuratorate.

Thus, by the end of 1954, the government had been centralised with a hierarchy of congresses and governments, extending right down to the level of the *xiang* and urban ward. Centralisation had been achieved at the expense of the former large administrative regions which, paradoxically some might say, harboured the most extreme exponents of centralisation within their own spheres of jurisdiction.

## The First Taiwan Straits Crisis

By 1954, it seemed that the Chinese government could chalk up notable successes in the field of foreign policy. The Chinese People's Volunteers had fought the United States and its allies to a standstill in Korea and an armistice had been signed. With the battle of Dienbienphu and the temporary ending of the Vietnam War, the socialist camp had been strengthened and, at Geneva, Zhou Enlai had emerged as a statesman of international standing. It is possible that the Gao Gang incident, which paralleled the struggle between Malenkov and Khrushchev in Moscow, had some immediate effect on relations between the Chinese and Soviet Parties but, whatever that effect might have been, relations between the two states and the two Parties were particularly good by the autumn of 1954.

The internal consolidation of the People's Republic and its improved international position was, of course, a serious concern for the Nationalist régime on Taiwan which had attempted to frustrate these developments since 1950. For four years, the Guomindang régime had maintained a blockade of Chinese shipping which was facilitated by its control over a number of offshore islands, notably Jinmen (Quemoy) and Mazu (Matsu) off Fujian province and the Dachen Islands off Zhejiang province. By 1954, the Guomindang forces had been considerably modernised, with United States help, and were ready to reinforce garrisons on the offshore islands.[45]

As reinforcement got under way, a clash occurred between United States and Chinese aircraft in late July which promoted bellicose noises from President Syngman Rhee of South Korea to the effect that a general war was threatened. After the inauguration of Jiang Jieshi for a second term as president, in the spring of that year, the posture of the Guomindang régime appeared much more aggressive and talk of Jiang's return became more frequent. In such an atmosphere Zhou Enlai, arriving back in China in August after the Geneva conference on Indo-China, was most vigorous in his expressions of determination that the current period of consolidation would be completed by the liberation of Taiwan[46] and, in September, a large-scale artillery duel began on the islands off Fujian province. In December, the Dachen Islands were blockaded and the United States and the Taiwan régime signed a mutual defence agreement.[47] Though there is some disagreement about exactly what the terms of this agreement meant, the upshot was that the Guomindang régime evacuated the vulnerable Dachens in February 1955 with American support and the United States seemed to have committed itself to defending the other offshore islands if any threat to them could be constituted as a threat against Taiwan.

In this dangerous situation, appeals were made from many sides for negotiations, though to little effect. Having been rebuffed by the UN Security Council in 1950 and having been branded an 'aggressor' in Korea, China was unwilling to send a representative to address the Security Council where Taiwan was a permanent member, and the subsequent visit of UN Secretary General Dag Hammarskjøld to China bore little fruit. As late as March 1955, United States Secretary of State Dulles still spoke of the possibility of escalation and there have been some suggestions that the United States attempted to use nuclear blackmail to solve the issue. The Soviet Union, for its part, offered only lukewarm support for China and official Soviet statements carefully avoided any reference to Taiwan.[48] There seemed little that any of the major parties to the dispute could do.

The attention of the United States and Soviet Union was now shifting to Europe and that of China to the wider field of relations with the states of south and south-east Asia. This had been China's major concern before the crisis and, as the situation in the Taiwan Straits froze once again, China's long-term policy which sought ultimately to isolate both Taiwan and the United States, was restressed. In April 1955, at the Afro-Asian conference of heads of government held in Bandung, Indonesia,[49] Zhou Enlai was most active in promoting the 'five principles of peaceful coexistence', namely:

1. Mutual respect for sovereignty and territorial integrity.
2. Mutual non-aggression.
3. Non-interference in each other's internal affairs.
4. Equality and mutual benefit.
5. Peaceful coexistence.

The five principles were not, of course, to cover relations between socialist and imperialist states and were seen essentially in a United Front context of rallying forces to oppose the United States. This is not to say, however, that China would not engage in dialogue with the United States on specific issues. At the conference Zhou, in fact, offered to negotiate the relaxation of tension in the Far East and abortive talks at ambassadorial level began in August. In the meantime, China's new outward-looking foreign policy achieved tangible results as more and more contacts were made with newly emergent nations.

## Conclusion

The Soviet model brought with it bureaucratism and managerial leadership. The verticalisation of administration, reversed temporarily during the mass movements of 1950–2, developed to a new intensity and the gap between élite and mass and urban and rural areas became serious. The rural revolution was in danger of grinding to a halt and the organic unity of soldiers and civilians, treasured since Yan'an days, was shattered. On the other hand, the defusing of the Taiwan Straits crisis, the inauguration of the 'Bandung spirit' and good relations with the Soviet Union saw China emerging as an independent force in the world. Civil administration now operated much more efficiently and there was something more like a single economy with the beginnings of a nation-wide planning system. By 1955, the First Five Year Plan was half over and its provisions were finally published;[50] in terms of sheer economic growth that plan was to enjoy considerable success. The problem in 1955 was how to reconcile central planning with the ideals of Yan'an. Those ideals were still very much alive and were still propagated. Before long, many people were to test those ideals against reality and to set out to change that reality.

## NOTES

1. Gittings, 1967, pp. 119–20.
2. *PR* 19, 8 May 1964, p. 14.
3. Rees, 1964, pp. 370–8.
4. Schurmann and Schell, 1967, Vol III, p. 257.
5. Gittings, 1967, p. 120; Friedman, 1971, p. 242.
6. Gittings, 1967, p. 129.
7. Schurmann and Schell, 1967, Vol. III, p. 259.
8. Gittings, 1967, p. 129.
9. *ECMM* 204, 14 March 1960.
10. Klein and Clark, 1971, pp. 211 and 433–44.
11. See Teiwes, 1979, pp. 191–4.
12. Schurmann, unpublished manuscript, II, pp. 14–15 and 28.
13. *Zhonggongye Tongxun* 30, 21 October 1953, pp. 30–1.
14. See Brugger, 1976, p. 134.
15. The following account is based on Schurmann, 1966; Brugger, 1976.
16. Vogel, 1971, p. 127.
17. The following account is based on Gittings, 1967, pp. 117–18.
18. Ibid., pp. 152–5.
19. Ibid., pp. 154–5.
20. *CB* 314, 18 February 1955, pp. 2–8.
21. Cited in Gittings, 1967, p. 157.
22. Schurmann, 1966, p. 438.
23. Ibid., pp. 438–9.
24. Ibid., p. 440.

25. Ibid., pp. 440–2.
26. See Bernstein, 1968.
27. Schurmann, 1966, pp. 444–5.
28. Ibid., p. 445.
29. Vogel, 1971, pp. 128–9.
30. This section is based on Schurmann, 1966, pp. 374–80.
31. Cohen, 1971, p. 35.
32. Ibid., p. 31.
33. Ibid., p. 32.
34. For a discussion of these concepts in a Chinese context see Kamenka and Tay, 1971, and Thomas, 1974.
35. Cohen, 1971, p. 35.
36. The following section is based on Teiwes, 1979, pp. 166–210.
37. PFLP, 1953.
38. CCPCC, March 1955, Chai, 1970, pp. 343–5.
39. Teiwes, 1979, pp. 88–91.
40. Ibid., pp. 205–7.
41. Ibid., p. 197.
42. PFLP, 1953.
43. *SCMP* 889, 16 September 1954, pp. 1–11.
44. PFLP, 1961, Selden, 1979, pp. 287–90.
45. H. Hinton, 1966, p. 260.
46. Zhou Enlai, 11 August 1954, *CB* 288, 16 August 1954, pp. 6–8.
47. H. Hinton, 1966, pp. 261–2.
48. Ibid., p. 262.
49. Ibid., pp. 30–3.
50. Li Fuchun, 5–6 July 1955, Selden, 1979, pp. 294–300.

# V
# THE GENERALISATION OF THE YAN'AN HERITAGE
## (1955 – 1956)[1]

Chapter 3 suggested that the mass movements of 1950 – 2 might be seen both as an attempt to restore the ideals of Yan'an, in the face of increasing corruption, and as a move to lay the basis for the system of centralised planning stipulated by the Soviet model. The extent to which these two aims might have been in contradiction was barely apparent at that time. By 1955, however, some people in China had become aware that many current problems might be systemic. Experience with the Soviet model, at first hand, had not been the most salutary of experiences.

What was lacking was an adequate theory specifying the systemic generation of social contradictions. It is perhaps strange that such a theory was not developed in China in the period after liberation. Mao's seminal essay 'On Contradiction'[2] was widely studied and there had been much discussion about the similarities between the policies of China in the early 1950s and the Soviet Union's New Economic Policy of the 1920s. The questions thrown up in that debate could have been subjected to the dialectical method exemplified in Mao's writings of the late 1930s. There was, however, a general poverty of theory on socialist transition and this might only be explained by the dead weight of Stalin's influence.

What was imported into China in the 1950s from the Soviet Union was not just a model of administration but a model of socialism itself. According to the view outlined by Stalin in 1936, socialism was seen not as the process whereby capitalism was negated but a static configuration of the productive forces and relations of production.[3] Stalin listed a number of attributes which he felt a socialist form of production should have and then proceeded to show how the Soviet Union had basically achieved them. Since capitalism was characterised by an increasingly sophisticated level of co-ordination within modern industrial enterprises in an external economy which was unco-ordinated and prone to crisis, socialism would come into existence when the same form of co-ordination existed in the economy as a whole as that which existed in industrial enterprises. When this occurred, one might consider the forces of production to be of a 'socialist' nature and one did not have to worry too much about the extent to which the relations of production and ideological forms might 'lag' behind them. Sooner or later conformity would be peacefully achieved.[4]

Since socialism was defined by Stalin in terms of the co-ordination of the economy and not in terms of the transition to a single form of ownership and 'real appropriation', socialist society was characterised by the existence of two classes (workers and peasants) and one stratum (the intellectuals). These two classes corresponded to the two dominant forms of ownership (state and co-operative) and the intellectuals were defined in terms of their function of promoting co-ordination. The relationship between these classes and this stratum was essentially non-antagonistic. The Stalinist method, therefore, precluded any consideration of the antagonism which might be generated within socialist society and, when forms of antagonism did manifest themselves in the late 1930s, Stalin could only offer external factors, such as imperialist influence, as explanations. The consequences of this were theoretical absurdity and the brutalisation of policy. Realising perhaps the problems which his earlier formulation gave rise to, Stalin attempted in 1952 to face up to the problem of the generation of antagonism in socialist society[5] but his efforts did not lead to any sophisticated Soviet explanation of systemic antagonism.

The poverty of theory of systemic contradiction is particularly important when one comes to consider events in China in the mid-1950s. To many people, it must have been obvious that the Soviet model itself gave rise to major problems. Yet, to others, problems could be explained away as due to external influences or 'counter-revolutionaries'. This chapter will demonstrate the contradictions generated by, on the one hand, an attempt to accelerate the process of transition to a Chinese equivalent of the 1936 Soviet model and, on the other, by a growing awareness of structural problems which were generated by that model itself.

### Sufan

In accordance with Soviet thinking, the Chinese Communist Party attempted, in mid-1955, to deal with current problems by launching a campaign to wipe out hidden counter-revolutionaries (*suqing ancang fangeming* or *sufan*). This campaign was a parallel to the earlier campaign for the suppression of counter-revolutionaries of 1951. The origins of *sufan* are unclear. Though there was probably some link between the campaign and the Gao Gang incident, I have seen no evidence for such an association. It has been argued, more forcibly, that the campaign grew out of a movement in the field of art and literature against the author Hu Feng[6] who, in 1954, had written a letter to the Party Central Committee protesting against restrictions on literary activity. After much academic discussion, the Hu Feng debate became openly political as Zhou Yang (later denounced in the Cultural Revolution as the 'literary tsar') mounted a full-scale attack against him. By January 1955, Hu had confessed his errors, but his confession was considered inadequate and a nationwide campaign of criticism began to unfold. In May, Hu Feng began to be denounced not merely as a 'petty bourgeois' writer but as a 'counter-revolutionary' and a number of documents appeared, annotated by Mao, which subjected him to severe criticism.[7] Such, it has been claimed, was the origin of *sufan* which soon enlarged its scope to investigate other 'counter-revolutionaries'.

The Hu Feng issue is extremely obscure, particularly since it involved both Mao Zedong and Zhou Yang, who later took very different lines on literary policy. In 1955, however, they seemed united in their attack, maybe because Hu Feng was something more than just a dissident intellectual, as the virulence of the condemnation suggests, maybe because Mao had yet to formulate a policy on intellectual criticism or maybe because he felt constrained by the Soviet model. It is difficult to be sure of what went on in the Party at this time beyond the fact that, by mid-1955, a major process of investigation was in full swing particularly amongst those Party members whose pre-1949 background was suspect.

As in the movements of the early 1950s, fixed quotas of cadres were singled out for investigation from above and chosen targets were required to write out their past histories and submit them for examination by higher authorities.[8] By September 1955, 2.2 million people were reported to have been investigated and 110,000 'counter-revolutionaries' unearthed. In Mao's view, there were 50,000 major suspects still around and, before the movement ended, 11-12 million people had to be investigated.[9] As it happened, very few people were finally designated as 'counter-revolutionaries'[10] and expelled from the Party and most of those were, at first, confined to their place of work and, at the end of the year, sent for labour re-education without sentencing by the courts.

In the view of one writer, who draws his evidence partly from statements by the Minister of Public Security, Luo Ruiqing, the exercise was designed to get opponents of the socialist transformation of industry and commerce out of the way.[11] That would explain why court sentences were not imposed (with fixed time limits), why many people were considered to have been wrongly accused[12] and why many of those sent for labour re-education were returned to their place of work once socialist transformation had been concluded.

In the light of considerations suggested at the beginning of this chapter, however, one might suggest less 'totalitarian' explanations. First, such a Soviet-style movement from the top down sought scapegoats for bureaucratism and yet by 1956, when the model was under full-scale criticism, it was seen that bureaucratism did not necessarily stem from active 'counter-revolutionaries'. Secondly, the movement might itself have generated hostility to the Soviet way of doing things.[13] It violated the earlier Chinese Communist tradition of 'curing the sickness to save the patient' and thus necessitated a reversal of policy the following year.

### The Unified Purchase and Marketing Movement[14]

Whatever the real purpose behind the *sufan* movement, it is true that the urgency of 'socialist transformation' of the economy had been foremost in cadres' minds since 1953. Within most sectors of the economy, 'The General Line of Transition to Socialism', put forward in October of that year, was taken very seriously even though it was not always clear whether that transition should be along Yan'an or Soviet lines.

In agriculture, the situation was particularly confusing. Not only had new rich peasants emerged, but the general level of political consciousness of rural cadres, burdened with a multiplicity of tasks, was low. The cost of China's mammoth industrialisation drive had to be borne by the peasants, and yet the Yan'an tradition of peasant support and peasant activism was still very much alive. This contradiction was nowhere more manifest than when the Party tried to implement unified purchase and marketing of grain as a first step in socialist transformation. Following the decision in November 1953 to impose a state monopoly upon trade in grain, attempts were made to reconcile low state prices (in one area reportedly 40 per cent lower than prices available on the private market) with demands for higher exactions of grain. If implemented properly, the unified purchase and marketing of grain could bring benefits to the peasants; they would no longer be fleeced by unscrupulous merchants, prices would be stable and the state could then mobilise relief grain more readily. On the other hand, if the process was handled bureaucratically or in a 'commandist' manner, peasants would suffer. In 1954, for example, grain quotas were often too high[15] and bureaucratically minded cadres sometimes applied quotas arbitrarily to areas both where there was a surplus and where there was a shortage. The planning system sometimes seemed incapable of accounting for regional natural calamities and there was considerable dissatisfaction.

To counter arbitrariness, misclassification and disorder, a 'three fix' (*sanding*) campaign was inaugurated in March 1955[16] whereby quotas were set for each *xiang* with regard to output, surplus and sale of grain and later in the year the assignment of quotas was extended down to households. In this campaign, work-teams investigated the situation at lower levels where it appeared that cadres could not be relied upon because of family ties or rich peasant influence. Such cadres, unsure of what to do in the new situation, had reacted to peasant dissatisfaction and rich peasant opposition by shifting from a policy that was 'commandist' to one which was 'tailist'. Many peasants had claimed to be in need of relief supplies of grain when they were not, and others had had themselves classified as in need merely because such a classification might help them resist grain exactions in the future. Such occurrences were explained not only as due to poor leadership at the local level but also due to the continuing influence of 'bad elements' and 'counter-revolutionaries'.

By April 1955, tension existed between higher and lower levels of rural administration. Each was suspicious of the other for being, in the case of the former, too harsh and, in the case of the latter, too lenient. The situation varied in different parts of the country and though, in general, older liberated areas found the job of rural transformation much easier than newly liberated areas, it was by no means certain that serious problems in the unified purchase and marketing of grain did not occur there too. One reason for this might have been that, in the former areas, the interval between land reform and the movement had been much longer and the reassertion of conservative values that much more developed.

On 28 April 1955, the Party Central Committee and the State Council turned their attention squarely to the problem of excess supply (relief grain) and work-teams busied themselves with mobilising peasants to part with their surplus. First, cadres were summoned to meetings at *xian* level, away from unhealthy local influences. Then, these cadres and work-teams went down, once again, to the villages to link up with Youth League or other activists who had begun to persuade peasants not to hoard or make unreasonable demands. During the course of the campaign, many peasants confessed their errors but in a climate very different from land reform, for techniques of 'struggle' were not used. At the same time, cadres who admitted their 'tailist' leadership remained at their posts and few active counter-revolutionaries were found. Despite the general implemention of the Soviet model in society as a whole, the Party, in the rural areas at least, still adhered to the Yan'an tradition of not imposing change too harshly from without.

## *Accelerated Co-operativisation of Agriculture*

Experience in the unified purchase and marketing movement convinced many in the Party that insufficient attention had been paid to the livelihood of peasants. In the spring of 1955, therefore, the burden of grain exaction was reduced,[17] both to maintain peasant support and to prevent the switch away from economic crops to the production of grain. More attention was paid to encouraging peasants to participate in decisions which affected them and attempts were made to strengthen rural leadership.

Since land reform, the transformation of traditional temporary mutual aid teams (*huzhuzu*) into permanent teams had been widespread but this development had not been matched by a growth in the rural Party network.[18] The Party was barely able to influence what happened in the teams, much less organise producer co-operatives. It was probably for this reason that attempts to speed up the process of co-operativisation, in the spring of 1953 and the autumn of 1954, had met with little success.

The initial co-ops—subsequently referred to as 'lower-stage co-ops' (*chuji hezuoshe*)—were four or five times the size of the mutual aid teams and consisted of some two to three dozen households. Members pooled most machinery, draught animals and all but about 5 per cent of their land ('private plots'). They received a share of the harvest after the co-op had paid land tax and had made its compulsory sale of grain to the state. Such a system was not considered to be a Soviet-type of 'socialist co-operative' since the allocation of produce and cash, deriving from the sale of grain, was made on the basis of not only the amount of labour contributed to the joint venture but also the resources pooled. Consequently, richer peasants, able to put more resources into the co-ops, did much better than poorer peasants and acquired a new institutional framework to cement their leadership over the villages.

Though many richer peasants benefited from their position in the co-ops, there remained at that time an important private rich peasant sector where superior resources often resulted in higher productivity. Frequently these richer peasants, outside the co-ops, put pressure on the co-op members to withdraw their resources to the point that many co-ops simply collapsed. In Zhejiang in 1953, for example, 15,000 out of a total of 53,000 co-ops had been dissolved at one blow. Despite such developments, however, the overall number of co-ops continued to rise. By 1954, there were some 114,000 but both the speed and nature of their development left much to be desired.

The need to strengthen Party branches in the rural areas being paramount, the First National Conference of the Party on Basic-level Organisational Work in the Villages resolved, in March 1955, to redirect the focus of Party recruitment from the cities (where it had rested since 1949) back to the countryside. Responsibility for a new co-operativisation drive was located at *xiang* level and attempts were made to ensure that at least one co-op existed in each of these administrative units as a model for the formation of others. We might surmise, therefore, that the bulk of new recruits to the Party which jumped from 7.9 million at the end of 1954 to 9.4 million by the end of 1955[19] might be found at *xiang* level.

Though, in the beginning, the new co-operativisation drive was initiated from above, it was not as bureaucratic as that might suggest. Since leadership at *xiang* level rested with the Party rather than the formal administration, it seemed that the intention was to repenetrate the villages and carry out mobilisation along Yan'an lines. Initially, however, since leadership talent was scarce, the *xiang* was probably a better unit to operate from than the village.

Shortage of leadership talent for the drive resulted also in the employment of large numbers of ex-servicemen with rural backgrounds who had been released from an increasingly technocratic army. It was felt that such cadres might achieve the correct balance between the two errors of subordination to local 'feudal' interests and the imposition of change from without. Perhaps the model was that of the immediate post-liberation period where transferred military cadres had played the midwife to local Party branches, since at least one of these transferred cadres was attached by the *xiang* Party branch to each co-op.

We have seen already that May 1955 was a crucial month in the development of this new period of radicalisation. It saw an upsurge in the *sufan* campaign, the redesignation of Hu Feng as 'counter-revolutionary' and an intensification of the campaign to propagate the value of unified purchase and marketing. By that time, the Gao Gang issue had been cleared up, the First Five Year Plan ironed out and Party control committees established at various levels. With the Fifth Plenum of the Seventh Central Committee in April, Lin Biao and Deng Xiaoping who may, at that time, have been advocates of rapid change, were elected to the Politburo and the tide was flowing against those who felt that co-operativisation should wait upon mechanisation.

As radicalisation accelerated the formation of producer co-ops, cadres involved in the 'three fix' campaign found themselves increasingly preoccupied with problems of co-operativisation and training activists. At the same time, attempts were made to ensure that the heads of co-ops were Party members, and frequently meetings of *xiang* Party committees consisted simply of such co-op heads. There were, however, considerable difficulties. Cadres were not always sure just how much pressure to put on richer peasants not to leave the co-ops without endangering the rural United Front. There were no clear directives on how to handle tension between middle peasants who enjoyed a privileged position and poorer peasants unable to negotiate loans to provide share capital for entering the co-ops. Though credit facilities were provided at *xiang* level, it was not always clear whether they could generate funds quickly enough.[20]

The fact that directives were seldom specific was perhaps a consequence of the Yan'an model which was in part revived here. For the Mass Line to operate, policies had to remain general; only that way could some of the errors of the Soviet collectivisation programme of 1928–9 be avoided. Indecision, therefore, was to be expected in the early stages though, to be sure, it was due in part to the low political consciousness of some newly recruited cadres.

Though the Yan'an model stipulated that directives should be general, they had to be consistent. It was clear, however, in the spring of 1955, that this was not always the case. Deep divisions existed at the highest levels of the Party concerning the speed of co-operativisation. Though the focus of Party work had been shifted to the countryside in preparation for accelerated co-operativisation, a rural work conference in May endorsed a plan submitted by Deng Zihui to cut back 200,000 co-operatives.[21]

Faced with what appeared to be too cautious an attitude, Mao Zedong decided to intervene directly in rural policy. After extensive talks with Party leaders from various parts of the country, Mao was convinced that the 1955 harvest would be a good one, guaranteeing adequate storage of grain to tide over any dislocations which rapid co-operativisation might cause. It also seemed obvious that co-operativisation was necessary to facilitate grain collections to fulfil the now fully formulated Five Year Plan. On 31 July, therefore, Mao delivered his famous speech 'On the Co-operative Transformation of Agriculture' which set the tone for the whole movement.[22] In the speech, Mao revealed that the original target for co-operativisation had been one million co-ops. Now the figure was set at 1.3 million for China's 200,000-odd *xiang* so that each *xiang* might have one or more semi-socialist co-operatives; the target date was the autumn harvest of 1956. The immediate task of the Party was to arrange for the campaign to go into operation after the autumn harvest of 1955. Mao Zedong was clearly in charge and full-scale mobilisation was to be undertaken; the more cautious were, for the time being, silenced.

## The Consequences of 'Collective Leadership'

In the last chapter, it was noted that one explanation of the Gao Gang issue dwelt upon the violation of 'collective leadership' which had been formally adopted by the Chinese Communist Party in December 1953. Collective leadership, however, applied not only at higher levels of organisation but at all levels. In some senses, it might have approximated to that kind of functional leadership which had been referred to contemptuously as 'multi-headed leadership' when the Soviet model was implemented.

In the light of subsequent revelations, it would seem that the more extreme patterns of vertical rule and one-person management, prescribed by the Soviet model, were adopted reluctantly and then only in a few areas such as north-east China. This might explain the fact that one-person management was seldom referred to by its name and was just called the 'system of sole responsibility by the factory general manager'.[23] In his excellent summary of the history of one-person management in China in the 1950s, Schurmann remarks on the apparent lack of enthusiasm with which the system was received.[24] By mid-1954, articles had begun to appear which revealed disquiet with this total revocation of the Yan'an tradition and the principle of Party leadership. Presumably under the protection afforded by the new principle of collective leadership, factories indicated their implementation of the principle of 'responsibility of the factory general manager under the unified leadership of enterprise Party committee' *despite* current policy. Other articles described the opposition which existed towards one-person management and the fact that the Party committee in some enterprises had been reduced to merely 'staff' status. Contrary to normal practice, little attempt was made to refute the critics.

By 1955, positive references to one-person management had virtually disappeared and criticism was made of the extent to which the system had, in the past, been introduced too precipitately.[25] Though the demise of one-person management was achieved quietly, the significance was as profound as anything which happened in the rural sphere. First, the principle of dual rule with all its implications for *horizontal* mobilisation was once again the order of the day. The Soviet stress on *managerial* as opposed to *cadre* leadership was under implicit attack. The process whereby institutional arrangements were created for the subordination of political to technological leadership was reversed. The 'virtue' and 'ability' (soon to be referred to as the 'red' and 'expert') dichotomy was given a new meaning and, with it, the orientation of educational policy. Finally, once the principle of vertical rule was questioned, it was possible once again to think of the decentralisation of operations. The implications for a country pursuing a Five Year Plan of Soviet inspiration, with its stress on heavy industry and the élite sectors of the economy, were shattering. It was to be some time, however, before all these implications became manifest and it was not until later in 1956 that one-person management was formally abolished.

## Criticism of the Control Structure

The decline of one-person management was remarkably similar to the decline of the system of external economic control. One of the characteristic features of the Soviet model was the creation of an elaborate control structure under the Ministry of State Control (established in 1954). The clearest example of this was a model introduced into the north-east railway network in 1954 known as the Harbin system, whereby a hierarchy of accounting offices was set up to check on the operation of railways in the north-east.[26] According to this system, the whole task of supervising economic performance was subordinated to a vertical chain of command which severed links with local Party and government organs.

Like one-person management, the external control system was strongest in the north-east but that was not only because the north-east was the region where the Soviet model was most thoroughly implemented. The one-person management system had been strengthened under Gao Gang, whereas external control was strengthened as a consequence of the *removal* of Gao Gang. Schurmann has suggested that, in 1954, control over the ministerial command structure centred on Shenyang required the strengthening of structures centred on Beijing. Consequently, when control cadres were criticised for being impervious to local authorities, such criticism might be from those who demanded a return to dual rule or from those who resented an erosion of the vertically organised ministerial structure based on Shenyang.[27]

In contrast to the position of Teiwes, discussed in the preceding chapter, Schurmann has concluded, therefore, that the issue of 'independent kingdoms' should be taken quite seriously. If one accepts Teiwes's position, the demise of the external control structure was not a consequence of the Gao-Rao case. On the contrary, that case led to a strengthening of external control. If, however, one accepts Schurmann's view, both the strengthening and the decline of external control might be related to the Gao-Rao case. External controls were strengthened until 'independent kingdoms' had ceased to exist and the decline of one-person management had led to an enhanced role for the enterprise Party committees. Then, once such Party committees were ready once again to assume the task of control and to integrate this duty with the work of local government according to the principle of dual rule, the external control network could be dismantled. This, it would seem, was an example of Mao's dialectical proposition put forward in 1949, whereby state forms might be strengthened to prepare for their own demise.[28]

By the Fourth National Control Work Conference in Beijing in April 1955, control cadres were unsure as to their proper function. The report of the Minister of State Control, Qian Ying, was contradictory.[29] She praised the work of control cadres in supervising the movement for the unified purchase and marketing of grain; yet she must have realised that this movement was a preparation for the co-operativisation drive which eventually would reassign rural control duties to the Party. She praised also the Harbin system (which had been introduced experimentally into various sectors of industry), mainly for its results in the railway network (which Schurmann takes as a reference to the north-east where five out of a total of 17 branch bureaux were located[30]) and textiles (located mainly in Shanghai—the former 'independent kingdom' of Rao Shushi). Other industries were now largely to control themselves. Qian Ying stressed that control cadres were to assist in the process of administrative simplification (which was to follow the completion of *sufan*) and to work with local Party committees and the People's Procuratorate, which were also engaged in the business of control. One wonders to what extent control cadres realised that administrative simplification might result in their own retrenchment once it was seen that there were perhaps too many bodies engaged in the same work.

By mid-1955, therefore, there was a shift from external back to internal controls and, with the *sufan* movement, from a separation of economic and political control back to their integration under Party leadership. Ironically this shift accompanied the replacement of the former loose network of Party commissions for inspecting discipline by a regular hierarchy of external Party control. One should not conclude, however, that the change was simply the replacement of one hierarchy of control by another similar body. The Party control hierarchy was not an economic agency; it was simply an institution charged with maintaining the integrity of the Party organisation.

The decline of the formal external economic control structure in 1955 proceeded in a manner similar to the demise of one-person management. In August 1955, articles appeared in the press praising the Harbin system but, in effect, warning against adopting it *in toto*.[31] As Schurmann sees it, the whole idea of external control implied intolerable rigidity. A body which stamped out illegality would also stamp out flexibility. The Yan'an model, which sought not to impose control from without but to effect change from within, was one which initially tolerated a certain amount of illegality, but under a Party which would choose the right moment to counter it either by internal rectification or by mass mobilisation.

### The Initial Acceleration of the Socialist Transformation of Industry and Commerce

The five anti movement of 1952 had left some 30 per cent of China's total production in private hands. With the 'General Line of Transition to Socialism' in 1953, however, it became clear that the private sector would soon be brought under state or joint public-private control. In September 1954, the State Council passed the temporary regulations on joint state-private enterprises which established 'joint public-private' (or 'joint state-private') as the prescribed form of operation for formerly private concerns following socialisation.[32] Small traders or service concerns, however, would be co-operativised rather than socialised.

The normal method of joint public-private operation would be for the state or local government to take over ownership of a concern, paying the former owner 1 to 5 per cent per annum 'fixed interest' (*dingxi*), while still employing him to manage the concern at a fixed salary. Though a former capitalist in this situation might not earn an income more than a few times that of the average worker (since unsocialised firms were usually quite small) and though he might be urged to spend his fixed-interest payments on government bonds,[33] the fact that he continued to enjoy the fruits of what was technically still 'exploitation' was later to cause some disquiet.[34] But before it could worry about such problems, the Party had to ensure that the socialisation process was achieved without too much disruption of production.[35]

Between 1952 and 1955, the state had made some headway in the process of socialisation but had been more concerned with establishing a planning network and articulating private concerns to it via contracts. Controls imposed over the distribution of certain goods effectively turned many private shops into agencies of the state marketing organs which had already come to control the bulk of wholesale outlets. Since price controls often left retailers small profit margins, a guaranteed 5 per cent per annum began to look attractive.

There were a number of problems, however, which suggested that the pace of socialisation should be forced. Shopkeepers, faced with eventual socialisation, were often unwilling to invest large sums of money in their businesses. Insufficient goods were purchased from wholesalers which led to stockpiling and waste. A black market for rural produce developed as 'capitalist-minded' peasants sought to bypass the state marketing system which paid low prices. Private industry tended to neglect quality as it sought to make as much money as possible before the axe fell, and private entrepreneurs seemed unwilling to share technical knowledge with those in the public sector. The planning machinery found it difficult to articulate production and distribution in both public and private sectors. At the same time, the general radicalisation in other areas of society highlighted these problems and led to pressure for the solution once and for all of the socialisation of industry and commerce.

By early 1955, the problems in the private sector were such that the government found itself supporting all sorts of conservative policies just to keep trade and industry moving. Trade fairs were organised which bypassed the state marketing organs. State banks made loans to private businessmen who were unwilling to continue investing capital in their concerns. Goods were redirected from co-operatives to private concerns, and regulations governing some goods were relaxed. Senior cadres were so concerned that production and distribution would be disrupted by a lack of business confidence that, once the rural sector radicalised after Mao's speech of 31 July 1955, they tried to convince businessmen that a similar radicalisation would not occur in the urban sector. They soon, however, set about making sure that it did, in fact, occur. Such action cannot be dismissed as hypocrisy. The situation is perhaps analogous to a country facing the possibility of a devaluation of its currency. All rumours of devaluation have to be denied right up to the last moment to prevent speculation, but unless those rumours are effectively squashed (and they rarely are), the rumours themselves bring about devaluation.

By August, plans were being actively pursued to effect socialist transformation. Investigation teams were formed. United Front-type organisations of businessmen such as federations of industry and commerce became active in preparing the ground and shops were reorganised according to specified lines of work (often through existing guilds). Here the Yan'an principle of transformation from within came into its own. Adherents of the Soviet model would surely have condemned the guilds as 'feudal'; now cadres used them as the basis for reorganisation of commerce under Party-led management bureaux. As in the rural sector, there was a need for more and more cadres to supervise the work. Some might be found in the labour unions but many were businessmen themselves who were retrained in numerous study courses. With the old lesson of democratic reform in mind, they were presumably somewhat suspect.

By October 1955, preparations were ready. In a way similar to the radicalisation of rural policy, Mao Zedong, at a joint meeting of the Politburo and Executive Committee of the All China Federation of Industry and Commerce, called for a radical speed-up in the socialist transformation of industry and commerce. Originally the target for completing the transformation had been 1962. In December, Mao called for 90 per cent completion by 1957.[36] The radical movements in countryside and city had joined.

## Socialist 'High Tide'

The parallel between 1951 and 1955 will by now be apparent. Just as in the earlier year the process of radicalisation got under way in May and intensified in the late summer, so in 1955 a similar process occurred. The immediate consequence of Mao's speech of 31 July, however, was not, as one might have expected, an immediate drive to step up the rate of co-operativisation. This may have been due to the opposition of senior Party leaders but it is more likely that it was because of the concern to initiate a thorough process of discussion and to draft plans which were to go into effect after the summer harvest. A 'backbone cadre' had to be created for each co-operative and a new drive had to be launched to recruit students and ex-servicemen to help with the movement. Accountants had to be trained to manage the books and new schools were set up for that purpose. The propaganda network also had to be enlarged and films and propaganda material prepared.[37]

At the Sixth Enlarged Plenum of the Seventh Central Committee in September-October 1955, Mao outlined his strategy.[38] In Mao's view, 'socialist transformation' would proceed over two or three Five Year Plans. He put forward, therefore, a series of very ambitious targets to be achieved within twelve years:

|  | 1955 output (official)[39] | 12-year targets (annual output)[40] |
|---|---|---|
| Grain | 175 million tonnes | 300 million tonnes |
| Cotton | 1.5 million tonnes | 6 million tonnes |
| Steel | 2.9 million tonnes | 18–20 million tonnes |
| Coal | 98 million tonnes | 280 million tonnes |
| Tractors | – | 183,000 |
| Motor vehicles | – | 208,000 |
| Machine tools | 14,000 | 60,000 |
| Cement | 4.5 million tonnes | 16.8 million tonnes |
| Chemical fertiliser | 0.3 million tonnes | 7.5 million tonnes |
| Crude oil | 1.0 million tonnes | 18 million tonnes |
| Electricity | 12 billion Kwh | 73 billion Kwh |

By 1967, the area under mechanical cultivation was to be increased to some 60 per cent of the total of 107 million hectares. Quite clearly, if these targets were to be achieved, a 'leap forward' in agriculture and industry was called for and the first step in this process was the rapid transformation of agriculture. As guidelines for this 'leap', a 17-point document was drawn up by Mao in consultation with the secretaries of 14 provincial Party committees. These 17 points, drafted in November 1955, were expanded into a 40-point document in January 1956, and, after amendment at a series of meetings, were incorporated into a 'National Programme for Agricultural Development (1956–67)'.[41] The details of this document, which were put forward at a Supreme State Conference on 25 January, were somewhat different from those submitted to the Sixth Plenum[42] and it was clear that some more cautious people had prevailed upon Mao to be more modest in his aims. None the less, the launching of the National Programme constituted a signal for China's first attempt at a 'leap forward'.

The new atmosphere was to lead to even more rapid co-operativisation. In most areas of the country, co-operativisation was to proceed in three waves, each in the winter and spring periods of 1955 – 6, 1956 – 7 and 1957 – 8; in a few national minority areas, however, co-operativisation might not be completed until 1960. Though the pace was to be fast, the experiences of the Soviet Union in the late 1920s were to be studied and 'left' excesses guarded against. Up to 1955, however, the main obstacles had come from the right and there is every indication that the Sixth Plenum was characterised by intense debate, during which Deng Zihui and the Party's Rural Work Department came under considerable criticism.[43] At the same time, it is said, Mao's close colleague Chen Boda became very influential in rural matters.[44] By September 1955, the conservative line of the early 1950s had been repudiated and the notion that collectivisation had to follow mechanisation was rarely heard. As Mao saw it, the Chinese countryside was ready for a much more intensified radical programme which should not and need not be forced. In Mao's words:

> We must attain our objective naturally and not by forcing ourselves. It is like a woman giving birth to a child. If we force the delivery after seven months, it is 'left'. If after nine months we do not permit the birth, it is 'right'.[45]

The radicalisation of the Party's line on co-operativisation was not just a question of increasing the number of co-ops and the rate at which they were formed but also of changing the rural class structure. Mao now insisted that reformed landlords and rich peasants could join the co-ops in order that such elements might be remoulded and fewer efforts were directed at patient persuasion. At the same time, more money was made available to lend to peasants who wished to purchase co-op shares. In general, therefore, a 'poor peasant line' was reborn.[46]

Following the Sixth Plenum and the formulation of detailed plans in local areas, the co-operativisation movement reached its 'high tide'. Quotas and targets were constantly revised to the point that, by the end of the year, 75 million peasant households (or 63.3 per cent of the total peasant population) had joined co-ops.[47] The sheer pace of change found many cadres wanting and sometimes resulted in 'formalism' where mutual aid teams were transformed into co-ops with very little other change. Once the breakthrough had been made, however, the process of strengthening and consolidation could proceed. Richer peasants could no longer resist the tide and began to join in ever greater numbers. An added incentive, perhaps, was the fact that grain collection was first done in the co-ops and then the responsibility for the collection from other sectors was assigned to co-op members.[48]

Once middle peasants had joined co-ops, it became possible to move to what in Soviet terms was considered to be a more 'socialist' form. The model for a new type of co-op—the 'higher-stage co-operative' (*gaoji hezuoshe*)—was clearly the Soviet *kolkhoz* (or collective farm). Those which were formed in 1955 varied considerably in size from a few lower-stage co-ops to collectives as big as a whole *xiang*.[49] They were similar to the earlier co-ops in that all land, draught animals, major production materials etc. were turned over to the collective and individual peasants retained a plot of land, a few animals and some tools. Provision was still made for share funds determined according to property and labour status but payment was now exclusively according to work, not according to resources originally pooled. Nevertheless, some compensation was made for loss of property.

By late 1955, success in the co-operativisation movement led, as we have seen, to the decision to bring forward to 1957 the target for completing the socialisation of industry and commerce.[50] In fact, it was to proceed even faster than anticipated. Despite constant urging not to be too precipitate, meetings of businessmen were hastily organised to petition local government to reorganise their concerns into joint public-private enterprises.[51] Mass meetings were held to hear reports on the need for socialisation and the target dates for socialisation were progressively brought forward. Such a situation was particularly remarkable since the person entrusted with overseeing the socialisation was Chen Yun who was usually portrayed as a cautious man concerned with maintaining production. He was, it seems, outpaced by Beijing's mayor, Peng Zhen, who managed to convert all private industry, commerce and handicrafts in the capital within the first twelve days of January 1956.[52] This pattern was soon copied in other cities, where United Front bodies, reminiscent of the five anti movement, busied themselves in assisting the reorganisation of whole lines of business and attending parades to celebrate the successful 'completion' of the task.

But what was implied by completion? It could not have meant that reorganisation had resulted in stable forms of management. Since inventories were often made before the State Council Regulations for Inventories and Assessments were promulgated, they were often quite inaccurate. Cadres were unsure, therefore, about the assets they were now to reallocate. Nor had cadres any guidelines on how the process of amalgamation was to proceed and firms often got bigger and bigger to the point where management became most confused. Faced with such a situation, Mao was somewhat critical of the Beijing experiences.[53]

In early 1956, with the escalating socialisation and co-operativisation, the Party began to discuss long-term economic policy and the optimum organisation of the collectives, co-operatives and joint enterprises. It seemed clear that the current drive would not finish until all private business had been socialised and the whole of the rural population had been brought into collectives. But at the very peak of this 'socialist high tide', a decision was taken to deradicalise policy.

Various scholars have debated the many possible causes for the deradicalisation decisions of 1956. One school of thought argues that the 'leap forward' had got out of hand.[54] The former private sector of industry and commerce was in disarray. Peasants had been coerced and were resentful. Livestock had been killed prior to collectivisation and there had been a marked decline in peasants' sideline agricultural activities. It is argued also that provincial authorities had escalated production targets beyond realistic levels and had used coercion to achieve them. They had imposed central policies upon peasants, who knew that such policies could not possibly work. Mao, for example, had promoted the mass production and distribution of a two-wheel double-bladed plough which often proved too heavy for draught animals and was not suitable to local soil conditions. There was a need, therefore, to adopt a more sane approach to rural policy. By April, there was much talk of 'reckless advance' and the need to 'seek truth in facts' rather than utopian wishes. This was to be the theme of a major editorial written by Deng Tuo, the editor of the Central Committee newspaper *Renmin Ribao* on 20 June 1956[55]—an editorial which Mao refused to read.[56]

Other scholars argue, however, that although occasional compulsion was used and although there was some slaughter of livestock before co-ops were organised, the principle of voluntarism seems to have been adhered to and change brought about from within according to the old Yan'an tradition.[57] If one compares the progress of co-operativisation in China with that of the Soviet Union, one may only conclude that the process was a very great success.[58] The movement had, moreover, facilitated the penetration of the natural village for the first time since the bureaucratisation of the early 1950s. Herein lay one of the strengths of the old Yan'an model which had been generalised and adapted to a very new situation.

In explaining the deradicalisation decisions, however, what is important is what various leaders thought the actual rural situation was rather than which explanation might have been the true one. In later years it was claimed that the major opposition to the 'reckless advance' came from Liu Shaoqi and Deng Xiaoping.[59] On the basis of the available evidence, however, it is difficult to substantiate such a charge.[60] It might be argued with equal force that the major opposition came from Zhou Enlai, who in early 1956 called for a more lenient policy towards intellectuals. Perhaps it came from economic planners such as Chen Yun who were involved in the socialisation of private industry and commerce. It might even be the case that Mao himself had come to the conclusion that the movement was getting out of hand. At the enlarged Sixth Plenum,

Mao had declared that he would regard as 'leftist' the attainment of 80 per cent co-operativisation by the end of 1956.[61] But that was precisely what looked like happening. Mao was to applaud that development. But had he changed his mind or was he just making the best out of the situation?[62] It might also be argued, moreover, that the deradicalisation decisions were due less to the economic situation than to events in the Soviet Union following the Twentieth Congress of the Soviet Communist Party. The implications of that congress will be explored in the next chapter.

### Criticism of Army Professionalism

The radicalisation of late 1955 and early 1956 was to have an impact far wider than rural co-ops and private industry. In the army where sovietisation was almost complete, the new radical atmosphere allowed those who resented the decline of old traditions to voice their complaints. They demanded that the army practise, once again, the Mass Line, the 'three military democracies' (political, economic and financial) and set up soldiers' committees.[63] No one doubted that army modernisation was very necessary but the aim was to gain experience, not to become isolated *professionals*.[64]

In response to Mao Zedong's twelve-year plan for agriculture, the Political Department of the PLA drew up a plan to support agricultural co-operativisation.[65] On the average, each soldier was required, during the course of the year, to devote five to seven free labour days to production,[66] though, in this period, it appears that this average was not reached. The PLA of some 2.5 million was to devote 12.5 to 17.5 million workdays in 1956, though it only reached the figure of four million.[67] Nevertheless, this was a considerable improvement on previous years. Soldiers were instructed, in particular, to use their spare time in the drive to eliminate four pests (rats, sparrows, flies and mosquitoes), and to assist in afforestation even to the point of planting trees in their barracks. Gifts of army 'night soil' were to be made to local peasants and military doctors were to make their services available to civilians. Army units in the countryside were instructed to raise livestock at a rate of one pig per 50 men and military engineering shops were to help repair agricultural machinery in the co-ops. Army units were to build electric power stations which were to be co-ordinated with local civilian requirements. Soldiers were to engage in propaganda and the Signals Corps was to set up broadcasting stations. Military units were to assist in the establishment of schools in the co-ops and soldiers had the duty of looking after the ideological training of their relatives. The army was to conduct an economy drive to save money for equipping tractor stations and was to provide personnel to run them. Perhaps most important of all, specific military units were to identify themselves with specific co-ops and accept the leadership of the local Party committee. An all-out attempt, therefore, was undertaken to reintegrate the army with society according to the Yan'an tradition.[68]

A far greater emphasis was now placed on political training in the army. Excessive and dogmatic reliance on the new disciplinary code was criticised as well as the dogmatic rejection of formality. Syllabuses for political study were prescribed for officers of a certain rank and political night schools were established. Training manuals were rewritten in accordance with Chinese geographical conditions, since handbooks produced in Moscow often said very little about tactics in rice-paddy country. In drafting these manuals, officers were to consult with the men in accordance with the old idea of military democracy.[69]

In all the discussions of the generalisation of the Yan'an heritage in the PLA, however, there was one area about which virtually nothing seems to have been written—the people's militia. With the introduction of conscription, the militia had atrophied and yet there was clearly some kind of militia in existence in early 1956, for reference was made to militia activities in PLA regulations.[70] In the plan to support agricultural co-operativisation, for example, provision was made for the militia to hunt wild animals, and yet not much was said about militia organisation in the various articles on organising co-ops and collectives. It was not until much later that elaborate plans were put forward to 'make everyone a soldier'. Such a demand would clearly not have met with much positive response immediately after the deradicalisation decisions of 1956.

## Conclusion

The initial decision to deradicalise seems to have been taken at an enlarged Politburo conference in early April 1956 though it was not fully implemented until June.[71] Even so, the sheer momentum of the collectivisation drive was such that central decisions could not prevent 83 per cent of all households being enrolled in co-ops by the end of the year, rising to 97 per cent in the summer of 1957.[72] They did, however, result in the shelving of Mao's twelve-year plan for agriculture. It is perhaps the case that the mass movements of 1955 – 6 went to such extremes that the deradicalisation decisions became inevitable but, as I have suggested, external factors were also important. Indeed, there was no Communist Party in the world which was not affected by Khrushchev's denunciation of the excesses of Stalin at the Twentieth Party Congress in February 1956.[73] As Chinese leaders asked how it had been possible for Stalin to abuse power in the way he was said to have done, the way was open for a new analysis of the systemic generation of contradictions in socialist society. It was possible, moreover, that China's *ad hoc* dismantling of the Soviet model of administration might be replaced by a theoretically informed restructuring of the newly socialised economy.

## NOTES

1. This term was coined by Benjamin Schwartz.
2. Mao Zedong, August 1937, *SW* I, pp. 311–47.
3. See Stalin, 25 November 1936, Stalin, 1947, pp. 540–68.
4. See Stalin, September 1938, ibid., pp. 585–6.
5. See Stalin, 22 May 1952, Stalin, 1972, p. 69.
6. Vogel, 1971, pp. 135–7; Goldman, 1962.
7. Mao's annotations in *SW* V, pp. 172–5 and 176–83.
8. Vogel, 1971, p. 136.
9. Mao Zedong, 11 October 1955, *JPRS*, 1974, p. 16 (the date given here is September 1955). The current revised version of this speech omits these figures, *SW* V, p. 215.
10. Mao Zedong (8 December 1956, *SW* V, p. 40) notes that, by December, four million people had been investigated and only 38,000 designated as counter-revolutionaries.
11. Vogel, 1971, pp. 137–8.
12. Mao apologised for people being wrongly accused in December 1956. Mao Zedong, 8 December 1956, *JPRS*, 1974, p. 41.
13. For a Cultural Revolution criticism of excessive Soviet influence during the campaign, see Xie Fuzhi, *SCMM* 641, 20 January 1969, pp. 20–2.
14. The following is taken from Bernstein, 1969.
15. See Mao's criticism. Mao Zedong, 13 January 1958, *JPRS*, 1974, p. 84.
16. SC, 3 March 1955, *CB* 318, 15 March 1955, pp. 1–7.
17. Mao Zedong, September 1955, *JPRS*, 1974, p. 18. A different version in *SW* V, p. 218.
18. The following is taken from Schurmann, 1966, pp. 442–7.
19. Ibid., p. 129.
20. Vogel, 1971, pp. 144–8.
21. Liu Shaoqi, summer 1967, Liu 1968, Vol. III, p. 366.
22. Mao Zedong, 31 July 1955, *SW* V, pp. 184–207; Selden, 1979, pp. 341–50.
23. E.g. *Zhonggongye Tongxun* 16, 1 June 1953, pp. 1–5.
24. Schurmann, 1966, p. 263.
25. Ibid., pp. 272–8.
26. Ibid., pp. 327–39.
27. Ibid., p. 331–5.
28. Mao Zedong, 30 June 1949, *SW* IV, p. 418.
29. Schurmann, 1966, pp. 340–4.
30. Ibid., p. 342.
31. Ibid., pp. 346–9.
32. Vogel, 1971, p. 157.
33. Ibid., p. 170.
34. Mao Zedong, 8 December 1956, *JPRS*, 1974, pp. 41–4.
35. The following description is taken from Vogel, 1971, pp. 156–64. See also Selden, 1979, pp. 300–9.
36. Mao Zedong, 6 December 1955, *JPRS*, 1974, p. 27.
37. Vogel, 1971, pp. 149–53.

38. Mao Zedong, September 1955, *JPRS*, 1974, pp. 14–26.

39. State Statistical Bureau, 1960, pp. 95–8 and 119.

40. Mao Zedong, 11 October 1955, *JPRS*, 1974, p. 16. Figures omitted from current official text, *SW* V, pp. 214–15.

41. See Chang, 1975, pp. 17–20.

42. Text in Bowie and Fairbank, 1965, pp. 119–26. This document does not give the targets stated in Mao's speech of 11 October. See also Selden, 1979, pp. 358–63.

43. Mao Zedong, September 1955, *JPRS*, 1974, p. 22.

44. Chang, 1975, p. 16.

45. Mao Zedong, September 1955, *JPRS*, 1974, pp. 24–5. My translation from Mao Zedong, 1969, p. 23.

46. Vogel, 1971, pp. 152–3.

47. Schurmann, 1966, p. 454.

48. Vogel, 1971, pp. 154–5.

49. Schurmann, 1966, p. 455.

50. See MacFarquhar, 1974, pp. 22–3.

51. See Vogel, 1971, pp. 164–73.

52. MacFarquhar, 1974, pp. 23–4.

53. Mao Zedong, 20 January 1956, Mao, 1969, p. 30.

54. See Walker, 1965, pp. 59–67.

55. *RMRB*, 20 June 1956, p. 1.

56. Mao Zedong, 12 January 1958, Mao, 1969, p. 152.

57. Nolan, 1976.

58. For an interesting comparison of the campaigns in the Soviet Union (1929–30) and China, see Bernstein, 1967; Nolan, 1976.

59. *RMRB*, 23 November 1967, *SCMP* 4068, 28 November 1967, p. 6.

60. See the discussion in Chang, 1975, pp. 13–14; MacFarquhar, 1974, pp. 86–8.

61. Mao Zedong, September 1955, *JPRS*, 1974, p. 24.

62. MacFarquhar, 1974, p. 25.

63. These are summed up in Tan Zheng, PFLP, 1956, Vol II, pp. 262–4.

64. See Gittings, 1967, Chapter VIII.

65. *SCMP* 1234, 24 February 1956, pp. 3–7.

66. Ibid.

67. Ibid., 1443, 4 January 1957, p. 9.

68. Ibid., 1234, 24 February 1956, pp. 3–7.

69. Gittings, 1967, pp. 164–71.

70. Ibid., p. 207.

71. See Chang, 1975, pp. 23–9.

72. Schurmann, 1966, p. 454.

73. Text in Rigby, 1968, pp. 23–84.

# VI
## 'SOCIALIST' CONSOLIDATION
### (1956)

Khrushchev's denunciation of Stalin, at the Twentieth Congress of the Communist Party of the Soviet Union, provided an opportunity for the leaders of both countries to embark upon a theoretical examination of the problems encountered in socialist transition. In practice, however, the Soviet leadership offered little more than an attribution of most ills to Stalin's personality. This chapter will note Mao's dissatisfaction with the Soviet position. In general, however, the policy of the Chinese Communist Party, throughout 1956, echoed the initiatives taken in the Soviet Union and Mao's role as leader was played down. Continued adherence to the Soviet model of socialism, though not to the Soviet model of administration, moreover, resulted in policies aimed at consolidating the gains of socialisation rather than continued social experimentation.

### The Chinese Response to Destalinisation

As has been noted, the deradicalisation decisions of 1956 were, in part, a reaction to the Soviet Twentieth Party Congress. At the April Politburo conference, where the decision was taken to modify radical policies, the main item for discussion was probably Khrushchev's secret speech. Right from the start, it seems, Mao was disturbed. In his concluding remarks at that conference, he expressed disquiet at Khrushchev's actions. He acknowledged that discipline within the Soviet Union had been too strict and that, if China persisted with a system of tight control from above, it would be tantamount to 'letting Gao Gang hold sway for another year'.[1] Mao opposed excessive centralisation and later was to castigate Stalin for occasional 'metaphysics and subjectivism', 'making mistakes in dialectics', failing to see that the October Revolution, which had negated capitalism, could itself be negated[2] and for using the public security organs exclusively in dealing with counter-revolutionaries.[3] What Mao was opposed to, however, was making the whole issue public. He considered that parts of the mass criticism campaign in the Soviet Union were suitable neither to China nor the Soviet Union[4] and urged that discussion of Stalin's bad points should be kept within the Party.[5]

The official Chinese position, which gradually evolved in early 1956, was that Stalin's errors should be seen not in terms of the Soviet leader's *personal* aberration but as the result of internal contradictions occurring in socialist society. The Chinese leaders were quite aware that the bureaucratic model they had begun to dismantle was essentially Stalinist but, as Marxists, they could not ascribe it entirely to Stalin's personality. This view was reflected in the first public statement on the problem of Stalin which was to appear in April 1956. The article 'On the Historical Experiences of the Dictatorship of the Proletariat'[6] went to great pains to point out that, at the height of the Yan'an movement of 1943, Mao had attacked any notion of the 'cult of the individual'. Furthermore, if it were true that Stalin was divorced from the masses, this only highlighted the importance of the Mass Line. The article also drew attention to some of Stalin's achievements, thus making the message abundantly clear: Stalin should not shoulder all the blame for what had happened in the Soviet Union, and even if he were guilty of certain errors, these errors were not paralleled in a China now engaged in a radical generalisation of the Yan'an heritage.

In April 1956, however, one could not be sure as to what curbs might be applied to the new 'leap forward'. Policies, therefore, which originated at that time were somewhat ambiguous and have been variously interpreted by Western scholars. At the April Politburo meeting, Mao called for a policy of 'letting a hundred flowers bloom and letting a hundred schools of thought contend'.[7] Thus, Mao's prescription for dealing with the contradictions generated by the Stalinist system was not to crush dissent but to let intellectuals and others voice their opinions and stand the full test of criticism. Such a policy might be interpreted in two very different ways. On the one hand, Mao's policy could be seen as a call for 'liberalisation' in order to allow people simply to let off steam. On the other hand, such a call might be interpreted as advocating open Party rectification, whereby non-Party people might help to reform the Party by criticising its leaders. The first interpretation saw the 'blooming of a hundred flowers' as a form of repressive tolerance. The second interpretation saw such 'blooming' as an integral part of Mao's desire to push ahead with the social revolution. Had Mao's call been made during the early part of the 'leap forward' of 1956, one might assume the latter interpretation. Had it been put forward later in 1956, when more cautious policies were in force, one might have more confidence in the former interpretation. But April 1956 was the very turning-point in radical policies and Mao's intentions remain obscure.

Another initiative by Mao was to occur at this important turning-point. This was his speech of 25 April, entitled 'On the Ten Major Relationships'.[8] Mao's speech, which constituted a direct attack on the Soviet model of administration, was, as MacFarquhar asserts, a complete rejection of Li Fuchun's 1955 outline of the First Five Year Plan. That plan had allocated 89 per cent of industrial investment to heavy industry and only 11 per cent to the consumer goods industries. Now Mao called for much greater attention to be given to light industry and agriculture. It was essential, Mao felt, to stimulate productivity by improving the livelihood of the peasants. Investment in light industry, moreover, would yield capital much more quickly. The response of Li Fuchun and other planners to the proposal was not particularly sanguine. They were even less happy with Mao's second proposal to shift a certain amount of heavy industrial development back to the coastal cities. In advocating the reduction of defence expenditure, however, Mao was probably at one with the planners, if not with senior generals in the army.[9] On other economic issues such as the promotion of an industrial wage rise, the discouragement of accumulation through the pricing of agricultural products and the decentralisation of economic decision-making, it is difficult to know how the planners reacted.

Concerning the relationship between industry and agriculture, therefore, there is some evidence that many of China's planners were reluctant to abandon the old Soviet model. What is important to determine here, however, is the direction of Mao's attack on that model. Was Mao advocating a more 'liberal' policy (with greater concessions to mass consumption, even if they led to greater inequalities) or a more 'radical' policy (aimed at a faster transformation of the relations of production)? It is extremely difficult to answer such a question. One might interpret concessions to peasant consumption both as a way of mitigating the hostility generated in the 'leap forward' of early 1956 and as a way of engendering mass commitment for further accelerated co-operativisation. The shifting of a small amount of heavy industrial investment back to the coastal cities might perpetuate the lopsided development strategy China had inherited from the past, but it might also require less investment for the same amount of increased output and so free future investment funds for development of the hinterland. There was no doubt, however, that the reduction of defence expenditure and the decentralisation of decision-making authority to the regions could facilitate the old Yan'an policy of military-civilian integration and dual rule and so assist future radicalisation.

Despite its ambiguities, most commentators see the speech 'On the Ten Major Relationships' as an attack on the Soviet model from the *liberal* direction. This seems clear also in its non-economic proposals. The national chauvinism, which accompanied the Stalinist policies, was criticised together with the attitude of 'Han chauvinism' towards national minorities. At the same time, a less authoritarian interpretation was given to the term 'dictatorship of the proletariat' and minority parties were given some encouragement. The speech called, moreover, for a mitigation of the harshness meted out to counter-revolutionaries, though executions would still continue.

In Mao's speech, however, it is possible to see issues of great importance to any *radical* strategy. I refer here not to matters such as the assessment of Stalin (70 per cent good and only 30 per cent bad) but to the policy of simultaneous advance on all fronts. Though Mao advocated policies which might be expected to exacerbate the differences between town and country, the injunction that agriculture, light industry and heavy industry should be pushed simultaneously was to become the major slogan of a new 'leap forward' which was to be much more radical than that of early 1956. The stress on sectoral balance in April 1956 was to lead to some rather unadventurous policies but, before long, it would be possible to read parts of Mao's speech in a way which would encourage 'dynamic disequilibrium'. In the meantime, however, the dominant ethos was to be a criticism of 'reckless advance' and most Party leaders devoted their attention to preparing for a new Party congress to formulate the new process of consolidation. Mao, moreover, supported their efforts[10] though we cannot be sure as to how he saw the function of the congress, particularly since the groundwork was laid at those very ambiguous meetings of April 1956.[11]

## The Problem of the Intellectuals

The focus of Mao's attention in the spring and early summer of 1956 was clearly upon the intellectuals. In January of that year, Zhou Enlai had spoken at length upon the subject and stressed opposition to rightist conservative ideology.[12] As Zhou saw it, Party attitudes towards the intellectuals were subject to two kinds of error—'sectarianism' and 'compromise'. The former, associated with an 'ultra-left' position, was élitist and, from a Mass Line perspective, reactionary, while the latter, which led to passivity, was conservative. In practice then, the 'ultra-left' could dialectically be linked with the right.

Zhou had spoken in an atmosphere which was still quite radical, when the campaign style of leadership was triumphant. Following the deradicalisation after April, however, Party 'sectarianism' came to be seen as a much more serious error than 'compromise' and efforts were made to enlist many more intellectuals in the service of socialist construction.

Greater emphasis was now given to the positive role of university academics. The attempt to draw up socialist legal codes, which had commenced in 1953, was speeded up under the guidance of Peng Zhen. At the same time, Liu Shaoqi pressed for a reform of the press and suggested that Western techniques should be emulated. In this respect, Hu Qiaomu, the author of a very influential short history of the Party, suggested that the Soviet news agency Tass was a very inadequate source of information. As a consequence, a limited-circulation news medium appeared entitled *Cankao Xiaoxi* (*Reference News*). This was based on Western news sources and was read most eagerly by many intellectuals. In 1956, China's intellectuals seemed never to have had it so good.[13]

If Mao's aim in launching the policy of 'letting a hundred flowers bloom and a hundred schools of thought contend' had been simply to satisfy the intellectuals, then it was enjoying much success in the summer of 1956. If, however, the aim had been to help reform the Party from without, then not much had been achieved. This second aim required much more than a liberalisation of policy towards universities, the law and the press. It required intellectuals actively to criticise the Party. This presumably was what had been implied in the policy of 'long-term coexistence and mutual supervision' whereby 'democratic parties and groups' could assist the Party by pointing out its errors (and, of course, vice versa). Yet very few democratic parties and groups did respond to Mao's call in 1956. They quite naturally feared a repetition of the Hu Feng case. The Party machine, for its part, also seemed unwilling to encourage criticism for fear of provoking further upheavals.

The reluctance of the Party machine to stimulate criticism in 1956 might also be explained by an adherence to the repressive tolerance interpretation of the hundred flowers policy. This implied that there was no necessary connection between rectification and the 'blooming and contending'. Various leaders may have seen the need for rectification in 1956 but this could have been interpreted not as a way of dealing with the criticism stemming from the 'blooming of a hundred flowers' but as a response to the strikes and disturbances which had developed in the wake of the Khrushchev revelations.[14] Though Mao did not think that such disturbances would reach the proportions of those in Eastern Europe,[15] they did require action by the Party and the imposition of penalties for lax and bureaucratic cadres. But such a situation could be handled by the time-honoured process of closed rectification organised from the top down without being mixed up with the criticism of intellectuals.

In any case, neither rectification nor the hundred flowers movement was to develop in mid-1956. This is particularly difficult to explain since very little comment was made about these matters in the subsequent Cultural Revolution. Material from that time focuses not so much on the movement, or lack of it, but on the 'perfidious' speeches of certain individuals. Lu Dingyi, the head of the Party Central Committee's Propaganda Department, for example, came under savage attack for a speech made in late May.[16] As Lu saw it, intellectual freedom had clearly to be under Party leadership and within prescribed lines. Nevertheless, this only applied to *political* freedom and, 'as everyone knows, the natural sciences including medicine, have no class character'. Such a position, which seemed the very antithesis of Mao Zedong Thought in the mid-1960s, might possibly have been endorsed by Mao in 1956. Lu was also charged with maintaining that since all exploiting classes had been eliminated, class struggle had basically come to an end. Yet, however 'revisionist' such a statement might appear later, it did seem to reflect the positive model of socialism adopted by the Party in 1956. Such conclusions have led scholars to assert that, although Mao might have been very frustrated by the lack of development of his hundred flowers policy in 1956, there was no evidence of any major theoretical cleavage amongst the central leadership. Contrary to the views on this subject expressed in the first edition of this book, this is a conclusion I must accept.

## Wage Reform

In his speech 'On the Ten Major Relationships' Mao called for a wage rise for industrial workers. Such a rise, which would exacerbate the urban-rural gap, could have been supported by Mao for many different reasons. It might have been seen as necessary in the light of developments in Eastern Europe. It may also have been a response to the industrial disturbances in China. Even more likely, Mao was merely echoing a policy agreed on before 1956.[17] In the period up to 1953, there had only been regional wage reforms, and in the period 1953–5, no wage reform at all. During those latter two years, the stress had been on a high rate of domestic saving which led to a drive to limit wage increases, practise strict industrial discipline and implement strict financial control. The former policy had been enforced by 'comrades' judicial committees' (*qiye tongzhi shenpanhui*) and the latter by strict accounting procedures (which may have led to friction between accountant and 'one-person manager' and contributed to the latter's demise).[18] While it lasted, the policy seems to have been effective since the rise in wages for industrial blue- and white-collar workers was only 5 and 3 per cent respectively compared with 17.4 per cent in the years 1950–3. In the atmosphere of centralisation after the Gao Gang affair, attempts to iron out regional differences and abolish non-monetary payment tended to lower wages and encourage demands for wage reform. The first steps in that direction were taken in the state and administrative system in October 1955 when formal salary scales were worked out for all cadres comprising some 30 salary grades with quite steep differentials.[19] Such a policy, quite clearly in line with the Soviet model, was now to be applied to the industrial sector in general but, it was anticipated, without a major increase in the average wage.

As policy was worked out in the deradicalised atmosphere of mid-1956, wage reform along Soviet lines stipulated that the differential between management/technical staff and workers should be increased, that managerial staff should have wages higher than technical staff and that differentials among skilled workers should widen. In addition, in marked contrast to 1955, an across-the-board wage rise became the primary object of reform. As *ad hoc* wage reform committees began their work at enterprise level, tensions developed since managers did not wish to lose their discretionary wage powers along with the other powers they had surrendered with the decline of one-person management.

By the completion of the wage reform in the autumn of 1956, the average wage had increased by nearly 20 per cent. In a few months, the reform had fulfilled the total rise in average wages planned for the whole of the First Five Year Plan. From a radical point of view, the results were alarming. Migration from rural areas intensified. The manifest gap between urban and rural incomes cancelled out some of the intended effects of co-operativisation. There was a great consumption boom in some of the major cities, leading to packed restaurants and the opening of clubs. Conflicts between labour and management over economic issues multiplied as labour unions once again began to walk the path of 'economism'. One wonders whether Mao had foreseen such developments in his speech 'On the Ten Major Relationships'.

## Consolidation of the Rural Sector

Though co-operativisation went on throughout the consolidation period which began in April 1956, the new stress on orderly administration had a significant impact on the villages. During the earlier 'high tide' of co-operativisation, there had not only been economic disruption but a certain amount of administrative confusion had been caused by a shortage of rural cadres. Since there had been insufficient cadres at village level, co-operativisation tended to be organised from *xiang* level, from whence cadres were sent down to the villages. This had then resulted in a shortage of cadres at *xiang* level and a pressure for *xiang* amalgamation. As *xiang* increased in size, a decision was taken in December 1955 to abolish the level of administration intermediate between *xiang* and *xian*, known as the *qu*. There was a need, therefore, to work out new prescriptions as to the size of the rural administrative units. This was particularly important if the new *xiang* were not to disrupt traditional marketing areas and if the new collectives were not to cut across lines of *xiang* jurisdiction.

In the spring of 1955, there had been some 219,000 *xiang*. By the time regulations were worked out as to optimum size in the autumn of 1956, there were only 117,000. These *xiang* were now divided into three categories—those on the plains with a population of 10,000 – 20,000 people, those in hilly areas with a population of 5,000 – 8,000 and those in the mountains with a population of 2,000 – 3,000.[20]

After fixing the size of the *xiang*, attempts were made to specify the size of the new collectives. In September 1956, this was to be 300 households in the plains, 200 households in hilly regions and 100 households in the mountains. Collectives were subdivided into *brigades* (corresponding often to the older co-ops and consisting of 20 – 40 households) and *teams* (often corresponding to the old mutual aid teams containing seven to eight households).[21] As time went on, the early very large collectives were reduced in size to correspond more nearly to the old natural villages where rich peasants still owned proportionally better land. With the old village reconstituted as a collective, there was understandable pressure to collectivise all its population. In the non-radical political climate of mid-1956, it became easier for richer peasants to join, though, as we have seen, not all wanted to and they may have been subjected to pressure. Some joined but then left again and were to be the butt of a later anti-rightist campaign. Still others assumed leading roles in the collective and propelled policy in a conservative direction.

The Model Regulations for Collectives, promulgated in 1956, demanded that the collective divide its gross income into four parts.[22] First, state taxes were to be paid and compulsory grain sales made to the state at fixed prices. Secondly, a sum was deducted for future production costs and the repayment of debts. Thirdly, a public accumulation fund and public benefit fund (not to exceed 8 per cent and 2 per cent of income respectively) were set up and finally the remainder was divided according to the work done by collective members, calculated as the amount of 'work-points' they had collected during the year. Payment to peasants, therefore, would consist of a small amount of cash which had accrued to the collective from the sale of grain and other goods plus a share of the harvest in kind. The calculation of individual income, however, was by no means an easy task. The ideal, rarely achieved, was that every single job of work, day in and day out throughout the year, had to be assigned a definite number of work-points. Accountants and administrators were needed in ever greater numbers and the problem arose of how one determined *their* income. It was to be extremely difficult moreover to work out equivalents between different types of farm work and between farm work and work in subsidiary industries set up by the collective.

The collectives were run by an administrative committee of nine to

19 members, which was elected by a members' council or members' delegates' council and was supervised by a control committee similarly elected. Wherever possible, a Party committee was also set up in the collective, the membership of which overlapped the management committee. Where the Yan'an model was effective, these structures helped younger men to assume leading roles in the village for the first time. Where it was a failure, however, older rich peasant leadership remained and frustrated social change. This latter situation was to occur quite frequently in the early period when problems of organisation led to bureaucratism and new young cadres were too inexperienced. Faced with a reversal of the early-1956 policies in order to overcome problems of rural dislocation, these young cadres did not know how to advise peasants on the relative importance to give to collective work or work on their private plots. They were not sure what kind of commercial network to set up in the collectives or how to draw the line between maintaining production and fostering a 'capitalist' mentality. Bureaucratic directives from above appeared in profusion but it was difficult to apply them in concrete situations and, as we have seen, the second half of 1956 was not noteworthy for clear Party leadership. Faced by supply problems in September 1956, the government responded by reopening rural markets.[23] How was the inexperienced cadre, who had just gone through the radical process of co-operativisation, to react, especially since he had just been engaged in the redrawing of *xiang* boundaries which may have involved the reorganisation of traditional marketing structures? A lot of serious rethinking needed to be done.

### National Minorities Policy

In the fields discussed above, the policy of late 1956 was one of consolidation after the radical movements of the 'leap forward'. With regard to policy towards national minorities, there had never been any radical movements. In a major work on the subject published in that year, Zhang Zhiyi,[24] one of the leading architects of the United Front, noted that the People's Republic of China differed from the Soviet Union in that it was a unitary and not a federal state. Although the Party had supported a policy of federalism from 1921 to 1940, the war had forced nationalities together so that by 1949 there was no need for a federal state. In any case, national minorities comprised less than 10 per cent of the population, whereas in Russia in 1917 more than half of the population were non-Great Russians, some of them more 'advanced' than the Great Russians themselves. The 1954 constitution, therefore, accepted the principle of self-government but not separation. Such a policy, Zhang admitted, was different from that of Lenin.

Although the Soviet Union had accepted the principle of separation, it was not permitted in practice and Soviet policy towards nationalities was, at times, quite brutal. In China on the other hand, although separation was not permitted, policy in the 1950s had been to interfere hardly at all. An assimilationist policy was ruled out, since such a policy could lead to national movements led by non-proletarian elements. Religion was to be tolerated, since any attempt to suppress religion only produced martyrs and a Marxist position held that it was pointless to attempt to destroy religion unless, at the same time, one destroyed its class basis.[25] In the early 1950s, there remained 5,000 Buddhist temples with 3,000 living Buddhas and 320,000 lamas. In Islamic areas there were 40,000 mosques and more than 100,000 imams and mullahs.[26] In some nationality areas, a system of slavery was still maintained (e.g. among the Yi).[27] In others, there existed monastic serfdom (Tibet), nomadic pastoralism (Inner Mongolia and Xinjiang), head-hunting (among the Wa in Yunnan) and slash-and-burn agriculture (among the Jingpo in Yunnan).[28]

To cope with the differences in social life and economic structure, attempts were made to define special national minority regions at provincial level, known as 'autonomous regions' (zizhiqu), at levels intermediate between province and xian, known as 'autonomous districts' (zizhizhou) and also at xian level and below. Within these administrative units, cadres busied themselves with educational work though this sometimes involved first inventing a written script. Reform was, in general, very slow.

During the high tide of co-operativisation of 1955–6, some areas had experienced change. By March 1956, 72.7 per cent of herding families in Inner Mongolia had been co-operativised though similar attempts to co-operativise the Kazakhs were less successful. In the Zhuang area of Guangxi, the Yanbian Korean Autonomous District and agricultural parts of Qinghai, 70–90 per cent of households had been co-operativised by 1956 and, in the Hui autonomous xian in Hebei, over 90 per cent had been so organised.[29] In other areas, however, social change was minimal.[30] Cadres were instructed not to antagonise local leaders and must have been extremely perplexed at how to deal with such practices as Yao 'witch vengeance' (like voodoo) or mating festivals, how one pursued a non-interventionist policy when musical instruments were made out of human skin, how to draft a directive to the effect that bugs should not be killed in areas where a belief in reincarnation was prevalent or whether to forbid the use of iron ploughs where tradition said that iron poisoned the soil.

One of the best accounts of how the extraordinarily moderate policy towards natural minorities worked is that of Alan Winnington. Describing the reforms of 1956 amongst the slave-owning Yi,[31] Winnington observed that only those who owned more than ten slaves were singled out as targets for reform. Even after the slave-owners had lost their slaves, however, they still enjoyed political rights and still remained influential in local government. Sometimes they were even paid compensation. In the Yi region, opium cultivation (the main agricultural activity) was still permitted for fear of damaging the local economy.

Such a moderate approach[32] could not but lead to resentment, especially among cadres who elsewhere had been active in land reform. They could not but feel disquiet at a policy of Party recruitment whereby, if Party committees refused membership to national minorities who refused to give up the customs and religions of their people, they were criticised from the highest level as 'great Han chauvinists'.[33] There were, of course, a lot of quite genuine cases of 'great Han chauvinism' where, for example, Muslims were forced to eat pork. Nevertheless, one cannot fail to observe that excessive moderation, in which attempts were made to effect the Yan'an model of transformation from within, could lead to the Party's being taken over by the people whom it was trying to reform. There was perhaps little danger of that in 1956, but many cadres were apprehensive.

## The Party in 1956

It was in an increasingly conservative climate that preparations were made for the Eighth Party Congress. On 6 July 1956, a Politburo conference worked out the congress agenda and, in late August, a somewhat confused Seventh Plenum of the Seventh Central Committee examined a political report to be submitted to the congress. That political report was later to be the subject of considerable polemic.

The Eighth Party Congress, which met on 15 September, was to endorse some of the measures already taken to replace the Soviet model of administration. It adopted, however, a model of *socialism* which was remarkably similar to that first put forward by Stalin in 1936. According to the congress resolution, since the exploiters had already been liquidated as classes, the basic contradiction in Chinese society was no longer a matter of class struggle but resided in the relationship between the 'advanced socialist system' and the 'backward productive forces'.[34] This implied that, since an 'advanced socialist system' (or model) was already in existence in part of society, any class struggle in the future would occur outside that system. There was no basis, therefore, for the systemic generation of antagonism except in relation to residues of the past. Consequently, policies ought to be directed primarily to developing the productive forces and expanding the 'socialist system' rather than fostering class struggle. This formulation was an official endorsement of the kind of position put forward by Lu Dingyi in May. As has been noted, it was later to be vigorously condemned as a violation of Mao Zedong Thought. If, however, Mao had any reservations about this formulation in September 1956, he left no record of them.[35]

Nor did Mao leave any record of his views of the official Party position on the role of the guiding ideology. The Seventh Party Congress in 1945 had established Marxism-Leninism and Mao Zedong Thought as the foundation of Party policy. The 1956 constitution however, omitted the reference to Mao Zedong Thought.[36] In the Cultural Revolution, this was held to be one of the 'crimes' of Liu Shaoqi and Deng Xiaoping. Commenting on this, MacFarquhar regards such a view as somewhat simplistic and, in his analysis of the events of the congress, suggests that there was a very clear difference of emphasis in the speeches of Liu and Deng.[37] In his view, Liu Shaoqi, in line with the criticism of the 'cult of personality' in the Soviet Union following the Twentieth Party Congress, wished to play down the role of Mao in the Chinese revolution. By stressing 'collective leadership', Liu may implicitly have criticised Mao's possible failure to consult his colleagues on the speed-up in the collectivisation drive of April 1955. It is possible also that Liu played a part in the drafting of an internal Party directive to the effect that no mention be made of Mao Zedong Thought in Party communications though Mao Zedong's *works* should continue to be stressed. Thus, in accepting the recommendation of Defence Minister Peng Dehuai that no reference be made to Mao Zedong Thought in the Party constitution, Liu might have demonstrated his personal agreement.[38] Deng Xiaoping, on the other hand, MacFarquhar argues, was the man most attuned to Mao's ideas. In 1954, he had been appointed Party secretary general (*mishuzhang*), but now in 1956 he was elevated to the new eminence of general secretary (*zongshuji*) at the head of a strengthened Secretariat. The influential Deng continued to stress Mao's symbolic importance. He insisted that there had been no problem of a 'cult of personality' in China and pointed to the fact that, before the founding of the Chinese People's Republic, the Party had forbidden the celebration of the birth-days of Party leaders and the naming of places after them.[39] Certainly Deng later admitted that he had withdrawn reference to Mao Zedong Thought in the Party constitution but, MacFarquhar says, this was probably only true in the sense that he had been a member of the drafting committee.[40]

Other writers, however, have challenged MacFarquhar's descrip-tion. Teiwes, for example, argues that the differences in Liu's and Deng's speeches merely reflect a division of labour among the central leadership.[41] As he sees it, Liu was, if anything, closer to Mao than Deng. In any case, it did not matter very much because the moves taken by Mao to prepare for his retirement suggest that Mao had full confidence in the Party leadership and that he did not object to the reformulation of the Party's theoretical line.

We shall perhaps never know what exactly Mao felt about the omission of Mao Zedong Thought in the 1956 constitution and it will probably be a long time before we may determine, with any precision, where various leaders stood on the different issues under discussion. But one thing does seem certain. Whatever cleavages did exist did not reflect the different sides taken by various leaders in what the Cultural Revolution of 1966 was to refer to as 'the struggle between two lines'. At that time, Liu Shaoqi, Deng Xiaoping, Peng Dehuai and Peng Zhen were considered to be 'revisionist'. Lin Biao and Kang Sheng, on the other hand, were considered to be adherents to Mao's 'correct line'. At the Eighth Congress, Deng Xiaoping and Lin Biao were promoted whilst Peng Dehuai, Peng Zhen and Kang Sheng were demoted.[42] This evidence, MacFarquhar suggests, shows that whatever policy differences there might have been had not crystallised into 'two lines' in September 1956.

The Eighth Party Congress noted that Party membership had risen to some 10.7 million.[43] Growth, since 1949, had been somewhat erratic. Though the worker component in the Party rose in the years 1950 – 3, the overall increase in membership was only from five million to 6.5 million. Following the Gao Gang affair, Party membership jumped 1.5 million in one year (1954) and again soared during the radical period after mid-1955 as attempts were made to establish a Party branch in each *xiang*. As a result of the expansion of rural membership, 7.4 million out of the 10.7 million membership at the time of the congress were classified as peasants (of whom 5.4 million were poor peasants and two million middle peasants). With the new policy towards intellectuals, the intellectual component was also expanded. By the autumn of 1956, there were 1.3 million people classified as intellectuals within the Party (and this was to expand to 1.9 million the following year). Though a Party of 10.7 million was very large in absolute terms, it only represented some 1.7 per cent of the total population and clearly there was room for far greater expansion.[44]

Few changes were made in the structure of the Party in 1956. The congress remained as the source of authority which determined the Party's general line and elected a Central Committee which was required to meet periodically in plenary session. These plenary sessions rarely initiated policy but, in the 1950s, were extremely important in making authoritative decisions.[45] Policy tended to be initiated either by the Politburo or sometimes, when the Mass Line was working effectively, at meetings of provincial Party secretaries. The two most important of these in the recent past had been held in July 1955 when Mao explored the ground for speeding up collectivisation and in April 1956 when Mao delivered his speech 'On the Ten Major Relationships'.

The Politburo, along with the chairman (Mao Zedong), vice-chairmen and general secretary, were elected by the Central Committee. In 1956, a new body was created, the Politburo Standing Committee, to manage the day-to-day business of this extremely important decision-making body. Around the time of the congress (though some sources refer to an earlier date), Mao divided this Standing Committee into two 'fronts'.[46] The chairman proposed gradually to remove himself from the day-to-day management of current affairs by the creation of a 'second front' to which he would eventually retire. When he finally took that step, operational decision-making would rest with the 'first front' consisting of Liu Shaoqi, Zhou Enlai, Zhu De, Chen Yun, Deng Xiaoping (and later Lin Biao).[47] Mao was obviously concerned about the issue of succession to the post of Party chairman. He noted that, in the Soviet Union, Malenkov had been unprepared to assume the supreme leadership and, to prevent a similar situation occurring in China, had created the institutional framework whereby others could assume greater responsibility.[48] In anticipation of Mao's retirement, the post of 'honorary chairman' was created but for the time being left vacant.[49]

A number of other bodies existed at the central level of which perhaps the most important was the Party Secretariat under Deng Xiaoping. This body, which handled the routine business of the Central Committee, served probably as an important link between the Politburo and local Party organisations. In the post-Twentieth Soviet Congress atmosphere of 1956, the fact was not lost on the Party leadership that it was from his position in the Secretariat that Stalin had risen to the supreme leadership in the Soviet Union and, although this body was strengthened by the Eighth Party Congress, there may be some truth in the suggestion that the Politburo Standing Committee was set up precisely to act as a curb on the Secretariat.[50] Another body was the Military Commission which was linked to a newly created General Political Department (*Zongzhengzhibu*) of the People's Liberation Army, the immediate task of which seemed to be to ensure that all PLA companies had established Party branches. Other committees existed to deal with propaganda and various branches of the economy, the latter running parallel to the state structure. There was also a Party Control Commission, headed by Dong Biwu which stood at the apex of the Party control hierarchy set up in the aftermath of the Gao Gang affair.

The local organisation of the Party[51] paralleled the state structure. With the abolition of the large administrative regions in 1954, the six associated central bureaux of the Party were also dissolved. There had existed, however, prior to 1954, a number of central branch bureaux in areas where there were particular problems (Inner Mongolia, Shandong, South China and Xinjiang). In 1954, the Shandong and South China branch bureaux were abolished and a new branch bureau created in Shanghai where the bulk of 'national capitalists' lived and where problems of socialisation were most acute.[52] After the formation of the Xinjiang Uighur Autonomous Region and the Inner Mongolian Autonomous Region, the only Party organisation between centre and provinces left, by the time of the congress, was in Shanghai and this remained in existence until 1958.

The organisation of the Party at provincial level was the same as at the centre. Provincial Party congresses elected committees, headed by a first secretary who was usually a member of the Central Committee. They set up a number of specialist committees to supervise various aspects of political and economic work and to supervise the 'Party fractions' (*Dangzu*) at various levels of administrative organisation. In view of the continuity of leadership in the provinces, it is highly likely that close links were maintained with the local military. At *xian* and city level, efforts were directed to recreating much the same kind of structure by abolishing many of the *ad hoc* committees which previously had been directly responsible to the Central Committee.

Basic-level Party organisations were formed according to both geographical and functional principles with particular emphasis on establishing Party committees in each *xiang*. By 1956, there were 538,000 of these basic-level organisations each headed by a secretary. The Party organisation at *xiang*, factory, school, military company, street, state organ and maybe collective was referred to as 'basic', in that it was the lowest level at which the principle of committee organisation applied. Though basic organisations could be set up where there were as few as three Party members, some of them were quite large and were subdivided into cells.

The only other local-level Party organisations which need concern us here were local control organs (which functioned in much the same way as the central control commission in checking up on the operation of lower levels) and the Party fractions which existed at most levels of administration.[53] Ideally, these fractions were the link whereby administrative organs were articulated to local Party committees according to the principle of dual rule. They had no decision-making function but could take the lead in any horizontal mobilisation campaign. According to the prescriptions of 1956, they were responsible only for Party members within any organisation and not for the general work of the organisation, though little guidance was given on how one made the distinction. Very soon it was to be quite clear that one could not.

We have seen that the attempts to specify Party structure in 1956 occurred in a tense political climate. The contradiction between the Party as a source of direction and the Party as a structured institution was still a very real one. One could straighten out Party organisation as much as one liked, but it would mean little if the Party were guilty of bureaucratism. The halt to radicalisation had left much work to be done and many errors to be combated. Mao Zedong, Liu Shaoqi and Deng Xiaoping all probably saw the need for rectification (though not much headway had been made in this regard since the early preparation for rectification in June). We cannot be sure, however, as to whether they all agreed on the methods to be used. In MacFarquhar's view, Liu attributed the major cause of error to 'subjectivism' which implied a stress on increased training in Marxist-Leninist theory and rectification from above.[54] Deng, on the other hand (and presumably Mao), attributed the major cause to 'bureaucratism' which reinforced Mao's call for the supervision of the Party from outside. To back up this point, Deng was most insistent on the need to reinvigorate the Mass Line in contrast to Liu's more élitist approach. Enough has already been said, however, to indicate that this was not the only possible reading of the evidence. Suffice it to say here that, whatever confidence Mao might have had in the new Party leadership and however content he might have felt about the new Party organisation, he did, in fact, delay his departure to the 'second front'.

## The Formal End of One-person Management and the Effective End of External Economic Control

Though the deradicalisation of 1956 halted some of the reforms set in motion in mid-1955, there were certain processes which could not be halted. Though rural collectivisation may have been slowed down, it still continued throughout the year. One-person management was by now a dead issue which probably could not have been revived even if anyone had wanted to. It was formally laid to rest at the Eighth Congress, though the manner of its passing was quite remarkable. In calling for its abolition, the head of the Party's Industry and Communications Department, Li Xuefeng, in effect, congratulated those cadres who had maintained the Yan'an tradition in resisting it.[55] A senior member of the Party was congratulating Party cadres for disobeying Party policy; the implications were profound.

The new policy in industry was the 'responsibility of the factory general manager under the unified leadership of the enterprise Party committee'.[56] In control work also, Party leadership over the external economic control structure was prescribed; this, in effect, meant internal political control according to the dual rule principle. The only exception here was Shanghai where the restoration of order, in what was the main centre of the former private sector, necessitated the continuance of external control.[57]

Major administrative simplification was to await a new radical upsurge in 1957. Although 'left' pressure had contributed to the decline of the cumbersome control bureaucracy, there is good reason to suppose that those of a less radical bent were also happy about its demise. It is not unreasonable to imagine that after Khrushchev's revelations, some people were worried about the growth of separate bureaucracies with powers of inspection. Stalin had depended on such a bureaucracy (The *Rabkin* or Commissariat of Workers and Peasants Inspection) and Stalin was currently the focus of Soviet criticism. Most Party leaders were concerned also that 'deviant tendencies' had developed in that other control organ, the public security network, which were noted by the Minister of Public Security Luo Ruiqing at the congress.[58] Few people wished to tolerate independent bureaucracies. Those who sought radical reforms did not like bureaucracies; those who were more cautious did not like independent ones.

### From Bandung to Hungary

Through much of the period covered in this chapter, China continued the foreign policy initiated after the Korean War and which was symbolised in the 'Bandung spirit'. At the Bandung conference of April 1955, China emerged as a major actor in the Third World and considerable cordiality was expressed by Zhou Enlai towards India's Nehru and Egypt's Nasser as representatives of more or less non-aligned countries. For many years, the Bandung spirit was to be the symbol of the growing unity of ex-colonial countries. Nevertheless, however successful Bandung might have been, it left no lasting organisation to promote that unity. In this respect, a more important conference, which took place just prior to Bandung, was the Asian Countries Conference in New Delhi. This meeting created a liaison group which, in January 1957, was to persuade Nasser to extend its scope to include Africa. Such was the genesis of the Afro-Asian Peoples' Solidarity Organisation based on Cairo in which China was to play a major role.

In the whole enterprise, the position of Nasser was crucial. In the face of growing Anglo-French hostility and the intransigence of Israel, Nasser, in 1955, began to purchase arms from Czechoslovakia and to establish trade relations with the socialist camp. In January 1956, Sino-Egyptian relations had improved to the point that a permanent trade office could be established in Cairo, thus signifying the first Chinese presence in the Arab or African world. By May, diplomatic relations between the two countries were announced with Chen Jiakang, a high-ranking cadre in the Foreign Ministry, as ambassador.[59] This was an important step, since Cairo was to become the major communications centre between three continents, the headquarters of the Afro-Asian Peoples' Solidarity Organisation, the political centre of the Arab world and the point at which African liberation movements made contact. Chen was to remain in this vital post until 1965.

The Chinese support for Third World unity was in many ways similar to current Soviet foreign policy. In his secret speech, Khrushchev had argued that 'a vast zone of peace' existed in which the socialist camp was linked to the emerging non-aligned countries. Where China and the Soviet Union disagreed, however, was on the tactics to be used by the socialist camp to counter imperialism. In the Soviet view, the world balance was shifting in the direction of the socialist camp and, provided nuclear war could be avoided, the socialist system would spread all over the world by peaceful means. The current tactic, therefore, should be to extend the hand of friendship to non-aligned countries and engage in 'peaceful coexistence' and 'peaceful competition' with the imperialist nations. In the meantime, Communist parties everywhere should endeavour to come to power by 'parliamentary' means to prevent the advent of world war.[60]

To those Chinese leaders who were wrestling with the problems of contradictions at home, the Khrushchev formula was unsatisfactory. Though their criticisms at this time were muted, they began to feel that one could not arbitrarily decide that all the contradictions in the world were 'non-antagonistic'. Any non-antagonistic contradiction might quite easily become antagonistic.[61] In Mao's view, the primary factor in change occurred because of contradictions inherent in a thing. External factors were only effective inasmuch as they acted on internal contradictions.[62] One could not, therefore, decide arbitrarily that the structure of class forces and antagonisms in the world had now become different just because there was a danger of nuclear war. As for the 'parliamentary road to socialism', devotees of the Yan'an experiences were all too aware that a Communist Party which wishes to effect changes from within can itself all too easily lose its independence once it plays by the rules of the host institution. The Chinese leaders were later to denounce the Soviet foreign policy stance of 1956 as 'revisionist' and this term was well chosen. As Marxists, the Chinese Party were all too aware of the 'revisionism' of the Second International where social democratic parties came to see themselves as *inheritors* waiting for the future that would inevitably be theirs. For the time being, however, the issue of 'parliamentary roads to socialism' was sidestepped in official Chinese pronouncements. The much clearer Bandung call for anti-colonial struggle was the watchword. According to the Bandung formula, 'peaceful coexistence' was accepted only as a relationship between socialist and Third World countries and not in the Khrushchevian sense of a relationship between socialist and *imperialist* countries.

By mid-1956, the eyes of the whole world were on Egypt. One week after the Chinese ambassador took up his post, the Egyptian government nationalised the Suez Canal. With the Anglo-French-Israeli invasion, China's response was reminiscent of the Korean War. A special committee was set up to mobilise support and, in November, China began enlisting volunteers to fight in Egypt though they were never called for. China immediately granted a loan of 20 million Swiss francs to Egypt[63] and it seemed quite clear that it envisaged a protracted struggle of the Korean type. By Christmas, however, Egypt had scored a major diplomatic victory and the dissension in the ranks of the 'imperialist powers' took everyone by surprise. Mao had always felt that imperialism was a 'paper tiger' but surely the paper could not be that flimsy! A reassessment of the world balance was to be made.

However critical the Suez crisis looked from the Chinese point of view, the simultaneous events in Hungary were of more immediate importance. Having begun the task of dismantling the Soviet model, most people in the Chinese leadership were probably quite happy to see devolution of power within the socialist camp, provided the camp itself remained intact. Accordingly, when the Soviet leaders contemplated using force to overthrow the increasingly independent Gomulka régime in Poland in October 1956, it was said that the Chinese restrained them.[64] Later in the year, the Chinese leadership also attempted to mediate between the Soviet Union and Yugoslavia.[65] Hungary, however, was a different matter. As the Chinese saw it, the Hungarian leadership had, in the past, committed much the same kind of error as the leadership in Poland or the Soviet Union. Agriculture had been neglected, there had been no Hungarian equivalent of the Mass Line and a policy of greater national independence was to be welcomed. But what could not be tolerated was the reaction of a government against Stalinist bureaucratism which looked like taking Hungary out of the socialist camp and playing into the hands of external 'imperialist powers'. It was in the interests of the unity of the socialist camp that China had made no official criticism of the new Soviet foreign policy line. Once that unity was seriously threatened, the Chinese leadership decided that it had no course but to urge Soviet invasion.[66]

## Conclusion

The period of consolidation in 1956 was relatively short and, unlike the previous one (1952–4), was somewhat unstable. On the one hand, it was to see the continued abandonment of many features of the Soviet model of administration. On the other hand, it was to result in the adoption of a static model of socialism which was a direct copy of Stalin's 1936 position. That model was eventually to be rejected by Mao but there is not much evidence that Mao was too unhappy with it at the time of the

Eighth Party Congress. Throughout 1956, leaders were to disagree on a host of policies. Mao's speech 'On the Ten Major Relationships' was not received warmly by people like Li Fuchun. Deng Zihui and leaders concerned with agriculture were, it seems, quite hostile to the continuance of the 'leap forward' in agriculture. Mao, moreover, was displeased with Peng Zhen's precipitate socialisation of Beijing's industry and commerce. But what was important about these disagreements was that they did not bring about any decisive antagonism amongst the leadership.

Mao, of course, had yet to work out a theory of antagonism and had yet to become identified with a distinct set of economic policies. There was no doubt that the rapid co-operativisation and the 'leap forward' of early 1956 had been carried out under his direct inspiration. We are not sure, however, just what part the chairman played in the deradicalisation decisions of April. Different opinions amongst Western scholars on this issue have led to conflicting interpretations of the purpose of both the 'hundred flowers' policy and Mao's speech 'On the Ten Major Relationships'. Yet one thing is certain: policy in 1956 was remarkably moderate.

A major factor in bringing about the deradicalisation decisions and the new period of moderate policies was China's response to events in the International Communist Movement. That response led not only to moderate policies but also to Mao's beginning to think about the structural generation of antagonism in socialist society. The first step in this process had been Khrushchev's secret speech. The second step was to be the Hungarian rising of late 1956. How had it been possible, Mao asked, for such a bitter reaction to occur against a socialist régime and what could be done to prevent a similar situation occurring in China? Mao's answers to that question were to lead to a renewed and much more vigorous programme of radicalisation which made the 'leap forward' of early 1956 seem insignificant by comparison.

## NOTES

1. Mao Zedong, April 1956, *JPRS*, 1974, pp. 30 – 5. On Gao Gang and Stalin, see Mao Zedong, 10 March 1978, Schram, 1974, p. 100.

2. Mao Zedong, January 1957, *JPRS*, 1974, pp. 49 – 50.

3. Mao Zedong, 8 December 1956, ibid., p. 40.

4. Mao Zedong, April 1956, ibid., p. 34.

5. Ibid., p. 35. For further views on Stalin, see Mao Zedong, 10 March 1958, Schram, 1974, pp. 96 – 103.

6. Text in Bowie and Fairbank, 1965, pp. 144 – 51.

7. Mao Zedong, April 1956, *JPRS*, 1974, p. 33.

8. Mao Zedong, 25 April 1956, *CB* 892, 21 October 1969, pp. 21 – 34. Reprinted in *SW* V, pp. 284 – 307.

9. MacFarquhar, 1974, pp. 61 – 74.

10. Mao Zedong, 6 December 1955, *JPRS*, 1974, p. 28.

11. *CB* 411, 27 September 1956, p. 3.

12. Zhou Enlai, 14 January 1956, Bowie and Fairbank, 1965, pp. 128–44.

13. MacFarquhar, 1974, pp. 75–85.

14. Mao Zedong, 27 February 1957, *SW* V, p. 414.

15. Mao Zedong, 8 December 1956, *JPRS*, 1974, p. 40; Mao Zedong, January 1957, ibid., p. 48.

16. Lu Dingyi, 26 May 1956, *CB* 406, 15 August 1956, pp. 3–18, and Bowie and Fairbank, 1965, pp. 151–62.

17. The following account is from Howe, 1973 (a), pp. 89–95. See also Selden, 1979, pp. 309–14.

18. On the role of the accountant, see Schurmann, 1966, pp. 248, 250 and 328.

19. Vogel, 1967, p. 51.

20. Schurmann, 1966, pp. 452–3.

21. Ibid., pp. 455–6; CCPCC, 12 September 1956, URI, 1971, pp. 407–30.

22. The following is taken from Schurmann, 1966, pp. 457–64.

23. Vogel, 1971, p. 185; Walker, 1965, p. 67.

24. Zhang Zhiyi's work has been translated in Moseley, 1966.

25. Ibid., pp. 113–14.

26. Ibid., p. 41.

27. For a fascinating account of the Yi slave system, see Winnington, 1959, Part I.

28. Ibid., Part II (Wa) and Part III (Jingpo).

29. Moseley, 1966, pp. 104–5.

30. Strong, 1965, p. 51.

31. Winnington, 1959, Part I.

32. The most succinct statement of this may be found in Moseley, 1966, p. 132.

33. Ibid., pp. 144–5.

34. CCP, 27 September 1956, PFLP, 1956, Vol. I, p. 116.

35. See MacFarquhar, 1974, pp. 160–4.

36. For a side-by-side comparison of these two constitutions, see *CB* 417, 10 October 1956, pp. 32–76.

37. See MacFarquhar, 1973 for specific textual analysis.

38. URI, 1968 (a), pp. 119–20; MacFarquhar, 1973, pp. 619–24.

39. Deng Xiaoping, 16 December 1956, PFLP, 1956, Vol. I, pp. 199–200.

40. MacFarquhar, 1974, p. 149.

41. Teiwes, 1979, pp. 227–9.

42. MacFarquhar, 1974, pp. 140–8.

43. Schurmann, 1966, p. 129.

44. Ibid., pp. 129–36.

45. On the loci of top-level decision-making, see Chang, 1970.

46. Mao Zedong, 25 October 1966, *CB* 891, 8 October 1969, p. 75. See also the discussion in MacFarquhar, 1973, pp. 629–34.

47. Lin Biao was appointed to the Politburo Standing Committee after the second session of the Eighth Party Congress in May 1958.

48. Mao Zedong, 24 October 1966, *CB* 891, 8 October 1969, p. 71.

49. See MacFarquhar, 1973, p. 631.

50. Schurmann, 1966, p. 146.

51. The following is taken from ibid., pp. 147–56.

52. The functions of central branch bureaux were somewhat vague. They seem, however, to have been specifically designed to deal with areas in which particular problems existed and where it might be necessary to adopt an approach to social transformation different from other parts of the country.

53. Schurmann, 1966, pp. 156–62.

54. MacFarquhar, 1973, p. 635.

55. Li Xuefeng, PFLP, 1956, Vol. II, p. 306.

56. See Schurmann, 1966, pp. 284–93.

57. Ibid., pp. 352–3.

58. Luo Ruiqing, PFLP, 1956, Vol. II, pp. 98–124.

59. Larkin, 1971, pp. 20–1.

60. Discussed in ibid., pp. 21–4.

61. Mao Zedong, 27 February 1957, in *SW* V, pp. 384–421.

62. Mao Zedong, August 1937, *SW* I, pp. 312–13.

63. *SCMP* 1411, 15 November 1956, pp. 42–4.

64. Zagoria, 1966, p. 56.

65. Ibid., pp. 58–65.

66. On Chinese reaction to events in Hungary, see Solomon, 1971, pp. 285–8; MacFarquhar, 1974, pp. 169–76.

# VII
# FROM 'BLOOMING AND CONTENDING' TO 'UNINTERRUPTED REVOLUTION'
## (1957)

This chapter will examine the origins of China's most radical experiment to restructure the Chinese economy and society—the Great Leap Forward. In the early part of 1957, the movement to 'let a hundred flowers bloom and a hundred schools of thought contend' finally got off the ground, whilst, in the second half of the year, that movement was brought to a sudden end and policies of mass mobilisation were initiated. The reversal of policy in mid-year has given rise to much controversy both in China and among Western scholars. The dominant view of the current (1979) Chinese leadership, which has attempted to restore many of the policies and institutions of early 1957, is that mid-1957 marked the point where the Chinese revolution went off the rails. There was, therefore, a fundamental disjunction between the policies of the early part of the year and those of the later part. This view is shared by many Western commentators, who regard the former policies as more 'liberal' and the latter policies as more 'radical'. Others, however, argue that one can see a continuity between the earlier policies and those which led to the Great Leap Forward. One cannot deny that an important watershed occurred in mid-year when criticism by intellectuals was brought to an end. It is argued, however, that the purpose of 'blooming and contending' had, all along, been to bring about a radical restructuring of society and, when blooming and contending did not work, other means were used with much more effect. At the root of the controversy, therefore, is an assessment of the purpose of the 'hundred flowers' and, as the last chapter showed, this is not altogether clear.

A second source of controversy amongst Western commentators concerns the alignment of various leaders on the question of 'blooming and contending'. In the first volume of his study of the origins of the Cultural Revolution, MacFarquhar has assembled much evidence to show that, with the exception of Deng Xiaoping and Zhou Yang who remained attuned to Mao's ideas, the leadership divided on the issue in a way which prefigured the subsequent divisions in the Cultural Revolution. Thus, Chen Boda and Kang Sheng supported Mao's call for 'blooming and contending' plus rectification, whilst Liu Shaoqi, Peng Zhen, Peng Dehuai and Lu Dingyi opposed it.[1] The question arises, however, as to which interpretation of the movement the various supporters adhered to. It is reasonable to suppose that Zhou Enlai and Chen Yun might have supported the liberal version but not necessarily the radical version. They might have accepted the mild policy known as 'gentle breeze and mild rain' (*hefeng xiyu*) but not necessarily the 'big blooming and contending' which subsequently developed. Unfortunately, we cannot determine the orientation of various leaders with any certainty and one scholar has gone so far as to deny that MacFarquhar's categorisation has sufficient documentatory verification. There is not enough evidence, Teiwes maintains, even to determine whether Mao and Peng Zhen disagreed on policy.[2] In assessing the movements of 1957, therefore, one must tread more warily than I did in the first edition of this book.

## The Correct Handling of Contradictions Among the People

The Hungarian uprising began on 23 October 1956, two days after the installation of the Gomulka régime in Poland. As the preceding chapter noted, the official Chinese position was to support the Polish demands for independence but to condemn the Hungarian intention to withdraw from the Warsaw Pact. But what was at stake was more than a question of foreign policy. On 11 November, Yugoslavia's Tito, whilst endorsing the Soviet intervention for the sake of preserving socialism, regretted most strongly that such action had become necessary. The situation which demanded intervention, Tito maintained, had been brought about by a combination of bureaucratic rule and the Stalinist 'cult of personality'. Tito's speech was made whilst the Second Plenum of the Eighth Central Committee of the Chinese Communist Party (10–15 November 1956) was busily discussing the East European crisis and the Chinese position, which was to emerge from that plenum, was to constitute a partial refutation of Tito's comments.[3]

The official Chinese assessment entitled 'More on the Historical Experiences of the Dictatorship of the Proletariat' was published on 29 December.[4] Echoing the earlier document, 'On the Historical Experiences of the Dictatorship of the Proletariat' issued nine months previously, the Chinese argued that all the evils which had occurred in the Soviet Union and Eastern Europe should not be blamed on Stalin. None the less, there were problems of bureaucratism in socialist societies and their structure should be reassessed. Though such socialist systems were basically sound, the contradictions which existed in certain links in these systems, could result in antagonism if leadership were incorrect. To prevent defects in leadership and Stalinist-type 'dogmatism', one should not engage in 'revisionist' capitulation to capitalism but should revitalise the Mass Line. In Hungary, the Petöfi Club, a clandestine group of dissident intellectuals which had been denied an opportunity to voice complaints, had played an important part in the rising. To prevent the formation of similar groups in China, the answer was not more repression but open criticism.[5]

Since the slogan 'let a hundred flowers bloom and a hundred schools of thought contend' was first put forward in April 1956, it had been associated in some leaders' minds with the idea of Party rectification and documents to assist such rectification had been issued in June 1956.[6] But the conservative climate of late 1956 had not been conducive to rectification and the stress, in Party work, was on regularising the Party structure. After Hungary, Mao felt himself in a position to press once again for 'blooming and contending'. As he saw it, the Party had nothing to fear from criticism:

It is correct to let a hundred flowers bloom and a hundred schools of thought contend. Truth develops in the struggle with falsehood. Beauty develops in comparison with and in struggle against ugliness. Good things and good men develop in comparison with and in struggle against bad men. Fragrant flowers develop in comparison with and in struggle against poisonous weeds. Materialism develops in comparison with and in struggle against idealism. Many people hate Jiang Jieshi but everyone is ignorant as to what kind of bad man he is. We must publish, therefore, *The Collected Works of Jiang Jieshi*, also *The Collected Works of Sun Zhongshan* (Sun Yat-sen) and *The Collected Works of Kang Youwei*[7] . . . We people in the Communist Party know too little of our opponents. We are somewhat simplistic and consequently cannot speak persuasively.[8]

Mao's attempt to get the hundred flowers movement off the ground in January 1957 was supported by some kind of agreement of rectification. But in the view of one scholar, this was to be an *internal* process of rectification[9] and not the open Party rectification which the radical interpretation of the hundred flowers movement would demand. In any case, the launching of that rectification movement was scheduled for 1958.[10] Considering the urgency with which Mao had insisted on the need for the 'hundred flowers' to 'bloom', it would appear that Mao's initiatives were being blocked. But who was doing the blocking?

One obvious source of opposition to Mao's policy was a certain high-ranking political commissar in the PLA by the name of Chen Qitong. In an article in *Renmin Ribao* on 7 January, Chen expressed considerable reserve towards the movement, implying that it was intellectuals who should be rectified rather than employed to rectify the Party.[11] The fact that the Central Committee newspaper was prepared to publish Chen's views suggests that Chen must have been backed by some quite powerful people. One of these was almost certainly Deng Tuo the editor of *Renmin Ribao* and others might have included Lu Dingyi and Hu Qiaomu who were active in propaganda affairs. But did the opposition to Mao reach any higher? MacFarquhar argues most persuasively that it did and included Peng Zhen and Liu Shaoqi.[12] Teiwes, on the other hand, points out that in the Cultural Revolution, whilst Lu Dingyi and Hu Qiaomu were blamed for obstructing Mao, Liu Shaoqi and Peng Zhen were not. Had Liu and Peng been opposed to Mao, the Cultural Revolution critics would not have lost the opportunity to denounce them.[13]

It is difficult, therefore, to ascertain the position of Liu and Peng in January 1957. It seems clear, however, that Mao's initiatives were viewed unfavourably by senior people in the propaganda network (who interestingly did not include that major target of the Cultural Revolution—Zhou Yang). It is equally clear that Mao was very concerned about the opposition in the Party as a whole. In fact, Mao was to remark that Chen Qitong represented 90 per cent of the comrades in the Party and that he (Mao) did not have any mass base.[14] It was to be some time, however, before Mao put forward the slogan that 'going against the tide' was a Marxist-Leninist principle.[15]

Although the opposition to Mao's initiatives appeared to be great, he was able, in February, to prevail upon the Party leadership to advance the date for commencing the rectification movement by one year. How was this possible? According to MacFarquhar, Mao achieved this through the efforts of Zhou Enlai who had returned from Eastern Europe with the message that 'blooming and contending' plus rectification would not weaken the Party. Peng Zhen, however, had returned from Eastern Europe with the opposite message, but was not so effective.[16] Having apparently prevailed on this important point, Mao was able to deliver his famous speech 'On the Correct Handling of Contradictions Among the People' which was the strongest call yet for 'blooming and contending'.

Mao's speech was presented to a Supreme State Conference on 27 February 1957. Though I have met people who heard the full text of the speech, no copy of it is available to the Western scholar. All we have is an abridged version which was published after the policy reversals of mid-year.[17] Dilution notwithstanding, the available version is still a very significant document. In 'On the Correct Handling. . .', Mao synthesised the themes elaborated in the various articles commenting on events in the Soviet Union and Eastern Europe, in his speech 'On the Ten Major

Relationships' and in his various calls for 'blooming and contending'. In short, Mao elaborated on the occurrence of contradictions in socialist society. These contradictions, Mao maintained, might under certain circumstances become 'antagonistic' and require a process of struggle before they could be resolved. To treat all contradictions as 'non-antagonistic' and amenable to resolution through debate was to court trouble. On the other hand, to treat all contradictions as 'antagonistic' (between the 'enemy' and oneself) was the surest way to tyranny and a violation of the Mass Line. The 'blooming of the hundred flowers' was necessary, therefore, to prevent 'non-antagonistic' contradictions becoming 'antagonistic' and endangering the revolution. Unity did not imply absence of conflict. Conflict was a force for progress but it had to be kept within bounds. If suppressed, tension would build up and the eventual explosion would be beyond control.

Though Mao might not have said so in his speech, there was a great similarity between the actions of those cadres who were everywhere rooting out 'counter-revolutionaries' and those of Stalin. Such actions, Mao felt, endangered the very life of the Party and perhaps obscured the real counter-revolutionaries. The Party, therefore, was oscillating between 'left' dogmatism of a Stalinist variety and 'right' revisionism where all group struggle and all class struggle was discouraged. In a vein reminiscent of 1942–3, Mao expressed his confidence:

> Marxism is scientific truth and fears no criticism . . . If it did, and if it could be overthrown by criticism, it would be worthless . . . Marxists should not be afraid of criticism from any quarter. Quite the contrary, they need to temper and develop themselves and win new positions in the teeth of criticism and in the storm and stress of struggle. Fighting against wrong ideas is like being vaccinated—a man develops greater immunity from disease as a result of vaccination. Plants raised in hot houses are unlikely to be hardy. Carrying out the policy of letting a hundred flowers bloom and a hundred schools of thought contend will not weaken, but strengthen the leading position of Marxism in the ideological field.[18]

## The Hundred Flowers

With his speech 'On the Correct Handling . . .', Mao issued a challenge to all those Party members of a 'left' dogmatist or 'right' revisionist variety. In the next two months, he busied himself seeing that organisational means existed for making his policy of 'blooming and contending' a reality. In early March, the Chinese People's Political Consultative Conference, which had been eclipsed by the National People's Congress on the formulation of that body in 1954, was revived as the most appropriate United Front organisation to initiate discussion. Before long, the various 'democratic parties and groups' also began discussing the policy of 'long-term co-existence and mutual supervision'[19] and in March, at a National Party Conference on Propaganda Work, Mao sought active support from rank-and-file Party cadres for the policy of 'blooming and contending'.[20]

The response of Party cadres was mixed. Zhang Zhiyi, who as we have seen took a very cautious line on work among national minorities, expressed fears that Mao's policy would endanger the United Front.[21] The propaganda apparatus, moreover, seemed reluctant to give publicity to the proceedings of the Supreme State Conference in late February and it was not until April that it published a self-criticism for its tardiness in criticising people like Chen Qitong.[22] We cannot be sure, however, whether the press was being used by senior opponents of the movement or was merely showing caution in the face of mixed feelings amongst the central leadership.[23] In MacFarquhar's view, Liu Shaoqi had distanced himself from Mao's call either by not attending the Supreme State Conference or, if he had attended, by refusing to allow his attendance to be publicised.[24] In a provincial tour in March and April, Liu gave the impression that social problems might be solved by economic means rather than by rectification.[25] Peng Zhen also showed a similar distance, by not addressing his own (Beijing) municipal Party conference after Mao had insisted that all first secretaries of the Party should personally take charge of ideological matters.[26] Progress at lower levels of the Party was likewise rather slow, perhaps because Party secretaries felt that there were senior leaders who did not support the movement. In the words of Qian Weichang, a member of the Central Committee of the China Democratic League (one of the 'democratic parties'), 'blooming and contending [would] not work because it [was] not supported by the line of Liu Shaoqi through Peng Zhen'.[27] At one time, Mao was said to have been so angered by Party resistance that he declared that he would rather not be chairman so that he himself could participate more actively in the movement.[28]

Though MacFarquhar's characterisation of the position of Liu Shaoqi and Peng Zhen is open to challenge, it cannot be denied that considerable opposition to the movement was expressed in many quarters after Mao's speech 'On the Correct Handling . . .'. By late April, however, due partly to the efforts of Zhou Yang,[29] the Party press had fallen into line behind Mao and soon both Liu Shaoqi and Peng Zhen were calling for 'blooming and contending'. Local Party cadres were urged not to bury their heads in routine tasks and were not to fear a loss of prestige.[30] Finally, at the end of the month, a formal directive was issued on the immediate launching of the rectification movement, which called upon first secretaries of Party organisations at *xian* level and above to assume personal leadership.[31]

Circumstantial evidence would suggest that the rectification decision of late April was arrived at in some haste.[32] Because all senior leaders did not have a chance to think through its implications, there was a difference of opinion as to the extent to which an open-rectification movement was called for. Such haste might have been due to Mao's exasperation with the press as was shown by his suggestion that each province should encourage the publication of a non-Party newspaper in competition with the official press.[33]

Once the rectification decision had been taken, however, the slow trickle of criticism changed into a steady flow and the 'blooming and contending' began to take the form of a mass movement. Forums of an increasing animation were convened and large character posters (*dazibao*) began to appear, specifying Party and government malpractice. Perhaps the most sensational of these were to appear on a newly designated 'Democracy Wall' at Beijing University. It was claimed that *sufan* had been too harsh and the distinguished non-Party minister Luo Longji proposed that a special committee be set up to examine excesses in the suppression of counter-revolutionaries. Such a demand was tantamount to the call for an examination not only of *sufan* but also the various movements of the early 1950s. Indeed, some people went so far as to demand that the Hu Feng case be reopened. Another prominent 'democratic personage' Zhang Bojun demanded the establishment of a 'political design institute' which would give substantive power to the Chinese People's Political Consultative Conference and so strengthen the United Front. Apparently, many critics felt that the United Front (the 'four-class bloc') had been ineffective and the Party had paid insufficient attention to the needs and desires of national capitalists. They were dissatisfied at the way the socialist transformation of industry and commerce had been carried out, since the process had often resulted in the victimisation of former owners of small businesses. At the root of this and many other problems was the exclusivity of the Party and numerous cases were cited of dogmatism, bureaucratism, corruption and favouritism. Particularly reprehensible, it was felt, was the blind copying of Soviet practices and numerous cadres were encouraged to engage in 'self-examination' (*jiantao*). The Party was, however, not only criticised on behavioural grounds. Many intellectuals felt that the Party's ideological control had been too tight. University academics demanded the abolition of Party fractions in universities, and the restoration of the critical functions of such disciplines as sociology and political science. They demanded also the completion of the work of legal reform which had been given much attention in late 1956.[34]

The criticisms voiced in May 1957 were not just confined to intellectuals. Even the PLA, which was undergoing a reassessment of the hastily imposed Soviet model, was affected. In the period 1955−6, attempts had been made to strengthen the Party system within the army and to impose limits on the professionalisation of what was rapidly becoming an officer corps. With the hundred flowers movement, further criticism of these developments was put forward though, this time, such criticisms were mixed with complaints that too much time had been spent on political study.[35] It might be argued, therefore, that some people in the army were using the hundred flowers movement to reinforce a professional orientation. It will be remembered that it was senior army personnel such as Chen Qitong who were most vocal in their doubts that people outside the Party could assist in its rectification. Perhaps their major target were those who advocated the depoliticisation of the PLA?

The doubts of people like Chen Qitong were also shared by the leaders of the All China Federation of Trade Unions (formerly known in English as the All China Federation of Labour).[36] The major problem in the first labour union crisis of 1951 (discussed on pp. 77−8) had been the fact that 'economist' labour unions would not subordinate themselves to Party leadership, and it was for that reason that Li Lisan had been replaced as effective head of the ACFL by Lai Ruoyu. Instead of implementing dual rule, however, Lai had built up an ACFTU hierarchy characterised by vertical rule. At the top of that hierarchy, Party control was quite strong but, at the bottom, union branches were often impervious to local Party influence. The old local craft unions were replaced by large industrial unions with a functional division of labour. Within the industrial network, specialist staff functions were paralleled by specialist union bodies, increasingly committed to technical expertise. Within enterprises, managerial wages and welfare sections were often joined by similar union bodies charged with the same functions and articulated to a parallel staff-line system.[37] In such a system, union activism was played down, except perhaps in the former private sector where unions assisted in the process of socialist transformation.

In early 1957, Lai Ruoyu complained that, during the First Five Year Plan, unions had become once again 'tails of management'.[38] This view was probably quite accurate but what Lai could not see was that the problem may have stemmed from the structure which he had been instrumental in creating. Lai's solution, therefore, was that the ACFTU hierarchy should be strengthened and made even less susceptible to interference by local Party committees. Greater Party control within the context of vertical rule implied independence of the union structure at lower levels. At a time when official management policy had shifted to the 'responsibility of the factory general manager under the unified leadership of the enterprise Party committee', such a policy could not but lead to tension.

In early 1957, the ACFTU sent out investigation teams to study the relations (contradictions) between Party and unions at local levels. In some cases, Party leadership was found to be too weak and, in others (from an ACFTU perspective), too strong. In Shanghai, for example, the local Party committee under Ke Qingshi insisted most strongly on the principle of dual rule and this led to friction between Shanghai and the ACFTU centre.[39] In other areas, investigation teams discovered a general lack of union influence among the workers. In the words of Li Xiuren, Deputy Director of the ACFTU General Office, who was sent on an inspection tour of the Beijing-Guangzhou railway, unions had everywhere 'been cast aside by the workers'; they were 'workers' control departments' or 'tails of management'; union cadres did not know whether to listen to the directives of the local Party committees or the demands of the masses. Many of them were again complaining that they were 'fourth class'. Party members with union affiliations, moreover, were said to be guilty of the 'three don't comes' (san bulai—they did not come to union meetings, they did not come to make reports and they did not come to pay union dues). It seemed that unions were once again being used as a vehicle for promotion to management or to Party posts and had little life of their own.[40]

Such reports as these were used to support Lai's demands for tighter vertical control. The last thing he seemed to want was the basic-level union structure to be further weakened by 'blooming and contending'. On 9 May, therefore, he declared his opposition to the policy. It was not possible, Lai maintained, to formulate one's own school of thought in labour union work and the views of the masses were not always correct.[41] In its reply to Lai's remarks, Renmin Ribao was most critical of labour union leadership[42] but Lai remained at his post. This might have been either the result of the support of senior Party leaders or that Lai's forthrightness was itself seen as within the spirit of the 'hundred flowers'.

But undoubtedly the most dramatic criticisms came from intellectuals and, by the end of May, some of these complaints grew into a criticism of the socialist system itself. Despite the attention given to them by Western observers such views were probably only a very small part of the movement as a whole.[43] Nevertheless, they did play into the hands of those who wished to bring the whole process of 'blooming and contending' to a close. By late May, the opponents of the hundred flowers policy seemed to be in the ascendant. A session of the National People's Congress, scheduled to meet on 2 June, was postponed, it has been argued, to give Peng Zhen time to prepare the ground for a new policy to be presented at the meeting.[44] Some circumstantial evidence exists that, at a Politburo meeting on 25 May, a decision was taken to reverse policy even though Mao still felt that 'rightism' within the Party was more dangerous than 'rightism' voiced outside it. Two weeks were to elapse, however, before the movement was finally terminated. This may have been because of opposition to the reversal of policy or because the advocates of termination wanted to give the non-Party 'rightists' enough rope to hang themselves. Some commentators have seen the whole hundred flowers movement as a trap to expose opponents of the régime. I have argued above that such a view is quite wrong. It is possible, however, that the trap explanation might have had some validity with regard to the final two weeks of the movement.

On 8 June, the hundred flowers movement turned abruptly into an anti-rightist movement in which the Party turned on its critics. This was to be one of the most important turning-points in the history of the People's Republic and, understandably, many scholars have debated just which leader stood on which side. As has been noted, one school of thought maintains that Liu Shaoqi and Peng Zhen had opposed the 'blooming and contending' all along and, once it got out of hand, were able to defeat Mao's policies. Thus, not long after the delayed session of the National People's Congress met on 26 June, Mao departed for Shanghai in order publicly to disassociate himself from the policies of Liu and Peng who were now directing the struggle against critics of the Party.[45] The Shanghai Party committee, under the leadership of Ke Qingshi, seemed consistent in its support for 'blooming and contending' and, thus, Shanghai was an excellent place to take stock of the situation. According to this view, it was no accident that a photograph appeared in the 11 July edition of *Renmin Ribao* showing Mao engaged in intimate conversation with non-Party Shanghai intellectuals.[46] In the same month, *Renmin Ribao* published criticism of Mao made by rightists.[47] Though these criticisms were subjected to severe attack, their very publication aided Mao's critics. Mao himself was, in fact, being associated with the 'rightists'.

Another school of thought rejects the above explanation, preferring to see the senior leadership responding to the changing situation. Mao had certainly been the prime mover behind the hundred flowers policy but there was insufficient evidence of a split amongst the senior leadership. When the movement got out of hand, Mao, Liu and Peng all agreed that the experiment had failed. The attempt to prevent a Hungarian situation occurring in China had resulted in 'tens of thousands of little Hungaries'.[48] Mao's support for terminating the movement was demonstrated by his allowing the text of 'On the Correct Handling . . .' to be revised with the addition of six criteria for distinguishing 'fragrant flowers' from 'poisonous weeds'. These were that actions had to be beneficial (1) to the unity of the various nationalities in the country, (2) to socialist transformation and socialist construction, (3) to the people's democratic dictatorship, (4) to the consolidation of democratic centralism, (5) to leadership by the Communist Party and (6) to the international unity of socialism and all 'peace-loving' peoples.[49] Mao would surely not have permitted the revision of his speech if he had wanted to distance himself from the decision to terminate the movement. According to this view, Mao's rapid departure for Shanghai might be explained according to the official reason given for his trip. He had gone to investigate the 'rightist' editorial policy of the non-Party newspaper *Wenhuibao*, then under criticism by the soon to be famous Yao Wenyuan.

An accurate explanation of Mao's position probably lies somewhere between the above two views. If the first view were correct, the critics in the Cultural Revolution were remarkably obtuse in not using the events of June 1957 to damn Liu and Peng. The second view, however, presents us with a picture of Mao's political style which is hardly flattering. Several times, it seems, Mao would launch a political movement and then, when it appeared to get out of hand and he was isolated in inner-Party circles, would lose his nerve and call the whole thing off.

If the first of the above views is correct, then it is difficult to see why Mao did not retire immediately to the 'second front' in late 1957. In fact, Mao was able rapidly to regain the initiative in the anti-rightist campaign. Here Solomon's explanation has a ring of plausibility. The hundred flowers movement had been committed to criticising 'rightist' bureaucratism within the Party. After the reversal of policy, although the Party was not going to allow too much criticism from outside, it remained committed to the struggle against 'rightism'. If the 'liberal' interpretation of rectification had really always been subordinate to the 'radical' interpretation, it was now possible for Mao to utilise the anti-rightist movement to oppose 'rightist' economic policy.[50] Non-Party intellectuals had proved themselves to be unreliable. But, from Mao's perspective, the same could be said for Party intellectuals who had promoted the cautious economic policies of late 1956. Thus, the strategy used to dislodge one set of intellectuals, who had been too critical in the hundred flowers movement, could be used to dislodge a different set of intellectuals who had resisted the radical restructuring of the economy.

### The Anti-rightist Movement

It is perhaps ironical that the anti-rightist movement should have been initiated by the publication, on 18 June 1957, by the revised version of Mao's 'On the Correct Handling. . .'. The original version of that speech had, after all, played a major part in the earlier movement of 'blooming and contending'. It was important, however, to give the reversal of policy Mao's imprimatur and to show continuity in policy before the important meeting of the National People's Congress which was to be a forum for attacks on 'rightists'. It was also probably the case that an unofficial copy of the original speech had found its way to Eastern Europe and that could have caused considerable embarrassment in the hands of the Soviet Communist Party.[51] An official version, therefore, had to be published.

The anti-rightist movement was to last well into 1958 but the initial stage, which dealt specifically with 'rightist' critics who had been vocal during the hundred flowers movement, was quite brief. Forums at which certain intellectuals and businessmen had spoken up were hastily reconvened and fresh judgements were made of the 'correctness' of the earlier criticisms. Newspapers published editorials outlining criteria for the evaluation of 'rightism' and organisational meetings were held to discuss how to deal with certain individuals. As the movement unfolded, a number of literary figures and leaders of the 'democratic parties' were denounced. Prominent amongst this latter group were Zhang Bojun and Luo Longji who were considered to be at the head of a conspiracy.[52] It was claimed also that some 1 to 3 per cent of all students were 'rightists' though in some places, such as Beijing University, up to 10 per cent were 'capped' (i.e. designated as 'rightists')[53] and sent for indefinite periods of manual labour. The press also came under attack, a particular target being Shanghai's *Wenhuibao* which had apparently taken too seriously the injunction to 'open wide the publication of criticism'.[54]

The *Wenhuibao* case, which it will be remembered involved the attentions of Chairman Mao, provides another instance of profound disagreement amongst commentators. It was in that newspaper that Zhou Yang had published one of the first calls for 'blooming and contending' and *Wenhuibao* had taken a lead in bringing the press into line behind Mao's original movement. In investigating *Wenhuibao*, therefore, one wonders whether Mao was particularly concerned about its 'rightism' or was in fact trying to protect it. A similar problem of interpretation concerns the Central Committee newspaper *Renmin Ribao*. In July 1957, Deng Tuo, the editor, was replaced by Wu Lengxi and 'promoted' to managing editor. Was this a reward for his reluctance to launch the 'blooming and contending' or was he being 'kicked upstairs' for giving in to the demands of that movement?[55]

Further controversy attends a speech made by Mao to a conference of provincial-level Party secretaries at Qingdao in the second half of July, in which Mao proposed guidelines for the anti-rightist movement. As MacFarquhar sees it, the speech was a clear example of Mao's redirecting the focus of attack back on to senior Party cadres, particularly in the economic field.[56] Indeed, after July, the movement became more and more concerned with economic matters rather than the original critics of May though at that stage there was no attempt made to mobilise the masses to achieve economic goals.[57] In such a climate, one might have expected that Lai Ruoyu's position would be re-examined. As long as criticisms were directed at those who had taken part in the 'blooming and contending', Lai, the opponent of that movement, had nothing to fear. Once, however, the focus had shifted to economic matters, then Lai Ruoyu's demands for union independence would surely have occasioned concern. The rectification of the unions, however, did not really get under way until the end of the year and, by that time, Lai was extremely ill. His death in May 1958 certainly spared him from quite severe censure.[58]

Within the army, also, there was a mild anti-rightist movement though the 'poisonous weeds' which were discovered were given less publicity. Here the main focus of attack were those who had sought to weaken Party leadership and who insisted on a 'purely military viewpoint'. It was said that certain military cadres stressed only technical modernisation and were guilty of a modern form of 'warlordism'. It was apparent, therefore, that the move to return to the revolutionary tradition of 'people's war' had been resisted and that certain senior military commanders might have been involved.[59]

By August 1957, it was clear that the anti-rightist movement was something more than a reflex action on the part of the Party machine. It had now been embraced by those of a more radical persuasion who wished to go further in dismantling the Soviet model. Thus, late in the month, serious criticisms began to appear in the press of that archtypical Soviet form of organisation, the Ministry of State Control.[60] Initial attacks centred on one Peng Da, who was accused of opposing the Party fraction in the ministry and the principle of dual rule. By December, criticism of 'rightism' in the ministry had escalated to include Wang Han, a deputy minister who had played an important part in the introduction of the Harbin system. In March 1958, most control work was to be handed down to local authorities which, in effect, meant being handed over to the Party and, by mid-year, references to the external control network disappeared. The ministry was not to be formally abolished until April 1959 but clearly the anti-rightist movement sealed its fate and signified the beginning of the end of Soviet-style central planning.

The anti-rightist movement was also to prepare the ground for the decentralisation of authority to local areas. But before this could be done, it had to destroy 'localism', defined here in a more traditional sense than the concept 'independent kingdom'. One of the most striking examples of such 'localism' in this period was that of Feng Baiju in Hainan Island. Feng had for long resisted the influence of cadres from the north and had complained to the Eighth Party Congress in September 1956 about outside interference in Hainan affairs.[61] In December of that year, the situation had become so bad that minor armed incidents took place. Some 'localists' had made much of the 'blooming and contending' policy, but by August 1957 full-scale criticism of 'localism' was in progress. Feng and other 'localists' elsewhere were to be removed from office.

## The Socialist Education Movement

The hundred flowers movement had little impact on rural cadres still busy with the tasks of collectivisation. In the countryside, policy was still unclear and there was much confusion. Throughout 1956, some cadres had discriminated against the private sector while others had done little to restrain peasants who wished to leave the collectives. Occasionally, rural leaders permitted a decentralisation of power to individual house-holds (*baochan dao hu*) or ignored what was happening provided that grain quotas were met. They permitted peasants to spend an increasing amount of time on their private plots and even began to act like 'rich peasants' themselves.[62]

To help retrieve the rural situation, a process of *xiafang* (sending down) had been employed. The notion of *xiafang* had been put forward by Zhou Enlai in his report to the Eighth Party Congress[63] though, in the conservative atmosphere of that time, it meant little more than the disposal of personnel made redundant by administrative streamlining; retrenched cadres did not usually take part in manual labour.[64] In his speech 'On the Correct Handling . . .', Mao hinted that rusticated cadres should 'share the sufferings of the masses' by engaging in productive labour[65] and this became official policy upon the promulgation of the hundred flowers movement.[66] In May, photographs appeared in the press showing leading Party figures doing manual work[67] and a Party directive was issued demanding that all Party members, regardless of rank, should assume the work of ordinary toilers.[68] Though various senior cadres might have been reluctant to participate in this work,[69] the publicity given to their manual labour had important implications for the *xiafang* process. People began to recall that the original *xiaxiang* move-ment of Yan'an days had an important educative function. But it was not only the city youth who were to be educated. The youth themselves could participate in the education of the rural population. Education, more-over, was not seen as a passive process of mutual learning. When Mao called for a Socialist Education Movement at the Qingdao conference in July, he had something more radical in mind.[70] A large-scale attempt was to be made to clean up the unhealthy tendencies which he felt had developed in the countryside.

The Socialist Education Movement of 1957 was not a mass move-ment. It bore some superficial resemblance to land reform in that 'monsters and demons' (*niugui sheshen*) were criticised but there were no 'struggle sessions' or 'speak-bitterness' meetings. Peasant associations were not reactivated and the initiative in detecting obstacles to collectivi-sation was taken by work-teams sent down from above. Despite its limited nature, the movement was to have a significant impact. In August, the State Council moved effectively to restrict rural markets. By

September, rural Party rectification could be undertaken in earnest and work was begun on co-ops with the most serious problems (the so-called 'third category' co-ops). Aiming to reduce the size of collectives to about 100 households, the work-teams were able to bring the average down from 246 households in 1956 to 169 in 1957.[71] By the autumn, rural petty capitalism had been checked, much of the power of the traditional village elders had been broken and leadership was in the hands of younger cadres. More and more the collectives began to resemble the Soviet *kolkhoz*.

Major problems, of course, still remained. In slack seasons there was temporary underemployment. In many areas, women were excluded from the main agricultural workforce except at harvest time. Perhaps most important of all, peasants had still not been mobilised to effect major changes for themselves. So much of what had been done was merely institutional engineering. The cautious approach to rural change, moreover, was still apparent in September 1957 when a Party directive declared that once the size of the collectives and brigades had been fixed, there should be no further changes for ten years.[72] Mao Zedong was not to be so easily satisfied.

From the countryside, the Socialist Education Movement spread to the cities in a milder form. In September and October, capitalist influences in industrial and commercial enterprises[73] were attacked and the 1956 wage reform reassessed.[74] Individual piecework, bonuses and an exclusive concentration on material incentive were denounced and moral incentive affirmed. In universities and schools, special 'socialist education' sections resolved to undertake the task of training 'revolutionary successors'.[75] As the elements of education in the Socialist *Education* Movement received belated stress, it was seen that reforms could not be carried out effectively in watertight compartments. Students and teachers had to integrate with the labouring people.

Perhaps the most notable achievement in 1957 was not so much the rectification of shortcomings by the Socialist Education Movement but the success of *xiafang*.[76] What started as mere administrative retrenchment had grown, by the end of 1957, into a major developmental policy. By the end of November, 303,000 out of a total of 575,000 cadres from 18 provinces and municipalities had gone to the 'labour front'. By February of the following year, the figure was to reach 1.3 million. A major attempt was under way to close the gap between those who laboured with their hands and those who laboured with their minds. *Xiafang* was no longer a remedial measure but a continuous process. Labour reform was no longer seen as a punishment but as an education and, although not all cadres were happy with their lot, most seemed content not merely to 'dismount and look at the flowers'.

## Towards a New Economic Strategy[77]

As the *xiafang* and Socialist Education Movement unfolded and the First Five Year Plan drew to a close in the summer and autumn of 1957, an intense debate arose on the question of development and economic strategy. The First Five Year Plan (1953–7) had given investment priority (over 50 per cent) to capital goods industries with a much smaller planned investment in consumer goods industries. Only 6.2 per cent of the state budget was devoted to agriculture though a considerable proportion of agricultural investment was not included in the state budget. The Soviet Union had agreed to provide about 300 modern industrial plants during the course of three five year plans at an estimated total cost of $US 3 billion and, by 1957, 68 of these projects had been completed. The bulk of Chinese indebtedness to the Soviet Union, however, resulted not so much from economic assistance as from the liquidation of Soviet shares in the former joint-stock companies in Lushun and Dalian and payment for Soviet military supplies delivered during the Korean War. Though there was some Soviet assistance in key areas, the bulk of capital investment was provided by the Chinese themselves and gross fixed investment rose from an estimated 5.5 per cent of GNP in 1950 to some 18 per cent in 1957.[78]

As one might expect, the annual growth rate of industrial output during the plan was spectacular. A rate of 14–19 per cent was higher than virtually every other country in the world and surpassed the industrial growth rate of the Soviet Union during its first two Five Year Plans (1928–37).[79] As a result of adherence to a Soviet economic model, heavy industry constituted as much as 48 per cent of total industrial output by 1957. In comparing China with the Soviet Union, however, one should remember that China started from a much lower base at the start of its plan.

Though economists differ as to their estimates of China's industrial growth during the period 1952–7, the differences in estimates are nowhere near as great as in the agricultural sector. Official figures claim that total farm output increased during the period by some 25 per cent, giving an annual growth rate of over 4 per cent, though it has been argued that these figures underestimate output for the early years. One estimate, that of Liu and Yeh, states that production increased by less than 9 per cent giving an annual growth rate of less than 2 per cent.[80] Economists argue amongst themselves as to the relative merits of estimates placed between these two extremes. It would seem, however, that the majority agree that food production roughly kept pace with the total population increase of from 11 to 12.5 per cent but did little more than that.[81] If this is so, two conclusions emerge. First, during a plan which only allocated 6.2 per cent of the state budget to agriculture, a major collectivisation of agriculture was carried through without a significant decrease in output per capita; this was no mean achievement. Secondly, with the bulk of capital investment being financed domestically, agricultural output had to increase quite substantially to avoid a major investment crisis. Since investment in heavy industry derived in large measure from agriculture via light industry, a Soviet-style concentration on heavy industry alone was inappropriate.

In the field of foreign trade, there was considerable expansion during the period, mainly with countries of the socialist camp. The average annual growth rate was soem 20 per cent for exports and 16 per cent for imports.[82] It seems, therefore, that trade was growing faster than industrial production. From a developmental perspective, it may be argued, such a situation could be potentially dangerous as the Chinese economy became plugged into a world economy the prices of which China was in no position to control. In the radical atmosphere of the late 1950s, China was to move to a more autarchic view of development.

The key question, therefore, in the autumn of 1957 was how to increase agricultural output to pay for industrialisation. The Soviet answer, which had been found wanting, was to predicate rural transformation on industrialisation. Mechanisation of agriculture was to precede social transformation. We have seen, however, that after the relatively poor harvests of 1953–4, Mao had taken the initiative in reversing this order of priorities. Social mobilisation itself was to increase productivity and thus generate funds for agricultural mechanisation which would make savings available for industrial investment. As Mao saw it, collectivisation was not an end in itself but was the first step in a process whereby a 'Great Leap Forward' would take place in production, according to the slogan of producing 'more, better, faster and more economically'. Such had been the basis of Mao's twelve-year plan for agriculture, so unceremoniously shelved in 1956. With the renewed radicalisation during the various movements in the summer of 1957, Mao was in a position to voice his strategy once again.

A second question concerned the location of operational economic decision-making. The Soviet answer lay in centralisation of both policy and operations. The revelations of Khrushchev had shown how wasteful such a system had been and, in China, one could also discern similar (though perhaps less serious) problems.[83] The question to be answered was, if there was to be decentralisation, what kind of decentralisation and to what level? The Yugoslav solution (which Schurmann designates 'decentralisation I')[84] was to transfer decision-making power down to the units of production themselves. This view, which was advocated in part by Chen Yun and Xue Muqiao,[85] looked very attractive from the point of view of involving all enterprise and co-operative personnel in decision-making, but there were considerable drawbacks. In a system where units of production were atomised, the only possible structure which could hold the economy together was the market and not the plan. Once free play was given to market forces, some people felt that there would be an inevitable tendency for industrial and agricultural units to produce solely for self-gain, the internal effects of which would be a stress on material incentive. In such a system, the articulation of the economy to regional and local government would break down, thus making the Party as ineffective as when it was subordinated to vertical decision-making structures. Far more attractive from a radical point of view than 'decentralisation I' was the decentralisation of policy and operational decision-making power to *local areas* (Schurmann's 'decentralisation II'), if only one could make it work. This was the strategy adopted in the Soviet Union in 1957 when regional economic councils (*sovnarkhozy*) were set up with broad powers.[86] The Soviet experiment, however, was not to be a success. Ministries were abolished and their powers transferred to branches of the State Planning Commission which then proceeded to function in much the same way as the old ministries. On the one hand there was partial recentralisation, and on the other the adoption of what some call more 'liberal' economic policies (the Chinese were to call them 'revisionist'), which resulted in a partial 'decentralisation' and the growth of the market at the expense of the plan. In 1957, however, these problems that were to plague the Soviet Union were but dimly seen.

By the autumn, a modified version of 'decentralisation II' became the accepted strategy. Not only was power decentralised to local areas[87] but a programme of decentralisation of power was also to be carried out *within* economic units.[88] The great virtue of 'decentralisation I' over 'decentralisation II' lay precisely in the scope that was given for mass participation in decision-making. The modified 'decentralisation II' adopted in China gave scope for that participation but located power both above and below the level of the productive unit.

It has been remarked that one of the decisive features of the Chinese planning system was that non-economic goals were fed into it.[89] I would argue, however, that the Chinese planners, of the late 1950s, would not accept such a description, since to them there was no such thing as a non-economic goal. All goals were both political and economic. The Great Leap Forward strategy was not aimed just at increasing productivity, with some human considerations taken into account. Rather it was aimed at the closure of the élite-mass and urban-rural gaps in both their economic and non-economic dimensions, and this within an atmosphere of expanding productivity whereby greater investment funds could be provided for all sectors of the economy. It was not to be, as it has sometimes been described, a shift from material to moral incentive but was rather a shift from the individual to the collective dimensions of both material and moral incentive. It was not merely to be an acceleration of the existing pattern of the modern-oriented First Five Year Plan with a slightly greater stress on agriculture, but was an exercise in creative imbalance or dynamic disequilibrium whereby sectors of the economy were thrown out of gear just to find out what the potential was. As a theoretical underpinning of the leap, Mao articulated the theory of 'uninterrupted revolution',[90] which he saw, not as Trotsky's theory of 'permanent revolution' whereby the socialist revolution might be launched before the democratic revolution was completed,[91] but as a continuous succession of revolutionary stages during which periods of consolidation would not endure long enough for institutionalisation to occur. As Mao put it in early 1958:

> Imbalance is a universal objective law. Things forever proceed from imbalance to equilibrium, and from equilibrium to imbalance, in endless cycles. It will be forever like this, but each cycle reaches a higher level. Imbalance is constant and absolute; equilibrium is temporary and relative.[92]

For Mao, even 'communism' was not an end but a revolutionary process.[93] The Great Leap Forward, then, was envisaged as part of this process of 'uninterrupted revolution' and there was nothing that was not to be pressed into its service. A policy of 'walking on two legs' was not just a device to utilise the old as well as the new, but implied a continuous state of flux in which the old became something even newer. It implied that both worker and peasant and both nuclear physicist and traditional practitioner of acupuncture and moxibustion were equally relevant. The Soviet-style planners, in many ways as conservative as any Western accountant, could not but be alarmed.

## Conclusion

This chapter, which has focused on one of the most important turning-points in the history of the People's Republic, has demonstrated the enormous problems one has in trying to interpret Chinese official statements. To some commentators, the period covered in this chapter saw the origins of what became known as the 'two-line struggle' in the Cultural Revolution of 1966–9. Others, however, maintain that the evidence does not warrant such a conclusion. Those who prefer to see Mao as a liberal-Marxist may find support for their position in his pronouncements early in the year. Others, however, may find support for the contention that both the 'blooming and contending' and the anti-rightist movement were means to the same end—the restructuring of the Chinese economy. By the end of 1957, a movement to effect such restructuring was, indeed, launched, but whether that was the intention of Mao in early 1957 and whether his intention was shared by other leaders is open to question. At the time of writing, there is much unofficial debate in China about whether Mao was outflanked in mid-1957 or whether he should be held responsible for what appeared to be a breach of faith. One cannot tell how the Chinese Communist Party will eventually settle that question. But, whatever decision it comes to, one may predict that scholars will continue to debate that extraordinary year—1957—a year which started with 'gentle breeze and mild rain' and finished with the Great Leap Forward.

## NOTES

1. MacFarquhar, 1974, pp. 248–9.
2. Teiwes, 1979, pp. 251–5.
3. MacFarquhar, 1974, pp. 171–4.
4. Text in Bowie and Fairbank, 1965, pp. 257–72. Note, in Mao's view this essay should never have been published in the form that it was, since it argued in terms of the inevitability of mistakes. Mao Zedong, January 1957, *JPRS*, 1974, p. 58, and *SW* V, p. 370.
5. See Solomon, 1971, pp. 285–8.
6. MacFarquhar, 1973, p. 634.
7. A late-nineteenth- and early-twentieth-century reformer.
8. Mao Zedong, January 1957, *JPRS*, 1974, p. 57. My translation from Mao, 1969, pp. 84–5. A quite different version appears in the official (1977) version. *SW* V, p. 366.
9. Solomon, 1971, p. 289.
10. MacFarquhar, 1974, pp. 177–8.
11. Chen Qitong *et al.*, *RMRB*, 7 January 1957, *SCMP* 1507, 9 April 1957, pp. 17–19.
12. MacFarquhar, 1974, pp. 191–6.
13. Teiwes, 1979, pp. 255–6.
14. Mao Zedong, January 1957, *JPRS*, 1974, p. 67.
15. Mao was to advance this principle in 1958.
16. MacFarquhar, 1974, pp. 180–3.
17. Mao Zedong, 27 February 1957, *SW* V, pp. 384–421.
18. Ibid., p. 410.
19. Solomon, 1971, pp. 296–7.
20. Mao Zedong, 12 March 1957, *SW* V, pp. 422–35.
21. Zhang Zhiyi, 31 March 1957, *SCMP* 1522, 3 May 1957, pp. 1–9.
22. *RMRB*, 10 April 1957, p. 1.
23. See Teiwes, 1979, pp. 250–1.
24. MacFarquhar, 1974, pp. 250–2.
25. Ibid., pp. 196–9.
26. Ibid., p. 195.
27. *RMRB*, 17 July 1957, p. 2, cited in Solomon, 1971, p. 304.
28. Ma Zhemin, *RMRB*, 18 July 1957, p. 10, cited in Solomon, 1971, p. 305.
29. MacFarquhar, 1974, p. 201.

30. *SCMP* 1512, 17 April 1957, p. 15; 1516, 25 April 1957, p. 2; 1518, 29 April 1957, p. 2.

31. CCPCC, 27 April 1957, URI, 1971, pp. 253−7.

32. MacFarquhar, 1974, pp. 207−10.

33. Mao Zedong, April 1957, *JPRS*, 1974, p. 68.

34. Vogel, 1971, pp. 192−9; MacFarquhar, 1974, pp. 218−49; Teiwes, Chapter VI.

35. Gittings, 1967, pp. 173−4.

36. The following is based on Harper, 1969, pp. 99−114.

37. See Brugger, 1976, Chapter VII.

38. *SCMP* 1535, 22 May 1957, p. 12.

39. Harper, 1969, p. 106.

40. *JPRS* 665, pp. 33−6; *SCMP* 1551, 17 June 1957, pp. 10−13.

41. *SCMP* 1535, 22 May 1957, pp. 8−11.

42. Ibid. 1536, 23 May 1957, pp. 1−3.

43. E.g. Tao Zhu noted in June that 90 per cent of the criticisms had been 'correct'. Vogel, 1971, p. 201.

44. Solomon, 1971, p. 314.

45. MacFarquhar, 1974, p. 281.

46. Reproduced in Solomon, 1971, p. 321.

47. Ibid., p. 322; MacFarquhar, 1974, p. 283.

48. Mao Zedong, 18 January 1961, *JPRS*, 1974, p. 238.

49. On the insertion of these six criteria, see MacFarquhar, 1974, pp. 265−6.

50. Solomon, 1971, pp. 325−7.

51. These explanations are discussed in Solomon, 1971, pp. 290−1. See also MacFarquhar, 1974, pp. 266−7.

52. See MacFarquhar, 1974, pp. 224−5, 271−3; Teiwes, 1979, pp. 300−6.

53. Teiwes, 1979, p. 297.

54. MacFarquhar, 1974, p. 279.

55. See ibid., p. 282.

56. Ibid., pp. 285−9.

57. Teiwes, 1979, pp. 290−1.

58. Harper, 1969, pp. 106−14.

59. Gittings, 1967, pp. 173−5, 226−7.

60. See the discussion in Schurmann, 1966, pp. 353−63.

61. Vogel, 1971, pp. 211−16. For other examples of 'localism', see Teiwes, 1979, pp. 366−74.

62. Vogel, 1971, pp. 204−5.

63. Zhou Enlai, PFLP, 1956, Vol. I, p. 324.

64. Lee, 1966, p. 44.

65. Mao Zedong, 27 February 1957, *SW* V, p. 418.

66. Lee, 1966, p. 44.

67. See Solomon, 1971, p. 310.

68. CCPCC, 14 May 1957, URI, 1971, pp. 259−63.

69. MacFarquhar, 1974, pp. 228−31.

70. The following is based on Vogel, 1971, pp. 205−9.

71. Schurmann, 1966, pp. 456−7.

72. Cited in ibid., p. 456.

73. Vogel, 1971, p. 210.

74. For criticism dating mainly from 1958, see *JPRS* 1337−N, 12 March 1959.

75. Vogel, 1971, p. 210.

76. The following is taken from Lee, 1966.

77. For an interesting discussion of the thinking which led to the Great Leap Forward, see Lippit, 1975.

78. Wheelwright and McFarlane, 1970, pp. 35−6.

79. Eckstein, 1973, pp. 223–4.

80. Ibid., pp. 214–19.

81. Ibid., p. 215.

82. Ibid., pp. 228–9.

83. See Zhou Enlai, PFLP, 1956, Vol. I, pp. 263–328.

84. Schurmann, 1966, pp. 175–8.

85. Ibid., pp. 196–208; Chang, 1975, p. 54.

86. Schurmann, 1966, p. 176.

87. SC, 18 November 1957; Selden, 1979, pp. 432–6.

88. See Andors, 1971; Selden 1979, pp. 444–8.

89. Wheelwright and McFarlane, 1970, p. 14.

90. See the discussion in Schram, 1971; Starr, 1971; Young and Woodward, 1978.

91. Mao Zedong, 28 January 1958, *Chinese Law and Government*, Vol. I, No. 4, Winter 1968–9, pp. 13–14.

92. Mao Zedong, 19 February 1958. This is taken from an untitled Red Guard pamphlet, p. 33. Another translation may be found in *CB* 892, 21 October 1969, p. 7. For an earlier formulation, see Mao Zedong, January 1957, *JPRS*, 1974, p. 49, and for a later one (20 May 1958), *JPRS*, 1974, p. 112.

93. 'On the Historical Experiences of the Dictatorship of the Proletariat' talks of the persistence of contradictions among the people even in communist society. Bowie and Fairbank, 1965, p. 148. See also Mao Zedong, 1959, *JPRS*, 1974, p. 221.

# VIII
# THE GREAT LEAP FORWARD
## (1958 – 1959)

The Great Leap Forward, which was ushered in by the Third Plenum of the Eighth Central Committee in September – October 1957, was to see changes in Chinese society more profound than at any other time in the history of the People's Republic (and here the Cultural Revolution is included). Scholars, the world over, have disagreed radically on their interpretations of this movement and, in China itself, the Great Leap continues to be the source of profound debate. Much of current (1979) Chinese thinking is quite critical of the events of that time but, because Mao Zedong was so intimately associated with the development of the Leap, criticism remains muted.

### The Third Plenum (20 September to 9 October 1957)

By the time of the Third Plenum in the autumn of 1957, Mao felt himself in a position to criticise the line of the Eighth Party Congress which held that the main contradiction in Chinese society was between the 'advanced socialist system' and the 'backward productive forces'.[1] As Mao saw it, the main contradiction was between the 'people' and the bourgeoisie. This position implied that 'class struggle' would be treated far more seriously than in the preceding period though Mao did not revoke the view put forward in 'On the Correct Handling . . .' that 'large-scale turbulent class struggles characteristic of times of revolution [had] in the main come to an end'.[2] This seemed to be because Mao was reluctant to abandon the positive model of socialism. It was, in fact, to be some three years before Mao saw the inherent contradictions in his position and began to work out a new formulation of socialist transition.

Mao's immediate concern in September 1957 was not socialist theory but how to promote radical economic policies and revive the 'leap

174

forward' of early 1956. At the Third Plenum, he was to enjoy considerable success and the rectification movement came increasingly to be interpreted in terms of attitude towards economic strategy. This, as Teiwes points out, was a significant departure in the policies of the Chinese Communist Party. Though one might wish to disagree with his view that the earlier rectification movements were concerned largely with matters of organisation and broadly defined ideology and that the Gao Gang affair did not involve policy issues, there is little doubt that the rectification movement, endorsed by the Third Plenum, was the first such movement in which economic policy was the *major* issue.[3] Such a development had only become possible once consensus on the Soviet model had completely broken down.

In economic policy, therefore, the Third Plenum was a watershed. It was as important as the decision to terminate 'blooming and contending' had been in the field of politics. That plenum endorsed the policy of 'decentralisation II' and the revival of Mao's twelve-year plan for agriculture[4] in revised form.[5] As one might imagine, such events did not occur without some opposition. It will be remembered that less than one week before the plenum, on 14 September, a Central Committee directive had struck a conservative note on rural organisation, declaring that, once the current programme of scaling down the collectives had been completed, there should be no change for the next ten years. This directive, which probably resulted from the conclusions of a national conference on rural work in early September, was not what one would have expected if the twelve-year plan was shortly to go into effect. In fact, the plenum only 'basically' adopted the plan (signifying agreement only in broad outline). Some scholars have concluded, therefore, that a reversal of policy occurred during the course of the plenum itself and that its proceedings were the scene of much disagreement. Further evidence for this view is provided by the fact that speeches to the plenum by Chen Yun (on economic administration) and Zhou Enlai (on wages and welfare) were never made public.

In retrospect, it seems that the Third Plenum marked the eclipse of the influential Chen Yun. In Teiwes's opinion, this was the first demotion of a senior leader on purely economic grounds[6] and, for that reason, Chen was not publicly criticised. At the highest levels, the norms of inner-Party democracy still held. But, as we shall see, at lower levels they were breaking down and a large number of economic 'conservatives' were to be removed from office and bitterly denounced.

## The Moscow Conference

The Great Leap strategy, initiated by the Third Plenum, was gradually to evolve in the last three months of 1957. It was based on the old Yan'an principle of 'self-reliance' (*zili gengsheng*) in all aspects, except for a portion of heavy industry which remained under central control. Here a continued reliance on the Soviet Union for the supply of capital goods was maintained and paid for by expanded exports of primary products and the products of light industry. The expansion of Sino-Soviet trade had become possible with a marked improvement in Sino-Soviet relations, once again in 1957, after the coolness following the Twentieth Congress. In June, Khrushchev had triumphed over an 'anti-Party clique' headed by Molotov and Kaganovitch. We cannot be sure as to the precise Chinese reaction to this development[7] but, whatever China's leaders felt, Khrushchev was much more conciliatory towards the Chinese in the aftermath of the crisis. *Pravda* declared that Mao's position, put forward in the speech 'On the Correct Handling . . .', constituted a development of Marxist-Leninist theory, and Khrushchev himself declared that China *especially* had the right to build socialism in accordance with its national characteristics.[8] On 26 August 1957, the Soviet Union successfully tested an intercontinental ballistic missile, followed on 4 October, while the Chinese Third Plenum was in session, by the launching of its first *Sputnik*. On 15 October, China and the Soviet Union signed an 'agreement on new technology for national defence' (perhaps involving nuclear weapons)[9] and, as the fortieth anniversary of the Bolshevik Revolution approached, it seemed that the balance of the world's forces was shifting in the direction of the socialist camp. In Moscow for a conference of representatives of Communist and workers Parties in November 1957, Mao was to make his famous remark that 'the East wind prevails over the West wind', referring here not to China but to the socialist camp.[10]

In the view of some commentators, the outward cordiality expressed between China and the Soviet Union in November 1957 is evidence that one should not date the origins of the Sino-Soviet dispute from the Twentieth Party Congress in 1956.[11] There is much evidence, however, that fundamental disagreements still existed and that Mao's role in Moscow in November 1957 was much the same as Zhou Enlai's role as conciliator after the Hungarian events in January 1957.[12] There is no evidence that the Chinese were prepared to accept the notion of 'peaceful competition' or 'peaceful coexistence' with *imperialist* countries; nor were they prepared to support Khrushchev's partial *rapprochement* with Tito, who developed a 'diplomatic illness' at the time of the Moscow conference.[13] In fact, the atmosphere of Sino-Soviet conciliation during the conference hardened the attitude of the CPSU towards Yugoslavia, then in receipt of American aid.

In the subsequent Sino-Soviet polemic on the General Line of the International Communist Movement, much was made of the conference declaration jointly sponsored by China and the Soviet Union with only Yugoslavia dissenting.[14] Khrushchev probably felt that the tone of the declaration was much the same as the position he had adopted at the Twentieth Party Congress, though some concessions had been made on wording. The declaration still held that war was not 'fatally inevitable', though there was now no reference to any change of heart on the part of Western leaders. 'Peaceful transition' to communism was still held to be possible, but only in advanced capitalist countries. There was also a new stress on wars of national liberation in the Third World. The notion of 'different roads to socialism' was still maintained, though in a watered-down form. Mao, on the other hand, though perhaps not completely at ease with the new formulation, probably saw Khrushchev as coming to a slightly more revolutionary position. The declaration insisted that imperialism was still the major enemy and that 'revisionism' was more of a danger than 'dogmatism'. What is perhaps most important, from Mao's point of view, was that there was now agreement that the national liberation struggle in the Third World should not be underestimated. The declaration had every appearance of a strongly debated compromise but one that both China and the Soviet Union could accept without very much departure from principles. Under the surface, however, the same divergencies that had existed since the Twentieth Congress remained and were soon to re-emerge.

Despite the fact that the fundamental differences between the Soviet and Chinese Parties still continued to rankle, the atmosphere of conciliation in October and November 1957 did ensure the prospects of increased trade and, therefore, guaranteed one crucial aspect of the Great Leap strategy.[15]

## Decentralisation

Exports to the Soviet Union were to depend upon the development of agriculture and light industry. Light industry, as defined here, did not just mean the consumer goods industries but all medium and small-scale industry whether concerned with producer or consumer goods.[16] Such industries obtained some 80 per cent of their raw materials from agriculture and were the important link through which agriculture provided investment in heavy industry.[17] Their development necessitated the rapid expansion of intermediate technology in rural and semi-rural areas in accordance with a policy known as 'get the best out of each area' (*yindi zhiyi*). With the decentralisation of control, the state was not going to provide much investment in this sector and local light industries were required to practise self-reliance. Finally, the very life of these light industries depended upon radical agricultural reorganisation. Unlike the radicalisation of 1955 which followed a good harvest, the radicalisation of 1957 came after a poor harvest. Unless something drastic was done immediately to boost agricultural productivity, rural light industries were not going to generate enough funds for heavy industrial development. Thus, radical rural reorganisation, the development of light industry and the continued growth of heavy industry were all linked in a programme of 'simultaneous development on all fronts'.

When, on 18 November 1957, the State Council published the decentralisation provisions all light industry was transferred to provincial control. In addition, all non-strategic heavy industrial enterprises, the timber industry, ports, many construction enterprises and some industries formerly under the Ministry of Communications were likewise transferred. Now, more of the revenue of industrial enterprises (20 per cent) could be retained locally as could the proceeds of a number of taxes, though the central government could, if it wished, compensate for this loss of revenue by altering its budget allocation to the local area the following year. Local governments could now raise funds by floating their own bonds and far greater provincial or municipal financial autonomy was enjoyed.[18]

At the same time, the planning system was simplified. Enterprises had now only to report on four instead of twelve planned targets and the former cumbersome 'two up and two down' planning procedure was replaced by a simpler 'two down and one up'. (This meant that the interval between the drafting of a plan and its final authorisation was shortened.[19]) With the reduction in the number of central ministries, there was also a decentralisation of personnel, which in effect meant an intensification of *xiafang*. As local power was strengthened, the dual rule system became more effective and even industries still under central control became subject to far greater regional co-ordination. Eventually, therefore, dual rule was to result in a dual system of planning in which provincial authorities played the dominant role.[20] At the same time, the commercial network was reorganised with far greater power to determine prices being located in the regions. Even the railways, where centralisation had been the main purpose of the Harbin system, were transferred to local authorities.[21]

The picture which emerged at the end of 1957 was one of far greater provincial and municipal independence, though some centralised financial controls (such as those exercised by the People's Bank) remained. In the following year, there was much discussion about the divisive effects of such a system and various plans were put forward for large economic co-operation regions,[22] though we are not sure how effective they were. With the strengthening of dual rule, the Party was stronger than ever and capable of effective horizontal mass mobilisation.

## Rectification

According to the Yan'an tradition, any programme of administrative decentralisation had to be accompanied by a centralisation of key policy-making. If local leaders were to be given greater power, then there was a corresponding need to invoke the process of rectification. The rectification movement endorsed by the Third Plenum was, as we have seen, a continuation of the closed movement implemented during the anti-rightist campaign but, like that closed movement which had taken place in Yan'an, it was linked to policies of mass mobilisation. Non-Party people were not able to criticise Party cadres in the same way as had been possible in the open movement of early 1957 but the performance of cadres in integrating with the masses and promoting mass mobilisation provided important data for the rectification process. A controlled process of 'blooming and contending', therefore, became legitimate once again.

As I have suggested, the economic interpretation of rectification in 1957 and 1958 meant that the targets for criticism were not just corruption, organisational indiscipline or a 'tailist' pandering to peasant superstitions, but could simply be disagreements with the radical economic strategy and a refusal to set targets high enough. Thus, amongst senior cadres at provincial level who were removed from their posts in 1958, there were not only those who had supported rightists in 1957, who had communicated false information to higher levels or who had tried to create 'independent kingdoms', but also those who persisted with the policy of reducing the size of co-ops and who failed to keep up with the increasing radicalisation.[23] In almost all the cases of punishment of senior cadres in the eleven months after December 1957, errors of rural policy were involved. Most significant here was the dismissal of Henan Party first secretary Pan Fusheng and his replacement by a fervent activist of Great Leap policies, Wu Zhipu.[24] It was no accident that Henan became a model of radical experimentation.

In early 1958, the lot of rural cadres was not enviable. This was not only because failure to be sufficiently enthusiastic about radical policies was a serious deviation but also because some of the aims of those policies might be in contradiction. In January 1958, for example, a brief 'two anti' (*shuangfan*) movement was launched against waste and conservatism.[25] But what happened when the consequence of combating conservatism was reckless experimentation which led to waste, and balancing the books to prevent waste might be defined as a form of conservatism? Yet for all the tensions such policies might have caused, the atmosphere in early 1958 was one of great excitement and large numbers of cadres vied with each other to be the first to engage in manual labour or go to the 'production front' as part of the new programme of *xiafang.* Coercion there might have been but much of the coercion was, in fact, self-coercion in the single-minded pursuit of production.

## The Water Conservancy Campaign

By the beginning of 1958, an economic strategy for the Great Leap had been initiated, power had been decentralised to local areas and an intense rural rectification had been launched. Now attention could be devoted to widespread mass mobilisation. Back in September, the Party had announced its annual policy of building and extending waterworks[26] and, in December, the Central Committee and the State Council demanded the movement be undertaken before the spring ploughing.[27] At first, as normally happened in such movements, the water conservancy work was confined to a few collectives, but it was soon seen that the demands of the twelve-year plan required the labour of several collectives to combine in order to complete major tasks. There was but a short step from this to the amalgamation of collectives into large units which divided out the work according to a rational division of labour. In this policy, Henan, which stood at the junction of a number of major rivers and which had suffered from drought in 1956-7, was once again to take the lead.[28] There and elsewhere, peasants for the first time found themselves working far away from their familiar land and yet still within the same collectively administered area. The terms 'brigade' and 'team' now meant something more than just a collective subdivision. The brigades and teams began to develop something like the spirit of a military unit engaged in a common struggle where the reward was collective benefit and from which they could not easily retire to till their private plot.[29]

As the pace of rural mobilisation intensified, a series of conferences of provincial Party secretaries and some Politburo members met to plan strategy. At the Hangzhou conference (early January 1958)[30] and the Nanning conference (late January),[31] Mao and others engaged in endless discussions on Great Leap strategies and put forward guidelines in the form of 'Sixty Work Methods'.[32] As the atmosphere became more and more heated, it became clear that the Second Five Year Plan (commencing 1958) would be drastically revised. In late 1957, national plans called for an increase of 4.7 per cent in agricultural production and 8 to 10 per cent in industrial production during the coming year.[33] These figures were soon to be substantially altered.

## The Taiwan Crisis

The Great Leap Forward took place in an atmosphere of growing international tension and any evaluation of the fervour engendered at that time must take into account sentiments of patriotism. The first Taiwan crisis had resulted in stalemate, though in 1956–7 tension had been somewhat eased. At the same time, China had become less affected by the Guomindang blockade.[34] Throughout 1956 and early 1957, there had been much talk of negotiations between Beijing and Taibei and it is said that, in the original version of the speech 'On the Correct Handling . . .', Mao had indicated the possibility of an agreement with the Guomindang. In May 1957, however, an agreement was signed between Taiwan and the United States whereby Matador missiles were to be placed on the island. These weapons could carry nuclear warheads and had an effective range of 1,000 kilometres. Faced with this military threat, China could only press even more strongly for some kind of diplomatic settlement, but Guomindang positions were hardening. The Taibei government was particularly worried that some kind of deal might be worked out between China and the United States at the Geneva ambassadorial talks. It felt also that Taiwan was now beginning to acquire the capability to invade the mainland and that this had to be carried out before China acquired nuclear weapons. As the United States greatly expanded its programme of military aid in early 1958, the Guomindang government embarked upon a 'forward-looking' foreign policy.[35]

The Taiwan question began to look even more ominous when, in early 1958, the United States reduced its representation at Geneva below the ambassadorial level. In the view of one writer, it is possible that the Chinese government interpreted this move as a preparation for a bid by Jiang Jieshi to return to the mainland before the expiration of his second term as president, the last allowed to him under the Republic of China's constitution. The fear, then, was a Guomindang invasion supported by American tactical nuclear weapons. In such a situation, the production drive of 1958 was geared not only to solving the investment crisis and reviving the Yan'an tradition of greater mass involvement and commitment but also to increasing defence potential and reaffirming the Yan'an tradition of people's war.

## The Great Leap Forward: Stage One (January-March 1958)

By early 1958, most of the features of the old Yan'an model were being actively promoted. Rectification of cadres was being undertaken to criticise not only 'rightist' thought but also the worship of foreign models. In the new radical climate, it was seen that one of the major errors of Stalin's policies in the Soviet Union had been a neglect of the Mass Line[36] and 'walking on one leg'[37] (an excessive concern with modern urban industry). As the principle of the Mass Line was given new stress, it was combined with the latter-day version of *xiaxiang* and decentralisation of authority. The decentralisation of 1957 – 8 placed much greater stress on the old ideal of 'cadre' leadership, dual rule and 'concentrated leadership and divided operations'.[38] As the Taiwan threat loomed large and the old idea of people's war was restressed, Mao was soon to note that the Communist Party could be grateful once again to Jiang Jieshi for helping the process of militia formation.[39] At the same time, the mass mobilisation effected during the water conservancy campaign led to a further reduction in the size of private plots,[40] the amalgamation of collectives and the redeployment of troops in the civilian rural sector.[41] Campaigns came thick and fast in the Chinese countryside and, following the promulgation of an 'eight-character constitution' for agriculture, further mobilisation became possible in a mass campaign to collect manure.[42]

As war was declared against natural obstacles, all efforts were bent in the direction of encouraging mass activism. Grain quotas were fixed at 1957 levels and were no longer to be adjusted annually; this meant that everything which was achieved above the quota could go into collective investment, to be decided by the collective itself.[43] Everyone was now instructed to help agriculture[44] and thus bring to an end the resentment felt by peasants that they were poor cousins of the industrial workers. By February 1958, there was every indication that the harvests in that year would be much better than in 1957 and this prospect added to the mood of tremendous optimism surrounding the launching of the Great Leap.

An immediate consequence of this optimism was the continual raising of planned targets. In Guangdong, for example,[45] the plan for 1958 (decided on in October 1957) called for a 6.6 per cent increase in agricultural production during the year. By December, this figure had been raised to 8 per cent with a planned rise in yields from three tonnes/hectare[46] to 5.25 tonnes/hectare by 1962 and 6.75 tonnes/hectare by 1967. In January, however, the target was raised to a 26 per cent increase in one year and a planned yield of six tonnes/hectare to be reached in the same period. Industrial plans underwent the same escalation. In the same province, planned industrial increase for 1958 stood at 5.8 per cent in October 1957, 12.4 per cent in early January 1958, 15 per cent later in January and 33.2 per cent in early February. It was, however, not only enthusiasm that accounted for this escalation. With the decentralisation of authority and the *xiafang* of statisticians, the mechanisms for reporting statistics were not all they might have been and occasionally resulted in serious errors. Secondly, since no one wanted to be criticised as a conservative, planning organs tended to accept the highest possible estimate of prospective output.

In a situation characterised by creative imbalance, it was extremely difficult to determine exactly what could be planned. When every single unit of organisation was encouraged to set up some kind of subsidiary plant, when factories were encouraged to till and sow any bit of land they might have, when schools took on productive functions, how could one possibly know what potential output might be? A mammoth drive was launched to discover oil (for China had hitherto been considered very poor in this crucial source of energy) and large new oil deposits were, in fact, discovered, causing a dramatic revision of China's future energy programme.[47] More and more seemed possible and more and more, in fact, became possible. It would be a very brave (or foolhardy) person who felt able, in the first few months of 1958, to make anything like a reasonable estimate of exactly what could be done.

Just as intensified *xiafang* aimed at the closure of the gap between mental and manual labour and between the leaders and the led, so attempts were made to deal with Mao's other major concern, the urban-rural gap. Steps were taken to establish some kind of industry in each *xiang* to manufacture agricultural tools, to produce fertiliser and to process food.[48] Attempts were also made to set up small furnaces at *xian* level and lower to turn out steel.[49] Here, however, the results were not successful and were admitted not to be by Mao. A lot of steel was produced but it was of low quality and not very serviceable.[50] The failures were on a mammoth scale but so were the successes. The growth of rural industries and intermediate technology in the first few months of 1958 was an irreversible process and one which was later considered to be a key feature of the success of the Chinese developmental model.

The policy of closing the urban-rural gap was aimed at the eventual transformation of peasants into workers. This did not mean the creation of factory-like organisations in the countryside, for socialist collectives still formed the majority of rural organisations. But in some areas, especially where land was being newly reclaimed, a 'state farm' form of organisation was set up where peasants became farm workers and received payment in the form of wages.[51] In general, however, peasants continued to receive a proportion of the harvest on the basis of work-points.

As the Leap intensified in early 1958, there was inaugurated what Mao referred to as a period of 'three years' hard struggle'.[52] Technical cadres were sent, in ever increasing numbers, to the countryside to participate in labour and to train other technicians. To this end, plans were put forward to have a secondary school in every *xiang*.[53] The schools were to pay particular attention to the experiences not of model organisations in the Soviet Union but to models within China itself. As we have seen, the Henan model was specified as an example of what could be done in the way of labour-intensive programmes on wheat lands[54] and was given particular support by the influential Tan Zhenlin. Similarly, the Shantou (Swatow) model was put forward in the field of rice cultivation.[55] A mammoth study programme was introduced with an urgency dictated by the ominous storm clouds over the Taiwan Straits. Plans for study or increased production were no longer just 'plans'. They were 'battle plans'.[56]

### The Great Leap Forward: Stage Two (March-August 1958)

In March 1958, in a manner similar to that of almost exactly two years previously, there were moves to begin a period of consolidation. Complaints of excesses began to appear in the press. Materials were said to be in short supply. The centre had begun to lose its grip on local developments. Local governments, finding it extremely difficult both to remit funds to the centre and to finance the burgeoning local investment, further decentralised authority to *xian* and minor municipalities. There was much talk of 'reckless advance' (which were precisely the words once used to describe the 'leap forward' of 1955 – 6) and of 'overcoming the ill wind of empty talk and false reports'.[57] Clearly some mistakes had been made but did this mean that the overall strategy was wrong or that some cadres had been found wanting?

In March 1958, all kinds of meetings were held to discuss how the new policies were working. Of these, the most important was one held in Chengdu where Mao suggested that the experiences in mass mobilisation already undertaken in Henan province might tentatively be emulated in other areas.[58] Mao, however, along with most leaders of the Party, clearly saw the need for more caution and, when the Eighth Party Congress was reconvened in May, many leaders stressed the need to take stock of the situation. In this respect, one of the clearest statements was made by Liu Shaoqi:

> Leaders . . . must combine revolutionary enthusiasm with business-like sense. They must be able not only to put forward advanced targets, but also adopt effective measures in time to ensure the realisation of the targets. They must not engage in empty talk and bluff. The targets we put forward should be those which can be reached with hard work. Do not lightly publicise as plan that which is not really attainable lest failure dampen the enthusiasm of the masses and delight the conservatives.[59]

There has been much speculation amongst commentators that Liu's comments constituted opposition to the radical policies promoted by Chairman Mao. Liu, however, had also criticised those who had spoken of 'reckless advance' and, once again, it is difficult to discern any marked difference between Liu's position and that of Mao. In February 1958,

Mao had expressed his intention to resign from the position of state chairman[60] (though to retain his Party post). This is precisely what he did do in late 1958 and such would surely not have occurred had Mao any reservations about his senior colleagues in May 1958. On the basis of the available evidence, it is difficult to come to any clear view on the possible differences between Mao and Liu. What is certain, however, is that the second session of the Eighth Party Congress initiated a programme of investigation and various Party leaders spent much of the summer touring the country to make an assessment of what was happening now that mass enthusiasm and local initiative was the order of the day.

There was a desire, therefore, to curb excessive radicalism. Such curbs, however, do not appear to have been very significant since the revised twelve-year targets approved by the congress were probably higher than those agreed to in late 1957.[61] The Fifth Plenum, immediately after the session of the Eighth Congress, moreover, promoted a number of people to senior positions who, in retrospect, were not noted for their caution. Lin Biao, for example, was elected Party vice-chairman. Ke Qingshi, who had resisted the erosion of the principle of dual rule in Shanghai, was elected a member of the Politburo, and Tan Zhenlin, a major architect of the ambitious Great Leap in agriculture, was promoted to that body.[62] But perhaps we may deduce little from an analysis of changes in leading personnel. When it came down to it, the sheer momentum of the Great Leap was such that restraints were rather insignificant.

In the field of foreign affairs, policy was also to remain radical. Back in November 1957, Mao Zedong had been particularly concerned about how much Yugoslavia had weakened the 'socialist camp' and the extent of its 'revisionism'. Now, in May 1958, China's objections were stated quite openly[63] and, in retrospect, it is not too difficult to read in them a criticism of the direction in which China felt the Soviet Union to be heading. The crucial question which faced China's leaders in the early summer of 1958 was the extent to which Soviet aid might be forthcoming in the event of a war in the Taiwan Straits. It was that question which probably dominated discussions at an extraordinary meeting of the Party Central Committee's Military Commission from 17 May to 22 July. The Soviet Union had apparently pressed for a joint Sino-Soviet naval command in the Far East, integrated air defences and perhaps the stationing of Soviet troops and emplacement of weapons on Chinese territory.[64] If this were acceded to, China would become no more than a Soviet dependency. In pressing for the rejection of the Soviet demand, Mao was quite adamant:

We must not eat ready-made food, for if we do so we will be defeated in war. This point should be conveyed clearly to the Soviet comrades.[65]

It was probably at this meeting of the enlarged Military Commission that a new Chinese defence strategy was worked out. Chinese independence had to be secured as soon as possible by the development of an independent nuclear capacity. At the same time, institutions should be created within China to undertake the task of people's war should the need arise. The Great Leap Forward then was not just to 'overtake Britain within fifteen years',[66] not just to solve the fundamental contradictions between élite and mass and city and countryside, not just to put China once again on a people's war footing but also to break its dependency on the Soviet Union once and for all.

There is evidence that the long meeting of the Military Commission was particularly tense. Its final communiqué stated that the meeting had been carried out 'using the method of the rectification campaign'.[67] Apparently there were some senior commanders of the PLA who still maintained the 'purely military viewpoint',[68] notably, it would seem, chief-of-staff Su Yu who was dismissed in October.[69] By the close of the meeting, tension hardly abated for, on 29 July, air clashes occurred over the Taiwan Straits and two days later no less a person than Nikita Khrushchev himself arrived in Beijing accompanied by Defence Minister Marshal Malinovsky.[70] We are not sure what happened at the meeting except that no agreement was reached on Taiwan; in fact the press communiqué did not even mention it. There was probably considerable disagreement, not only between Mao and Khrushchev but also between Mao and Chinese Defence Minister Peng Dehuai,[71] on both Sino-Soviet relations and response to the Taiwan crisis. Whatever happened, less than three weeks after Khrushchev returned to Moscow, the shelling of Jinmen began (23 August) and a United States taskforce was sent to the area.[72] Just at that crucial juncture, the Great Leap entered its third and most radical phase.

### The Great Leap Forward: Stage Three (August-December 1958) —Rural People's Communes

The extended debate on defence in the summer of 1958 led to a qualitatively new stage in the Great Leap Forward. The campaign to build waterworks, in the winter of 1957–8, had resulted in the amalgamation of some collectives and the advancement of the principle of a mobilised and potentially transferable rural workforce. At that time, the absence of men in the work brigades had resulted in more and more women being engaged in agricultural tasks in the slack season and in the provision of communal mess facilities. The establishment of some industrial plants in the countryside had demanded the resources of more than one collective and had aided the process of collective amalgamation. The provision of secondary schools at *xiang* level had led people to consider that perhaps the *xiang* might be a more suitable collective unit than the smaller agricultural producers' co-operative. The final step in this whole process was when considerations of defence suggested the merger of productive units with militia organisations.[73]

We have seen that, in the old days of the Soviet model, the people's militia had been allowed to atrophy. Even the co-operativisation movement of 1955–6 had done little to revive militia organisation in the countryside. In 1957, however, as part of the radicalisation of the PLA, the militia was merged with the reserve. Demobilised soldiers and those eligible for conscription but not chosen were organised into a new 'backbone militia' which, in 1957, expanded quite considerably.[74] Doubtless one of the key issues in the defence debate of 1958 was the role of the militia, and it was stated that:

> Some comrades take a purely military viewpoint in the militia organisation and overlook the part played by the militia organisations in promoting socialist construction; or else they take the view that the war for national defence and against aggression is the business of the army and not the whole people.[75]

The new slogan was to be 'everyone a soldier' (*quanmin jiebing*),[76] resulting in a militia enrolment by January 1959 of 220 million people. The way was now open for the creation of new units in the countryside which would combine agricultural and industrial production, administration, education and defence. These were to be the people's communes.

As we have seen, the amalgamation of collectives dates from, at the latest, early 1958 and 'communes' may have begun to appear in the model Henan province as early as April. They were to be officially endorsed in that province at a meeting in Zhengzhou in July, with the blessing of Tan Zhenlin (and maybe Mao).[77] It is perhaps ironical that the first model commune in that province was named after one of the Soviet achievements which initiated the radicalisation of late 1957—*Sputnik* (*Weixing*).[78] By the end of July, 5,376 agricultural collectives in the Henan region had become 208 large people's communes with an average population of 8,000 households.[79] It would appear that communisation had taken place with Mao's approval but without any central Party directive and, on his inspection tour in August, Mao did not appear to have grasped all the intricacies of this development.

> In Shandong, a reporter asked me 'is the commune good?' I said 'good' and he immediately published it in the newspaper. This might be due to some petty-bourgeois fervour. Hereafter newspaper reporters should leave [me alone].[80]

Mao was soon in little doubt, however, that the 'communes' which had appeared were, in fact, 'good' and at an enlarged Politburo conference, attended by provincial Party secretaries and others at Beidaihe from 17 to 30 August, a 'Resolution on the Establishment of People's Communes in the Rural Areas' was adopted.[81] The term 'commune' (*renmin gongshe*) was well chosen. Before the Beidaihe conference, Chen Boda, the editor of the Party Central Committee's new journal *Hongqi* (*Red Flag*), had pointed out that industry, agriculture, commerce, education and militia should be combined into single large 'communes', the inspiration for which could be found in Mao's report of November 1956, 'On the General Line for the Building of Socialism'.[82] As Schurmann has pointed out, the fundamental principle of the people's commune was the unity of work and arms; such its proponents considered had also been the principle of the Paris Commune in 1871.[83] The people's commune (together with the General Line and the class struggle) was henceforth to become one of the 'three red banners' of China's radical development programme.

Although the Beidaihe conference accepted the idea of communes, the communiqué which followed was a very cautious document. Cadres were instructed not to disturb the villages too much and to take existing collectives as communal sub-units.[84] Though transformation from within was an essential feature of the Yan'an model, it is possible that some Party leaders were worried about the destabilising effects of new rural organisations. Ideally, the commune was to replace the *xiang* as the basic level of rural administration and the former collectives would become its brigades and the former brigades its teams. In addition, specialist teams might be formed to undertake light industrial or special agricultural work. The *xiang*-level school system, separate tractor stations and marketing co-ops were merged into a single organisation under the leadership of a Party committee and an elected management committee. Now, with everything happening in an area consisting of a number of villages under the control of a tangible authority, much closer identification of the peasant with the collective might be made. Some peasants were reluctant to give up their private plots and some complained that the food in the communal mess halls was not very palatable. The point was, however, that the provision of communal messing facilities, communal child-care centres and 'homes of respect for the aged' freed a lot of people for productive labour who could now be absorbed in the subsidiary industries, not only at harvest time but also in the slack season. The formal economic basis for equality between the sexes was laid. In so far as the prescribed policy of paying individuals and not families at harvest time was adhered to, the structure of the paternalist gerontocratic family life could undergo change.

Many people were understandably excited. To them, the commune was a fusion of state and society and the beginnings of a process whereby the state would begin to wither away.[85] To Nikita Khrushchev, convinced that the most advanced form of rural organisation to date was the Soviet *kolkhoz*, this was a very unwelcome suggestion. Even more disturbing was the intention to introduce a partial free-supply system within the communes, signalling the initiation of a transition from the 'socialist' principle of 'payment according to work' to the 'communist' principle of 'payment according to needs'. From the vantage point of the Soviet Union, the shift from individual material incentive to, at least, group material incentive and, at most, group moral incentive was premature. Both Soviet and Chinese observers must also have been quite disturbed by some of the excesses which occurred in the whirlwind process whereby 90 per cent of the Chinese rural population were organised in communes within a few months. Sometimes, overzealous cadres confiscated personal property such as radios, bedding and watches. Domestic sideline operations were suppressed and instances of excessive egalitarianism were frequently noted. One particular practice, which later merited official condemnation, was known as 'one equalisation and two transfers' (*yiping erdiao*), where the income of each peasant was equalised, the property of wealthy brigades above the average was transferred to other brigades and the labour force from brigades was transferred elsewhere without compensation.[86]

There has been much argument amongst Western commentators as to the extent to which such 'ultra-leftist' practices were encouraged by members of the Chinese leadership. The Shanghai activist Zhang Chunqiao, for example, published an article calling for the total restoration of the Yan'an supply system and the abolition of the current 'bourgeois' wage system.[87] This, Wu Lengxi, the new editor of *Renmin Ribao*, considered to be in accord with the views expressed by Mao at the Beidaihe conference.[88] Wu maintained, moreover, that Mao had ordered the publication of Zhang's article and had personally written the accompanying editorial note. We shall discuss later the association between Mao and Zhang, though it is difficult to decide, on the basis of pieces of evidence such as this, that Mao was a firm advocate of what became known (pejoratively) as 'the communist style'. Mao's editorial note was, to say the least, only mildly approving.[89] In fact it is more likely that Mao shared the dominant view that the changes proposed in 1958 were long term. The original idea of 30 per cent payment according to labour and 70 per cent according to 'needs' was hardly ever carried out, though less ambitious payments according to 'need' were more widespread. The family structure in the villages and the role of 'family head' (*jiazhang*) remained much as before.[90] But still the intention remained, to create an organisation whereby the end of communism should not be perverted by the means used to reach it.

In the autumn of 1958, it seemed that many cadres interpreted the Beidaihe resolution quite permissively. In August, it had been decided that communes should consist of about 2,000 households. In practice, however, the initial communes became bigger and bigger. The largest commune, to my knowledge, embraced a whole *xian*[91] though, in general, the size of most communes was roughly equivalent to the old *qu* (or intermediate level between *xiang* and *xian*) with some 5,000 – 11,000 households.[92] As such, they may have cut across the old 'standard marketing areas' and contributed to rural dislocation.[93]

The major problem which came to the fore in the autumn of 1958 was the contradiction between the commune as a do-it-yourself exercise in organisation and as a process whereby the Party organisations mobilised people to undertake tasks for which they were unprepared. The situation was new and cadres could quite easily fall into one of the two extremes of 'commandism' or 'tailism'. In general, however, peasant morale was very high and seemingly quite impossible construction tasks were undertaken. We shall perhaps never know just how spectacular the production increases in the bumper harvest year of 1958 actually were, for statistics continued to be inflated and unreliable. Whatever the shortcomings and errors, and there were many, China had embarked upon a course that has radically altered all existing theories of development.

### The Great Leap Forward: Stage Three (August-December 1958) —Urban People's Communes

The rural people's communes sought to bring some degree of industry to the countryside—in short to make the countryside just a little bit more like the city. Not long after their formation, some experiments were undertaken to achieve the reverse—to make the cities or parts of the cities a little more like the countryside.[94] In the countryside, a major economic problem had been low productivity. In the urban areas, the problem was a rapidly expanding drift of people from the countryside, many of whom were dependent relatives who could not find employment. Since 1949, the urban population had increased from some 58 million (out of 540 million) to 92 million (out of 657 million).[95] In a survey of 15 cities, it was found that from 1953 to 1956 the basic population had increased by 28 per cent, the service population by 5 per cent and the dependent population by 70 per cent.[96] The rural people's communes were seen eventually as a way of stemming the drift to the cities (though initially they were unsuccessful in this respect). The *urban* communes were to rapidly expand the opportunities for city employment.

The model put forward in 1958 was the Zhengzhou urban people's commune.[97] Here a factory became the nucleus of a people's commune which took in the entire surrounding population of 10,500 people. New satellite factories were set up around the core factory to employ dependants and process waste. All commercial and service facilities in the area (formerly run by the city) were now taken over and run by the commune. A 'red and expert' university was set up together with elementary and night schools. The entire neighbourhood was organised into a militia unit and, perhaps most significant, two agricultural production brigades and one sheep milk station were attached. The keynote was 'self-sufficiency'; not that the agricultural land was expected to feed the entire population, but it could at least help. Since a primary aim was to provide full employment for all able-bodied people, the same kind of facilities as could be found in rural communes were organised, though probably with much greater ease, for restaurants, barbers' shops etc. already existed before communisation. With the formation of urban communes, the shift in policy was away from control to activism, and it is significant that the old residents' committees and street officers did not seem to play a large part, at least in this type of urban commune.

The Zhengzhou commune was, of course, just a model and most of the communes formed in late 1958 fell short of its ideals. It had been possible to undertake such an ambitious venture in a city like Zhengzhou because it was in Henan, which had stood at the forefront of the rural communisation movement. Also, funds were available for the relocation of housing where necessary, and furthermore most of the city was not very old with established residential, commercial and industrial districts. Not much, for example, could have been done with Shanghai without colossal expense, amongst other things, because there was just no agricultural land available in many industrial areas. A lot of communes, therefore, were just simply amalgamations of the former network of street administrations which, although useful in generating employment, were nothing like as comprehensive as the Zhengzhou type and in some cities it seemed that no attempts were made to establish communes at all.

Even the model Zhengzhou commune experienced serious problems. The Zhengzhou core factory was technically provincially owned whereas the other property was collectively owned. There were thus conflicting lines of authority. Secondly, there were wide disparities in wage structures; the workers in the core factory were paid at a much higher rate than those in satellite factories and the peasants still operated according to a work-point system. All these problems could, in theory, be solved though it would take time. One could not ask the workers to reduce their wages immediately. There was not, however, to be enough time and the urban commune experiment was to be given up.

### *The Great Leap Forward: Stage Three (August-December 1958) —Other Aspects*

Reforms in urban and rural administration in the autumn of 1958 were accompanied by reforms in industrial management. The demise of 'one-person management' had led to the system of 'responsibility of the factory general manager under the unified leadership of the enterprise Party committee'. In 1958, this was supplemented by a policy known as the 'two participations' and 'triple combination'.[98] The 'two participations' were that of the cadre in manual labour and of the worker in management, and the 'triple combination' consisted of teams of workers, technicians and management cadres which made technical innovations and operational decisions. The idea was that Party committees should confine themselves to overall questions of *politics* (to see that the activity of factories was in harmony with long-term strategies), whereas the factory general manager should now share *operational* decision-making power with these 'triple combination' teams, which would hopefully cut through bureaucracy and implement some kind of functional leadership. Congresses of white- and blue-collar workers had been revived to discuss broad questions, but democracy within the plant was now seen to be better served in a *participatory* sense rather than in the *representative* sense which had failed so miserably in the early 1950s. As far as incentive policy was concerned, piecework was, in general, abolished and the ratio of highest to lowest paid in factories reduced to about three or four to one.[99] Though there was some talk of greater egalitarianism and even of the introduction of a 'free-supply element', I know of no case where this was actually carried out.[100]

Though it is probably true that the army was the area in which Great Leap policies were most strongly resisted, 1958 saw a massive involvement of the army in civilian activities.[101] In 1956, the PLA had contributed some four million workdays to agricultural and industrial production. In 1957, this had risen to 20 million. The planned figure for 1958 was 30 million though, in fact, the figure actually claimed was 59 million (but along with other figures this might be an exaggeration). Whether it was an exaggeration or not, however, some military commanders probably suggested that, in the face of the Taiwan Straits crisis, far too much time was spent on production work. In one city alone, Nanjing, 82 factories were said to have been built with PLA aid.[102] As well as participating in normal civilian economic activities, the army also engaged in its own economy drive, considerably reducing its logistics departments and economising on fuel. The main aim of all this was, of course, not just economic; great stress was laid on maintaining harmonious relations with civilians according to the Yan'an tradition and civilians were urged to voice their grievances against the military. The military was now compelled to pay overdue rent, to return land appropriated during the Korean War, and to compensate for requisitioned property. As a result, 72,400 civilian houses were returned. Within the army itself, the soldiers' committees were strengthened and a movement launched known as 'officers to the ranks'. Every serving officer was required to serve for a time in the ranks as an ordinary private soldier.[103]

## Foreign Policy in 1958

The sheer scope of the reforms undertaken in the autumn of 1958 was quite staggering. They took place in a quasi-wartime situation but, by September, it was fairly clear that the Taiwan Straits crisis would not result in all-out war. On 6 September, Premier Zhou Enlai proposed talks with the United States[104] and, once it was clear that neither America nor China wanted armed confrontation, Khrushchev announced that 'an attack against China [was] tantamount to an attack on the Soviet Union'. One does not know what would have happened to Sino-Soviet relations in 1958 had Khrushchev made the announcement when he visited China. As it stood, however, the Soviet Union seemed only prepared to support China when it had nothing to lose.[105] It was probably with the Soviet Union in mind, therefore, that in October 1958 Mao's statements to the effect that all reactionaries were 'paper tigers' were given great stress.[106] Khrushchev had been seen to bow before the 'paper tiger'.

Back in the old days of the Cold War, it used to be argued in the West that the Great Leap Forward brought to an end the Bandung period in Chinese foreign policy and somehow *caused* China to take a hard line in international affairs. Though, quite clearly, patriotic incentive served the interests of the radical Chinese leadership and the Taiwan crisis gave the Great Leap its sense of urgency, there is ample evidence that, in general, many features of the Bandung period remained[107] and where there was a change in policy it was, more often than not, a reaction to circumstances beyond China's control. For example, China was alarmed at the attempts to bring down the elected Communist government in the Indian state of Kerala, the right-wing reaction in Algeria and the American-backed attempted coup in Indonesia.[108] Sino-Indian relations were very cordial until well into the Great Leap period[109] until Nehru expressed the intention of visiting Lhasa[110] and perhaps attempting to alter the People's Republic's policy towards Tibet. Before long, the Chinese government published a map showing that it had constructed a road, it is said, without the knowledge of the Indian government, across the remote disputed frontier region of Aksai Chin.[111]

What worried the Chinese above all in 1958 was that not only did imperialism seem suddenly more aggressive but that the Soviet Union did not appear to be doing anything about it. In Syria, for example, in September the Soviet government repeated its performance over Taiwan by supporting the left-wing government only after the United States government had declared that it would probably not invoke military action under the 'Eisenhower doctrine'. When the Syrian crisis blew up again in October, the main result of Soviet interference was to drive Syria into the arms of an increasingly anti-Communist Egypt which was no longer the object of Chinese admiration.

Following the American landing in Lebanon in the summer of 1958, the stand of the Soviet Union was hardly decisive and, after the revolution in Iraq on 14 July when it was rumoured that the United States might intervene, all the Soviet Union could do was attempt to convene a conference, which at one time might even have included Taiwan in its capacity as a permanent member of the UN Security Council.[112]

It would be somewhat misleading to suggest, however, that Chinese foreign policy in 1958 was completely reactive. It must surely be partly due to the reaffirmation of the concept of people's war that China was the first major power to grant recognition to the Algerian Provisional Government proclaimed by the FLN in the autumn[113] and to express support for the victories of Fidel Castro in Cuba. Here the Soviet Union remained cautious, for Castro's communist credentials were still unproven.[114]

It would perhaps be wrong also to suggest that the implementation of Khrushchev's policy of 'peaceful coexistence' had, by 1958, resulted in a complete sell-out to the United States. The truth of the matter was that Soviet eyes were firmly riveted on Berlin with the aim of eliminating it as a possible source of war. Though Soviet pressure on Berlin was, in the long run, linked to the policy of 'peaceful coexistence' and 'peaceful competition' with the United States, Khrushchev was still bold enough to offer the Western powers a six-month ultimatum in November 1958. What the Chinese felt to be the real Soviet sell-out was yet to come.

### The Wuchang Plenum (28 November to 19 December 1958) and its Aftermath

After the 'high tide' of the Great Leap Forward in the summer and autumn of 1958, a number of serious problems had been encountered. One of the aims of the Leap had been to deal with rural underemployment. It had perhaps been too successful in that, by September, China was plagued by a labour shortage.[115] At the same time, inexperience occasionally resulted in a waste of labour power and cadres initiating construction tasks which later proved worthless. There were sometimes severe dislocations in the supply and marketing network now that power was decentralised to commune level[116] and, once again, cases of excessive 'commandism' were noted. Occasionally richer collectives had refused to combine with poorer ones and friction had resulted. Perhaps the most serious problems resulted from the very enthusiasm for the Leap itself. Inflated statistics of grain production led to a consumption boom in late 1958 and the belief that the problem of food supply had been solved. Overconfidence caused many communes to believe they could implement immediately a ten-year plan to reduce the area sown in grain by 30 per cent.[117]

By November, it was quite evident to most members of the Party leadership that urgent corrective measures were necessary. These were put forward at a conference in Zhengzhou in November and at the Sixth (Wuchang) Plenum in December. In his speech to that plenum, Mao admitted that a number of problems had arisen with the formation of communes and that cadres had exaggerated production statistics.[118] He felt, however, that only some 1 to 5 per cent of cadres were guilty of violating discipline and had resorted to 'commandism'. In his view, the original aim 'basically to transform the country within three years' was overoptimistic. He therefore cautioned cadres not to be in so much of a hurry. At the same time, Mao urged that they should devote more time not only to practical investigation but also to the study of economics and dialectics. He firmly refuted the idea that pockets of communism should develop in socialist society but not that communist elements should be incorporated into socialist policy. Though he welcomed changes in the orientation of the army in 1958, he acknowledged that there was a tendency to disregard military training. Mao's speech to the Wuchang Plenum was, therefore, a cautious appeal for a period of consolidation. In no way, however, did he call for the abandonment of the Great Leap. The new stress on the principles of Yan'an was welcomed and the shortcomings had by no means negated the growth in mass enthusiasm which promised even more spectacular results in the future.

There has been much debate as to whether everyone in the Party leadership shared Mao's view of the situation in the aftermath of the Wuchang Plenum and, indeed, just how far Mao was prepared to go in curbing excesses. On the one hand, Mao was optimistic about a new round of the Great Leap Forward in 1959. For all the talk about realistic targeting, the Wuchang targets were even higher than the official targets for 1958. It was anticipated, for example, that grain production could increase to 525 million tonnes and steel to 18 million tonnes.[119] Mao, moreover, welcomed the splits which had occurred in the leadership of half the provinces in 1958[120] (for only by struggle could one advance to a new stage of unity). On the other hand, Mao seemed genuinely to have been in agreement with the moderate approach to policy implementation laid down at Wuchang. He obviously could not but respond to the reports of investigation teams which had gone to the countryside in the aftermath of the Zhengzhou meeting. These teams discovered massive problems. Decentralisation had sometimes resulted in extreme 'localism' and 'departmentalism': commune planning had broken down and many communes operated on a day-to-day basis. The mess hall experiment had resulted in much peasant dissatisfaction. The 'communist style' which had been criticised at Wuchang still continued into the new year and it seemed that the curbs prescribed by Wuchang did not go far enough.[121]

In such a situation, Mao was to describe himself as a 'middle of the roader'.[122] At a policy level, he affirmed the ideals of the Great Leap but, at an operational level, he supported conservative measures to restore order. It was not always easy, however, to make the distinction between general policy and specific operations. In opposing the position of Anhui first secretary Zeng Xisheng who felt that keeping targets low was a form of 'right opportunism',[123] Mao obviously thought he was dealing with an operational matter. But in early February, when he said that the 'cutting back' of the preceding two months should come to an end and that one should once again 'go all out',[124] he was obviously raising an issue of major policy. Mao's position, and attitudes in general, therefore, were marked by considerable ambivalence. The press talked about observing objective economic laws independent of human will and also of the need to mobilise mass enthusiasm. It spoke both of cold scientific analysis and maintaining revolutionary fervour. It attempted, moreover, to combine the attack on 'blind optimism' and 'right conservatism'. One would have had to be a superb dialectician to sort out so many contradictions.

But overall, the first two thirds of 1959 were to see a general drift to the right both in policy and operations. Not long after Wuchang, limits were imposed on horizontal Party mobilisation. Far greater powers were placed in the hands of formal administrative structures (such as commune management committees). The 'free supply' element in payment became less and less important. Dislocations in the supply and marketing network were dealt with by the partial revival of free markets.[125] Furthermore, there was endorsed once again the old (Soviet model) notion of no fundamental rural reorganisation before adequate mechanisation had been achieved,[126] but what that might have meant after the events of 1958 escapes me.

At another conference in Zhengzhou in late February and early March, attempts were made to sort out the ownership levels within the communes. The Wuchang Plenum had established the production brigade as the basic unit of account but its gains and losses were still pooled in the commune as a whole. Now the brigade became an independent unit of ownership with the right to allocate its own resources.[127] In effect, this meant that the old property status of the higher-stage collective was restored and the commune returned property formerly owned by the collective. Mao, it seems, endorsed this change and noted that accounting at commune level usually only comprised some 10 – 30 per cent of the total, with the bulk of economic activity being run at brigade level. In opposing excessive accumulation targets decided on at commune level, Mao adopted a cautious position in favour of a federal commune structure which would only be completely unified after several years.[128] He supported, therefore, the decentralisation of the unit of account to brigade or even team level,[129] though one should bear in mind that, in early 1959, when there was an average of some 5,000 households in the commune, the team was sometimes as big as the old higher-stage collective.

Once the relationship between the various components of the commune had been decided upon, it became possible to strengthen planning in the rural sector. Relationships both between communes and within communes were to be regulated by means of contracts and attempts were made to work out a system of responsibility at all levels.[130] This new stress on tightening up the planning system was reflected at a national level in the new policy of 'taking the whole country as a co-ordinated chess game'.[131] This policy, attributed to Mao, called for the replacement of dual planning by a single national plan and for far greater centralisation. Speaking on the subject, Chen Yun suggested that only when a national industrial complex had been built could one set up regional industrial complexes and only when one had set up regional industrial complexes could one set up provincial industrial complexes.[132] As such, Chen's comments constituted a denunciation of the whole policy of 'decentralisation II' which had been pursued since the Third Plenum in November 1957.

As policies drifted to the right, one would have imagined that the grandiose targets approved by the Wuchang Plenum would be scaled down. At an enlarged Politburo conference in Shanghai in late March, however, the majority resisted such a move, revealing once again the extraordinary ambivalence in policy during this period.[133] Mao, it seems, supported the majority though was now even more critical of unrealistic exaggeration. This was the theme of a letter in late April[134] which was apparently resisted by Sichuan First Secretary Li Jingquan who accused Mao of 'blowing a cold wind' whilst 'right opportunism' was rife at all levels in the Party.[135] Was Mao himself considered to be a 'right opportunist'? Alas, we cannot be sure since for every cautious statement of the chairman there was another which proclaimed adherence to the impending revival of the Leap.

Though the position of Mao and other Party leaders was ambiguous, there was no doubt that the Soviet leadership, exasperated by claims for the Leap, was quite pleased with what was happening. In early 1959, therefore, relations between China and the Soviet Union began to improve. Khrushchev made available to China more industrial aid[136] and soon Defence Minister Peng Dehuai was to go on a tour of Eastern Europe where he found Party leaders most congenial. But just as domestically there was a disjunction between operational measures designed to clear up problems created by the Leap and a policy commitment to the ideals of 1958, so in relations with the Soviet Union there was a disjunction between better diplomatic relations and the Chinese commitment to its new form of social organisation. At the Twenty-first Congress of the CPSU, in January 1959, Khrushchev insisted that all socialist states would attain communism more or less simultaneously.[137] This was, of course, perfectly in accord with the Chinese line and with that of Mao himself.[138] Nevertheless, though Mao had rejected the notion of pockets of communism, he presumably did not accept the implication of Khrushchev's remarks that the commune was no better than the Soviet *kolkhoz*. Nor would he have accepted another Khrushchevian implication that socialist states could not slip backwards. After the Seventh Plenum approved his retirement in April 1959 from the state chairmanship,[139] Mao announced that he wished to devote more of his time to ideological issues. This presumably meant that he wished to examine the roots of the ideological divergence with the Soviet Union. Now that Khrushchev had begun to make comments about internal Chinese affairs, Mao came gradually to see those affairs in a different light. He was prepared, it seems, to accept and endorse all kinds of criticism of the Leap, provided that it did not come from Khrushchev or anyone Mao considered to be his spokesman. It was, I believe, considerations of this kind which lay behind the crisis which was to erupt in the summer of 1959 and which will be the subject of the next chapter.

### The Tibetan Rebellion (March 1959)

Though, in some national minority areas, exasperation with the previous gradualist policy and the demands for independence made by 'rightists' during the hundred flowers movement resulted in radical policies in 1957–8,[140] Tibet remained relatively untouched.[141] In some minority areas, during the Great Leap, communes were formed and cadres strove to bring about a situation where minority nationalities 'caught up' with Han areas in three to five years.[142] But in Tibet the old system of monastic serfdom was still supreme. In his speech 'On the Correct Handling . . .', Mao had expressly stated that no changes should take place in Tibet during the Second Five Year Plan (up to 1962) and it was an open question as to whether they should take place in the Third (up to 1967).[143] Little was done during the most radical period of the Great Leap in 1958, and it is strange, therefore, that a major crisis did not occur in Tibet until policies of consolidation had been introduced in early 1959. The timing of the Tibetan rebellion of March 1959, in my opinion, has less to do with any excesses of the Leap than to a changing international environment. It has been reported that during the Taiwan Straits crisis in the second half of 1958 arms were dropped to dissident elements in Loka,[144] though this has not been confirmed. What *The Pentagon Papers* tell us, however, is that a CIA-run air company had made overflights of Tibet during that period[145] and the United States was definitely interested in the area. We have seen also that, in April 1958, Nehru had expressed a determination to involve himself in China's Tibetan policy and that, by the end of the year, Sino-Indian relations had deteriorated considerably. At the turn of the year, Nehru and Zhou Enlai exchanged notes on the Aksai Chin highway, each claiming it was in their own territory[146] and it was in this tense atmosphere that the Tibetan rebels chose to act.

The rebellion of March 1959 was put down quite rapidly[147] by Chinese troops and the Dalai Lama fled to India. He immediately issued a stream of condemnatory speeches. Perhaps the strongest of these, on 30 June, denounced every act of the Beijing government towards Tibet from the 1951 agreement onwards. The Dalai Lama now declared that he would no longer attempt to deal with China directly but only through a third power (India?).[148] The Chinese response to this was to publish his charges alongside the extravagant praise the Dalai Lama had lavished on Beijing's policies since 1951. It was perhaps ironical that the source of all Tibet's ills should be assigned to Mao Zedong whose deeds the Dalai Lama had, less than five years previously, compared with the Lord Brahma, creator of the world.[149] The Dalai Lama seemed to have burned his boats and thrown in his lot with India but was nevertheless recognised in Beijing as Tibet's titular head and member of the Standing Committee of China's National People's Congress until December 1964.

Upon the Dalai Lama's departure, the State Council moved, on 28 March, to abolish the traditional government (the *Kashag*) and transfer power to the Preparatory Committee for the Tibet Autonomous Region.[150] This body had been set up in 1955 with the eventual aim of replacing the *Kashag*,[151] though it is unlikely whether anyone at that time envisaged that it might do so as early as 1959. Though the titular head of the committee remained the Dalai Lama, its effective head was now to be the Banqen Erdini who celebrated his installation by reciting *sutras* with two living Buddhas.[152] Hardly a radical act to commence a new stage in Tibet's history!

Nevertheless, the policies to be pursued by the new government were, by Tibetan standards, highly revolutionary. While the fighting was still going on, the PLA spread the slogan of 'land to the tiller' and the first 'law and order groups', which were formed under PLA auspices to round up rebels, were expanded into peasant associations.[153] Following the first session of the new government in April, the Banqen Erdini left for Beijing and, on his return in July, the second session approved a series of measures for 'democratic reform'. The operative slogan was *'sanfan shuangjian'* ('three abolitions and two reductions'). The 'abolitions' here referred to rebellion, forced labour and personal servitude and the 'reductions' to land rent and interest. The land of all rebels was confiscated and the crops handed over to the tillers. The land of other nobles was made subject to rent restrictions and later compulsory purchase.[154]

The abolition of serfdom was carried through rapidly with many of the techniques of the old land reform. Nobles implicated in the rebellion were made to stand with heads bowed and hear the former serfs 'speak their bitterness'.[155] As in land reform, the aim was to raise the level of class consciousness but here there were many more problems. During the Civil War, work-teams and peasant associations did not have to contend with peasants anxious to protect their *karma*. The price of overthrowing a Tibetan lord or abbot was felt to be reincarnation as a lower being.

The task of education was perhaps made easier once the corruption of the monastic élite was revealed. One might have reverence for a 'living Buddha' who claimed to have chosen to remain in the world of men rather than advance to Nirvana, but not after one had heard that he had purchased his title of 'living Buddha' from the *Kashag*.[156] One might acquire a different view of monastic hierarchy once the leadership of monasteries became democratised.[157] With the confiscation of monastic lands, it was surely only a matter of time before the number of monks that each monastery could support would decrease.

Much ink has been spilled on the events in Tibet in 1959. It is probably true that large numbers of Han were moved into the area but it is a peculiar twisting of the word to call it 'genocide'.[158] It is probably true that the abolition of serfdom and the suppression of rebellion were occasionally brutal, but this should occasion no shocked surprise. It is true also that sporadic fighting was to continue for many years, but fighting in Tibet, especially where the Khambas were concerned, had gone on for decades, whatever the government in Lhasa. It might perhaps be argued that the PLA did not have the right to take the action it did in March-April 1959, and many jurists have belaboured precisely that point, but then the *Kashag*, and for that matter the Indian government, had accepted the authority of Beijing over Tibet.[159] Legal issues aside, it may be said that no nation has the right to impose its will over another but then one must establish an adequate non-legal definition of 'nation'. Finally, I suppose, the debate must turn on questions of actual and perceived interest and such a debate, though important, is endless.

In conclusion, I can only make three points. First, it is the opinion of most travellers to Tibet, in the period after 1959, that the material lot of ordinary Tibetans has improved considerably;[160] the travellers, of course, cannot speak for the Tibetan's *karma*. Secondly, events in Tibet extinguished what was left of the *entente* between China and India though border disagreements had already eroded much of the former goodwill. In subsequent years, the idea of Indian non-alignment was to appear highly questionable and to have meaning only in the sense of India's attempts to play off the United States against the Soviet Union. India's China policy was to remain implacably hostile until the late 1970s. Thirdly, there was a sharp disjunction between the radical moves undertaken in Tibet after March 1959 and the policies of consolidation pursued in the rest of China.

## Conclusion

By the spring and summer of 1959, China's countryside had undergone the most profound changes yet. These changes had given rise to considerable disagreement about the preferred organisation and size of the communes and whether the 1958 policy of mass mobilisation was to be resumed. There had been a retreat from the optimistic policies of August 1958, but, even in the atmosphere of consolidation of early 1959, it seemed impossible to go back on the idea of a communal self-reliant structure in the Chinese countryside. Some leaders were not tardy in pointing out that people's communes need not necessarily be self-reliant[161] but, whatever happened, the old idea of an urban-oriented Soviet-style developmental strategy could probably never be restored.

The Great Leap Forward had caused much dislocation and chaos but some might argue that this was a small price to pay when one takes the longer perspective, since tremendous creative potential had been released. Small-scale plants had mushroomed. The reactivation of the *minban* concept of education had resulted in a phenomenal rise in the number of people striving to raise themselves from a state of illiteracy. The notion of 'part-work and part-study' had called into question developmental strategies which gave primacy to formal academic education. The explosion of job opportunities in the cities had not meant that the problem of rural-urban drift had been solved, but the communal strategy of transferring industry to the countryside offered a glimpse of an eventual solution. There had been supply difficulties due to bad communications between communes and between cities and countryside, but the new egalitarian ethos in the countryside meant that it would be unlikely that, in the immediate future, the former situation would recur in which there were great variations of wealth within the same marketing area.

Economists, both Chinese and Western, will no doubt continue to argue at great length about the positive and negative features of the policies pursued in 1958. Political scientists also will debate as to whether the origins of what later became known as the 'two-line struggle' might be found in the events of that time. In the sense that different policy groups coalesced around Mao Zedong and Liu Shaoqi, they will find insufficient evidence. In the sense, however, that attitude towards economic policy had begun to be seen as a source of antagonism, then one can see a number of policy positions which could lead later to bitter struggle. At the Third Plenum, Chen Yun had been demoted for advocating a mixture of central control and 'decentralisation I'. He had, however, not been denounced and was able to repeat his demands in early 1959. In early 1958, however, opposition to Great Leap strategies on the part of provincial leaders was seen as a manifestation of antagonism. Finally, in late 1959, what appeared to be an endorsement of Khrushchev's negative assessment of the people's communes was to see the demise of a very senior leader. The next chapter will note the beginnings of a polarisation which was to eventuate in the Cultural Revolution. In early 1959, however, as far as intra-Politburo affairs were concerned, contradictions were still 'among the people'.

## NOTES

1. Mao Zedong, 7 October 1957, *JPRS*, 1974, p. 75.
2. Mao Zedong, 27 February 1957, *SW* V, p 395.
3. Teiwes, 1979, p. 362 and pp. 379–83. Teiwes notes, however, that the major deviation was seen as organisational indiscipline.
4. URI, 1971, pp. 109–10.
5. The revised plan, dated 22 October 1957, is in Chao, 1963, pp. 157–79. There were, in fact, few differences between this and the 1956 text. On the importance of the plenum, see Schurmann, 1966, pp. 195–205; Chang, 1975, pp. 38–40 and 55.
6. Teiwes, 1979, pp. 342–6.
7. Zagoria, 1966, p. 378.
8. Clark, 1967, pp. 97–8.
9. Gittings, 1967, p. 228.
10. Speech to Chinese students in Moscow, 17 November 1957, *CB* 534, 12 November 1958, p. 12. This was only Mao's second trip abroad.
11. Clark, 1967, pp. 95–8.
12. See Gittings, 1968, p. 70.
13. Zagoria, 1966, p. 178.
14. Text in Hudson, Lowenthal and MacFarquhar, 1961, pp. 46–54. See the highly imaginative discussion in Crankshaw, 1965.
15. Schurmann, 1966, p.203. Chang (1975, pp. 65–6), however, believes that Mao's failure to secure further Soviet credits in November 1957 was a factor in the new stress on self-reliance.
16. For a discussion of the Chinese meaning of the terms 'heavy' and 'light' industry, see Donnithorne, 1967, pp. 140–1; Schurmann, 1966, p. 202.
17. The following discussion is taken from Schurmann, 1966, pp. 202–10; Chang, 1975, pp. 55–61.
18. Vogel, 1971, p. 225.

19. SC, in *SCMP* 1665, 5 December 1957, pp. 4–5.

20. Chang, 1975, pp. 59–61. This was not formalised until September 1958.

21. Schurmann, 1966, p. 209.

22. Ibid., p. 210; Chang, 1975, pp. 63–4; Mao Zedong, 20 March 1958; Schram, 1974, p. 106.

23. Teiwes, 1966; Teiwes, 1979, pp. 349–66.

24. Chang, 1975, pp. 40–6, 81–2.

25. *SCMP* 1734, 19 March 1958, pp. 1–4.

26. CCPCC, 24 September 1957, URI, 1971, pp. 517–22.

27. Schurmann, 1966, p. 466.

28. Chang, 1975, p. 80.

29. Schurmann, 1966, pp. 466–7.

30. Referred to in *CB* 892, 21 October 1969, p. 1.

31. See Mao's speeches at the conference, 11 and 13 January 1958, *JPRS*, 1974, pp. 77–84.

32. Mao Zedong, 19 February 1958, *CB* 892, 21 October 1969, pp. 1–14.

33. *SCMP* 1612, 18 September 1957, pp. 14 and 16.

34. The following is based on H. Hinton, 1966, pp. 263–70. The Guomindang blockade had been in existence since 1949.

35. Kallgren, 1963, p. 38.

36. Mao Zedong, May 1958, *JPRS*, 1974, p. 121.

37. Mao Zedong, November 1958, ibid., p. 129.

38. Mao Zedong, 19 December 1958, ibid., p. 143.

39. Mao Zedong, 30 November 1958, ibid., p. 136. Mao was referring specifically to the summer crisis.

40. Vogel, 1971, p. 231.

41. *SCMP* 1682, 2 January 1958, p. 27.

42. CCPCC and SC, 24 September 1957, URI, 1971, pp. 517–22.

43. Vogel (1971, p. 231) notes that this provision was often disregarded.

44. Ibid., pp. 228–9.

45. The following is taken from ibid., pp. 233–5.

46. The late 1957 NPAD target for South China was six tonnes/hectare by 1967.

47. The famous Daqing oilfield dates from this time. See PFLP, 1972 (b).

48. Vogel, 1971, p. 235.

49. Mao Zedong, 23 July 1959, URI, 1968 (a), p. 25.

50. Ibid.; Mao Zedong, 19 December 1958, *JPRS*, 1974, p. 147; Mao Zedong, 1959, *JPRS*, 1974, p. 223.

51. Vogel, 1971, p. 236.

52. Inaugurated at the Nanning conference. See Mao Zedong, 19 December 1958, *JPRS*, 1974, p. 141.

53. Vogel, 1971, p. 237.

54. Mao Zedong, 20 March 1958, Schram, 1974, p. 104.

55. Vogel, 1971, p. 238.

56. Ibid., p. 237.

57. See ibid., pp. 241–3.

58. Mao Zedong, 20 March 1958, Schram, 1974, p. 104.

59. PFLP, 1958, p. 61; Liu, Vol. III, 1968, p. 36.

60. Mao Zedong, 19 February 1958, *CB* 892, 21 October 1969, p. 13.

61. Chang, 1975, pp. 78–9.

62. CCPCC, 25 May 1958, URI, 1971, p. 111. See also Chang, 1975, pp. 67 and 77.

63. *RMRB*, 5 May 1958, p. 1.

64. See URI, 1968 (a), p. 202; Garthoff, 1966, p. 90.

65. Mao Zedong, 28 June 1958, *Chinese Law and Government*, Vol. I, No. 4, Winter 1968–9, p. 19.

66. Mao Zedong, 20 March 1958, Schram, 1974, p. 111.

67. *SCMP* 1822, 30 June 1958, p. 1.

68. Zhu De, *CB* 514, 6 August 1958, pp. 1–2.

69. Hsieh, 1962, p. 122.

70. H. Hinton, 1966, p. 266; Gittings, 1967, p. 230; Clark, 1967, p. 100.

71. URI, 1968 (a), p. 202. See also the discussion in Solomon, 1971, pp. 386–7. Teiwes (1979, pp. 423–8), however, thinks that military issues were not decisive in the Peng Dehuai case.

72. H. Hinton, 1966, pp. 266–7; Clark, 1967, p. 100.

73. Schurmann, 1966, p. 478.

74. Gittings, 1967, pp. 207–8.

75. Cited in ibid., p. 211.

76. *SCMP* 1856, 18 September 1958, pp. 17–19.

77. See Mao Zedong, 19 December 1958, *JPRS*, 1974, p. 140 (on the April date). Chang (1975, p. 84) believes that the first communes did not appear until after the Zhengzhou meeting. On the amalgamation of collectives, see ibid., pp. 75–6.

78. Bowie and Fairbank, 1965, pp. 463–70; Selden, 1979, pp. 397–401.

79. Schurmann, 1966, p. 473.

80. Mao Zedong, 23 July 1959, *Chinese Law and Government*, Vol. I. No. 4, Winter 1968–9, p. 41.

81. CCPCC, 29 August 1958, URI, 1971, pp. 299–304; Selden, 1979, pp. 401–5.

82. According to Chen Boda, 1 July 1958, Bowie and Fairbank, 1965, p. 453.

83. Schurmann, 1966, pp. 477–8. For a different view, see Chang, 1975, p. 83.

84. CCPCC, 29 August 1958, Bowie and Fairbank, 1965, pp. 454–6.

85. This is not to say that there was much official support for the idea that pockets of communism had already arrived. See Xu Liqun, Bowie and Fairbank, 1965, pp. 479–83.

86. Chang, 1975, pp. 98–101.

87. *RMRB*, 13 October 1958, p. 7.

88. Wu Lengxi, *Chinese Law and Government*, Vol. II, No. 4, winter 1969–70, pp. 74–5.

89. Ibid., pp. 84–5; *RMRB*, 13 October 1958, p. 7.

90. Vogel, 1971, p. 251.

91. Ibid., p. 248. This was Panyu *xian* in Guangdong province; population 276,358.

92. Chang, 1975, pp. 97–8. The average was 4,600 household, ranging from 1,400 in Guizhou to over 11,000 in suburban Beijing and Shanghai.

93. Skinner, 1965, Part III.

94. See Salaff, 1967.

95. Schurmann, 1966, p. 381.

96. Ibid., pp. 381–2.

97. The following description is taken from ibid., pp. 387–91; Salaff, 1967; Selden, 1971, pp. 454–64.

98. Andors, 1971, pp. 406–7.

99. Ibid., p. 409.

100. See the various articles collected and translated in *JPRS* 1337–N, 12 March 1959.

101. The following is taken from Gittings, 1967, pp. 181–95.

102. Ibid., p. 183.

103. Chen Zaidao, *CB* 579, 25 May 1959, pp. 5–8.

104. Zhou Enlai, 6 September 1958, *SCMP* 1851, 11 September 1958, p. 2.

105. People's Republic of China spokesman, 1 September 1963, Garthoff, 1966, p. 233.

106. *CB* 534, 12 November 1958, pp. 1–14.

107. H. Hinton, 1966, p. 34.

108. Ibid.
109. Zhou Enlai, 10 February 1958, Bowie and Fairbank, 1965, pp. 401–10.
110. Patterson, 1963, pp. 159–60.
111. On the Aksai Chin road, see Maxwell, 1972, pp. 82–4.
112. H. Hinton, 1966, pp. 36–7.
113. *SCMP* 1861, 22 September 1958, p. 42.
114. H. Hinton, 1966, p. 38. China had, however, no illusions about Castro being a Communist at that time.
115. CCPCC, 10 December 1958, URI, 1971, p. 139.
116. Skinner, 1965, Part III.
117. Walker, 1968, pp. 444–5.
118. Mao Zedong, 19 December 1958, *JPRS*, 1974, pp. 140–8.
119. See Chang, 1975, p. 104.
120. Mao Zedong, 19 December 1958, *JPRS*, 1974, p. 146.
121. Chang, 1975, p. 105.
122. Mao Zedong, 23 July 1959, URI, 1968 (a), p. 23.
123. Mao Zedong, 19 December 1958, *JPRS*, 1974, p. 142.
124. Mao Zedong, 2 February 1959, ibid., p. 151.
125. *SCMP* 2055, 15 July 1959, p. 19.
126. Xie Yinqi, ibid. 1986, 6 April 1959, p. 3.
127. Chang, 1975, p. 105. See also Zhou Enlai, 26 August 1959, *PR* 35, 1 September 1959, pp. 13–14.
128. Mao Zedong, 21 February 1959, *JPRS*, 1974, pp. 160–1.
129. Mao Zedong, 15 March 1959, ibid., p. 167.
130. *RMRB*, 17 February 1959, p. 1.
131. Ibid., 24 February 1959, p.1. For Mao's comments, see Mao Zedong, 21 February 1959, *JPRS*, 1974, p. 162.
132. Chen Yun, *RMRB*, 1 March 1959, pp. 1–2.
133. Teiwes, 1979, p. 393.
134. Mao Zedong, 29 April 1959, *JPRS*, 1974, pp. 170–2.
135. Teiwes, 1979, p. 394.
136. Zagoria, 1966, p. 128.
137. Ibid., p. 127.
138. Mao Zedong, 19 December 1958, *JPRS*, 1974, p. 145.
139. The communiqué noted that a decision had been reached on candidates for leading posts in state organs. CCPCC, 2–5 April 1959, URI, 1971, pp. 149–50.
140. Dreyer, 1968, pp. 98–9.
141. See Strong, 1965, Chapters III and IV.
142. Dreyer, 1968, p. 99.
143. Mao Zedong, 27 February 1957, *SW* V, p. 406.
144. Strong, 1965, p. 67.
145. Gravel edition, Vol. II, pp. 648–9.
146. See the collection of documents in PFLP, 1962 (a).
147. Strong, 1965, pp. 73–81.
148. Ibid., p. 71.
149. Ibid., p. 65.
150. SC in URI, 1968 (c), pp. 357–8.
151. Adopted 9 March 1955, URI, 1968 (c), pp. 141–3. It was formally established in April 1956, ibid, pp. 144–55.
152. Strong, 1965, p. 77.
153. Ibid., p. 81.
154. Ibid., pp. 83–4. See also Ngapoi Ngawang-Jigmi, URI 1968 (c), pp. 394–403.
155. Strong, 1965, pp. 168–90.

156. Ibid., p. 235.

157. Ngapoi Ngawang-Jigmi, URI, 1968 (c), pp. 394–403.

158. International Commission of Jurists, 1960, pp. 11–63.

159. As late as 7 September 1958, Nehru told the Indian Parliament: 'so far as I know, there is not one country in the world which recognised the independence of Tibet; we definitely have not', cited in Wilson, 1966, p. 115.

160. See e.g. Gelder, 1964.

161. *SCMP* 1939, 22 January 1959, pp. 29–30.

# IX

# THE CASE OF PENG DEHUAI
# AND THE BRIEF REVIVAL OF
# THE GREAT LEAP
## (1959 – 1960)

The preceding chapter noted the ambiguity in the statements of senior Chinese leaders in early 1959. On the one hand, there was a desire to rectify the problems caused by the Great Leap in 1958 and, on the other, a consistent affirmation of the need for a new round of the Great Leap in 1959. Such a situation was to give rise to an intense debate on developmental strategy. At the centre of that debate was Defence Minister Peng Dehuai. In the subsequent Cultural Revolution, Peng was accused of a host of 'crimes' including maintaining relations with Nikita Khrushchev who regarded the Great Leap as a utopian adventure.[1] Some two years after the death of Mao, however, it was alleged that Peng's position was the proper response to the unrealistic escalation of targets.[2] Amongst Western scholars, the case of Peng Dehuai has given rise to many and varied interpretations. Some accounts focus on Peng's military élitism, seeing Peng as a military technocrat who consistently opposed the reintegration of the PLA in society. Others, however, regard military issues as only secondary since very little was done in subsequent years to impart any substance to the charge that Peng was the representative of a 'bourgeois military line'.[3] Some accounts make much of Peng's alleged desire to maintain the Soviet alliance for the sake of military protection. Others, however, reject this view and prefer to discuss Peng's criticism of the Great Leap Forward. Indeed, there is much more material on this last aspect than on any other, though it is possible to find evidence to support any of the above interpretations.

This chapter will give a chronological account of the Peng Dehuai case and will attempt to integrate it with some of the different interpretations. It will note that the removal of Peng cleared the way for a partial revival of the Great Leap policies. These, however, took place in a deteriorating economic situation and the Leap was soon to collapse. But was this collapse due to the mistakes of 1958, because of 'sabotage' on the part of senior Party leaders, or because of bad climatic conditions? To what extent, moreover, was it due to the Sino-Soviet dispute which reached a new intensity after the dismissal of Peng and resulted in the cancellation of Soviet economic assistance?

## The Case of Peng Dehuai

Like most Chinese leaders, Peng Dehuai undertook tours of inspection in the autumn of 1958 to evaluate the progress of the Great Leap and probably attended the Wuchang Plenum for a short time in late November and early December. The fact that he was absent from most of the discussions, however, does not suggest that at that stage he was particularly influential in criticising the Leap.[4]

In the period immediately following the plenum, articles began to appear in the press criticising those who sought to set up 'independent kingdoms' of the Gao Gang type[5] and people were warned not to look after their own sphere of interest at the expense of the whole.[6] Though such cases of 'departmentalism' might have included the advocates of a more independent army, the main object of criticism might just as well have been the activities of regional leaders who were tardy in taking the whole country as a 'co-ordinated chess game'. After January, the Minister of Public Security, Luo Ruiqing, began to relinquish some of his duties, in preparation, it may be argued, for appointment to a senior position in the PLA; though one might also surmise that his actions were designed to give himself more time to concentrate on problems of public security which had arisen during the Leap.[7] Some time in early 1959, key personnel changes also occurred in the PLA, especially in the Beijing Military Region. This could have been brought about in order to rid sensitive commands of those who sought greater army independence but there is no evidence that they were necessarily aimed at weakening the position of Peng Dehuai. In April, Peng was conspicuously absent from the meeting of the National People's Congress which endorsed the new state leadership. This could have signified a fall from power or simply that Peng was too busy preparing for a visit to the Soviet Union and East European countries.

On the basis of the above evidence, Simmonds speculates that Peng was being sent out of the country to prepare for his removal.[8] Thus, he left China on 24 April, before the newly elected National Defence Council met under the new state chairman, Liu Shaoqi. At the same time, Vice-Foreign Minister Zhang Wentian (later criticised as Peng's accomplice) also went to Eastern Europe, in his capacity as Chinese observer at meetings of the Warsaw Pact, and Luo Ruiqing (later to replace Huang Kecheng as chief-of-staff) was promoted to vice-premier.

While the value of such speculation is questionable, one cannot deny the significance of Peng's overseas trip. It is almost certain that one of the assignments given to Peng was to explain to Khrushchev why the enlarged meeting of the Military Commission the previous summer had rejected the Soviet plans for a joint Sino-Soviet defence arrangement. In the light of Peng's commission, senior Party leaders within China could not but be suspicious about the apparent warmth of the reception Peng received in the Warsaw Pact countries, and in particular the cordiality between Khrushchev and Peng at their meeting in Albania. At that time, Khrushchev was trying to coerce a recalcitrant Albania and the last thing most leaders in China wanted was any suggestion of Chinese endorsement of Khrushchev's position. The condemnation of Peng's activities in Albania, published during the Cultural Revolution, was both crude and pithy:

> He [Peng] informed bald-headed Khrushchev of the shortcomings of the Great Leap Forward and the latter encouraged the former to go home and oppose Chairman Mao.[9]

One suspects that the above quote misses some of the subtlety of Peng's position but, whether it were substantially true or not, we do know that many of China's leaders had good cause to be dissatisfied with Peng's tour. On 20 June, less than one week after his return, the Soviet Union cancelled the agreement on new technology for national defence.[10] This agreement, which was said to have involved the principle of nulcear sharing, was highly important and its cancellation might have been related to a possible Soviet-American understanding on halting nuclear proliferation, whereby the United States would resist West Germany's demand for nuclear weapons if the Soviet Union did the same with China.[11] If that interpretation is correct, it could surely not have been perceived by the Chinese leadership in June 1959. A more likely Chinese interpretation of the cancellation, therefore, was that Khrushchev was attempting to do to China precisely what he was trying to do to Albania —to force that country back into the Soviet-controlled bloc. To some Chinese leaders, one would surmise, Peng had, at best, failed to restrain Khrushchev and, at worst, was in league with him.

Peng returned to China on 13 June to find that the Chinese leadership was embarking on one of its periodic series of inspection tours to assess the situation in the wake of the curbs applied to the Great Leap. It is possible that Peng himself undertook an inspection tour of the north-west at that time.[12] We do not know what he discovered but it was probably no different from that of many other leaders. There were still tremendous problems in rural organisation and the general mood of the Party seemed opposed to further radicalisation. In June, the influential Tao Zhu suggested that people should be bolder in their discussions of the short-comings of the Great Leap even if nine-tenths of Great Leap policies had been correct.[13] At the same time, Wu Han, the deputy mayor of Beijing (a confidant, it is said, of Peng Zhen), wrote a number of articles which purported to be discussions of history but which could be read as criticisms of the Great Leap.[14] Even Mao himself was on record as criticising many Great Leap developments, though he seemed to believe that most problems associated with the communes had been solved by April.[15]

In such an atmosphere, an enlarged Politburo conference met at Lushan to assess the results of its members' inspection tours. Here, on 14 July, Peng offered his criticism of the Great Leap strategy in the form of a letter of opinion:

> Petty bourgeois fanaticism causes us easily to commit 'left' errors. In the course of the Great Leap Forward of 1958, I, like many comrades, was led astray by its achievements and the ardour of the mass movement. 'Left' tendencies developed to an appreciable extent. All the time, one wanted to leap into communism in one bound. The idea of taking the lead took possession of our minds and we pushed to the back of our minds the Mass Line and the style of seeking truth from facts which had been formulated by the Party over a long period. In our method of reasoning, we often confused strategic dispositions with concrete operational measures, long-term policies with the minor collective.[16]

Though forthright, Peng's letter was, in many respects, quite cautious. What he specifically repudiated were the mistakes made in 1958 before the Wuchang Plenum. He was apparently quite happy with current Party policy. It was possible, therefore, that Peng's comments could have been accepted under the rules of inner-Party democracy, as Tao Zhu's seem to have been.[17] There is also probably some truth in the current (1979) claim of Lu Dingyi that Peng was not speaking simply for himself. According to Lu, Peng had incorporated some of Lu's own suggestions into his 'letter of opinion' as well as, more importantly, those of Premier Zhou Enlai.[18]

In Lu Dingyi's opinion, therefore, Peng's letter was not meant to be inflammatory. This view is shared by some Western commentators. Teiwes and Joffe, for example, argue that Peng felt that Mao's attitude on the Great Leap was flexible, and thus tried to win Mao over to his position.[19] After all, Mao had been at odds with the 'left' in the Party and, in his criticism of Li Jingquan, had called himself a 'conservative'. Mao, moreover, had aligned himself with some people whom the 'left' had considered to be 'right opportunist'.[20] There may even be some truth, Teiwes believes, in Peng's subsequent claim that his real object of criticism was not Mao but Liu Shaoqi.[21]

Yet Mao was to react most bitterly to Peng's criticism and was to brand Peng a 'right opportunist'. Why was this? One explanation might be that Mao was taken by surprise. Though, at an operational level, Mao endorsed a lot of criticism of the Leap and, in March, had been even more 'conservative' on the question of the unit of account in the communes than Peng's alleged accomplice, Zhou Xiaozhou (first secretary of Hunan province), he was optimistic about the 'bright future' and could not accept what seemed to be a frontal attack on the 1958 policies. Despite his self-characterisation as a 'middle of the roader', Mao had a deep psychological involvement with the commune programme.[22] But such an explanation is not very satisfying, since Mao had praised a lower-level planning official for making much the same kind of criticism as Peng.[23] For an adequate explanation, therefore, one must look at the timing of Peng's comments and the political position of Peng himself.

On the question of timing, it must be noted that Peng's criticisms were made at a time when a number of senior leaders of the Party were wavering on the question of the Great Leap. Li Xiannian and Bo Yibo, for example, were uncertain as to what attitude to take and they probably reflected a widespread view in the Party. Perhaps Mao felt that he should demonstrate a strong stand on the Great Leap Strategy by denouncing a leading critic, even though policies of consolidation might be continued. Indeed, Mao had no great love for the Minister of Defence who was renowned for his sharp and acerbic tongue. He was thus not reluctant to make an example of him. It may also have been the case that Mao genuinely believed that Peng was at the head of a conspiracy. Why else would a Minister of Defence, who was not known for his interest in economic policy, suddenly become the spokesman on the 'three red banners'? It will also be remembered that some association had been drawn between Peng Dehuai and Gao Gang. However fantastic the existence of such a conspiracy might have been, it is possible that Mao believed in it, and noted, with the gravest suspicions, that the letter had been circulated on 14 July, three days before the chairman received it.[24] Was Peng mobilising support for a bid for power?

In my view, however, none of the above explanations is very convincing. Contrary to Teiwes, I feel that the crucial element in the explanation must be the attitude of the Soviet leaders. On 18 July, in Poznan, Poland, Khrushchev reversed his Twenty-first Congress line on China and spoke of how 'the co-operative way was the surest way for the peasant'. He implied that, in setting up communes, the Chinese had a 'poor understanding' of how to build communism and stated that, when the Soviet Union had experimented with communes, the communes had failed because the material and political prerequisites for their establishment had not existed.[25]

Upon the publication of Khrushchev's speech on 21 July, it must have seemed to Mao that Khrushchev was echoing Peng Dehuai and was trying to push the Politburo conference in a conservative direction. This was what made Peng's actions inflammatory and it was not strange, therefore, that associations between Peng and Gao Gang would soon be made explicit.[26] Gao, after all, was said to have had secret dealings with Moscow. On 23 July, two days after the public disclosure of Khrushchev's speech, Mao counter-attacked:

> I never attack others if I am not attacked. If others attack me, I always attack back. Others attack me first, I attack them later.[27]

To make certain that he had adequate support, Mao was to summon other members of the Party Central Committee to Lushan and expanded the enlarged Politburo conference into a regular plenum.[28] He was determined for a showdown. In his speech to the enlarged Politburo conference on 23 July and subsequently in his speech to the Eighth Plenum, Mao proceeded to defend the Great Leap Forward. He was concerned to explain what, in his view, constituted mistakes and shortcomings in Party work and readily recognised that he had committed errors. He urged other comrades to make a similar acknowledgement:

> The chaos caused was on a grand scale and I take responsibility. Comrades, you must all analyse your own responsibility. If you have to shit, shit! If you have to fart, fart! You will feel much better for it.[29]

He rejected, however, the idea that the Party should be cowed into a conservative position because of any 'mess' that might have been caused.

> Whenever they speak, they say we are in a mess. This is fine. The more they say we are in a mess, the better, and the more we should listen . . . Why should we let the others talk? The reason is that China will not sink down, the sky will not fall. We have done some good things and our backbones are strong. The majority of comrades need to strengthen their backbones. Why are they not all strong? Just because for a time there were too few vegetables, too few hair grips, no soap, a lack of balance in the economy and tension in the market, everyone became tense. People became psychologically tense. I did not see any reason for tension, but I was also tense nevertheless; it would be untrue to say I wasn't. In the first part of the night you may be tense, but once you take your sleeping pills the tension will go away for the rest of the night.

Mao was most indignant that a movement based on mass activism should be dismissed as (in Peng's words) 'petty bourgeois fanaticism'.

> The people in Henan and Hebei have created the truth from experience, they have smashed Roosevelt's 'freedom from want'. How should we look upon such enthusiasm for communism? Shall we call it petty bourgeois fanaticism? I don't think we can put it in that way. It's a matter of wanting to do a bit more; it's nothing else but wanting to do a bit more a bit faster . . . We must not pour cold water on this kind of broad mass movement. We can only use persuasion and say to them: Comrades, your hearts are in the right place. When tasks are difficult, don't be impatient . . . They [the cadres] are very active . . . Do you think this is petty bourgeois fanaticism? They are not the petty bourgeoisie; they are the poor peasants, proletarians and semiproletarians.[30]

Mao admitted that there had been some cases of 'petty bourgeois fanaticism' but these had long since been corrected. He was convinced that one should look on the bright side. Originally he had been prepared for the collapse of up to one-half of the communes but not one had, in fact, collapsed. True, he had expected more of the movement than had been realised, but perhaps it was natural to be impatient. In Mao's view, the lesson that had been learned was that one could not apply the logic of the accountant to what had been a supreme act of spiritual liberation.

By the time Mao had delivered his defence of the Great Leap at the Lushan Plenum, many members of the Central Committee had deserted Peng Dehuai. Li Xiannian, for example, acknowledged that he changed sides and Bo Yibo scrapped a speech he had written which presumably echoed Peng's views. The editor of *Renmin Ribao*, Wu Lengxi, admitted he had been 'taken in'. But his colleague in propaganda affairs, Hu Qiaomu, could not think of an adequate defence and suffered a loss of power for about a year. This was not to say, however, that Peng remained undefended. The veteran 'father of the PLA', Zhu De, for example, spoke in his defence. In general, though, the private feelings of many Party leaders remained unspoken and, in retrospect, it seems that many of those feelings were quite intense. Quite a few leaders felt that Mao had violated the norms of inner-Party democracy and even Li Jingquan who, on Great Leap policies, had stood far to the left of Mao, was unhappy with the way Peng had been treated. Most ironical of all, Li Lisan, who had been in Mao's eyes the author of the 'second left line' in the 1930s which replaced inner-Party democracy by 'ruthless struggle and merciless blows', was critical of Peng's dismissal. As Teiwes sees it, the roles of Li and Mao had now been reversed. Mao, the champion of inner-Party democracy, had on this occasion himself become its major violator. A precedent had been set which was to be of great importance in the subsequent Cultural Revolution.[31]

Whether or not one accepts Teiwes's explanation as to the role of Mao depends upon the evidence concerning conspiracy and whether Mao's view of the position of the Soviet leaders was accurate. The evidence is, unfortunately, still incomplete. The evidence is inadequate also to answer the vital question as to the role of Liu Shaoqi. In the Cultural Revolution Liu was, as one would expect, closely associated, in the minds of critics, with the position of Peng Dehuai. We know, however, that at the crucial moment Liu, like so many others, backed Mao. But had Liu been critical of Peng all along? They had apparently exchanged sharp words at Lushan and Peng was later to claim that the focus of his criticism at Lushan was directed at Liu. Indeed, it seems that Liu and Peng were frequently at odds and Liu was not unhappy with Peng's demise. Liu, in fact, is reported to have persuaded an unwilling Lin Biao to replace Peng as Minister of Defence.[32] But here we are in very murky realms of Peking-ological speculation. Suffice it to say that, when most of the central leadership rallied against Peng, he could only confess,

> At the group Meeting of the Lushan Conference, I expressed a series of right opportunist absurdities, especially in my 14 July letter to Comrade Mao Zedong. I attacked the Party's general line of going all out and aiming high for greater, quicker and more economical results in the construction of socialism. At the same time, I attacked the activism of the broad masses of the people and cadres and damaged the prestige of the Party Central Committee and Comrade Mao Zedong. I now understand that this was a crime.[33]

In its resolution 'concerning the anti-Party clique headed by Peng Dehuai' of 16 August, the Eighth Plenum seemed particularly sensitive to Peng's alleged Soviet connections, noting that his attack came at a time when 'the reactionary forces at home and abroad were exploiting certain transient and partial shortcomings'[34] in the Great Leap Forward. Much was made of a remark by Peng to the effect that if the Chinese workers and peasants had not been as good as they were, a Hungarian incident would have occurred in China and it would have been necessary to invite Soviet troops in.[35] It was stated also that, at the time of the Gao Gang incident, Peng had been warned for supporting Gao's anti-Party activities.[36] The message was very clear.

In a letter to Chairman Mao on 9 September, Peng Dehuai apologised and begged to be allowed to participate in manual labour on the communes. His appeal for leniency seems to have been heard, and it was not until the Cultural Revolution that Peng was subjected to public criticism. With the appointment on 17 September of Lin Biao as Minister of Defence and Luo Ruiqing as chief-of-staff of the PLA, it would seem that the eighth of the ten crises in the history of the Party had ended. We shall see, however, that the eighth crisis was but the harbinger of the ninth and tenth. The ninth crisis was to start as a criticism of those who wished to see Peng Dehuai rehabililated and the tenth crisis was to see the defeat of Peng's allegedly reluctant replacement.

## The Revival of the Great Leap

The leniency accorded to Peng Dehuai was reflected in the use of the term 'right opportunist'. This was a much less serious charge than 'revisionist' or even 'rightist', and signified that the errant cadre might eventually be rehabilitated. Indeed, the campaign against 'right opportunism', which was to get under way in the wake of Lushan, did not affect many senior leaders of the Party. But though criticism at the top was mild, the movement was far more wide-reaching at lower levels and whole groups of cadres came under severe censure. Setting the pace in this respect was Sichuan's Li Jingquan who aimed to discipline some 20 – 30 per cent of all cadres. Similar targets, moreover, were announced in Yunnan.[37] Though these targets were perhaps exaggerated, there seemed no doubt that continuing problems, in the rural areas, resulted in quite strict organisational sanctions. This was perhaps the case because the 1959 harvest had been poor and peasant ardour had declined. 'Tailism', therefore, became a major deviation.

But, although organisational sanctions at lower levels were quite strict, the overall policies of the revived Great Leap were much more modest than those of 1958. The Lushan Plenum scaled down the targets for the Leap, requiring some 275 million tonnes of grain.[38] This was still unrealistic and it appears that statistics as well as targets were still not reported accurately. It was announced, for example, in April 1960 that the average income in the rural areas had reached ¥85[39] but, since 1977 reports speak of a mere ¥60 at that time,[40] one can only look at such figures with scepticism. The twelve-year plan for agriculture was now, once again, given a new lease of life but its final form in early 1960 only reflected the targets specified at the Third Plenum and not those agreed to at the second session of the Eighth Party Congress in May 1958.[41] But even these were still too ambitious. In the communes, the principle of decentralisation (according to the three-level ownership formula) was still officially endorsed.[42] In the field of rural trade, although free markets were restricted once again, they were not totally abolished, the policy being 'freedom but not disorder, control but not strangulation'.[43] It was admitted also that attempts to employ handicraft workers in factories had been premature and many were returned to their former trades.[44] Although cadres who had permitted the large-scale restoration of private plots were branded as 'right opportunists', moves to restrict private family activities were cautious.[45] In short, the Great Leap of late 1959 and early 1960s was but a pale reflection of that of 1958. But, given the bad climatic conditions, could it have been anything else?

Perhaps the most difficult task facing any leader in the revived Leap of 1959 was that which confronted Lin Biao, who was entrusted to counter the 'purely military viewpoint' in the army. In his first major statement as Minister of Defence in September 1959, Lin reasserted Mao's slogan that men were superior to weapons but also paid considerable attention to the importance of military technology. In defending the idea of military democracy, Lin also gave particular stress to combating anarchism and egalitarianism.[46] The reform of the PLA was evidently to be carried out under conditions of strict discipline.

The revival of the Great Leap, therefore, was to be a cautious one. None the less, there was a certain atmosphere of excitement in the autumn of 1959 which reached its high point by the tenth anniversary of the founding of the Chinese People's Republic on 1 October 1959, and it was in a moderately radical atmosphere that Mao greeted perhaps the most distinguished guest to attend the celebrations—Nikita Khrushchev.

## The Spirit of Camp David

Although Khrushchev had been conciliatory towards China at the Twenty-first Congress of the CPSU in January 1959, he could not disguise the fact that the Party programme had effectively thrown out the Leninist thesis on imperialism and had reinforced the notion of 'peaceful competition'. The Chinese leaders had never accepted Khrushchev's formulation, although in the cautious climate of early 1959 they had muted their disquiet. At a time when the Soviet press was full of Khrushchev's 'creative development of Marxism-Leninism', all *Hongqi* could say, in February, was that Khrushchev had made the creative suggestion that socialist countries would more or less simultaneously pass to the higher state of communist society.[47]

After the replacement of US Secretary of State Dulles by Christian Herter in April 1959, Khrushchev, having seemingly forgotten about the Berlin ultimatum, moved towards *détente* with the United States, much to the chagrin of the Chinese. As the Chinese leaders saw it, American foreign policy did not depend upon personalities but upon the requirements of monopoly capital, and *détente* would only be possible once the United States withdrew its forces from Europe and Asia. In the summer and autumn of 1959, Chinese suspicion of the Soviet Union grew as Kassem bore down on Iraqi Communists and the Soviet Union seemed to demand that Iraqi insurgents take a more conciliatory line.[48] As Nasser stepped up his anti-Communist crusade in Egypt, the Soviet Union showed no willingness to modify its programme of economic assistance.[49] On the Algerian question, the Soviet Union seemed more concerned with winning De Gaulle away from NATO than supporting the FLN.[50] Perhaps most galling of all, as Sino-Indian relations worsened in the aftermath of the Tibetan rebellion, Soviet-Indian relations were never better. In this atmosphere of suspicion, Khrushchev not only dropped his bombshell of 18 August when he declared his opposition to communes, but also announced his plan to visit the United States. On 16 September, the very day Khrushchev arrived in America, a *Hongqi* article laid particular stress on the struggle against imperialism,[51] in marked contrast to the article prepared by Khrushchev for the American establishment journal *Foreign Affairs*.[52]

Unlike President Eisenhower, who had embarked upon a European tour prior to his meeting with Khrushchev, the Soviet leader had apparently consulted no one.[53] As far as China was concerned, he was probably convinced that any agreement he might reach on *détente* would automatically be accepted by the Chinese, who were too dependent upon the Soviet Union to be anything but compliant. He was quite mistaken. Upon his arrival in China on 30 September, flushed with his new-found understanding with Eisenhower (referred to at the time as the 'spirit of Camp David'), Khrushchev was faced with severe Chinese criticism. In his speeches within China, Khrushchev reiterated the uncompromising version of his Twentieth and Twenty-first Congress lines,[54] and appeared impervious to Chinese criticism. In a speech to the Supreme Soviet on 31 October, the Soviet leader implied that the Chinese were taking much the same position as Trotsky who, at Brest Litovsk, was said to have opposed Lenin's moves to conclude a temporary peace with Germany.[55] Was Khrushchev suggesting that the Chinese should do to Taiwan what the Soviet government had done to parts of European Russia in 1918? In any case, the Trotsky analogy could only be a calculated insult. With regard to the Sino-Indian border dispute, Khrushchev assumed a neutral stance and, in the same speech, endorsed De Gaulle's demand for a ceasefire in Algeria.

Khrushchev had failed to bring China to heel during the Lushan meetings. He had failed to subdue China during his visit to Beijing in October and his Supreme Soviet speech could only provoke even further Chinese criticism. In the new year, Khrushchev was to think of even more direct methods of applying pressure.

### The Worsening Sino-Soviet Dispute

By early 1960, it seemed to the Chinese that the American moves towards *détente* were aimed at buying time to close what was believed to be a wide missile gap.[56] They were particularly wary of any moves towards disarmament or any negotiations which did not involve all members of the socialist camp. On the ninetieth anniversary of Lenin's birth in late April, the Chinese press produced a series of articles outlining in detail the Chinese position under the title 'Long Live Leninism',[57] to which the Soviet press replied. Both the Soviet Union and China adhered to the notion of 'peaceful coexistence', although the Chinese felt that this notion should not be used to impede wars of national liberation. Both sides felt that a general war was not inevitable, but the Chinese felt that at least it was possible as long as imperialism existed.[58] The Chinese were most dismayed at Kuusinen's use of a quote from Lenin to the effect that wars would become so destructive as to be impossible, to negate Lenin's much more important thesis that so long as imperialism existed there would be a danger of war. The Soviet position was based on two notions —that technology had changed the nature of war and that there were more reasonable men in power on the other side. To the Chinese, technology might make war more destructive but it could not change the nature of imperialism and a general war would not be the outcome of the reasonableness or unreasonableness of certain individuals. The Chinese could not accept that a 'parliamentary road to socialism'[59] was to be preferred in the Third World and that all local wars should be avoided regardless of the reasons for their occurrence. The argument of Soviet spokesman Sovetov that the existence of the socialist camp had made local wars less likely was most unconvincing.

Following the polemics of April and May 1960 and the abortive Paris summit, the dispute entered its most intense phase yet. At a meeting of the World Federation of Trade Unions in Beijing from 5–9 June, the Chinese delegate Liu Changsheng attacked most strongly the Soviet Twenty-first Congress line, declaring that disarmament was an illusion,[60] and this was followed by the publication in the Soviet press of discourses on Lenin's 'Left Wing Communism, An Infantile Disorder'.[61] A feature of such a 'disorder', it was claimed, was the advocacy of a policy of skipping over historical stages, which was one of the 'rightist' criticisms of the Great Leap.

At the Third Congress of the Communist Party of Rumania, which met in Bucharest in late June, it is reported that Khrushchev himself attacked Mao Zedong by name, suggesting that he was guilty of Trotskyist deviations, and of knowing nothing of the military realities of the modern world.[62] Khrushchev's Bucharest explosions were followed, in July, by a plenum of the CPSU where much discussion was given over to 'left-wing sectarianism' and the 'manifestation of narrow nationalistic tendencies'.[63] At about the same time, the journal of the Sino-Soviet Friendship Society *Druzhba* (*Friendship*) was suspended, and explicit attacks on China began to appear in the journals of Moscow-line Communist parties. The Indian paper *Blitz*, for example, published an article entitled 'Moscow "Boxes the Ears" of Peking Trotskyites'.[64]

The culmination of escalating Soviet attacks on the Chinese Party came in August with the unilateral withdrawal of Soviet aid, technicians and blueprints,[65] right at a time when China was about to experience its second year of poor harvests. The Chinese leadership would, however, not be brought to heel and the blunt response of Li Fuchun, the chairman of the State Planning Commission, was to call for even greater 'self-reliance'.[66]

A final attempt was made to reach agreement on the General Line of the International Communist Movement in the autumn of 1960. As plans were under way for a World Conference of Communist Parties to meet in Moscow in November, a preparatory commission was set up which became yet another forum for polemic.[67] A final declaration was, in fact, agreed upon in Moscow but it in no way signified that a *modus vivendi* had been reached. The declaration dealt with four major questions—the character of the present epoch, problems of war and peace, paths of transition to socialism and the unity of the International Communist Movement (including rules governing the relations between fraternal parties). On the first question, some concessions were made to the Chinese position that the era was one of the collapse of imperialism and the development of national liberation struggle, but the Soviet insistence that transition to socialism would come about largely because of the (economic) strength of the socialist camp rather than revolution, was maintained. On the second question, the resolution accepted both the Chinese assertion that imperialists would continue to start local wars and the Soviet view that they could be deterred. The Soviet contention that there was a real possibility of excluding world war, even while imperialism still existed, was retained. On the third question, the Soviet version of the principle of 'peaceful coexistence' was retained though it was no longer referred to as the 'General Line' and, on the fourth question, the Soviet Union was called the 'universally recognised vanguard of the International Communist Movement' rather than the 'head' (as in 1957).

The Moscow declaration, therefore, was no more than a collation of views.[68] It implied, however, a far greater degree of independence for individual Communist parties. At least that was how the Albanian Party leader Enver Hoxha interpreted it. On 16 November, he reportedly affirmed the Chinese line and criticised Khrushchev's accusations against the Chinese made at Bucharest.[69] The split between Moscow and Tirana was now final and, in subsequent months, the Soviet press pointedly used the codeword 'Albania' when it really meant China. Such was the international environment within which China faced its most serious economic crisis since liberation.

### The Worsening Economic Situation

In 1959, China suffered from its worst natural calamities for several decades. Farmlands affected by drought exceeded 40 million hectares (some 40 per cent of the land under cultivation).[70] At the same time, other areas experienced severe floods. In the years 1959–60, approximately half the land under cultivation was hit by bad weather. In 1957, the official figure for grain production had been some 185 million tonnes and this figure has been accepted by most Western commentators. The official figure for 1958 was 250 million tonnes, which in view of the current tendency to inflate statistics, Western observers feel to be an overestimate. Most of them agree, however, that grain production for that year was well over 200 million tonnes.[71] As for 1959, Li Fuchun claimed that food production reached 270 million tonnes.[72] Most foreign economists dismiss this figure and some of them place grain production for that year as low as 170 million tonnes. Similar foreign estimates for 1960 are around 160 million tonnes with a slight rise in 1961.[73]

There can be no doubt that the official Chinese figures were inflated, though I do not propose here to go into the bitter polemic which exists among economists as to the degree of that inflation. What I must do, however, is spell out the various positions taken in the debate about the causes of the economic crisis.

A common attitude adopted in the West is that the crisis of 1959–61 was directly attributable to the Great Leap Forward.[74] Dislocations which occurred during the formation of communes had been so severe that the autumn harvest of 1958 was not gathered in entirety. A reduction of the area sown in grain in the winter of 1958 led to a food shortage and the situation was further exacerbated by the poor harvests of 1959. Moreover, a premature reduction of material incentives and the abolition of the private sector led to a loss of peasant confidence. The boom of 1958 encouraged rather than reversed the drift of peasants to the cities and resulted in a rural labour shortage which hindered production. According to this view, therefore, the Great Leap was responsible for the crisis and the bad harvests of 1959–61 merely emphasised the problems.

A contrary view maintains that the primary cause of the crisis was flood and drought. It admits there had been dislocations, inflated statistics and an excessive reduction in the area sown in grain. It stresses, however, that the commune organisation in the countryside which facilitated grain distribution caused the burden of insufficient food to be shared and prevented mass starvation.[75] There was little evidence that material incentives had been reduced prematurely and a loss of peasant morale was to be expected at a time of extraordinarily adverse weather conditions. Such rural labour shortage as existed would in the long run be solved by the very commune organisation which had been designed (amongst other things) to facilitate rural industrialisation and halt the drift to the cities. In the meantime, an excess urban population must be compelled to return to the communes. How one evaluates these two views will depend upon an assessment of the adequacy of the evidence about malnutrition and starvation in this period. There is, indeed, much evidence of severe deprivation but, it might be argued, there was nowhere near the level of mass starvation which used to occur in similar natural catastrophies in the pre-1949 situation.

Whatever the causes of the economic crisis of 1960, the overwhelming problem which faced China's leaders from the beginning of 1960 to the end of 1962 was how to feed the population. Though people might disagree on their interpretations of the Great Leap and how to modify its policies, there was no doubt that some modification had to be made. The initial response to the food crisis was in line with the radical policies of the Leap. What remained of the private plots (restored and then restricted again in 1959) was, in 1960, frequently handed over to commune and brigade canteens in order to keep the supply of public meals going.[76] A major problem was that communes and production brigades had little surplus to distribute to peasants. Once the grain earmarked for animal fodder was consumed by humans, animals were killed and thus the supply of animal fertiliser was reduced. This, in turn, reduced the quality of the crops and further lowered output. The tremendous pressure to restore the level of food production led now to a reduction in the area of land given over to industrial crops. Since it was mainly these industrial crops which provided much of the raw material for local light industry, many small light industrial plants had their activities severely restricted. Industrial plants in the towns were also affected and factories, operating at reduced capacity, scoured the countryside for raw materials and, where possible, entered into contracts with local communes and brigades regardless of any local planning directive.[77]

Though the people's communes were originally seen as do-it-yourself exercises in organisation and although few people were particularly worried about planning in the period of creative imbalance in 1958, it was always anticipated that, once communes had been consolidated, a new planning structure would be ironed out. Unfortunately, once the Party moved to consolidate the rural situation in 1959–60, food shortages had resulted in a mass of *ad hoc* contractual and other relationships which made control extremely difficult. The immediate response of the Party to the problems of 1959–60 was to greatly accelerate the process of *xiafang*. In 1959–60, large numbers of cadres, intellectuals, students and PLA soldiers were sent to the countryside to re-establish control and to reduce the food supply problems in the cities. In the countryside, all sorts of systems were publicised in the press whereby administrative cadres spent greater amounts of time at lower levels. According to the 'two-five' system in Hebei, for example, cadres spent two days engaged in study, attending conferences and undertaking research projects followed by three days actually working in the teams.[78] According to the 'three-seven' system of Jilin province, three levels of cadre (*xian*, commune and brigade) divided each ten-day period into three days' study, investigation and allocation of work with the remaining seven devoted to production.[79] In some areas, *xian*-level cadres were given administrative jobs within the brigades, but the problems were immense and often beyond the abilities of newly retrenched cadres. It was precisely in this critical situation that the Soviet Union withdrew its technicians, aid and blueprints, thus causing more of industry to run at reduced capacity and, indeed, preventing many uncompleted industrial plants from coming into operation at all.

### The Worsening Urban Situation

The worsening food supply situation in the cities led, in early 1960, to a new drive to create urban communes.[80] The communes of 1960 were very different, however, from the Zhengzhou model of 1958, which reveals the fact that they were less the product of organisational inspiration and more an attempt merely to solve the problems of food production and distribution and keep small industry in the cities alive. Wherever possible, city suburbs were combined with agricultural production brigades to produce communes more or less self-sufficient in food. Most of the 1960 communes were not combined with regular industrial enterprises and consisted largely of housewives and family dependants with many of the male residents leaving the commune every day to work in regular factories. Such a situation was perhaps not the best way to form integrated urban units generating mass commitment.

These later communes tended to be huge. The original Red Flag Commune of Zhengzhou expanded sevenfold from 4,684 households in 24 streets to 150,000 people, and consisted of subdivisions each larger than the original commune.[81] The process here was the exact opposite of what was happening in the rural areas, where communes were in fact getting smaller to correspond more with the old *xiang*. In the rural areas then, communes were narrowing down to fit in with ecological conditions whereas in the cities they were expanding more and more to correspond to artificial administrative areas. It is probably because of this that many of the urban communes, which continued in existence throughout the 1960s, were little more than synonyms for urban wards (*qu*).

Although the 1960 urban communes were not very successful *qua* communes, various policies with which they were associated continued to be very important throughout the 1960s. Many of the locally run child-care centres and service points set up at that time remained, and the urban commune policy, whereby urban residents combined and pooled their own funds to set up small industries, continued. Perhaps in the really critical years of 1960−2 their activities were limited, but in the period immediately prior to the Cultural Revolution, I saw many such industries that seemed remarkably successful. One might argue that street co-operatives and street industries were sometimes inefficient but this would really be to miss the point. The resources that they mobilised would not usually be collected for use elsewhere. Secondly, most of these industries were run by women who, for the first time in their lives, were liberated from the home and introduced to technology, however primitive. I can remember visiting a shoe polish co-operative run largely by women in Taiyuan. Another observer of the same co-operative has described how chaotic the organisation was.[82] It is true that much money was wasted in the early years producing inferior shoe polish without any expert guidance at all but, by 1965, a product was made which was exportable and this fact gave to a group of men and women a sense of achievement that perhaps could have come from nowhere else. Such was the legacy of the urban commune movement or perhaps the legacy of the Great Leap Forward itself. With the decline of the urban communes in late 1960 and early 1961, the Great Leap Forward was really at an end but it had created a desire amongst many ordinary people to produce goods for themselves and to become inventors. It was the beginning of a process of emancipation that no amount of economic bungling, 'commandism' or utopian thinking could render less worthwhile.

## The Reform of the People's Liberation Army

The food shortages of 1960−1 inevitably affected the People's Liberation Army. In early and mid-1960, the army became heavily involved in agricultural work. As the situation worsened in November 1960, army rations were cut.[83] In the winter of 1960−1, it was estimated that 5 per cent of personnel in the armed forces suffered from oedema.[84] Even in this critical situation, however, Lin Biao, who noted that some 4 per cent of army units had 'fallen into the hands of the enemy',[85] proceeded gradually to carry out the task with which he had been entrusted—to raise the morale and political consciousness of the PLA after the dismissal of Peng Dehuai. At an enlarged conference of the Military Commission in September and October 1960, a 'Resolution on the Strengthening of Political and Ideological Work in the Armed Forces' was adopted. Lin proposed a policy known as the 'four firsts'—'man' first in the relationship between man and weapons, 'politics' first in the relationship between political and other work, 'ideology' first in the relationship between routine and ideological political education, and 'living thought' first in the relationship between book-learning and practice. What Lin strove to overcome was formalistic political training where military cadres went by the political book in the same way as they adhered to the military manual.[86] The 'four firsts' were to be the first of a series of numerical slogans such as 'five good soldiers', 'four good companies', the 'three-eight working style' etc., which were to form the basis for political training in the army.[87]

The enlarged conference of the Military Commission noted that, despite the many policies to that end which had been put forward over the past four years, there were still no Party branches in one-third of all PLA companies and the Party organisation below that level was often non-existent.[88] In the winter of 1960–1, considerable attention was devoted to building up the Party network at lower levels in the army and to restoring the old political commissar and company political instructor system that had existed from the days of the Civil War. By April 1961, it was reported that all companies now had Party branches and 80 per cent of platoons had organised cells.[89] Later in that year, the functions and duties of company Party branches were spelt out.[90] Party branches were given control not only over political training but also over promotions and were also given some say in military training and operations. At the same time, attempts were made to revive the soldiers' clubs with elected committees. Once the Party organisation had been strengthened, the structure of the Communist Youth League could also be built up to undertake the political education of the bulk of recruits who were aged about 18 or 19. Young privates were instructed to make a particular study of the revolutionary traditions of the army and to interview old people and veterans about their experiences in the old society.[91] Under no circumstances was the old technocratic military élitism to be allowed to recur.

### The Decision to Deradicalise (late 1960 and early 1961)

Since the revival of the Great Leap after the Lushan Plenum in 1959, attempts had been made in both the military and civilian spheres to keep the radical policies in operation. In this respect, the army had been much more successful than the civilian sector. Much of the credit for this belonged, of course, to Lin Biao, but one should note also that, if there was one area in which most people in the Party were united, it was in the belief that deteriorating Sino-Soviet relations and increasingly serious border disputes demanded a strengthening of military discipline. The army was to be made ready to stand on its own if China were attacked.

Whatever the economic cost, nothing should be done to demoralise the troops nor to slow down China's determination to develop an independent nuclear deterrent. Whatever the options open to China's military leaders, there was one option that now seemed closed—the integration of the Chinese armed forces into the network of the Warsaw Pact.

In the civilian sphere, however, despite the renewed *xiafang* of 1959 – 60, it was extremely difficult to keep the spirit of the Great Leap Forward alive. By mid-1960 Great Leap policies were, in many areas, no longer implemented,[92] and Mao could only admit that, by that time, building communism was 'unacceptable'.[93] He had certainly rejected the idea of pockets of communism but was not prepared to reject completely the principle of free supply. As we noted in the preceding chapter, Mao was no dogmatic believer in the instant application of commune-level accounting. He did believe, however, that, over a period of time, the unit of account should be switched from team to brigade and then to commune and that finally communal ownership would be synonymous with state ownership.[94] In 1960, the reverse was happening. After the decentralisation of some powers to brigade and team levels in 1959 (which Mao seemed to see as a necessary first step in consolidation), further moves seem to have been taken, towards the end of 1960, to transfer the bulk of decision-making power to the (by now much smaller) teams.

With the publication of a twelve-article directive on rural work towards the end of the year,[95] *de facto* decentralisation to team level took place and this move was confirmed at the Ninth Plenum of the Eighth Central Committee in January 1961. The team (which usually corresponded to the old lower-stage co-op) was now given full rights over the use of labour, land, animals, tools and equipment. They key slogan of the Ninth Plenum was 'agriculture as the base and industry as the leading factor', which had been put forward in March 1960[96] and was precisely the policy pursued during the Great Leap. What was essentially different in the new policy was not that agriculture was considered to be primary but that industry was severely cut back. Secondly, the primacy of agriculture was interpreted in such a way that it amounted to a general concession to the development of petty capitalism in the countryside.[97] It would appear, therefore, that the gust of wind from the 'right' which Mao had perceived in 1960[98] continued to blow throughout 1961 and, in his speech to the plenum, Mao noted that the deradicalisation of 1959 had led to a restoration of the power of former landlords.[99] The policies of the Ninth Plenum seemed to offer little chance that this situation would be remedied.

One decision taken by the plenum, however, probably caused little contention. This was the ratification of an earlier proposal, made by a central work conference in July – August 1960, to re-establish six regional bureaux of the Central Committee.[100] This decentralisation of Party authority seemed in no way a return to the pre-1954 situation whereby local leaders might re-establish 'independent kingdoms'. It signified only the Party's attempt to co-ordinate activities following the decentralisation of power to provincial levels after November 1957. The move was probably an extension of the idea of large economic co-operation regions implemented during the Great Leap.

## Conclusion

By 1960 the Great Leap had ground to a halt in the midst of an economic crisis. The Sino-Soviet split had developed to the level of bitter polemic and members of the Chinese leadership were divided in their assessment of the causes of the present troubles. At the beginning of the Cultural Revolution many people were to trace back the origins of what became known as the 'two-line struggle' to this time and members of China's present (1979) leadership echo that view though from the opposite perspective. In the words of Lu Dingyi:

> The original objective of the Lushan meeting in 1959 was, in the spirit of seeking truth from facts, to examine shortcomings in our work and apply corrective measures. It changed, however, into a meeting to oppose the correct views of Peng Dehuai. The more it proceeded, the more 'left' it became. This kind of leftist error subsequently developed into a line which was only rectified with the overthrow of the 'Gang of Four' in October 1976.[101]

The crucial question, however, is at what point did the differences of opinion amongst China's leaders become 'antagonistic'. Was the crucial turning-point the Lushan conference where (depending on one's point of view) Mao violated inner-Party norms or responded to 'conspiracy'? Or did the turning-point come much later? In Teiwes's opinion, the turning-point did not come until 1962 or perhaps even 1965. Throughout the period considered in this chapter, Mao still proclaimed his adherence to inner-Party norms and, with the single exception of the Peng Dehuai group, was to tolerate quite a lot of dissent in top Party circles. Mao, moreover, was, as much as anyone else, concerned to restore order to the economic situation. At lower levels of the Party, however, there were severe problems. The campaign against 'right opportunism' could not survive conditions of economic hardship and, as more and more corrective measures were applied, the target of criticism switched to the 'leftist' excesses attributed to the Great Leap. Through all this, the Party was to suffer a loss of prestige. In such a situation, contention amongst the senior leadership became sharper. Such contention will be examined in the following chapter.

# NOTES

1. URI, 1968 (a), p. 14.
2. Lu Dingyi, *RMRB*, 8 March 1979, p. 2.
3. Teiwes, 1979, pp. 423–8. Joffe (1975, pp. 12–19), on the other hand, argues that military issues were very important.
4. Simmonds, 1969, p. 124.
5. Shu Tong, 24 January 1959, *ECMM* 169, 25 May 1959, pp. 1–18.
6. Ke Qingshi, ibid. 165, 20 April 1959, p. 39.
7. See Simmonds, 1969, pp. 125–6.
8. This is suggested in ibid.
9. URI, 1968 (a), p. 204.
10. See Gittings, 1968, pp. 102–9.
11. Suslov noted that the Soviet Union considered it inexpedient to help the Chinese produce nuclear weapons because such a course would lead to the acquisition of nuclear weapons by West Germany and Japan. See Gehlen, 1967, p. 286.
12. Simmonds, 1969, pp. 132–4.
13. Tao Zhu, *RMRB*, 3 June 1959, p. 7. For a discussion of Tao's position, see Moody, 1973, pp. 279–80.
14. *RMRB*, 16 June 1959, p. 8 (under the pseudonym Lin Mianzhi).
15. Teiwes, 1979, pp. 403–5.
16. Peng Dehuai, 14 July 1959, URI 1968 (a), p. 400; Selden, 1979, p. 479.
17. Moody, 1973, p. 280.
18. Lu Dingyi, *RMRB*, 8 March 1979, p. 2.
19. Teiwes, 1979, p. 412; Joffe, 1975, p. 11.
20. See p. 197.
21. *SCMP* 4032, 2 October 1967, p. 7.
22. Teiwes, 1979, pp. 415–16; Joffe, 1975, p. 20.
23. Mao Zedong, 26 July 1959, *Chinese Law and Government*, Vol. I, No. 4, Winter 1968–9, pp.47–51.
24. URI, 1968 (a), p. 400.
25. Zagoria, 1966, p. 134.
26. URI, 1968 (a), p. 426.
27. Mao Zedong, 23 July 1959, ibid., pp. 19 and 407. See also Schram, 1974, p. 137.
28. Chang, 1975, pp. 117–18.
29. Mao Zedong, 23 July 1959; Schram, 1974, p. 146.
30. Ibid., pp. 132–3.
31. Teiwes, 1979, pp. 437–8.
32. Gigon, cited in Dittmer, 1974, p. 41.
33. URI, 1968 (a), p. 419.
34. Ibid., p. 423.
35. Ibid., p. 424.
36. Ibid., p. 426.
37. Teiwes, 1979, p. 432.
38. Zhou Enlai, 26 August 1959, *PR* 35, 1 September 1959, p. 17.
39. Tan Zhenlin, 6 April 1960, *PR* 15, 12 April 1960, p. 12.
40. CCPCC, *Zhongfa* (1979) 4, 11 January 1979, *Issues and Studies*, Vol. XV, No. 7 July 1979, p. 106.
41. Chang, 1975, p. 124. Text in Kuo, 1972, pp. 243–62.
42. *PR* 35, 1 September 1959, pp. 7–8.
43. CCPCC, SC, 23 September 1959, *SCMP* 2108, 2 October 1959, pp. 6–9.

44. *SCMP* 2078, 18 August 1959, p. 43.
45. Ibid. 2099, 21 September 1959, p. 38.
46. *PR* 40, 6 October 1959, pp. 13 – 20.
47. *ECMM* 159, 2 March 1959, p. 11.
48. Zagoria, 1966, pp. 258 – 60.
49. Ibid., pp. 260 – 2.
50. Ibid., pp. 270 – 6.
51. *PR* 38, 22 September 1959, pp. 6 – 11.
52. Khrushchev, 1959.
53. Zagoria, 1966, p. 277.
54. *PR* 40, 6 October 1959, pp. 7 – 10, reprinted in Hudson, Lowenthal and MacFarquhar, 1961, pp. 61 – 3.
55. Zagoria, 1966, pp. 281 – 4.
56. Ibid. p. 238.
57. PFLP, 1960.
58. For Mao's views on the likelihood of war, see *JPRS* 1974, p. 265.
59. For Mao's views on this, see ibid., p. 251.
60. *PR* 24, 14 June 1960, pp. 13 – 14, reprinted in Hudson, Lowenthal and MacFarquhar, 1961, pp. 123 – 6.
61. Shevlyagin, 10 June 1960, Hudson, Lowenthal and MacFarquhar, 1961, pp. 127 – 9; Matkovsky, 12 June 1960, ibid., pp. 129 – 31.
62. See Crankshaw, 1965, pp. 107 – 9. I am not sure about the authenticity of Crankshaw's account. The official speech of Khrushchev may be found in Hudson, Lowenthal and MacFarquhar, 1961, pp. 132 – 9.
63. According to Mao, Khrushchev's actions here were designed to strengthen his position at home. Mao Zedong, 18 January 1961, *JPRS*, 1974, p. 238.
64. Zagoria, 1966, pp. 327 – 8.
65. See Gittings, 1968, pp. 129 – 43.
66. Li Fuchun, *PR* 34, 23 August 1960, p. 15.
67. PFLP, 1965, pp. 83 – 9.
68. Zagoria, 1966, pp. 367 – 8.
69. Crankshaw, 1965, pp. 131 – 2.
70. Li Fuchun, *PR* 14, 5 April 1960, p. 7.
71. Eckstein, 1973, p. 216.
72. Li Fuchun, *PR* 14, 5 April 1960, p. 6.
73. Eckstein, 1973, p. 216.
74. E.g. Walker, 1968, pp. 444 – 5.
75. Robinson, 1969, p. 35.
76. Zhao Ziyang, *SCMP* 2262, 20 May 1960, p. 23.
77. Vogel, 1971, p. 272.
78. *RMRB*, 16 June 1960, p. 1.
79. Ibid., 29 June 1960, p. 5.
80. See Vogel, 1971, pp. 266 – 8.
81. Salaff, 1967, p. 108.
82. Fokkema, 1971, pp. 103 – 4.
83. Cheng, 1966, p. 37.
84. Information from Nanjing and Fuzhou military regions and army units under general (rear services etc.) departments. Cheng, 1966, p. 296 (from report of general rear services department, 20 Feburary 1961).
85. Mao Zedong, 18 January 1961, *JPRS*, 1974, p. 240.
86. *PR* 42, 18 October 1960, pp. 7 – 8.
87. Gittings, 1967, p.246.
88. Cheng, 1966, p. 81.

89.  Powell, 1963, p. 8.
90.  Gittings, 1967, p. 248.
91.  Ibid., p. 249.
92.  Vogel, 1971, p. 271.
93.  Mao Zedong, 1960(?), *JPRS*, 1974, p. 233.
94.  Mao Zedong, 1960(or 1961–2), ibid., p. 256.
95.  Selden, 1979, p. 516. See also Walker, 1968, p. 446.
96.  Vogel, 1971, p. 273.
97.  Ibid., pp. 275–92.
98.  Mao Zedong, 18 January 1961, *JPRS*, 1974, p. 244.
99.  Ibid., pp. 237–8.
100.  Chang, 1970, p. 189. The date of this decision is taken from a Red Rebel source.
101.  Lu Dingyi, *RMRB*, 8 March 1979, p. 2.

# X
# 'REVISIONISM'?
## (1961 – 1962)

This chapter will examine a period which in the subsequent Cultural Revolution was considered to be characterised by 'revisionism'. The issue of 'revisionism', amongst Marxist-Leninists, is sorely vexed. If Marxism-Leninism is not to be considered as static dogma, there must be some sort of theory which will distinguish between a 'revisionist capitulation to capitalism' and the creative adaptation to changed circumstances. It was doubtless the case that the policy-makers in Beijing, in the years 1960 – 2, saw what they were doing in terms of the latter and their interpretation has, by and large, been supported by the present (1979) leadership. It seems also that Mao Zedong, after Lushan, endorsed their position and that Peng Dehuai was referred to as a 'right opportunist' rather than a 'revisionist'. But, sometime in the period before August 1962, Mao appeared to change his mind, considering that the line between adaptation and 'revisionism' was being crossed. He did not offer the clearest guidelines as to how he conceptualised the dividing line, but his comments on events in the Soviet Union and, in particular, on a Soviet textbook on political economy do reveal that the chairman was engaged in a fundamental reassessment of the process of socialist transition. Those comments were only the beginnings of a reconceptualisation. They did not constitute a theory, and the theoretical confusion which was to plague China in subsequent years was due, in part, to the chairman's failure to develop the ideas traced out in this period. But, before examining Mao's thoughts, the objective economic situation must be described.

### The New Economic Policy[1] in the Countryside

The key slogan of the post-Ninth Plenum period was 'consolidation, filling out and raising standards'.[2] There was much talk of 'balance' rather than the old Great Leap Forward affirmation of the positive role of disequilibrium. Stress was placed on the realisation of short-term economic goals rather than on any long-term perspective. Instead of mass mobilisation, there was now to be sober book-keeping. These new policies were spelt out in the 'twelve articles' of late 1960 and a new sixty-article document issued on 12 May 1961.[3] This latter document endorsed the reduction in the size of the communes to that of the old *xiang*. Thus, the communes changed from units of some 5,000 households in 1959 to units of less than 2,000 in 1961.[4] At the same time, the rights of the teams, as basic accounting units, were affirmed. Brigades were instructed to guarantee to the teams a fixed amount of labour power, land, animals and tools. The teams' production targets were to be arrived at by consultation between various levels and incorporated in contracts. Under no circumstances were targets ever to be imposed from above.

Not only did the new regulations guarantee the integrity of the team, they also guaranteed the peasants' private plots. These plots, partially restored in 1959, then restricted in the same year and perhaps handed over to communal mess halls during the revival of the Great Leap, were now handed back to individual peasants. At first, some 5 per cent of land was reassigned for private cultivation with peasants allowed to derive 20 per cent of their income from private business.[5] By 1962, however, reports appeared that some 20-50 per cent of land in some areas was under private cultivation.[6] Once peasants were allowed to sell the produce of their private plots, there inevitably developed thriving rural markets. The new regulations, therefore, specified what goods might be privately traded. Goods were divided into three categories. The first category consisted of those which were required to be sold to the state at fixed prices; the second category could be sold on the open market once the state plan had been met and the third category could be disposed of in any way the peasant saw fit.[7] Although 'free markets' were officially sanctioned, they were required to be under some kind of official control. But it soon became difficult to know exactly what kind of transactions were going on and local cadres were unable to keep their fingers on the pulse.[8]

According to the new economic policy after 1961, attempts were made to combine the restoration of the planning system with the integration of industry and agriculture through the market. Various industrial departments frequently held 'commodity exchange conferences' where contracts were signed with rural units for the supply of raw materials and the sale of industrial goods. At the same time, 'hook ups' were established between customers and markets.[9] Thus, local production teams, brigades or communes entered into direct dealings with consumer co-operatives or urban department stores. Such a situation, which Schurmann describes as 'decentralisation I', had been rejected in favour of regional decentralisation in late 1957 on the grounds that strengthened market relations would lead to the development of capitalism. Now Chen Yun, the advocate of 'decentralisation I' plus limited recentralisation, was brought back into policy-making circles once again, and in 1962 was made head of a financial group under the Central Committee.[10]

The decentralisation of decision-making power to the team in 1961 as a form of 'decentralisation I', was to weaken the commune. None the less, the commune still maintained authority over some agricultural and industrial activities according to the 'three-level system of ownership'. This point needs to be given particular stress since, until quite recently, it was the conventional wisdom in the West that the measures of 1961 destroyed the commune as anything but an administrative unit. Though the industrial activities of communes were limited, the importance of the commune, even in 1961, was underlined by the fact that all sorts of provisions had to be worked out, specifying the permissible contractual relationships which might exist between the various levels of rural organisation.[11] There were, however, a number of serious consequences of decentralisation within the communes. First, communes and brigades were more able to set aside sums of money for capital accumulation whereas it was much more difficult for teams to do the same; in fact, regulations forbade teams to set aside more than 3 per cent in their accumulation fund. Similarly, it was easier for welfare facilities to be co-ordinated at commune or brigade level and regulations forbade teams to set aside more than 3.5 per cent for this purpose.[12] In an increasingly 'economist' atmosphere, smaller units were perhaps less likely to subscribe to a policy of delayed gratification. Decentralisation, therefore, hindered capital accumulation and the provision of welfare. A second consequence of decentralisation within the communes was that leadership at team level was more likely to reflect old values than at commune level, especially since many of the Great Leap activists sent down to team level were under a cloud for alleged 'commandism'. The older leadership probably contained a sizeable proportion of former 'prosperous middle peasants', oriented towards making a profit on the market and not so much towards collectivist goals.[13] They could ideally be checked by the large numbers of younger people sent down to the countryside during the 1960 *xiafang*, were it not for the fact that many of the latter were still 'wet behind the ears' and were sometimes resented by peasants tired of the countryside being used as a dumping ground for intellectuals.[14]

Once economic decision-making had been located at team level and once limits were placed on the volume of light industry which might be organised at brigade or commune level, it was inevitable that there should be an increase in the number of small rural industries which enjoyed independent responsibility for their operations. Teams, in 1961, had been reduced in size from some 40 households (1959) to some 20-30 households though with considerable local variations.[15] It is very difficult to imagine just what kind of control organisations of that size could have exercised over light industrial undertakings.

The extension of plots for private use, the expansion of the free markets and the increase in the number of small enterprises with sole responsibility for their own profits and losses were, as we have seen, the results of official policy. In the Cultural Revolution, they were to be condemned as three of the four elements in a notorious policy known as *sanziyibao* (three 'self' and one guarantee). The fourth element in this policy, 'the fixing of output quotas on individual households', was not, as far as I know, made part of central policy, though it was endorsed in some provinces. In Anhui, for example, it was officially adopted as part of a 'responsibility system'[16] designed to restore production after the bad summer harvest of 1961. In the Cultural Revolution, *sanziyibao* was directly attributed to the initiative of Liu Shaoqi.[17] It has been pointed out, however, that contemporary evidence suggests that the first three elements were part of official central policy agreed to perhaps by Mao himself. The fourth element had been proposed by Deng Zihui but no links with Liu Shaoqi have been conclusively established.

But whether Mao agreed with them or not, the various elements of *sanziyibao* were clearly a negation of the policies of the Great Leap Forward. The private sector was larger than for several years and the 'free market' sometimes bordered on the 'black market'. One way, of course, of countering 'black market' tendencies was to extend the scope of government markets to include off-ration goods at higher prices.[18] This may have been effective but hardly socialist. There were, indeed, many other unsocialist developments. The new stress on economic rationality and the operation of the 'law of value', for example, meant that many rural organisations which did not pay were closed down regardless of the services they performed. A lot of the *minban* schools, set up on the old Yan'an model during the Great Leap, were also deemed to require too much local expenditure for the relatively low standards they achieved and were thus abolished.[19] As one might have expected, the bulk of these were in the poorer areas. Unless something were done quite drastically, the urban-rural gap would continue to grow.

The architects of China's new economic policy in 1961–2 were, however, concerned more with maintaining a minimum level of production than dealing with the urban-rural gap. They were preoccupied also with restoring order in the countryside and with the low reputation of the local Party organisations. Ironically, the measures taken to rectify local cadres were often to damage that reputation even further.[20] Singled out for criticism were what were known as the 'five styles' (or 'five winds').[21] These were 'the communist style', 'the style of exaggeration', 'the commandist style', 'the privileged style' and 'the style of leading production blindly'. Most of these erroneous 'styles' were directly attributed to the

Great Leap Forward. Cadres were denounced for exceeding the spirit of directives from above, of pushing too far the idea of mess halls, of collectivising too much private property and of being insufficiently concerned with the livelihood of the masses. Doubtless much of this criticism was just, but the spectacle of cadres being disciplined for being too enthusiastic about the Great Leap Forward could not have contributed to the Party's prestige.

As Teiwes points out, the rectification movement of 1960 – 1 had a lot in common with that of 1947 – 8 which had also been designed to curb 'leftist' excesses.[22] At the Ninth Plenum, Mao had called for the formation of peasant associations[23] and sometimes what were known as 'poor and lower-middle peasant core groups' (*pinnong xia zhongnong hexin xiaozu*) assisted work-teams in denouncing cadres.[24] It was, therefore, a modest open-rectification movement. Mobilisation, however, was not always carried out and sometimes work-teams descended on the villages and did little more than subject local cadres to humiliation before meetings of peasants.[25] As long as peasants had a clear knowledge of all the intricacies of developmental policy, there was probably little damage done. But if all peasants learned from the experience was that the Party was bent on punishing excessive zeal, the implications for future programmes of mass mobilisation were not encouraging.

One wonders also about the extent to which the punishment fitted the 'crime'. Could it have been that the severity of punishment was not so much a reflection of a particular cadre's mistakes but of the state of the economy in the area? At a provincial level, a number of cadres were either dismissed or demoted. These included the Great Leap activist Wu Zhipu who was reduced to the rank of second secretary of the Henan Party committee. In his survey of such punishments, Teiwes points out that the heaviest sanctions occurred in the most 'leftist' provinces (Henan, Anhui etc.) but there was also a strong correlation between the severity of punishment and the extent to which a particular province had experienced natural calamities. Anhui, for example, had suffered from the flooding of the Changjiang.[26] Was it sensible to damage the prestige of the Party in the areas where strong leadership was needed most?

## Industrial Policy

As has been noted, the new economic policy consisted in that mixture of 'decentralisation I' and partial centralisation advocated in 1957 by Chen Yun and Xue Muqiao. In industry, therefore, the power of central ministries was strengthened whilst industrial enterprises were allowed much greater operational independence.[27] In the Cultural Revolution, this situation was felt to have led to the worst of both the old policies of the Soviet model and modern Libermanism (the belief in a 'socialist market'). Now as factory general managers acquired many more powers over production decisions and the disposal of profits, economists once again began to write about the virtues of market relationships and the profit motive.[28] From the point of view of the advocate of rapid socialist transformation, there was nothing wrong with the criterion of profit as a success indicator; in fact such an indicator was essential if accounting was to be in terms of money as well as gross output. The radical critique centred not on profit *per se* but on the 'profit motive', whereby the *raison d'être* of an industrial concern became the degree to which its sales exceeded capital and labour inputs, regardless of the criterion of service to the wider community. By 1961, the Chinese were quite convinced that Yugoslavia was no longer a socialist country[29] and yet it was precisely the same sort of policies which had characterised that country's development.

Nevertheless, in 1960–1, it would appear that the question of the profit motive was not so important as it was later to become. The main bone of contention seemed to be the extent to which 'politics' should be 'in command' of industrial work and the extent to which 'experts' should make policy and operational decisions. What in Yan'an days were referred to as the concepts of 'ability' (*cai*) and 'virtue' (*de*) had been revived in the mid-1950s as the concepts 'expert' (*zhuan*) and 'red' (*hong*).[30] Though Party secretaries may have been somewhat cavalier in their treatment of technicians and engineers in the days of the Great Leap,[31] there was never, to my knowledge, any condemnation of the notion of expertise. What was condemned were those *professionals* who neglected political questions and whose view of 'rationality' was limited to an excessively economic view of production and all that that involved. These people had been the 'one-person managers' of the early 1950s and had been subjected to Party control in the Great Leap. Anxious that this type of manager should not run industrial enterprises once again, Mao, at the tail-end of the Great Leap Forward on 22 March 1960, had put forward a constitution for the mammoth Anshan Iron and Steel Corporation which he hoped would be a model for industrial enterprises elsewhere. The Anshan constitution affirmed the notion of 'politics in command' and the importance of Party leadership. It called for the launching of vigorous mass movements, the implementation of cadre participation in productive labour and worker participation in management, the reform of irrational and outdated rules and regulations, the close co-operation between workers, cadres and technicians and a fostering of the movement for technical innovation.[32] The Anshan constitution, however, was not to be adopted until 1970.[33] It was alleged in the Cultural Revolution that it had been resisted by a 'revisionist' Party leadership led by Liu Shaoqi, which countered it by a constitution deriving from the Soviet city of Magnitogorsk.[34] Like so much else in the Cultural Revolution, this claim is difficult to assess, but one cannot deny that the Anshan constitution disappeared from view.

Although some of the descriptions of the restoration of one-person management in the early 1960s are quite lurid,[35] it is likely that, in the atmosphere of the Cultural Revolution in which they were written, there was much exaggeration. In his extremely interesting account of industrial management in China, Andors has put forward the view that, in general, many of the reforms of management instituted during the Great Leap were retained including the 'two participations' and the 'triple combination',[36] which both figured in the Anshan constitution. Perhaps the extremes of one-person management were isolated occurrences; for, quite frankly, in the light of the unpopularity of that system in the early 1950s, it is highly unlikely that such a policy would have made much headway in China *after* the Great Leap, no matter how different overall industrial policy might have been.

## The Huixiang Movement

Just as, in the industrial sphere, the period after January 1961 saw an odd combination of a return to Soviet-model practices, concessions to market socialism and a retention of some of the reforms of the Great Leap, so, in urban administration, a similar situation prevailed. With the decline of urban communes, the old Soviet-style network of street offices with parallel street committees was revamped, even though the name 'commune' might be retained. At the same time, many of the street industries and services (which were a radical legacy of the Great Leap) remained. So long as the primary concern of urban cadres was maintaining food supplies, *ad hoc* policies were the order of the day.

As we have seen, a major problem which the Great Leap Forward set out to solve, but in fact did not, was the constant drift of peasants into the cities. By the spring of 1962, the government had no course but to transfer physically large numbers of the urban population to the rural areas. A campaign was launched in April 1962 known as *huixiang* ('back to the village') whereby people were urged to return to their native areas (even if they were 'ancestral homes' with which their connection was purely historical). The movement was very different from the *xiafang* of the Great Leap Forward which had manifest educational aims and which transferred people usually to places with which they were unfamiliar. All *huixiang* appeared to be was a last-ditch measure to solve the urban food problem. Although there was some propaganda associated with the movement, the process was uncharacteristic in that sometimes very crude techniques were used, such as closing down small factories and leaving workers very little option but to return from whence they came. It was largely the *huixiang* movement, combined with a straitened situation in the countryside, which, in Schurmann's view, led to the mass exodus to Hong Kong in April 1962 and this was made much easier by the relaxation of border controls.[37]

There has been much speculation as to why border controls were, in fact, lifted for a time in April 1962. It could be that local officials in Guangdong just despaired of the situation or, as Vogel suggests, that they knew that, once the Chinese side relaxed border controls, the British would immediately tighten them to prevent a rapid rise in the Hong Kong population.[38] Whatever the truth of the matter, about 15,000 got through and about 60,000 were rounded up by the British and sent back to Guangdong. In Schurmann's opinion, what was really significant about the exodus to Hong Kong in April 1962 lay not in the sphere of macro-politics, nor in the fact that Hong Kong was a *capitalist* city, but simply that it was a city which extended kinship and quasi-kinship networks out into the surrounding countryside be it socialist, capitalist or feudal.[39] The rush into Hong Kong in April 1962, therefore, gives us a very good idea of exactly how serious pressure on the cities must have been during the economic crisis of the early 1960s.

## A 'Capitulationist' Foreign Policy?

It was later claimed that certain Party leaders 'capitulated' not only to 'domestic reactionaries' but also to modern revisionists (the Soviet Union) and to imperialism (mainly the United States) in the period 1961 – 2. The assertion of 'three capitulations' together with 'one annihilation' (of national liberation struggles) was clearly an exaggeration.[40] None the less, there is evidence that, in 1961 – 2, the former hard line in foreign policy began to soften.

Let us look first at 'capitulation' to the Soviet Union. It was extremely strange that the Chinese could possibly have accepted the Moscow declaration of November 1960, which was largely a 'victory' for the Soviet Union. One might note, however, that it was accepted in the very month that a Politburo conference laid the groundwork for the deradicalisation of policy prior to the Ninth Plenum. By the new year, there was clearly an outward show of cordiality between the two countries and there was even talk of a return of Soviet technicians.[41] In February 1961, a Soviet economic mission arrived in Beijing and the eleventh anniversary of the Sino-Soviet alliance of 1950 was celebrated with great fanfare. In this new atmosphere of cordiality, the Chinese government seemed to be putting up with actions which radical critics must later have found intolerable. In 1961, the Soviet Union and some East European countries strengthened economic sanctions against Albania,[42] while in February and April China had concluded economic aid agreements with that country.[43] In June, the Soviet Communist Party put forward a new Party programme (the first since 1919) which declared that the Soviet Party was now engaged in 'building communism'. Communism, however, was defined very largely in economic terms and was later to be bitterly denounced by the Chinese as 'goulash communism'.[44] But in mid-1961, the Chinese seem to have been strangely reticent with their criticisms. In October, at the Twenty-second Congress of the CPSU, Khruschev denounced Albania for opposing destalinisation and departing from 'the commonly agreed line of the whole World Communist Movement.'[45] This attack, which was directly aimed at China, did result in a walk-out by the Chinese delegate Zhou Enlai[46] and the partial resumption of polemics using the code words 'Albania' (meaning China) and 'Yugoslavia' (meaning the Soviet Union). There were some clashes at international Communist forums but by March 1962 the atmosphere was still surprisingly calm. Under the surface, however, those who shared Mao's opinions were most indignant. At a talk to an enlarged central work conference, attended by 7,000 cadres, on 30 January 1962 (but not made public until the Cultural Revolution), Mao pulled no punches.

> The Soviet Union was the first socialist country, and the Soviet Communist Party was the Party created by Lenin. Although the Party and the state leadership of the Soviet Union have now been usurped by the revisionists, I advise our comrades to believe firmly that the broad masses, the numerous Party members and cadres of the Soviet Union are good; that they want revolution, and that the rule of the revisionists won't last long.[47]

Nevertheless, Mao's words were said *in camera* and policy remained cautious. In the summer of 1962, however, the atmosphere became somewhat heated when Khrushchev sought once and for all to heal the breach with Tito of Yugoslavia, but it was not until the Cuban missile crisis of October that the full fury of Chinese indignation broke out and resulted in the dispute becoming public in December 1962. In the meantime, what had happened in China itself was the Tenth Plenum which sought to reverse the current Party line and inaugurate a new period of radicalism. If the above account of events is correct, then one may understand why critics, in the later more radical climate, saw the policies of 1961–2 as a 'capitulation' to the Soviet Union.

The second charge that Party conservatives 'capitulated' to the United States is somewhat more difficult to evaluate, especially since the Chinese were most critical of Kennedy, the new president.[48] In my view, the charge of 'capitulation' to imperialism can only refer to Indo-China. In Laos, in August 1960, a 'left neutralist' military officer Kong Lae took control of Vientiane and invited Prince Souvanna Phouma to resume the post of premier to maintain Laotian neutrality. United States aid, however, went in increasing measure to the rightist General Phoumi, who proceeded to move against both the Pathet Lao and the neutralists, and to drive Souvanna Phouma out into Cambodia. By the end of December 1960, Phoumi was in control of Vientiane and the neutralists and Pathet Lao made their headquarters on the Plain of Jars. Despite massive American aid, the Phoumi régime suffered repeated defeats, forcing the Kennedy government to consider cutting its losses and to urge negotiations. Faced with the possibility of a second Dienbienphu, the American government pressed for a ceasefire and threatened the neutralists and Pathet Lao with the might of SEATO. The Chinese response to this threat was to declare that, if SEATO became involved and if Souvanna Phouma's government requested help, China would not stand idle.[49] In this tense situation, however, China agreed to participate in a 14-nation conference at Geneva which met intermittently from May 1961 to July 1962. The final agreement guaranteed for Laos a very precarious neutrality which did not, in fact, last very long. Laos was soon to become once again a sphere of American military activity and, in retrospect, the Chinese actions of 1961 might indeed have seemed like a 'capitulation' to the United States and an 'annihilation' of the national liberation struggle.

### The Third Taiwan Straits Crisis

However 'capitulationist' or 'annihilationist' the Chinese may have been in other areas of foreign policy in 1962, these epithets surely did not apply to Beijing's relations with Taiwan. Since the crisis of 1958, a state of stalemate had existed, with both sides dug in and the shelling of Jinmen and Mazu being carried on on alternate days. In 1962, however, the situation began to change as the Guomindang began to think of taking advantage of China's natural calamities. Jiang Jieshi's new year message was more bellicose than usual and, in the early spring, large numbers of new recruits were taken into the Guomindang army. In May, a new tax was imposed specifically to support the 'return to the mainland' and a number of American officials were seen to visit Taiwan (whether to encourage Jiang or to restrain him we do not know). Was it just a coincidence that the new United States ambassador to Taiwan, appointed in May, was none other than Admiral Alan G. Kirk, an authority on amphibious operations?[50]

The crisis came to a head in June, when both sides considerably reinforced their troops and a Chinese statement was issued assuring the American-supported Guomindang army that any invasion would be crushed.[51] At a meeting of United States and Chinese ambassadors in

Warsaw, however, the United States disavowed any intention to support Jiang and this was endorsed by President Kennedy. The Chinese appeared to believe the American assurance and the crisis began to subside. Then just as tension relaxed, Khrushchev announced, on 2 July, that any attack on China would be rebuffed by the people of the socialist camp.[52] It was 1958 all over again!

## The Growing Sino-Indian Border Crisis

Another area in which the charge of 'capitulationism' will not stand up was Sino-Indian relations. By the end of 1960, Sino-Indian border negotiations had broken down. Under military pressure, the Indian government proceeded to step up the reinforcement of its frontier posts which had begun back in 1959 as part of a 'forward policy' and which could not but provoke severe Chinese censure.[53] In mid-1960, India had purchased a number of aircraft from the United States and, in the autumn, even larger amounts of military hardware from the Soviet Union. In early 1961, Indian troops began to move forward in the western sector claimed by China and had established 43 posts on disputed territory by the autumn of 1962.

As has been noted, June 1962 was a time of crisis for Chinese foreign policy. Not only was the economy still suffering the effects of natural calamities, there was also a danger of war over the Taiwan Straits. At the same time, a rising had occurred among the Kazakhs in the Yining region along the Soviet-Xinjiang frontier,[54] allegedly at Russian instigation, which was to result in the closure of Soviet consulates in Xinjiang.[55] It is probably not too much of an exaggeration to say that China was faced with a strategic threat on three fronts. By late June, however, it seemed that the Taiwan situation had reverted to stalemate and Khrushchev seemed to be too preoccupied with his Cuban adventure to fully exploit the situation in Xinjiang. In this situation, the Chinese decided to attempt to halt the Indian advance into the disputed territory. On 21 July, the first major armed clash since 1959 occurred along the frontier and China demanded immediate negotiations.[56] But the minimum Indian condition for negotiations was complete Chinese withdrawal from the disputed territories and this the Chinese found completely unacceptable. On 20 October, full-scale war broke out.[57] After four days' fighting, which saw considerable Chinese successes, China proposed a ceasefire and a border settlement based upon its proposals of 1959.[58] These proposals were, however, formally rejected in mid-November and fighting was resumed. On 21 November, after a complete rout of the Indian forces, the Chinese unilaterally withdrew to the *de facto* border proposed in the original offer of a ceasefire.[59]

We shall return to the implications of the Chinese victory which coincided with the Cuban missile crisis (in *China: Radicalism to Revisionism, 1962–1979*). My point here is simply to demonstrate that, although the fighting along the Sino-Indian border took place during a new period of radicalism, the decision to take a firm line had been made in the so-called 'capitulationist' period prior to the Tenth Plenum of September 1962. On this score, no section of the Chinese leadership could have been charged with 'capitulationism'.

## The Revival of the 'Hundred Flowers' Policy

In 1961–2 the old slogan of 'let a hundred flowers bloom; let a hundred schools of thought contend' was once more put forward.[60] The present (1979) Chinese leadership has done much to show the connection between this revival and the original movement of 1957 and to invest it with the authority of Zhou Enlai. Zhou, apparently made a number of important speeches on the policy in the early 1960s and one of these, delivered on 19 June 1961 but apparently suppressed for 18 years, was finally issued for publication in February 1979.[61] Since this speech is similar in part to remarks made by Foreign Minister Chen Yi in August 1961 which were released at the time,[62] I am inclined to believe that it is substantially genuine. It echoes Mao's 1957 position and, in some ways, calls for even greater boldness in seeking literary and artistic freedom. The content of Zhou's speech, however, does not convince me that the movements of 1957 and the early 1960s were qualitatively the same.

First, the 1961–2 movement was informed all along by Mao's 'six criteria' whilst the earlier movement had started without these constraints. Secondly, in 1957 it was Mao Zedong who inspired the movement, seeking widespread criticism of the Soviet model throughout Chinese society. His aim was to revitalise the Party from without. This may perhaps have been Zhou Enlai's aim in 1961 and also the aim of some other Party leaders. In practice, however, the main participants in the movement seemed less interested in revitalising the Party from without than in mobilising support within the Party to discredit the policies of the Great Leap Forward. It is significant to note, in this respect, that some of the most important material to be produced during this period came not from non-Party intellectuals but from senior cadres in the Central Committee's Propaganda Department and the Beijing Party Committee—the very people who had launched the movement in the first place.[63]

The origin of the new policy may be traced back to the Ninth Plenum in January 1961 when particular stress was given to scientific standards.[64] It was felt that the standards of scientific research had fallen during the

Great Leap and that this situation ought to be rectified. From an academic point of view, it was probably true that standards had fallen during the Great Leap but, at that time, the stress had been on widespread popularisation of scientific method; and supporters of the Leap could quite easily argue that a campaign for mass technological innovation was probably worth more than a particular breakthrough in pure mathematics—at least in the context of the tasks to be undertaken at that time. Nevertheless, the new policy in 1961 was designed to give scientists more time for individual (as opposed to group) research, greater material incentives and greater responsibility.

In the discussion above concerning industrial policy, it was noted that 1961 saw a reassessment of the policy of combining 'red' and 'expert'. This, of course, had enormous implications for educational and scientific work. This reassessment was quite apparent in the speech of Zhou Enlai which has been referred to but, unlike other contents of Zhou's speech, was aired quite openly in the press. As Chen Yi noted in August:

> At present we should stress specialised studies because failure to do so will keep our country perpetually backward in science and culture. In the early years of the liberation it was completely necessary for the Party and the government to stress political study. In the past several years, thanks to the correct leadership of the Party, our institutes of higher education have made outstanding achievements in political teaching . . . Today there is a need for us . . . to train a large number of specialists . . . This is our greatest political mission. To make efforts in the study of his special field is the political task of the student . . . The students . . . should devote most of their time and efforts to specialist studies. Of course, these students should also study politics to equip themselves with a certain degree of political consciousness.[65]

It might be useful at this point to compare Chen's remarks with Mao Zedong's Great Leap Forward formulation:

> The relationship between redness and expertness, politics and work, is the unity of two opposites. The tendency to pay no attention to politics certainly must be criticised and repudiated. It is necessary to oppose the armchair politicians on the one hand and the pragmatists who have gone astray on the other. There is no doubt whatever about the unity of politics and technology. This is so every year and will forever be so. This is red and expert. The term 'politics' will continue to exist in the future but the content will be changed. Those who pay no attention to politics and are busy with their work all the day long will become economists who have gone astray and are dangerous. Ideological work and political work guarantee the accomplishment of

economic work and technical work and they serve the economic base. Ideology and politics are also the supreme commander and the soul. As long as we are a bit slack with ideological work and political work, economic work and technical work will surely go astray.[66]

Unless Mao had completely changed his mind on this extremely important theoretical issue, one would suspect that he would have felt that many people who were making policy in 1961 had 'gone astray and were dangerous'. There were evidently quite a few 'economists' who seemed to have deviated from the hitherto accepted interpretation of Marxist-Leninist political economy, for this was the period when the first discussions of Liberman-type proposals on the profit motive began to be heard.[67] Alas, we cannot be sure how Mao responded to Chen Yi's remarks and it is not until we come to the evidence for 1962 that we may begin to deduce Mao's attitude on such contemporary developments.

The period 1961 – 2 also saw an attempt to re-evaluate parts of China's cultural tradition. During the final gasp of the Great Leap in July 1960, Professor Feng Youlan, the author of *A History of Chinese Philosophy*, had come under some criticism for making positive remarks about Confucius.[68] In the atmosphere of 1961 – 2, however, the issue of Confucius could be debated quite openly.[69] There had been a long tradition in China of interpreting Confucius as a 'progressive' according to whatever criterion of progressive was currently in vogue. Once again in 1961, some philosophers declared that Confucius was a progressive because he was a herald of the new feudal society of the sixth century BC who opposed the old slave society that had existed up to that time. Others argued, however, that Confucius, in fact, strove to maintain slave society against the inroads of feudalism and was therefore reactionary. One may regard such debates, which turn on obscure questions such as whether the Chinese word *ren* (man) referred (in the sixth century BC) to all people or just the ruling class, as highly academic and rather abstruse but, in the light of the subsequent campaign against Lin Biao and Confucius (1974 – 5), a case might be made that the Confucius debates of 1961 – 2 turned on the Great Leap Forward in exactly the same way as later debates turned on the Cultural Revolution. Would it be rash to conclude that those who wished to rehabilitate Confucius were, in reality, opponents of the reforms of 1958?

There was also much debate at that time arising out of the issue of 'socialist realism' and 'revolutionary romanticism' in literature and art. In the old days of the Soviet model, considerable attention had been paid to stereotyped 'socialist realism', which in 1958 had been criticised by Mao's close associate Guo Moruo, who insisted that 'socialist realism' should be combined with 'revolutionary romanticism'. In 1961 – 2, however, intellectuals insisted that neither of these two models was wholly adequate and suggested experimentation with other artistic forms.[70] In reality, this often meant no experimentation at all but a return to more traditional forms and genres in Chinese art.

## More Specific Attacks on the Great Leap Forward

The relationship of the above features of the 'blooming and contending' of 1961 – 2 with the Great Leap Forward is perhaps a little oblique. In the fields of short-story writing and drama, however, the criticisms of the Leap seem clearer. At Dalian in August 1962, for example, a conference met under the aegis of Zhou Yang to discuss short stories about the countryside and finished up denouncing mass campaigns, crash programmes and the general Great Leap Forward strategy. Writers, it was claimed, were urged to portray the events of that time as a tragedy. They were to guard against 'excessive romanticism'. Officials in the Propaganda Department, who had denounced Hu Feng, now began to voice much the same kind of criticism as Hu. Writers were urged to portray 'middle characters' and avoid painting everything in black and white terms as had been the fashion during the Leap.[71]

What was potentially more explosive than the efforts of short-story writers, however, was the publication of plays which might be interpreted not only as satirising the Leap but also as indirectly calling for the vindication of Peng Dehuai. It has been argued that from January 1961 to September 1962, a determined effort was made, by critics of the Lushan decisions, to rehabilitate the former Minister of Defence and Peng himself petitioned for his case to be reopened. It is in this connection, Cultural Revolution accounts suggest, that Liu Shaoqi's book *On The Self Cultivation of a Communist Party Member* (better known in English as *How To Be A Good Communist*) was republished, precisely because one of its major themes was the need to combat 'ultra-leftism' and the need for peace within the Party.[72] At the tail-end of the preceding radical period, there had been published, with much fanfare, the fourth volume of *Selected Works of Mao Zedong*. This volume, which dealt with the Civil War before 1949, could have been used to demonstrate the 'correctness' of Mao's long-term judgement.[73] Could it have been the case, therefore, that someone was trying to make a point by republishing Liu's work in 1962?

Perhaps the most critical comment on the Great Leap in the period 1961 – 2 was to emanate from senior members of the Beijing Municipal Party Committee. According to Cultural Revolution sources, Peng Zhen, the mayor of Beijing, initiated in May 1961 a series of investigations into all activities of the Party during the Great Leap. It was alleged that this major investigation was launched by Peng, in his capacity as a provincial-level official, without the authorisation of the Central Committee and could thus be considered conspiratorial. In November of that year, a group of senior cadres in the Beijing administration gathered at a place called Grandview House in the suburbs of Beijing to study a series of Great Leap documents and issued a report which amounted to a forthright condemnation of the policies of that time. That report was, however, never tabled and was not used by Peng Zhen to attack the Great Leap.[74]

The account of the 'Grandview House incident' may well have been a Cultural Revolution fabrication. But one cannot fail to observe that it was from Beijing that some of the most notorious satirical pieces of writing emanated. The most famous play which was subsequently felt to have been a defence of Peng was written by Wu Han, the deputy mayor of Beijing, entitled *Hai Rui Dismissed from Office*.[75] Hai Rui had been a high official of the Ming dynasty, stationed in the Suzhou area from 1569 – 70. At that time, according to Wu Han, the peasants were in a sorry plight because their land had been confiscated by local officials. Despite threats from these officials, the 'noble' Hai Rui took the side of the peasants and ordered the death of a landlord's son who had killed a peasant. The local landlords and officials, however, appealed to the Emperor against Hai Rui's verdict with the result that the landlord's son was spared and Hai Rui unjustly dismissed. The theme of this play, which was similar to Wu Han's essay published in *Renmin Ribao* during the earlier period of consolidation on 16 June 1959, was later considered by Mao to have been a direct satire on the Great Leap Forward. Hai Rui was allegedly Peng Dehuai; the Emperor who had lost touch with reality was supposed to be Mao Zedong and the process whereby land had been unjustly taken away from the peasants was, in fact, the Great Leap Forward. Current (1979) Chinese accounts deny that the play was an attack on the people's communes [76] and some Western commentators have come independently to a similar conclusion. As Teiwes sees it, the objects of the satirical attacks of 1961 – 2 could have been many different people and many different policies. There is insufficient evidence that the play about Hai Rui was a criticism of Mao and a different reading of the play could see Hai Rui as a loyal and dutiful subject. Nor is there any evidence that Mao interpreted it as an attack when it was first produced.[77] One might argue, however, that Mao could have been reluctant to voice his criticism at that time, either because he had not mobilised sufficient support or because, whilst economic conditions were still bad, he did not want to draw any further attention to the problems of the Leap.[78] The important point, however, is that, in 1965, Mao did see the play as an attack and the official rehabilitation of the play about Hai Rui was not made until after the official vindication of Peng Dehuai in late 1978.

The man who in the Cultural Revolution was felt to be the most out-spoken of the satirists of 1961 – 2 was Deng Tuo, the former editor of

*Renmin Ribao* and director of ideological and cultural activities in the Beijing Party committee. The most notorious of his works of the early 1960s was *Notes on the Three Family Village*, which he composed together with Wu Han and another official of the Beijing Party Committee, Liao Mosha, and a series of articles entitled *Evening Talks at Yanshan*, which appeared in the Beijing Party press.[79] Like Wu Han, Deng Tuo was said to have implied that Mao had been misled by flattery, that he was stubborn and cut off from reality. He was also subsequently accused of suggesting that Mao suffered from a particularly acute form of amnesia which caused him to go back on his word and which, if not treated, would result in insanity. He prescribed a long rest.[80] All sorts of implied criticism of the Great Leap policy have been attributed to Deng Tuo,[81] such as a denunciation of 'grandiose schemes which could not be realised'[82] and 'throwing out one's teacher'[83] (the Soviet Union). Finally it was said that Deng Tuo might have suggested reconciliation with the United States for, since the Chinese discovered America in the fifth century, Sino-American relations were worth treasuring.[84] Though it is possible to read all sorts of things into Deng Tuo's historical writing, it is not easy to be convinced by the current (1979) claims that Deng Tuo did not oppose Mao Zedong Thought and was merely echoing Mao's criticism of the 'ultra-leftism' of 1958.[85] Most significant, in this respect, is the fact that Deng Tuo's satirical comments ceased on 2 September 1962, just prior to that historic meeting which was to revive the radical spirit.

## Mao Zedong and Liu Shaoqi

The cessation of Deng Tuo's articles was, it seems, a response to a central work conference which met at Beidaihe in August and September 1962, in preparation for the Tenth Plenum of the Eighth Central Committee which was convened in September. At the Beidaihe meeting, Mao was to be most critical of the handling of national affairs since he had retired to the 'second front' and such criticism might be interpreted as directed against Liu Shaoqi.[86] 1962, therefore, was to see Mao's first serious misgivings about Liu.[87] In recapitulating the events of 1959 – 62, many scholars cannot find much evidence that Mao disagreed with the general thrust of Party policy before 1962 and, with the single exception of the Lushan meetings, was quite prepared to tolerate all kinds of dissent in the highest Party circles.[88] Something very important, therefore, must have happened in 1962.

At first sight, one might suspect that Mao's dissatisfaction with Liu dated from the conference attended by 7,000 cadres in January 1962, and much was made, in the Cultural Revolution, about the bitter 'struggle between two lines' at that time. At the conference, Liu Shaoqi remarked that, whilst in Hunan, peasants had told him that only 30 per cent of the difficulties in production had been caused by natural calamities, whereas the remaining 70 per cent had been caused by man-made factors. Liu suggested, moreover, that it might have been better had communes never been established.[89] This was the kind of remark which had damned Peng Dehuai in 1959 and, indeed, Liu pointed out that some of Peng's comments had been correct. Liu went on, moreover, to criticise the campaign against 'right opportunism' which he equated with erroneous 'leftist' campaigns in pre-liberation days. But Liu did not endorse Peng's 'conspiratorial' activities and affirmed the basic correctness of the Great Leap.[90] Mao, therefore, did not seem to object to Liu's forthrightness. In his speech to the conference, Mao did not address all the problems raised by Liu. He did, however, endorse Liu's speech and struck the same kind of note as Liu in calling for the restoration of the norms of inner-Party debate after the abnormal situation in previous years.[91] Clearly, Mao was very angry with some people at the conference:

> Those of you who shirk responsibility or who are afraid of taking responsibility, who do not allow people to speak, who think that you are tigers, and that nobody will dare touch your arse, whoever has this attitude, ten out of ten of you will fail. People will talk anyway. You think that nobody will really dare to touch the arse of tigers like you. They damn well will.[92]

It would seem, however, that the target of such remarks was not Liu Shaoqi.

In February 1962, Liu began to be much more critical of current economic policy which, he felt, had not solved most of the problems left over by the Leap. At that time, the programme of retrenchment developed even further in the single-minded desire to restore production. This was the period in which *sanziyibao* was recommended as a general policy by Deng Zihui[93] and when Deng Xiaoping made his famous remark to the effect that it did not matter what colour a cat might be so long as it caught mice.[94] Deng seemed to imply that one should not worry what the ideological implications of a particular policy might be, so long as it increased production. The accelerated retrenchment was no doubt dictated by the announcement of a huge budget deficit. But when confronted with that fact, Mao simply replied that a five-year period of consolidation would sort things out.[95] Such a remark did not suggest that Mao looked forward to impending radicalisation. One suspects, however, that Mao might have been disturbed by the qualitative change in retrenchment policies. By August 1962, he had become suspicious of Liu Shaoqi. But was this just because of the acceleration of retrenchment in 1962? Had Mao been hostile to the retrenchment policies all along and was he waiting for an improvement in the harvest conditions before launching an attack? Had he been stung by the new genre of satirical writing? Was he alarmed about the large-scale rehabilitation of former rightists? Had he come to the view that Liu's pressure for even stricter controls was a sign that Liu had lost his nerve and was not equal to the task with which he had been entrusted? Or were there other reasons?

We cannot be sure as to what made Mao come to this view in the first few months of 1962. A plausible explanation, however, might be found in Mao's long analysis of problems of political economy which he was undertaking at that time. It is possible that he began to see Liu and, for that matter, many other leaders of the Party as products of a set of structural relationships which were not conducive to socialist transition. 1962 marked the end of Mao's first serious analysis of political economy and, by that time, he was coming to a new view of socialist transition. Mao's writings on political economy were not intended for publication in the form in which they were subsequently released[96] and they contain many contradictions and much incoherence. None the less, in his comments on a Soviet textbook on political economy, Mao appears for the first time as a political economist of some originality and it is important to examine his writings and the comments of various scholars who have attempted to piece together what was distinctly new in Mao's approach.

## Towards a Reformulation of the Process of Socialist Transition

In his writings of the early 1960s, Mao seemed above all to be concerned with working out a theoretical explanation of 'revisionism'. Up to that time, the term had been treated merely as a behavioural characteristic amenable to arbitrary interpretation. Now, Mao attempted to depict a number of stages through which the socialist revolution would pass and to define revisionism as the adoption of policies which belonged to a superseded stage.

The problem of the stages of revolution has always been a very contentious one among Marxist-Leninists. In telescoping the bourgeois democratic stage of revolution into the socialist stage, Trotsky had incurred the ire of the whole of the Stalinist establishment. Thus, when Mao put forward his ideas on 'uninterrupted revolution' in the Great Leap Forward, he made the point that he was not adopting a Trotskyist position and still conceived of discrete stages.[97] Schram, who translates the term 'uninterrupted revolution' (*buduan geming*) as 'permanent revolution' (the term used by Trotsky and by Mao in his criticism of Trotsky), is unconvinced by Mao's defence.[98] Levy, on the other hand, who focuses on Mao's writings of 1960–2, is convinced that Mao had worked out a coherent 'timing theory'.[99] Though each of Mao's transitional stages established the preconditions for the next, it was quite discrete. The first of these in modern Chinese history constituted the bourgeois democratic revolution which ended in 1949 with the seizure of power.[100] Here, Mao revised the earlier view that the bourgeois democratic revolution had continued through the new democratic stage of the early 1950s. The second stage constituted the socialist transformation which was completed by the mid-1950s. Here, Mao was careful to avoid saying that socialism had been achieved[101] and there is some evidence that he had come to reject the static model of socialism which Stalin had laid down in 1936 (see pp. 109–10). The third stage, which began in the mid-1950s, was marked by the co-existence of 'co-operative ownership' and 'ownership by the whole people', though one is never quite sure which elements of the Chinese economy belonged to which category. The fourth stage, which had yet to be embarked upon, was to be characterised by 'total ownership by the whole people' and the fifth stage was, in fact, communism. After that there would be other stages which no one at present could define.[102]

Having elaborated these stages, it was possible to develop a critical theory of developments in the Soviet Union. As Mao saw it, the Soviet leadership applied principles valid for one stage to completely different stages. Stalin, for example, did not see the different roles played by commodities in the different stages of socialist transition. Both Mao and Stalin agreed that labour power could no longer remain a commodity once the socialist revolution had begun. Both also agreed that commodity production was necessary so long as co-operative ownership coexisted with 'ownership by the whole people';[103] only that way could exchange between the two sectors be ensured. They differed, however, with regard to the commodity feature of the means of production. As Mao saw it, Stalin regarded the replacement, by planning, of the commodity feature of the means of production as a key element of socialism.[104] Stalin, therefore, applied policies appropriate to the stage of 'total ownership by the whole people' to the stage where that form of ownership still coexisted with co-operative ownership. Thus there was a premature and excessive reliance on the planning machinery and an inefficient centralisation which dampened mass initiative.

Though Stalin had erred by implementing, in the current stage, policies appropriate to another stage, his error was qualitatively different from that of the Soviet leadership in the early 1960s. Stalin, in applying policies appropriate to a *future* stage, had committed a 'leftist' error. The current Soviet leadership was implementing policies appropriate to a superseded stage. They were thus 'revisionist'. If the above is a correct interpretation of Mao's views, then the implications for Chinese policies were most profound. Unfortunately, Mao was reluctant to draw those implications, probably because he had supported most of the policies of retrenchment since 1960. It is possible that Mao viewed the situation at two levels. On the one hand, he supported measures designed to restore the economy and foster the norms of inner-Party debate. On the other hand, he surely could not fail to notice that those policies might also be seen as belonging to a superseded stage of development and could be described as 'revisionist'. If Mao had followed through his theoretical discussion, he might have concluded that *sanziyibao* constituted a retreat to the second or even the first stage. The same may be said for the 'four freedoms' (to engage in usury, hire labour, sell land and run private business), if indeed those 'freedoms' were more than a Cultural Revolution fabrication. Other policies might be seen as appropriate for the current stage in terms of ownership but in terms of Mao's other two criteria for evaluating a particular stage—the relations between people at work and the reciprocal relations between production and distribution.[105] Thus, the Magnitogorsk constitution was less appropriate to the relations between people at work than the Anshan constitution which it was said to have replaced. Similarly, the adoption of policies appropriate to the third stage, which stipulated the 'socialist' principle of 'from each according to his/her ability, to each according to his/her work', in practice, resulted in a revival of piecework, the negation of 'politics in command' and its alleged replacement by 'work-points in command' and 'money in command'; these were appropriate more to the first stage.

There is, of course, no record that Mao made such a diagnosis of current Chinese policies in the early 1960s, though he was to be concerned with all the above aspects in the Cultural Revolution. My point is simply that the above diagnosis seems to follow logically from the kind of analysis of Soviet society which Mao was undertaking. If 1962 was the turning-point in Mao's ideas, it is not unreasonable to infer that Mao began to perceive a disjunction between the policies he had supported and his theoretical analysis. Once, moreover, Mao had made the jump from policy to theory, then questions of inner-Party norms of debate did not appear as very important and he had a theoretical basis with which to 'go against the tide'.

But any Marxist has to go much further than examining policies. A Marxist must ask about the class origin of those policies. Throughout the 1950s, Chinese thinking on the transformation of classes in Chinese society had been very inadequate. In the early 1950s, when the orthodox Soviet view of socialism was dominant, classes were seen exclusively as residues of the past. At the time of liberation, a complex system of class analysis had been adopted in which individuals were assigned to one of several dozen categories. These categories were based on relationships to the means of production but also included groups which would not ordinarily be considered in a class context (e.g. revolutionary soldiers).[106] Throughout the 1950s, individual class designations (*jieji chengfen*) remained even though changes in socio-economic structure radically altered the situation. Even in 1957, when Mao Zedong offered a new approach to social analysis, the residual view was strong. In his speech 'On the Correct Handling . . .', Mao differentiated between two kinds of social contradictions—those 'among the people' (capable of peaceful solution) and those 'between the people and the enemy' (capable only of forceful resolution). Observing Mao's contention that non-antagonistic contradictions, handled inappropriately, might grow into antagonistic contradictions, one writer has suggested that such was the basis of a new generative theory of class.[107] Others, however, argue more convincingly that the analysis of 'uninterrupted revolution', at that time, was outside the framework of classes and a residual view was still characteristic of Mao's thought.[108] When it came down to it, the concept 'the people' was treated as a behavioural rather than a substantive category.

By the early 1960, it was evident that Mao was becoming more and more concerned that new privileged groups might provide the basis for the formation of a new bourgeoisie. He spoke of 'vested interest groups' (*jide liyi jituan*)[109] stemming from the 'three major differences' which had taken on a hereditary nature.[110] At the conference attended by 7,000 cadres in January 1962 he was quite explicit:

> In our country, the system of man exploiting man has already been abolished as has the economic basis of landlords and bourgeoisie. Since the reactionary classes are now not so terrible as hitherto, we speak of them as remnants. Yet on no account must we treat these remnants lightly. We must continue to engage in struggle with them [for] they are still planning a comeback. In a socialist society [moreover] *new bourgeois elements may still be produced.* Classes and class struggle remain throughout the entire socialist stage and that struggle is protracted, complex and sometimes even violent.[111]

Thus the slogan 'never forget the class struggle', which was to dominate Mao's thinking during the next few years, though governed mainly by the residual view, contained the germs of a generative view of class. The implications of this generative view are quite profound. It now became conceivable that newly generated classes might be found in the leadership of the Communist Party itself. Socialism could now be viewed not as a model to be achieved and consolidated but as the whole process of transition from capitalism to communism. It was, moreover, reversible. A restoration of capitalism could now be conceived as taking place not only because of the actions of enemy agents (as it was according to the view of the early 1950s), not only because of the inappropriate handling of contradictions (as it was according to Mao's managerial view of the mid-1950s), but because of inequalities generated in the process of economic development.

But how was the generation of these new classes to be prevented? Here we must look at Mao's discussion of the relationship between the productive forces and the relations of production. Since Mao ignored the old problem in Marxism which stems from Marx's location of the relations of production in both the economic base and the ideological superstructure, his views on this subject tend to be somewhat crude. Nevertheless, following Levy, I am convinced that it is possible to see in Mao's writings of the early 1960s the germs of a theory of cultural revolution. Mao felt that the process, described by Marx, whereby a revolution is caused by productive forces outstripping the relations of production—i.e. when the superstructure lags behind the economic base—was valid only for advanced capitalist societies. In more backward countries, a revolution begins in the superstructure because that is the weakest link in the chain of capitalist control.[112] Thus, the relations of production may be transformed before the corresponding productive forces have fully developed, and the superstructure, instead of lagging behind, provides the conditions to push the productive forces forward. A *cultural* revolution, therefore, precedes a social revolution. Such an interpretation is, I believe, an accurate reflection of Mao's views. What is more contentious, both in interpretation and in substance, is Levy's suggestion that the above conclusion was seen by Mao as valid not only for major revolutions marking a seizure of power but for qualitative leaps in the process of socialist transition. Together, these leaps might be seen as part of a continuing process of revolution and the excessive consolidation of any stage in the transition process would create obstacles for the development of the next.[113] To prevent excessive consolidation in any stage, a number of measures had to be taken which were, in the first instance, *superstructural*.

The above formulation was markedly different from most Soviet views of the determining role of the productive forces. The official Soviet view was not a mechanistic one where changes in the productive forces automatically produced changes in the relations of production, or where the latter were simply a drag on the former. Indeed Stalin, in 1952, castigated the would-be textbook writer Yaroshenko for absorbing the relations of production into the productive forces and reaching a mechanistic view of communism as rational organisation.[114] Nevertheless, Mao gave a far greater weight to the active role of the superstructure than Stalin; he even criticised Stalin on precisely that point.[115]

If the above is a correct description of Mao's position, then he had revised the orthodox view of cultural revolution. This held that changes in ideas lag behind changes in material forces and a revolutionary process is necessary to bring them back into correspondence. This had been the view which had informed Mao's mid-1950s view of uninterrupted revolution and it continued into the 1960s. Indeed, in the same work in which

Levy suggests Mao might be arguing in favour of superstructural push, one may still find paragraphs discussing cultural lag.[116] Of course, superstructural push and cultural lag need not necessarily be in contradiction but one cannot use both theories to describe the same period. Yet Mao seemed to be doing precisely that. But perhaps one may understand his reluctance to abandon the theory of cultural lag in favour of initial superstructural push. After all, it could lead to a charge of 'idealism'. It is debatable, however, whether the notion of superstructural push leads inevitably to idealism. Nowhere is it argued that the preconditions for revolution are created in people's minds, merely that the precipitant is, in fact, located in the superstructure and that the initial role of leadership in that sphere is crucial. Surely this is what Lenin's theory of a Bolshevik Party, where a vanguard leads the proletariat from trade union consciousness to revolutionary consciousness is all about. It is not my intention here to evaluate whether such an argument is tenable or whether Mao's extension of Lenin's idea about the 'weakest link' is valid; nor do I wish to enter the savage polemic about Mao's Marxist credentials.[117] I wish merely to describe Mao's early thinking about cultural revolution which was to play such a major part in Chinese politics for a decade and a half. What must be stressed, however, was that the above generative view of class and the notion of superstructural push remained only as one strand in Mao's thought. This strand coexisted with previous thinking about the residual view of class and the notion of cultural lag. The ambiguity in Mao's thinking contributed to the theoretical confusion which dominated Chinese politics until the strand of thought, developed by Mao in the early 1960s, was expunged from the official theory of the Communist Party after Mao's death.

*China: Radicalism to Revisionism, 1962–1979* will explore the fate of Mao's generative notion of class. All which need be noted here is that, once class antagonism had been conceptualised in non-behavioural terms and once it was conceded that such antagonism might exist at the very highest levels of the Party, it became possible to view with suspicion those whose behaviour was impeccable from an inner-Party point of view but who were associated with policies which could lead to class polarisation. Since Mao himself had been associated with such policies, one might question his right to assign blame to Liu Shaoqi. But there were few senior members of the Party who, at one time or another, had not been associated with policies which were later considered to be excessively 'left' or excessively 'right'. After 1962, 'the past' was to 'serve the present' and, in the context of that time, Mao had decided that Liu Shaoqi and many others were on the 'right'. The result was to be a breakdown of Party norms, much chaos and confusion, but also a major element of liberation.

## Conclusion

Mao's new concern with class struggle was to usher in a new stage in the history of the Chinese People's Republic. It was articulated at a time when the period of natural calamities seemed to be coming to an end and the harvests had improved. The consolidation period of 1960–2, however, stood in marked contrast to the earlier periods of consolidation. It was this time much more difficult to chalk up the successes.

The people's communes in the countryside had been weakened and those in the cities had virtually disappeared. The full employment of 1958 had given way to widespread underemployment. Many of the light industrial enterprises in the countryside had ceased to operate and some of the smaller factories in the cities had closed. Some of the large industrial enterprises, started during the Great Leap, remained uncompleted. Much of the economy seemed to be regulated more by the market than by either central or local planning and there were many cases of corruption and bureaucratic inefficiency.

The above, however, is only one side of the coin. Although the people's communes were but a shadow of their former selves, commune-type organisations, some would argue, had helped to ward off famine during the bad years. Now that the weather had improved, one might anticipate that the communes would be strengthened. Though urban communes, in their original form, had perhaps been somewhat premature, they had helped to institute street industries which, potentially at least, offered great prospects for generating employment. Above all, the spirit of do-it-yourself organisation had been established. It could surely only be a matter of time before small industries, closed during the bad years, would be reopened once a sufficient agricultural surplus began to appear. It might be some time before some of the larger industrial concerns, which had depended on imports of technology from the Soviet Union, could operate according to the spirit of 'self reliance', but China had learnt the lesson of avoiding too great a dependence on the Soviet Union.

As for the growth of the market, a tremendous battle had yet to be fought to establish exactly what degree of market relationships might be permissible at what stage of socialist construction. At the conference attended by 7,000 cadres in January 1962, Mao expressed the gravity of this task:

> If our country does not establish a socialist economy, what kind of situation shall we be in? We shall become a country like Yugoslavia, which has actually become a bourgeois country; the dictatorship of the proletariat will be transformed into a bourgeois dictatorship, into a reactionary fascist type of dictatorship. This is a question which

demands the utmost vigilance. I hope comrades will give a great deal of thought to it.[118]

In the field of foreign policy, 1962 saw China standing much more alone than in 1959. In 1962, China was faced with a strategic threat on three fronts. The Sino-Soviet dispute was by that time insoluble and the United States had cut its losses for the time being in Laos only to strengthen its position in Vietnam. By the end of the year, India had been rebuffed but that country seemed no longer non-aligned but aligned with both the superpowers at the expense of China and, as such, was an intermediate source of danger to China's security. Nevertheless, Mao felt that there was no virtue in maintaining an alliance with an increasingly 'revisionist' Soviet Union. China had stood on its own in the past and could do so again. After all, the one sector in society which seemed effectively to be repudiating a 'revisionist' path was the PLA which was gearing itself both to the old tradition of people's war and the possibility of China becoming a nuclear power. Mao was soon to place a much greater confidence in the social role of the army—a confidence which, in retrospect, might have been misplaced. But that is a subject to be considered in *China: Radicalism to Revisionism, 1962–1979*. All we need note here is that, in September 1962, Mao returned to the 'first front' and initiated a series of movements which were eventually to convulse Chinese society.

## NOTES

1. One of the first accounts to note the similarity with the Soviet NEP is Schurmann, 1964.

2. Bo Yibo, *PR* 8, 24 February 1961, p. 5.

3. Though a version of the original document is available in the United States, the only version I have consulted is the one revised by the Tenth Plenum. *Issues and Studies*, Vol. XV, No.10, October 1979, pp. 93-111; ibid., No.12, December 1979, pp. 106–15.

4. Schurmann, 1966, p. 493.

5. Vogel, 1971, pp. 279–80.

6. Chen, 1968, p. 781; *FEER*, Vol. LIX, No.5, 1 February 1968, p. 193.

7. Vogel, 1971, p. 280; *SCMP* 2421, 20 January 1961, pp. 1–3.

8. Vogel, 1971, p. 281.

9. *PR* 38, 20 September 1960, pp. 21–2.

10. See Chang, 1975, pp. 138–40; Liu Shaoqi, 23 October 1966, Liu, Vol.III, 1968, p. 361.

11. Vogel, 1971, p. 283.

12. Ibid., p. 281.

13. Mao observed that, in Hebei, some 15 per cent of teams were dominated by wavering middle-peasant elements. Mao Zedong, 1960 (or 1961–2), *JPRS*, 1974, p. 255. See also Vogel, 1971, p. 284; Schurmann, 1966, p. 494.

14. In this regard, see the poster which appeared on 14 January 1967, translated in *CQ*

30, 1967, pp. 207–9. Though this belongs to a later period, it was probably indicative of long-term peasant feeling.

15. On the different sizes of production teams in 13 communes in 1965 (from seven members to 153), see Burki, 1970, p. 8.

16. Chang, 1975, pp. 138–9.

17. On the connection with Liu, see Domes, 1973, pp. 126–7.

18. Vogel, 1971, pp. 290-1.

19. Ibid., p. 286.

20. Teiwes, 1979, p. 459.

21. Mao Zedong, 18 January 1961, *JPRS*, 1974, p. 239 (translated here as 'five habits'). See also Teiwes, 1979, pp. 450–4.

22. Teiwes, 1979, p. 460.

23. Mao Zedong, 18 January 1961, *JPRS*, 1974, p. 244.

24. Teiwes, 1979, p. 465.

25. Vogel, 1971, pp. 277–8.

26. Teiwes, 1979, p. 470.

27. Schurmann, 1966, p. 218.

28. Meng Gui and Xiao Lin, *SCMM* 539, 29 August 1966, pp. 1–12.

29. Mao Zedong, 30 January 1962, Schram 1974, p. 167. The reference to Yugoslavia was deleted in the official version published in 1978, *PR* 27, 7 July 1978 p. 11.

30. Mao Zedong, 19 February 1958, *CB* 892, 21 October 1969, p. 6.

31. Schurmann, 1966, p. 295.

32. *PR* 16, 17 April 1970, p. 3; ibid. 14, 3 April 1970, p. 11.

33. Ibid. 16, 17 April 1970, p. 3.

34. Ibid. See also Mao Zedong, March 1960, *JPRS*, 1974, p. 230.

35. E.g. *SCMP* 4369, 5 March 1969, pp. 7–10.

36. Andors, 1974.

37. Schurmann, 1966, pp. 399–402.

38. Vogel, 1971, p. 295.

39. Schurmann, 1966, p. 399.

40. Mao Zedong singled out Vice-Foreign Minister Wang Jiaxiang as guilty of this charge. Mao Zedong, March 1964, *JPRS*, 1974, p. 345. See also Zhou Enlai, December 1964, *PR* 1, 1 January 1965, p. 13.

41. Crankshaw, 1965, p. 137.

42. Zagoria, 1961, p. 7.

43. Ibid., p. 8.

44. *PFLP*, 1965, p. 465.

45. Zagoria, 1966, pp. 370–83.

46. Crankshaw, 1965, p. 142.

47. Mao Zedong, 30 January 1962, Schram, 1974, p. 181. See also *PR* 27, 7 July 1978, p. 19.

48. E.g. Tan Wenrui, *PR* 15, 14 April 1961, pp. 11–13.

49. Chen Yi, ibid., p. 5.

50. H. Hinton, 1966, p. 271.

51. *PR* 26, 29 June 1962, pp. 5–7.

52. H. Hinton, 1966, p. 272.

53. On the Indian forward policy, see Maxwell, 1972, pp. 179–273.

54. H. Hinton, 1966, p. 318, 324–5 and 328.

55. Ibid., p. 324.

56. *PR* 30, 27 July 1962, p. 6.

57. Ibid., p. 387; Maxwell, 1972, p. 387.

58. *PR* 43, 26 October 1961, pp. 5–6.

59. Ibid. 47/48, 30 November 1962, pp. 5–7.

60. Ibid. 12, 24 March 1961, pp. 6–9.

61. Zhou Enlai, 19 June 1961, abridged version in *BR* 13, 30 March 1979, pp. 9–16.

62. Chen Yi, 10 August 1961, *CQ* 8, 1961, p. 231 (from *Zhongguo Qingnianbao*, 1 September 1961).

63. See Goldman, 1969, p. 68.

64. Ibid., p. 61.

65. Chen Yi, 10 August 1961, *CQ* 8, 1961, p. 231.

66. Mao Zedong, 19 February 1958, *CB* 892, 21 October 1969, p. 6.

67. Goldman, 1969, p. 63. For a criticism of these views, see *PR* 44, 28 October 1966, pp. 32–5.

68. Goldman, 1969, p. 63.

69. The culmination of the Confucius debate occurred in late 1962 at a symposium organised by the Shandong Historical Institute. See Wilhelm, 1965, p. 130.

70. Goldman, 1969, p. 64.

71. Ibid., pp. 69–73.

72. *PR* 22, 12 May 1967, pp. 7–11.

73. Ibid. 40, 4 October 1960, pp. 7–19. On the significance of this, see Joffe, 1975, pp. 22–3.

74. See Joffe, 1975, pp. 33–6.

75. See Pusey, 1969. In Pusey's view, the 1959 letter under the pseudonym Liu Mianzhi was a far more severe criticism than the play (p. 15). During the more radical period after Lushan, Wu Han's writings on Hai Rui struck a different note (ibid., p. 17) in which he obliquely criticised Peng Dehuai. The play was written in November 1960 and first staged in Beijing in February 1961. It was suspended after only a few performances. Wu Han was subsequently held to be guilty of 'using the past to satirise the present' (*yi gu feng jin*) as opposed to Mao's slogan of 'making the past serve the present' (*gu wei jin yong*).

76. *BR* 10, 9 March 1979, pp. 6–7 and 27.

77. Teiwes, 1979, pp. 476–9.

78. Joffe, 1975, pp. 37–8.

79. Deng Tuo, 1963 (I have already taken the following from Goldman, 1969, and checked the original).

80. *CB* 792, 29 June 1966, p. 4.

81. Deng Tuo, 1963, pp. 78–80.

82. Ibid., p. 180 (a reference to Wang Anshi).

83. Ibid., pp. 34–6.

84. Ibid., pp. 97–9.

85. Zhang Yide, *GMRB*, 26 January 1979, p. 3, *FBIS* CHI-79-029-E 2–8, 9 February 1979; Su Shuangbi, *GMRB*, 28 January 1979, p. 3, *FBIS* CHI-79-029-E 8–11, 9 February 1979.

86. Joffe, 1975, pp. 48–50; Chang, 1975, p. 142.

87. *SCMM* 652, 18 April 1969; Teiwes, 1979, p. 480.

88. Teiwes, 1979, pp. 441 et seq.

89. *SCMM* 652, 28 April 1969, pp. 25 and 27. See also the discussion in Joffe, 1975, pp. 39-46.

90. See Joffe, 1975, p. 51.

91. Mao Zedong, 30 January 1962, Schram, 1974, pp. 158–87. An amended version of this speech was issued publicly in 1978. *PR* 27, 7 July 1978, pp. 6–22.

92. Schram, 1974, p. 167 *PR* (27, 7 July 1978) translation on p. 11.

93. Mao Zedong, March 1964, *JPRS*, 1974, p. 345.

94. *CB* 874, 17 March 1969, p. 6; Joffe, 1975, p. 24.

95. Rice, 1972, pp. 189–90.

96. *JPRS*, 1974, pp. 247–318; Mao Zedong, 1977.

97. Mao Zedong, 28 January 1958, *Chinese Law and Government*, Vol.I, No.4, Winter 1968–9, pp. 13–14.

98. See Schram, 1971.

99. See Levy, 1975. Much of the following is based on Levy, and is taken from Brugger, 1978, pp. 20–6.

100. Mao Zedong, 1960 (or 1961–2), *JPRS* 1974, p. 252.

101. Ibid., p. 268. Here Mao qualifies the Soviet assertion that China 'accomplished' the socialist revolution, preferring the term 'won decisive victory'.

102. Ibid., pp. 264 and 273.

103. Mao defended Stalin against the charge that he wished to abolish all commodity production. Ibid., p. 298.

104. Mao Zedong, November 1958 (or 1959), *JPRS* 1974, p. 130. Discussed in Levy, 1975, pp. 103–4.

105. Mao Zedong, 1960 (or 1961–2), *JPRS* 1974, p. 270.

106. For a survey of class categorisation, see Kraus, 1977.

107. Starr, 1971, pp. 620–1.

108. Young and Woodward, 1978.

109. Mao Zedong, 1960 (or 1961–2), *JPRS*, 1974, p. 273, Mao 1969, p. 351.

110. Kraus, 1977, pp. 63–4, based on Mao Zedong, 1960 (or 1961–2), *JPRS* 1974, p. 306 (on the highly educated people with large salaries who are also stupid); Mao Zedong, 1960 (or 1961–2), *JPRS*, 1974, p. 273 (on the airs put on by cadres' children).

111. Mao Zedong, 30 January 1962, Mao, n.p. n.d. (probably 1967), pp. 68–9, emphasis added. Slightly different translations are in Schram, 1974, p. 168; *PR* 27, 7 July 1978, p. 12.

112. Levy, 1975, pp. 107–8, based on Mao Zedong, 1960 (or 1961–2), *JPRS*, 1974, pp. 258–9.

113. Mao Zedong, 1960 (or 1961–2), *JPRS*, 1974, p. 272.

114. Stalin, 1952, pp. 60–86.

115. Mao Zedong, November 1958 (or 1959), *JPRS*, 1974, p. 130.

116. Mao Zedong, 1960 (or 1961–2), *JPRS*, 1974, p. 280.

117. See the debate between Pfeffer, 1976; Schwartz, 1976; Walder, 1977; Wakeman, 1977; Schram, 1977.

118. Mao Zedong, 30 January 1962, Schram, 1974, p. 167.

# CONCLUSION

## The Models

This volume has examined two models of administration, which were employed in China in the 1940s and the early 1950s, and modified thereafter. The Yan'an model, articulated in 1942–3, had at its core a process of rectification whereby leaders learned how to apply Marxism-Leninism and general Party policy to a concrete environment and were made to answer for their conduct in the field. In that process, a new leadership type was prescribed—the 'cadre'—committed to change within a network of human solidarity and with an orientation which was both 'red' and 'expert'. The cadre operated in a situation where a distinction was drawn between policy and operations. He was committed also to the principle of the Mass Line which reconciled central policy with mass sentiments. Administration was organised according to a principle of dual rule and political campaigns were effected by horizontal mobilisation under the leadership of local Party branches. To prevent a growing division of labour between leaders and led, a programme of *xiaxiang* (later called simply *xiafang*) was introduced, whereby cadres engaged for periods of time in manual labour and helped peasants construct an informal or semi-formal *minban* education system. Throughout this whole process, units (both civilian and military) were encouraged to become self-sufficient and competent in both production and other duties. Rural co-operativisation, therefore, was by no means merely an agricultural programme and attempts were made to integrate agriculture, industry, administration, education and defence, insofar as wartime conditions allowed.

In the early 1950s, faced with the problems of administering large urban as well as rural areas, the general inexperience of cadres, the Cold War and economic blockade, decisions were taken to implement a model of administration which derived from the contemporary Soviet Union.

259

As an imported model, it was applicable neither to the objective situation in China in the early 1950s nor to the tradition of the Chinese Communist Party. The Soviet model, which was often implemented dogmatically, tended to prescribe a leadership type which was more that of the manager than that of the cadre. The new leader was still committed to change but within a network of technological solidarity. In a situation where both policy and operational decision-making were centralised, the commitment of leaders was to 'expertise' rather than to political values and the quality 'virtue' ('red') was interpreted increasingly in technological terms. The culture-hero frequently became the engineer and model worker rather than the political activist and the powers of local Party branches tended to be eclipsed in a centrally organised, vertical bureaucracy. In such a situation, *xiaxiang, minban* education and the Mass Line became less important, a slow programme of co-operativisation tended to be run from the top down and the army became separated from the rest of society.

The Soviet model of administration was, however, only imperfectly implemented and, in the mid-1950s, certain of its features came under attack. By the Great Leap Forward of 1958–9, the model was dismantled and many elements of the Yan'an tradition were adapted to the changed situation. The original Yan'an model had been formulated in a period of moderate radicalism. In 1958–9, however, the political climate often went to radical extremes and an excessive concern with production and 'ultra-left' idealism resulted in 'mistakes'. The debates of the early 1960s focused on these mistakes. At issue here was the role of the Great Leap Forward in bringing about the economic crisis of 1960–2. Various leaders disagreed on the extent to which one should assign blame to the policies of 1958–9 or to the three years of very bad harvests which China experienced at that time. A major cleavage, however, did not occur until 1962 when Mao decided that the policies of post-Great Leap retrenchment had gone far enough.

This volume has speculated on the reasons why disputes remained constrained by a basic policy consensus until 1962. Though no definitive conclusion has been reached, it is argued that 1962 was important in marking the beginning of Mao's fundamental reappraisal of the process of socialist transition. The 'new democratic' formula, adopted in the 1940s and early 1950s, was not particularly concerned with defining socialism, since the current 'new democratic revolution' was seen as a species of 'bourgeois democratic revolution'. During that revolution, it was believed that a 'four-class bloc' would eradicate the landlords together with the bureaucratic and comprador bourgeoisie. By the 1950s, however, as the Chinese engaged in 'socialist construction', they came to see 'socialism' as a static model in much the same way as Stalin had conceived the term in 1936. At that time, Stalin had outlined a number of features of 'socialism' in order to demonstrate how the Soviet Union had basically achieved them. The Stalinist model had been criticised by Trotsky on the grounds that socialism had been pitched at too low a level.[1] What was more to the point, however, was that the Stalinist model lacked a diachronic element. Mao was to remark on Stalin's poor knowledge of dialectics. But, when he made those remarks, Mao did not see that China, in abandoning the Soviet model of administration, had not abandoned the Soviet model of socialism.

Thus, Mao's seminal essay 'On the Correct Handling . . .', whilst rejecting many of the Soviet ways of doing things, still adopted a managerialist method of 'handling contradictions' in order to make the model work more effectively. What was new about Mao's conceptualisation of 'uninterrupted revolution', in January 1958, was his attitude towards the duration of periods of consolidation between the various stages in the construction of socialism.[2] It was, however, still informed by the 1936 Stalinist view, reiterated in 'On the Correct Handling . . .', that 'large-scale turbulent class struggles characteristic of times of revolution [had] in the main come to an end'. Though it might have been the case that Mao was sympathetic to those who claimed, in 1958, that the socialist revolution might be growing over into communism, there is no evidence that he was prepared, at that time, to incorporate such considerations into his theoretical view of socialist transition. He thus found it quite easy, in the subsequent period, to condemn the 'communist style'.

It was a consideration of events in the Soviet Union which led Mao to reformulate his views on socialist transition. In analysing what was particularly 'leftist' about the mistakes of Stalin, Mao began to come to a view on what constituted 'revisionism'. By 1962, 'revisionism' was seen not simply as a behavioural characteristic but also as the fostering of conditions under which policies appropriate to a superseded stage of development might be implemented. It arose from a disjunction between three elements of the relations of production (the pattern of ownership, the relations between people at work and the reciprocal relations between production and distribution). As Mao began to move away from a behavioural to a more substantive conception of 'revisionism', he must surely have begun to take stock of conditions in China which, in many ways, mirrored the 'reforms' then under way in the Soviet Union. The decentralisation of decision-making power to local areas, fostered during the Great Leap, was giving way to a mixture of recentralisation and decentralisation of power to units of production. Atomised units, therefore, began to be linked more by the market than by the plan and economists had come forward to promote the virtues of 'market socialism'. These were the same conditions which had produced 'revisionism' in Yugoslavia—a country which Mao became convinced was no longer socialist. The Soviet Union, moreover, seemed to be heading in the same direction.

The reason why Mao did not come to this view until 1962 might have been because he was preoccupied with the economic damage resulting from natural calamities and from the Great Leap. It might also have been the case, however, that he had not had time to study political economy until after he had retired to the 'second front' in 1959. Whatever the reason, the period 1960–2 did see Mao's first serious study of political economy. But he was still a novice and his notes, written at that time, reveal much inconsistency and confusion.

Mao's new thoughts about the structural conditions for 'revisionism' led him quite naturally to a reformulation of 'class struggle'. There had been much talk about 'class struggle' during the Great Leap, but one gets the impression that it was still seen in the old Soviet sense; it resulted from the persistence of remnant classes and their ideology which were supported by external forces. But by the early 1960s, Mao began to feel that, in socialist society, certain structural conditions might produce *new* bourgeois elements. This generative view of class had very important implications for domestic politics. It implied that the revolution was constantly in danger of sliding backwards. Thus, socialism came to be seen not as a model to be achieved and consolidated but as the whole process of transition from the old society to communism. It was, moreover, a *reversible* process. Mao had, indeed, begun to add a diachronic element to his view of socialist transition. There was now no room for models.

## Inner-Party Struggle

Mao's move away from considerations of behaviour to considerations of structure had very important implications for the way debate was conducted in the top policy-making circles. The conscientious adherence to Party norms of debate was no longer to be any guarantee that one would not be seen as the promoter of 'antagonistic' structures. Up to 1962, it seemed that the process of decision-making was able to accommodate all sorts of deviant and heterodox views, provided that organisational norms were adhered to. The Gao Gang and Peng Dehuai cases, however, appear as major aberrations. This may have been because Mao believed, in each case, that the existence of an independent power base suggested a conspiracy to seize supreme power. In each case also, a belief in a Soviet connection lent weight to such a view. But the important point is that whereas in the case of Gao Gang most Party leaders were prepared to support the conspiracy theory, in the case of Peng Dehuai many were not. To such people, it must have seemed that Peng had been victimised simply for his views on the Great Leap and a very unfortunate precedent had been set. Earlier, Chen Yun had lost power because of a similar opposition to the Great Leap but the case of Peng Dehuai did seem to be the first time that a senior leader had been publicly humiliated for such a position. Whether that assessment was correct or not is an open question. Suffice it to say that, in the future, many more cases like that of Peng Dehuai would occur.

At lower levels of the Party organisation, the norms of inner-Party debate had started to break down much earlier than the Peng Dehuai case. The collapse of consensus at the highest levels was not to occur until Mao had discarded much of the Soviet model of *socialism*. At lower levels, concerned more with operational matters, consensus began to break down as soon as the Soviet model of *administration* had been discredited. Thus, many people were capped as 'rightist' in 1957 – 8 purely because of their expressed attitudes and not because of any physical act of opposition. Such a situation was to affect quite profoundly the way rectification movements were carried on. Following Teiwes,[3] this volume has considered two kinds of rectification movement—the open type and the closed. The Yan'an movement had been a closed process of rectification, though the materials used to assess cadres were based on reports of their performance in the field. The 1947 – 8 movement, in contrast, was an open movement which resulted in much mass response and much confusion. The movement of 1950 was once again a closed movement as the Party strove to restore order, though elements of open rectification appeared in the subsequent three and five anti movements of 1951 – 2. When the Soviet model was implemented, the rectification movements were, once again, closed but, unlike that closed movement in Yan'an, were not reliant on material solicited by Mass Line techniques. The Party, therefore, became more and more exclusivist and cut off from the masses. This prompted Mao's call for an open process of rectification in 1957 which, after much opposition, finally got off the ground and then quickly got out of hand. One cannot be sure whether Mao supported the reversal of policy in mid-1957, but that reversal did signify a return once again to closed rectification. If Solomon is right and Mao was able to steer the subsequent anti-rightist movement on to specifically economic targets, then we might have the basis for an understanding of the excessive 'commandism' which sometimes developed during the Great Leap. Ideally, at that time, since open rectification could no longer be implemented, the closed process of rectification should have been informed (in the Yan'an style) by a parallel development of the Mass Line. But when the pace of change was too quick for mass comments to be solicited, the Great Leap might actually have contributed to the exclusivity of the Party and occasioned the complaints which were voiced in 1960 – 1. In contrast to the 1959 campaign against 'right opportunism', the movement of 1960 – 1 was again relatively open but took place in such an atmosphere of demoralisation that one wonders whether the masses were mobilised actively to remedy the situation. All too often, it seems, the masses might have been persuaded merely to endorse the decision of work-teams to blame the bad economic conditions on local cadres, regardless of their actual guilt. But significantly, the campaign of 1960 – 1 did give rise to the formation of new peasant associations and these were to become quite important in subsequent years. It would seem, therefore, that, after Yan'an, closed rectification movements led to Party exclusivity and open rectification movements led to confusion. By the early 1960s, the attempt to get back to the spirit of Yan'an by combining closed rectification with the implementation of the Mass Line had failed. What was more important, however, was that once Mao had decided that elements of a new bourgeoisie might develop in the Party structure itself, then the only kind of rectification movement which he could promote would be the open type. Mao, therefore, had to take the risk of whatever confusion might occur. Such was the thinking which led eventually to the Cultural Revolution.

### The Decision-making Process

The apparent ease with which Mao returned to the 'first front' in 1962 has given much weight to a view of Chinese politics which sees Mao as the consistent drafter of the political agenda. According to this view, Mao constantly shifted his position between radical and more conservative policies. This was because of changing information from below, produced either by Mass Line techniques or invented by close advisers such as Chen Boda or Kang Sheng. Thus, a 'conservative' or an 'ultra-leftist' was simply someone who did not keep up with Mao's changing position. There can be no doubt about the extraordinary power enjoyed by Mao both before and after the Party began to talk about 'collective leadership' in the 1950s. Indeed, the case of Peng Dehuai could be interpreted as showing that Mao was quite capable of taking a personal initiative in launching a surprise attack against someone who thought he was adhering to the norms of inner-Party debate. At times, Mao must have been a very difficult person to live with. Yet, if one looks at the whole period covered by this volume, despite the occasional criticism of Mao's personal style, one gets the impression that Mao did not often act in that way. In fact, Mao seemed particularly responsive to the opinions and pressures of the various groups in the senior echelons of the Party. Unlike Chang, I will not describe the decision-making process as 'pluralist'[4] because key personnel often occupied a number of roles, and interest groups were extremely difficult to pin down. Nevertheless, it does seem that the 'totalitarian' implications of the first view are open to question.

Mao, it appears, would frequently call meetings of provincial Party secretaries or Supreme State Conferences, at which he could nominate the audience. One could interpret these as means by which Mao could bypass the regular decision-making channels and get his way; and, in the case of the 1955 acceleration of co-operativisation, this is almost certainly what he did do. On the other hand, such forums might also be seen as a way of circumventing the constraints of the Soviet model of administration and making the Mass Line work more effectively.

In expressing reservations about the 'Mao in command' view, however, I must acknowledge that very significant contributions have been made to our understanding of Chinese politics by adherents to this view. The work of Teiwes, for example,[5] has caused me to modify considerably the rather crude categorisation of 'two-line struggle' expressed in the first edition of this book. It has caused me also to question the conclusions of MacFarquhar[6] who, in what is generally an extremely interesting and useful book, argues that the origins of the 'two-line struggle' might be traced back to the hundred flowers movement. Nevertheless, the picture of politics presented here still adheres to a conflict view, even if that conflict was, in Mao's words, 'non-antagonistic'.

## The Cycles

In the Preface, I suggested the reasons why I chose to play down the notion of cycles which figured so large in the first edition. This, it will be remembered, was not because I no longer subscribe to them (at least in the period covered by this volume) but because they raised a series of questions which could not be explored in an introductory textbook. At this point, however, it might be useful to recapitulate them in the hope that they might suggest questions for future study. The first cycle (which covers Chapters 1 and 2) started with a moderate period of radicalism (the Yan'an model), accelerated into a major mass movement during land reform in the early Civil War and then deradicalised in the rectification movement after 1948. That cycle came to an end with the moderate policies pursued after the establishment of government. The second cycle (which covers Chapters 3 and 4) started with a moderate rectification movement in 1950, accelerated into the mammoth three and five anti movements of 1951 – 2 and deradicalised as the Soviet model of administration was implemented. That cycle came to an end after the new permanent government structure had been consolidated. The third cycle (which covers Chapters 5 and 6) started with a Soviet-style campaign to suppress counter-revolutionaries and a moderate drive for co-operativisation, accelerated during the major co-operativisation drive in late 1955 and the 'leap forward' of 1956 and deradicalised in the second half of that year. That cycle came to an end after the Party structure had been regularised at the first session of the Eighth Party Congress. The fourth cycle (which covers Chapters 7 and 8) started with the 'blooming of a hundred flowers', accelerated during the Great Leap Forward and deradicalised after the Zhengzhou and Wuchang meetings of late 1958. That cycle came to an end as a series of measures were taken to restore order in the wake of the first round of the Great Leap Forward. The fifth cycle (which covers Chapters 9 and 10) started with the Lushan Plenum, accelerated into a campaign against 'right opportunism' and deradicalised in 1960 in the face of severe economic hardship. That cycle came to an end in 1962 amid quite bitter debate about the extent of retrenchment.

Each of the above cycles was seen, in the Chinese idiom, as 'saddle-shaped' (*maanxing*),[7] consisting of a high point, a trough and an even higher point. The high points of the 'saddle' represented periods of radicalism and the trough represented a period of consolidation. Ideally, each synthesis was to be at a point higher than the last when measured against the yardstick of overcoming the division of labour inherited from the old society and inherent in any transitional period. Different people, however, could be expected to disagree as to the degree of radicalism and the point at which a period of consolidation was to begin. But it would appear that, when the radical period of the fifth cycle came to an end at a point which few people could agree was higher than the last, disagreements occurred over the nature of the yardstick itself. After that, the notion of cycles appeared not to be of much use. My error, in the first edition of this book, was to extend the use of cycles after 1962, but in the period covered by this volume I think they are worth considering.

In reviews of the first edition, I was criticised on the grounds that I merely described the cycles of radicalism and consolidation whilst the need was to *explain* them.[8] That explanation is surely quite simple. Cycles occurred because the leaders of the Communist Party expected them to. They were promoted because the Chinese leaders felt that to foster development in a cyclic manner was the best way to prevent inertia. Cycles continued, therefore, so long as basic consensus applied to development policies—that is throughout the whole period covered in this volume.

### The Situation After 1962

*China: Radicalism to Revisionism, 1962–1979* will explore the consequences of the breakdown of basic consensus on developmental strategy and Mao's new conception of class struggle. In the period after 1962, the general contours of Chinese politics began gradually to change and to reflect greater degrees of antagonism. With the collapse of the old 'socialist camp', new and competing views of foreign policy were also to emerge. After that odd mixture of emancipation and repression, experimentation and chaos, which characterised the Cultural Revolution, and after the attempt to revive its spirit in the final years of Mao's life, there was to be a return to the policies of the mid-1950s which have been outlined in this volume. After that, there was a return to the policies of 1962. That is why a study of the events covered in this volume is so essential to understanding China after Mao. At the time of writing, however, even the 1962 scenario is giving way to something new. By observing the situation in 1980, we may get some idea of what might have happened had Mao not intervened so decisively in August and September 1962.

## NOTES

1. Trotsky, 1972 (original 1937), pp. 62–3.
2. Mao Zedong, 28 January 1958, *Chinese Law and Government,* Vol. I, No.4, Winter, 1968–9, pp. 13–14.
3. Teiwes, 1979.
4. Chang, 1975, pp. 176–96.
5. Teiwes, 1979.
6. MacFarquhar, 1974.
7. Mao Zedong, 23 May 1958, *JPRS*, 1974, p. 116; Liu Shaoqi, 5 May 1958, Liu, Vol. III, 1968, p. 19 (in the official English translation, the term is 'U-shaped').
8. Goodman, *International Affairs*, Vol. LIV, No. 1, January 1978, pp. 173–5.

# BIBLIOGRAPHY

Letters (a,b or c) have been inserted after some dates to facilitate identification of notes.

Alley, R. *Yo Banfa*, Shanghai, China Monthly Review, 1952

Andors, S. 'Revolution and Modernization: Man and Machine in Industrializing Society, the Chinese Case' in Friedman and Selden (eds.), 1971, pp. 393–444

_____ 'Factory Management and Political Ambiguity: 1961–63', *CQ* 59, 1974, pp. 435–76

_____ *China's Industrial Revolution: Politics, Planning and Management, 1949 to the Present*, New York, Pantheon Books, 1977

Barnett, A. *China on the Eve of Communist Takeover*, New York, Praeger, 1963

_____ (ed.) *Chinese Communist Politics in Action*, Seattle, University of Washington Press, 1969

Barrett, D. *Dixie Mission: The United States Army Observer Group in Yenan 1944*, Berkeley, University of California, Center for Chinese Studies, *China Research Monographs*, No. 6, 1970

Beal, J. *Marshall in China*, Toronto, Doubleday, 1970

Belden, J. *China Shakes the World* New York, Monthly Review Press, 1970

Bernstein, T. 'Leadership and Mass Mobilisation in the Soviet and Chinese Collectivisation Campaigns of 1929–30 and 1955–56: A Comparison', *CQ* 31, 1967, pp.1–47

_____ 'Problems of Village Leadership after Land Reform', *CQ* 36, 1968, pp.1–22.

_____ 'Cadre and Peasant Behaviour Under Conditions of Insecurity and Deprivation: The Grain Supply Crisis of the Spring of 1955' in Barnett (ed.), 1969, pp.365–99

268

Bowie, R. and Fairbank, J. (eds.) *Communist China 1955–59: Policy Documents with Analysis*, Cambridge, Mass., Harvard University Press, 1965

Brugger, W. *Democracy and Organisation in the Chinese Industrial Enterprise*, Cambridge University Press, 1976

———— (B.) (ed.) *China: The Impact of the Cultural Revolution*, London, Croom Helm, 1978

Buck, J. *Land Utilisation in China: A Study of 16,786 Farms in 168 Localities and 38,256 Farm Families in Twenty-Two Provinces in China 1929–1933*, New York, Paragon Book Reprint Corp., 1964

Burki, S. *A Study of Chinese Communes, 1965*, Cambridge, Mass., Harvard University, East Asian Research Center, *Harvard East Asian Monographs*, No. 29, 1970

Carr, E.H. *The Bolshevik Revolution*, Vol. I, Harmondsworth, Penguin, 1966

Carrère d'Encausse, H. and Schram, S. (eds.) *Marxism and Asia*, London, Allen Lane, 1969

Chai, W. (ed.) *Essential Works of Chinese Communism*, New York, Pica Press, 1970

Chang, P. 'Research Notes on the Changing Loci of Decision in the Chinese Communist Party', *CQ* 44, 1970, pp. 169–94

———— *Power and Policy in China*, University Park, Pennsylvania State University Press, 1975

Chao Kuo-chün (ed.) *Economic Planning and Organization in Mainland China: A Documentary Study (1949–1957)*, Cambridge, Mass., Harvard University, East Asian Research Center, *Harvard East Asian Monographs*, No. 7, 2 vols., 1963

Chassin, L. (trans. Osato and Gelas) *The Communist Conquest of China: A History of the Civil War 1945–49*, London, Weidenfeld and Nicolson, 1966

Chen, C. and Ridley, C. (eds.) *Rural People's Communes in Lien-chiang: Documents Concerning Communes in Lien-chiang County, Fukien Province, 1962–1963*, Stanford, Hoover Institution, 1969

Ch'en, J. *Mao and the Chinese Revolution*, London, Oxford University Press, 1965

———— and Tarling, N. *Studies in the Social History of China and South East Asia*, Cambridge University Press, 1970

Chen Pi-chao 'Individual Farming After the Great Leap: As Revealed by the Lien Kiang Documents', *Asian Survey*, Vol. VIII, No. 9, September 1968, pp. 774–91

Cheng, J. (ed.) *The Politics of the Chinese Red Army: A Translation of the Bulletin of Activities of the People's Liberation Army*, Stanford, Hoover Institution, 1966

Cheng Tsu-yüan *Anshan Steel Factory in Communist China*, Hong Kong, Union Research Institute, 1955

Cheng, Y.K. *Foreign Trade and Industrial Development of China*, Washington DC, University Press, 1956

Chesneaux, J. *The Chinese Labour Movement, 1919–1927*, Stanford University Press, 1968

————— *et al. China: The People's Republic, 1949–1976*, New York, Pantheon Books, 1979

Chiang K'ai-shek, see Jiang Jieshi

Clark, G. *In Fear of China*, Melbourne, Landsdown Press, 1967

Cohen, J. 'Drafting People's Mediation Rules' in Lewis (ed.), 1971, pp. 29–50

Compton, B. (ed.) *Mao's China: Party Reform Documents 1942–44*, Seattle, University of Washington Press, 1952

Cowan, C. (ed.) *The Economic Development of China and Japan*, London, George Allen and Unwin, 1964

Crankshaw, E. *The New Cold War, Moscow v. Peking*, Harmondsworth, Penguin, 1965

Croll, E. *Feminism and Socialism in China*, London, Routledge and Kegan Paul, 1978

Dallin, A. (ed.) *Diversity in International Communism*, New York and London, Columbia University Press, 1963

Davin, D. *Women-work, Women and the Party in Revolutionary China*, Oxford, Clarendon Press, 1976

Deng Tuo (pseud. Ma Nantun) *Yanshan Yehua*, Beijing Chubanshe, 1963

Dittmer *Liu Shao-ch'i and the Chinese Cultural Revolution: The Politics of Mass Criticism*, Berkeley, University of California Press, 1974

Djilas, M. *Conversations with Stalin*, Harmondsworth, Penguin, 1969

Domes, J. (trans. Rüdiger Machetzki) *The Internal Politics of China, 1949–1972*, London, Hurst & Co., 1973

Donnithorne, A. *China's Economic System*, London, George Allen and Unwin, 1967

Dreyer, J. 'China's Minority Nationalities in the Cultural Revolution', *CQ* 35, 1968, pp. 96–109

————— *China's Forty Millions*, Cambridge, Mass., Harvard University Press, 1976

Eckstein, A. 'Economic Growth and Change in China: A Twenty-Year Perspective', *CQ* 54, 1973, pp. 211–41

————— *China's Economic Revolution*, Cambridge University Press, 1977

—————, Galenson, W. and Liu Ta-chung (eds.) *Economic Trends in Communist China*, Edinburgh University Press, 1968

Esherick, J. 'Harvard in China: The Apologetics of Imperialism', *Bulletin of Concerned Asian Scholars*, Vol. IV, No. 4, December 1972, pp. 9–16

Feuerwerker, A. *China's Early Industrialization: Sheng Hsüan-huai*

*(1844 – 1916) and Mandarin Enterprise*, Cambridge, Mass., Harvard University Press, 1958

_____ 'China's Nineteenth Century Industrialisation: The Case of the Hanyehp'ing Coal and Iron Company Limited' in Cowan (ed.), 1964, pp. 79 – 110

Fokkema, D. 'Chinese Criticism of Humanism: Campaign against the Intellectuals, 1964 – 1965', *CQ* 26, 1966, pp. 68 – 81

_____ *Report from Peking*, Sydney, Angus and Robertson, 1971

Fong, H.D. *Industrial Organisation in China*, Tianjin, Nankai University, Institute of Economics, 1937 (originally in *Nankai Social and Economic Quarterly*, Vol. IX, No. 4, January 1937, pp. 919 – 1006)

Friedman, E. 'Problems in Dealing with an Irrational Power: America Declares War on China', in Friedman and Selden (eds.), 1971, pp. 207 – 52

_____ and Selden, M. (eds.), *America's Asia: Dissenting Essays on Asian-American Relations*, New York, Vintage Books, 1971

Gardner, J. 'The Wu-fan Campaign in Shanghai: A Study in the Consolidation of Urban Control' in Barnett (ed.), 1969, pp. 477 – 539

Garthoff, R. (ed.) *Sino-Soviet Military Relations*, New York, Praeger, 1966

Gehlen, M. *The Politics of Coexistence: Soviet Methods and Motives*, Bloomington, Indiana University Press, 1967

Gelder, S. and R. *The Timely Rain, Travels in New Tibet*, London, 1964

Gittings, J. *The Role of the Chinese Army*, London, Oxford University Press, 1967

_____ *Survey of the Sino-Soviet Dispute: A Commentary and Extracts from the Recent Polemics, 1963 – 1967*, London, Oxford University Press, 1968

_____ 'The Great Asian Conspiracy' in Friedman and Selden (eds.), 1971, pp. 108 – 45

_____ *The World and China: 1922 – 1972*, London, Eyre Methuen, 1974

Goldman, M. 'Hu Feng's Conflict with the Communist Literary Authorities', *CQ* 12, 1962, pp. 102 – 37

_____ 'The Unique "Blooming and Contending" of 1961 – 62', *CQ* 37, 1969, pp. 54 – 83

Gongren Chubanshe *Wusan Gongchang Gonghui Gongzuo Jingyan (The Experiences of Labour Union Work in the Wusan Factory)*, Beijing, 1953

Gravel (ed.) *The Pentagon Papers: The Defence Department History of United States Decisionmaking on Vietnam*, Vol. II, Boston, Beacon Press, 1971

Gray, J. (ed.) *Modern China's Search for a Political Form*, London, Oxford University Press, 1969

_____ 'The High Tide of Socialism in the Chinese Countryside' in

Ch'en and Tarling (eds.), 1970, pp. 85–134

_____ 'The Two Roads: Alternative Strategies of Social Change and Economic Growth in China' in Schram (ed.), 1973, pp. 109–57

Guillermaz, J. 'The Nanchang Uprising', *CQ* 11, 1962, pp. 161–8

Harper, P. 'The Party and the Unions in Communist China', *CQ* 37, 1969, pp. 84–119

Harrison, J. 'The Li Li-san Line and the CCP in 1930', *CQ* 14, 1963, pp. 178–94; *CQ* 15, 1963, pp. 140–59

He Ganzhi (Ho Kan-chih) *A History of the Modern Chinese Revolution*, Beijing, PFLP, 1959

Hinton, H. *Communist China in World Politics*, London, Macmillan, 1966

Hinton, W. *Fanshen: A Documentary of Revolution in a Chinese Village*, New York, Vintage Books, 1966

_____ *China's Continuing Revolution*, London, China Policy Study Group, 1969

Ho Kan-chih, see He Ganzhi

Ho Ping-ti *The Ladder of Success in Imperial China: Aspects of Social Mobility, 1368–1911*, New York, Columbia University Press, 1962

Hofheinz, R. 'The Autumn Harvest Uprising', *CQ* 32, 1967, pp. 37–87

Howe, C. *Employment and Economic Growth in Urban China, 1949–1957*, Cambridge University Press, 1971

_____ *Wage Patterns and Wage Policy in Modern China, 1919–72*, Cambridge University Press, 1973(a)

_____ 'Labour Organisation and Incentives in Industry, before and after the Cultural Revolution' in Schram (ed.), 1973(b), pp. 233–56

Hsiao Tso-liang 'Chinese Communism and the Canton Soviet of 1927', *CQ* 30, 1967, pp. 49-78

Hsieh, A. *Communist China's Strategy in the Nuclear Era*, Englewood Cliffs, N.J., Prentice-Hall, 1962

Huadong Renmin Chubanshe *Tewu Pohuai Gongchang de Zuixing (The Crimes of the Special Agents who Sabotage Factories)*, Shanghai, May 1951

Hudson, G., Lowenthal, R. and MacFarquhar, R. (eds.) *The Sino-Soviet Dispute*, London, *The China Quarterly*, 1961

International Commission of Jurists *Tibet and the Chinese People's Republic: A Report to the International Commission of Jurists by its Legal Inquiry Committee on Tibet*, Geneva, International Commission of Jurists, 1960

Isaacs, H. *The Tragedy of the Chinese Revolution*, Stanford University Press, 1961 (note: this is not the original text)

Israel, J. *Student Nationalism in China, 1927–1937*, Stanford University Press, 1966

Jiang Jieshi (Chiang K'ai-shek) *China's Destiny and Chinese Economic Theory*, New York, Roy, 1947

Joffe, E. *Between Two Plenums: China's Intraleadership Conflict, 1959 – 1962*, Ann Arbor, University of Michigan, Center for Chinese Studies, *Michigan Papers in Chinese Studies*, No. 22, 1975

Johnson, C. *Communist China and Latin America, 1959 – 1967*, New York, Columbia University Press, 1970

Johnson, C. *Peasant Nationalism and Communist Power*, Stanford University Press, 1962

*JPRS* (ed.) *Miscellany of Mao Tse-tung Thought (1949 – 1968)*, 2 vols. (*JPRS* 61269—1 and 2), Arlington, Va., 20 February 1974

Kallgren, J. 'Nationalist China's Armed Forces', *CQ* 15, 1963, pp. 35 – 44

Kamenka, E. and Tay, A. 'Beyond the French Revolution: Communist Socialism and the Concept of Law', *University of Toronto Law Journal* V, 21, 1971

Khrushchev, N. 'On Peaceful Coexistence', *Foreign Affairs*, Vol. XXXVIII, No. 1, October 1959, pp. 1 – 18

Klein, D. and Clark A. *Biographic Dictionary of Chinese Communism, 1921 – 1965*, 2 vols., Cambridge, Mass., Harvard University Press, 1971

Kraus, R. 'Class Conflict and the Vocabulary of Social Analysis in China', *CQ* 69, March 1977, pp. 54 – 74

Kuo. L. *The Technical Transformation of Agriculture in Communist China*, New York, Praeger, 1972

Laodong Chubanshe Bianshenbu *Qiye Guanli Minzhuhua* (*The Democratisation of Enterprise Management*), Shanghai, July 1951

Larkin, B. *China and Africa, 1949 – 1970: The Foreign Policy of the People's Republic of China*, Berkeley, University of California Press, 1971

Lee, C. *Communist China's Policy Toward Laos: A Case Study, 1954 – 67*, Lawrence, Kansas, University of Kansas, Center for East Asian Studies, *International Studies: East Asian Series, Research Publication*, No. 6, 1970

Lee, R. 'The Hsia Fang System: Marxism and Modernisation', *CQ* 28, 1966, pp. 40 – 62

Levy, M. *The Family Revolution in Modern China* (1949), New York, Octagon Books, 1971

Levy R. 'New Light on Mao: His Views on the Soviet Union's "Political Economy" ', *CQ* 61, 1975, pp. 95 – 117

Lewis, J. (ed.) *The City in Communist China*, Stanford University Press, 1971

———— 'Commerce, Education and Political Development in Tangshan 1956 – 69' in Lewis (ed.), pp. 153 – 79

Lieberthal, K. 'Mao Versus Liu? Policy Towards Industry and Commerce', *CQ* 47, 1971, pp. 494 – 520

———— 'The Suppression of Secret Societies in Post-liberation Tientsin', *CQ* 54, 1973, pp. 242 – 66

Lindsay, M. 'The Taxation System of the Shansi-Chahar-Hopei Border

Region, 1938–1945', *CQ* 42, 1970, pp. 1–15

Lippit, V. 'The Great Leap Forward Reconsidered', *Modern China*, Vol. I, No.1, January 1975, pp. 92–115

Liu Shaoqi (Liu Shao-ch'i) *Collected Works*, Vol. II (1945–57), 1969; Vol. III (1958–67), 1968; Hong Kong, URI

_____ *On the Party*, Beijing, PFLP, 1950

_____ et al. *Xinminzhuzhuyi Chengshi Zhengce* (*New Democratic Urban Policy*), Hong Kong, Xinminzhu Chubanshe, 1949

Liu Ta-chung 'Quantitative Trends in the Economy' in Eckstein, Galenson, and Liu (eds.), 1968, pp. 87–182

MacFarquhar, R. 'Problems of Liberalization and the Succession at the Eighth Party Congress', *CQ* 56, 1973, pp. 617–46

_____ *The Origins of the Cultural Revolution*, Vol. I, *Contradictions Among the People: 1956–1957*, New York, Columbia University Press, 1974

Mao Zedong *Selected Works*, Beijing, PFLP, Vol. I, 1965; Vol. II, 1965; Vol. III, 1965; Vol. IV, 1961; Vol. V, 1977

_____ *Quotations from Chairman Mao Tse-tung*, Beijing, PFLP, 1966

_____ *Selected Readings*, Beijing, PFLP, 1971

_____ *Miscellany of Mao Tse-tung Thought* (*1949–1968*), see *JPRS* (ed.), 1974

_____ *Mao Zhuxi Wenxuan*, n.p. n.d. (probably 1967)

_____ *Mao Zedong Sixiang Wansui*, n.p., 1967(a), p. 46

_____ *Mao Zedong Sixiang Wansui*, n.p., 1967(b), p. 280

_____ *Mao Zedong Sixiang Wansui*, n.p., 1969

_____(ed.) *Muqian Xingshi he Women de Renwu* (*The Present Situation and Our Tasks*), Jiefangshe, November 1949

_____ *A Critique of Soviet Economics* (trans. M. Roberts with introduction by J. Peck), New York, Monthly Review Press, 1977

Maxwell, N. *India's China War*, Harmondsworth, Penguin, 1972

Meisner, M. *Li Ta-chao and the Origins of Chinese Marxism*, Cambridge, Mass., Harvard University Press, 1967

_____ *Mao's China: A History of the People's Republic*, New York, The Free Press, 1977

Moody, P. 'Policy and Power: The Career of T'ao Chu:1956–66', *CQ* 54, 1973, pp. 267–93

Moore, B. Jnr *Social Origins of Dictatorship and Democracy: Lord and Peasant in the Making of the Modern World*, Boston, Beacon Press, 1967

Moseley, G. (ed.) *The Party and the National Question in China*, Cambridge, Mass., The MIT Press, 1966

Myers, R. *The Chinese Peasant Economy, Agricultural Development in Hopei and Shantung, 1890–1949*, Cambridge, Mass., Harvard University Press, 1970

Nolan, P. 'Collectivisation in China: Some Comparisons with the

USSR', *Journal of Peasant Studies*, Vol. III, No. 2, January 1976, pp. 192–220

Patterson, G. *Peking Versus Delhi*, London, Faber and Faber, 1963

PFLP *The Marriage Law of the People's Republic of China*, Beijing, 1950

_____ *The Electoral Law of the People's Republic of China*, Beijing, 1953

_____ *Eighth National Congress of the Communist Party of China*, 3 vols., Beijing, 1956

_____ *Second Session of the Eighth National Congress of the Communist Party of China*, Beijing, 1958

_____ *Long Live Leninism*, Beijing, 1960

_____ *Constitution of the People's Republic of China* (20 September 1954), Beijing, 1961

_____ *The Sino-Indian Boundary Question*, Beijing, 1962(a)

_____ *Workers of All Countries Unite, Oppose Our Common Enemy*, Beijing, 1962 (b)

_____ *The Polemic on the General Line of the International Communist Movement*, Beijing, 1965

_____ *The Seeds and Other Stories*, Beijing, 1972(a)

_____ *Taching: Red Banner on China's Industrial Front*, Beijing, 1972(b)

Perkins, D. 'Industrial Planning and Management' in Eckstein, Galenson and Liu (eds.), 1968, pp. 597–635

_____ 'An Economic Reappraisal', *Problems of Communism*, Vol. XXII, No. 3, May–June 1973, pp. 1–13

Pfeffer, R. 'Mao and Marx in the Marxist-Leninist Tradition: A Critique of "The China Field" and a Contribution to a Preliminary Reappraisal', *Modern China*, Vol. II, No. 4, October 1976, pp. 421–60

Pien Hsi 'The Story of Tachai' in PFLP, 1972(a), pp. 166–93

Powell, R. *Politico-Military Relationships in Communist China*, US Department of State, External Research Staff, Bureau of Intelligence and Research, 1963

Pusey, J. *Wu Han: Attacking the Present through the Past*, Cambridge, Mass., Harvard University Press, 1969

Rádvanyi, Janos 'The Hungarian Revolution and the Hundred Flowers Campaign', *CQ* 43, 1970, pp. 121–9

Rees, D. *Korea: The Limited War*, London, Macmillan, 1964

Rice, E. *Mao's Way*, Berkeley, University of California Press, 1972

Riesman, D., Glazer, N. and Denney, R. *The Lonely Crowd*, Garden City, New York, Doubleday, 1953

Rigby, T. (ed.) *The Stalin Dictatorship*, Sydney University Press, 1968

Robinson, J. *The Cultural Revolution in China*, Harmondsworth, Penguin, 1969

Rue, J. *Mao Tse-tung in Opposition, 1927–1935*, Stanford University Press, 1966

Salaff, J. 'The Urban Communes and Anti-City Experiment in Communist China', *CQ* 29, 1967, pp. 82 – 109

Scalapino, R. (ed.) *Elites in the People's Republic of China*, Seattle, University of Washington Press, 1972

Schram, S. (ed.) *Documents sur la Théorie de la 'Révolution Permanente' en Chine: Idéologie Dialectique et Dialectique du Réel*, Paris, Mouton, 1963

_____ *Mao Tse-tung*, Harmondsworth, Penguin, 1966

_____ 'Mao Tse-tung and the Theory of the Permanent Revolution, 1958 – 69', *CQ* 46, 1971, pp. 221 – 44

_____ (ed.), *Authority Participation and Cultural Change in China*, Cambridge University Press, 1973

_____ (ed.) *Mao Tse-tung Unrehearsed*, Harmondsworth, Penguin, 1974

_____ 'Some Reflections on the Pfeffer-Walder "Revolution" in China Studies', *Modern China*, Vol. III, No. 2, April 1977, pp. 169 – 84

Schurmann, H. 'China's "New Economic Policy"—Transition or Beginning', *CQ* 17, 1964, pp. 65 – 91

_____ *Ideology and Organization in Communist China*, Berkeley, University of California Press, 1966

Schurmann, H.F. and Schell, O. (eds.) *China Readings II, Republican China; China Readings III, Communist China*, Harmondsworth, Penguin, 1968

Schwartz, B. *Chinese Communism and the Rise of Mao*, Cambridge, Mass., Harvard University Press, 1966

_____ 'The Essence of Marxism Revisited', *Modern China*, Vol. II, No. 4, October 1976, pp. 461 – 72

Selden, M. *The Yenan Way in Revolutionary China*, Cambridge, Mass., Harvard University Press, 1971

_____ (ed.) *The People's Republic of China: A Documentary History of Revolutionary Change*, New York, Monthly Review Press, 1979

Seybolt, P. 'The Yenan Revolution in Mass Education', *CQ* 48, 1971, pp. 641 – 69

Shanghai (n.p. n.d.) *Jiefanghou Shanghai Gongyun Ziliao* (*Materials on the Shanghai Workers Movement after Liberation [May-December 1949]*), Hong Kong, reprint

Shanghai Zonggonghui Wenjiaobu (Shanghai General Labour Union Cultural and Education Department) (ed.) *Gongchang zhong de Xuanchuan Gudong Gongzuo* (*Agitprop Work in Factories*), Shanghai, Laodong Chubanshe, October 1950

Shewmaker, K. 'The "Agrarian Reformer" Myth', *CQ* 34, 1968, pp. 68 – 81

Simmonds, J. 'P'eng Te-huai: A Chronological Re-Examination', *CQ* 37, 1969, pp. 120 – 38

Skinner, G. 'Marketing and Social Structure in Rural China', *Journal of Asian Studies*. Vol. XXIV, No. 1, November 1964, pp. 3 – 43 (Pt 1);

No. 2, February 1965, pp. 195 – 228 (Pt II); No. 3, May 1965, pp. 363 – 99 (Pt. III)

Smedley, A. *The Great Road: The Life and Times of Chu Teh*, New York, Monthly Review Press, 1972

Snow, E. *Red Star Over China*, New York, Grove Press, 1961

Solomon, R. *Mao's Revolution and the Chinese Political Culture*, Berkeley, University of California Press, 1971

Stalin, J. 'On the Draft Constitution of the U.S.S.R.', 25 November 1936, in Stalin, 1947, pp. 540 – 68

_____ *Problems of Leninism*, Moscow, Foreign Languages Publishing House, 1947

_____ *Economic Problems of Socialism in the U.S.S.R.* (1952), Beijing, PFLP, 1972

Starr, J. 'Conceptual Foundations of Mao Tse-tung's Theory of Continuous Revolution', *Asian Survey*, Vol. XI, No. 6, June 1971, pp. 610 – 28

State Statistical Bureau *Ten Great Years: Statistics of the Economic and Cultural Achievements of the People's Republic of China*, Beijing, 1960

Stone, I. *The Hidden History of the Korean War*, New York, Monthly Review Press, 1970

Strong, A. *When Serfs Stood Up in Tibet*, Beijing, New World Press, 1965

Swarup, S. *A Study of the Chinese Communist Movement*, Oxford, Clarendon Press, 1966

Teiwes, F. 'The Purge of Provincial Leaders, 1957 – 8', *CQ* 27, 1966, pp. 14 – 32

_____ *Politics and Purges in China: Rectification and the Decline of Party Norms: 1950 – 1965*, White Plains, N.Y., M.E. Sharpe, 1979

Thomas, B. 'China in Transition: Society and Criminal Law', *Flinders Journal of History and Politics*, Vol. IV, 1974, pp. 14 – 60

Trotsky, L. *The Revolution Betrayed* (1937), New York, Pathfinder Press, 1972

Tsou Tang *America's Failure in China, 1941 – 50*, 2 vols., University of Chicago Press, 1967

Tuchman, B. *Sand Against the Wind: Stilwell and the American Experience in China*, London, Macmillan, 1970

URI (ed.) *The Case of P'eng Teh-huai*, Hong Kong, 1968(a)

_____ (ed.) *CCP Documents of the Great Proletarian Cultural Revolution, 1966 – 67*, Hong Kong, URI, 1968(b)

_____ (ed.) *Tibet 1950 – 1967*, Hong Kong, 1968(c)

_____ (ed.) *Documents of Chinese Communist Party Central Committee*, Hong Kong, 1971

Vogel, E. 'From Revolutionary to Semi-Bureaucrat: The "Regularisation" of Cadres', *CQ* 29, 1967, pp. 36 – 60

_____ *Canton Under Communism: Programs and Politics in a Provincial*

*Capital, 1949–1968*, New York, Harper and Row, 1971

Wakeman, F. 'A Response', *Modern China*, Vol. III, No. 2, April 1977, pp. 161–8

Walder, A. 'Marxism, Maoism and Social Change', *Modern China*, Vol. III, No. 1, January 1977, pp. 101–18; Vol. III, No. 2, April 1977, pp. 125–60

Walker, K. *Planning in Chinese Agriculture: Socialisation and the Private Sector, 1956–1962*, London, Frank Cass, 1965

————— 'Organisation of Agricultural Production' in Eckstein, Galenson and Liu (eds.), 1968, pp. 397–458

Waller, D. *The Government and Politics of Communist China*, London, Hutchinson, 1970

————— *The Kiangsi Soviet Republic: Mao and the National Congresses of 1931 and 1934*, Berkeley, Center for Chinese Studies, *China Research Monographs*, No. 10, 1973

Wang Gungwu *China and the World Since 1949: The Impact of Independence, Modernity and Revolution*, London, Macmillan, 1977

Wheelwright, E. and McFarlane, B. *The Chinese Road to Socialism*, New York, Monthly Review Press, 1970

Whiting, A. *China Crosses the Yalu: The Decision to Enter the Korean War*, Stanford University Press, 1968

Whitson, W. 'The Field Army in Chinese Communist Military Politics', *CQ* 37, 1969, pp. 1–30

Wilbur, C. 'The Ashes of Defeat', *CQ* 18, 1964, pp. 3–54

Wilhelm, H. 'The Reappraisal of Neo Confucianism', *CQ* 23, 1965, pp. 122–39

Wilson, D. *A Quarter of Mankind: An Anatomy of China Today*, Harmondsworth, Penguin, 1968

————— *The Long March*, 1935, London, Hamish Hamilton, 1971

Winnington, A. *The Slaves of the Cool Mountains*, London, Lawrence and Wishart, 1959

Wright, M. *The Last Stand of Chinese Conservatism: The Tung-chih Restoration, 1862–1874*, Stanford University Press, 1957

Young, G. 'Conceptions of Party Leadership in China: The Cultural Revolution and Party Building', unpublished PhD thesis, Adelaide, Flinders University, 1979

————— and Woodward, D. 'From Contradictions Among the People to Class Struggle: The Theories of Uninterrupted and Continuous Revolution', *Asian Survey*, Vol. XVIII. No. 9, September 1978, pp. 912–33

Zagoria, D. 'Khrushchev's Attack on Albania and Sino-Soviet Relations', *CQ* 8, 1961, pp. 1–19

————— *The Sino-Soviet Conflict, 1956–61*, New York, Atheneum, 1966

Zhonghua Quanguo Zonggonghui Shengchanbu (All China Federation of Labour: Production Department) (ed.) *Shengchan Gongzuo Shouce*

(*Production Work Handbook*), Vol. I, Beijing Gongren Chubanshe, May 1950

Zhonggong Yanjiu Zazhi she (ed.) *Liu Shaoqi Wenti Ziliao Zhuanji* (*A Special Collection of Materials on the Question of Liu Shaoqi*), Taibei, 1970

Zhongguo Minzhu Tongmeng Zongbu Xuanchuan Weiyuanhui (China Democratic League, General Office, Propaganda Committee) (ed.) *Zengchan Jieyue Fan Tanwu Fan Langfei Fan Guanliaozhuyi* (*Increase Production and Practise Economy: Oppose Graft, Waste and Bureaucratism*), 1951

# INDEX

accounting: agricultural 122, 137, 231; economic accounting system 79–80; industrial 135, 235; level of commune 196–7, 211, 225, 231–3; *see also* communes, Harbin system, planning
Acheson, D. 63–4
activism and activists (*jijifenzi*) 41, 55, 59, 72, 81, 85, 95, 115, 182, 232, 260
administrative streamlining 33, 95, 119, 165
Africa 146–7
Afro-Asian Peoples' Solidarity Organisation 146
agriculture: eight character constitution 182; forty points (1956) 122; mechanisation 115, 122–3, 168, 196; seventeen points (1955) 122; sixty articles (1961) 231; twelve articles (1960) 225, 231; twelve year plan (NPAD) (1956–67) 122, 126–7, 168, 175, 180, 215; *see also* communes, co-operatives, economic crops, landlords, land reform, mutual aid teams, natural calamities, peasants, rural administration, Socialist Education Mvt, state farms, unified purchase and marketing mvt, villages
air force *see* People's Liberation Army
air raids 37, 63
Aksai Chin 193, 199
Albania 209, 219, 237–8
Algeria 193–4, 217
Andors, S. 236
Anshan Iron and Steel Corporation 45, 79; constitution 235–6, 250
art and literature 38, 111, 241, 243–4
autonomous regions, districts and *xian* 139, 144

bandits 21
Bandung Conference 106–7, 146–7, 193
banking and insurance 58, 84, 120, 178
Banqen Erdini Quoiqyi Gyancan 71, 199–200
*baojia* 19
Barnett, A. 54
Beidaihe Conferences 188–90 (1958), 246 (1962)
Beria, L. 93
Berlin 194
'blooming and contending' *see* 'hundred flowers'
bonds 58, 120
Bo Yibo 211, 213
Britain 21, 50, 146, 148, 186, 237
Bucharest Conference (1960) 218–19
Bulganin, N. 90
bureaucracy, modern and traditional 17–8, 30–1
bureaucratism 27, 56–7, 59–62, 68, 78, 81–2, 91, 97–8, 112, 134, 138, 144–5, 148, 153, 158, 162, 254

cadres: as leadership type 30–1, 94, 259; 'fourth class' (union) 61, 82, 160; guerilla 68, 72; legal 100–1; rural 33, 42–4, 56, 72–3, 76, 98, 112–16, 122, 125, 136, 138, 165–6, 179–80,

280

THE LIBRARY
ST. MARY'S COLLEGE OF MARYLAND
ST. MARY'S CITY, MARYLAND  20686